Successful Leasing and Selling of Office Property

Developed by
Real Estate Education Company
in cooperation with
Grubb & Ellis Company

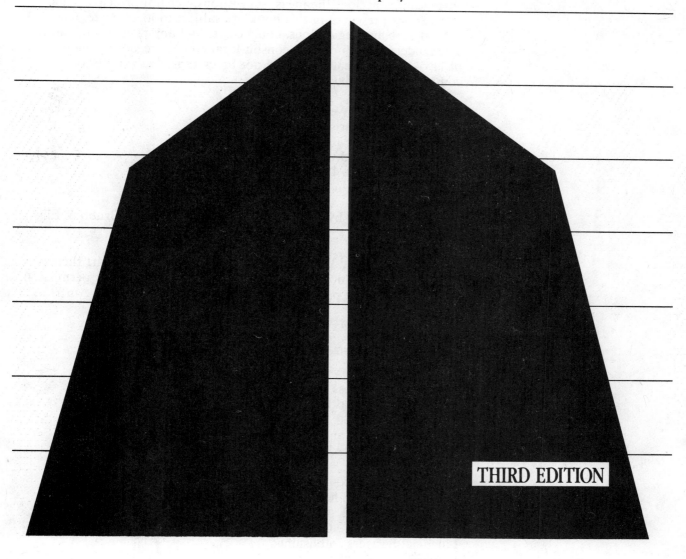

THIRD EDITION

 REAL ESTATE EDUCATION COMPANY
a division of Longman Financial Services Institute, Inc.

While a great deal of care has been taken to provide accurate and current information, the ideas, suggestions, general principles, and conclusions presented in this book are subject to local, state, and federal laws and regulations, court cases, and any revisions of same. The reader is thus urged to consult legal counsel regarding any points of law—this publication should not be used as a substitute for competent legal advice.

Executive Editor: Wendy Lochner
Project Editor: Chris Christensen
Copy Editor: Dale Bovoriak
Interior Design: Edwin Harris
Cover Design: Vito Depinto
Indexer: Rita Tatum

89 90 91 10 9 8 7 6 5 4 3 2 1

Library of Congress Cataloging in Publication Data
Main entry under title:

Successful leasing and selling of office property/Grubb & Ellis
    Company.—3rd ed.
        p.   cm.
    Includes index.
    ISBN 0-88462-108-1
    1. Offices. 2. Office leases. 3. Office Buildings. 4. Real
estate business. I. Grubb & Ellis Company. II. Longman
Financial Services Publishing.
HD1393.55.S92 1988
333.33'7—dc19   88-17544
                                                     CIP

Contents

Preface

Longman Financial Services Publishing developed this program during several years of work with Grubb & Ellis Company.

Grubb & Ellis Company is one of the country's largest companies providing a full range of real estate services. With headquarters in San Francisco, California, the company has over 160 offices throughout the United States.

The association between Grubb & Ellis Company and Longman Financial Services Publishing began with Grubb & Ellis Company's recognition of the need to adequately train great numbers of new salespeople. The company developed and proved many techniques and procedures for leasing and selling real property that contributed to its continued success. The challenge was to organize and convey the knowledge, skills and experience necessary to make the new people coming into the organization successful as quickly as possible.

Because of Grubb & Ellis Company's extensive commitment to the development of highly qualified salespeople, Longman was given the task of developing training programs and materials in many facets of the company's operations. The materials that resulted represent the combined contributions of many highly successful Grubb & Ellis Company salespeople, managers and training staff and professional educators and trainers from Longman Financial Services Publishing.

Because of the proven effectiveness of these materials and the basic selling procedures and techniques they reflect, Grubb & Ellis Company agreed to make several of these programs available for general distribution to the industry. *Successful Leasing and Selling of Office Property* has two companion programs dealing with specialized phases of the real estate industry: *Successful Leasing and Selling of Retail Property* and *Successful Industrial Real Estate Brokerage.* They are also available from Longman Financial Services Publishing, Chicago, Illinois.

Introduction

Successful real estate salespeople are well-paid for their services. They should be—the profession requires a very special kind of person. Many attributes go into successful selling, but one stands out: real estate sales representatives are constantly making decisions. The typical office worker makes essentially one daily decision: whether to get up and go to work that day. When such a worker arrives at the office, the job itself takes over. Phones must be answered. Supervisors devise tasks. The worker's day is a series of reactions to outside simuli.

Not so the days of real estate sales representatives! These salespeople work largely on their own, organizing their own tasks and assigning their own priorities, while coping with the unexpected and making quick adjustments to new situations.

As a specialist in office properties, you will deal with sophisticated business people. You will be working with very complicated, difficult transactions. This manual has been devised to help you not only recognize and meet the challenges involved but enjoy the process as well. You will get lots of help. Teamwork is an important component of office property brokerage. Furthermore, as your efforts and the efforts of other salespeople in your office help to increase your firm's dominance in the field, you will have an even greater opportunity to achieve the high degree of financial success that is so rare in almost every other profession. Simultaneously, you will enjoy the high measure of personal satisfaction that comes only with real accomplishment.

The program of instruction you are about to begin has been carefully structured. It begins with the nuts-and-bolts information you will need in order to understand your product thoroughly. Only after you know the general characteristics of office property, without which knowledge you could not hope to meet your prospect's needs, will you proceed to the marketing techniques and selling skills so necessary to your own personal and financial satisfaction.

You will be introduced first to the physical aspects of office buildings, and from that proceed to their economics. Here you will learn, among other things, why rents are priced as they are. After a look at the legal aspects of leasing and selling, you will find a detailed discussion of office leases. The chapter on marketing includes a description of a unique team method of area coverage and a consideration of your place in that picture. Selling skills will be outlined next, followed by a look at a case history. The manual ends with a Glossary, which you may want to refer to as you study the material.

This program has been developed to help you to become an effective, successful office-property salesperson. To accomplish this is not easy— it will come about only as the result of your own hard work. The manual attempts to ease that task as much as possible, but it represents only one of many types of experience that will mold you into a professional. To be fully effective, the program must be combined with your other real estate activities—weekly sales meetings, special training sessions, related books and audio cassettes, outside courses and seminars, your own independent reading, and, most important of all, the learning experiences you encounter in the actual practice of your profession.

To get the most benefit from the program, you must actively participate by answering questions, evaluating hypothetical situations and completing exercises. These tasks are designed to help you become thoroughly familiar with the material. Consider each question carefully, write your response and check your answer against the answer given in the manual. Many of the questions are broad-based and may have no one right answer.

Remember, this manual is only a starting point. Many of the subjects presented will merit further discussion with your managers and colleagues. Some chapters will provide the basis for special office training sessions.

All of the material in this program reflects practices and attitudes that have proved successful over the years for experienced office property salespeople. Yet it also offers maximum flexibility. If you discover a solution that works for you better than the one presented here, by all means use it. In some cases, too, practices will vary from one geographical area to another.

In today's fast-paced world of real estate brokerage, personal development is a never-ending process. For that reason, this program should be of value to the experienced salesperson as well as to the beginner.

Physical Aspects of Office Buildings

INTRODUCTION

All good salespeople must be thoroughly familiar with their product. That is no less true in marketing office properties than in any other field. The product in your case, of course, is the office space for which you want to find clients. Unless you are thoroughly familiar with certain physical features of that product, all the selling skills in the world will be of little use to you. This program begins by exploring some terms and building features that you will hear repeatedly in discussions with building owners and developers. Familiarizing yourself with these terms is a prerequisite to understanding the economics of office buildings, a topic examined in the next chapter.

BUILDING TYPES

High Rise

The definition of the term "high rise" varies from market to market. In some markets a building is not a high rise until it is 40 stories tall. In other markets it might be only ten. A safer way to define this type of building is by method of construction. In general, a high rise is a multi-story building of steel and concrete structure with an exterior of plastic, steel or precast concrete.

Low-rise or Mid-rise

Low- or mid-rise is generally a building of concrete construction, the height of which is regulated by construction limitations for concrete buildings. This classification is relative to the market, so an eight-story concrete building in a typically high-rise market (e.g., San Francisco) would be classified a low- or midrise building, while in a garden-office market it would be considered a high rise despite its method of construction.

STRUCTURE

The Shell

The building shell can be thought of as the skeleton to which the finished exterior and interior are applied. Although all three building types have a shell, the high-rise shell is the easiest one to describe. It is the foundation plus the steel girders that you see during the initial stages of construction.

The Skin

The skin is all the materials that cover the shell. It would include such features as flooring and exterior spandrells. Some of the finished features inside a building come under the heading "tenant improvements." These are interior office improvements made for the tenant, and will be discussed later.

Certain internal features are of special importance to the office marketing sales representative. As you read about these features, bear in mind that, although high rises will be stressed in examples, the information applies equally to all three classes of buildings.

THE CORE

Each floor of an office building contains an isolated area not generally accessible for office use by the building's tenants. In larger buildings this will consist of the elevator shafts, stairwells, rest rooms and service rooms for mechanical, electrical, telephone and air-conditioning equipment. Such areas are usually near the center of the building, although they are sometimes off center. The shape of the core and its location are of tremendous importance to users in certain businesses. These factors are, therefore, important to you as a marketer of office space.

The floor plan in figure 1–1 shows a central-core situation. The plan in figure 1–2 represents a radically off-center core. The effects on space planning of each floor plan will be considered in detail. Meanwhile, even a glance at the two illustrations will give you some feel for the types of space planning required in the different situations.

When examining unfamiliar office space, you should immediately do three things:

1. Establish the location of the core.

2. Determine the overall floor space by measuring it or checking reliable documents.

3. Determine the distance from the outer core wall to the window area.

This last measurement is particularly critical in determining what type of tenant will be most attracted to the space. Depending upon the expected space use and the tenant's needs, the distance from core wall to window—or the bay depth—should be 30–45 feet.

Some tenants will need 30–35 feet for optimum efficiency, while larger tenants will prefer a bay depth of 40–45 feet. Speculative multi-tenant buildings, for instance, often have the 45-foot bay depth to allow for the needs of a wide range of possible tenants.

A building that is basically square, has a square or rectangular centrally located core and measures 30–35 feet from core wall to window (figure 1–1) can be used most efficiently and flexibly by full-floor tenants in prestige businesses such as accounting or law firms. Such a floor plan permits offices all along the window lines with plenty of internal space for secretarial stations, aisles and hallways. The 30–35 rule is vital here. Less than 30 feet from core to window indicates cramped space.

Now look again at figure 1–2. This is a perfectly adequate floor design for a business with a high proportion of clerical and secretarial workers. Here, having large open spaces is more important than having many executive-type offices. An insurance company, for example, could use such space very well. So could a company looking for a large floor area for a sophisticated computer operation. The off-center core would also fit the needs of many companies looking for flexible space that could be altered from time to time with movable wall partitions, or of companies or government agencies that desire open-space planning.

In general, if an operation is people-intensive and plush offices are not a requirement, the off-center core building is a fine solution to a space problem.

A good rule of thumb to help you estimate a client's office-space needs is to check the number of employees the company has. If the business is a people-intensive operation, such as an insurance company, multiply the number of employees by 100 or 150. This will give a fair approximation of the company's space needs in square feet. If your client is a professional firm looking for a plush showplace for its business, use 200–250 as your multiplier. Many less people-intensive businesses require 250 square feet per person, and some law firms as high as 550.

So far, only single-tenant floors have been discussed. But what about the needs of companies that occupy a multitenant floor? Figure 1–3 shows the off-center-core floor plan again, this time divided for multi-tenant use. This floor plan is inefficient, because extra hall space is needed to reach all offices—extra hall space that the tenants will pay for in their rent. (This problem will be discussed in more detail later.) Actually, buildings with off-center-core areas often have even worse space

FIGURE 1.1   Central-Core Floor Plan

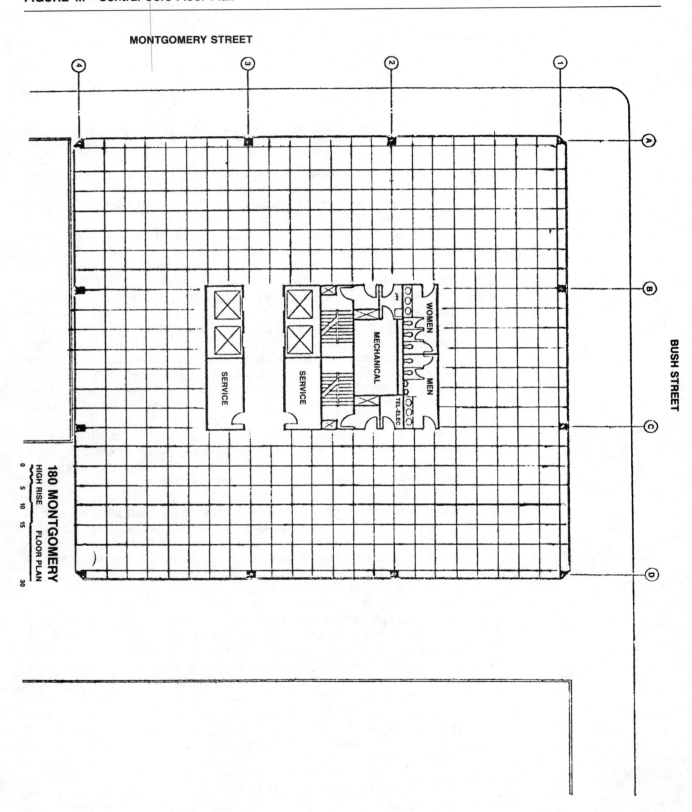

FIGURE 1.2   Off-Center-Core Floor Plan

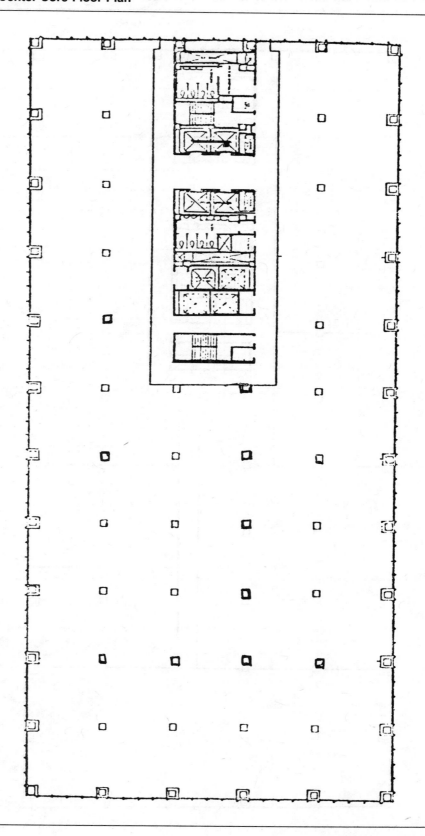

FIGURE 1.3   Off-Center-Core Floor Plan Divided for Multitenant Use

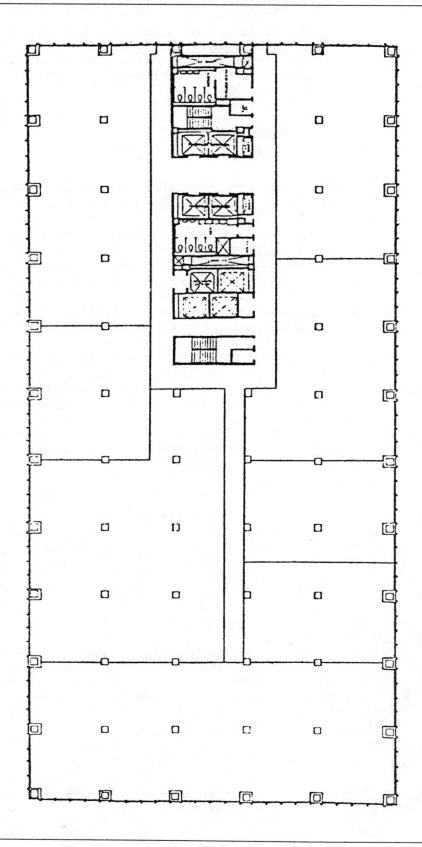

divisions than that in the example. Some tenants may wind up with no windows at all!

The second advantage of central-core buildings with proper bay depths is the ability to minimize hall space and maximize window space in multitenant situations. Figure 1–4 demonstrates this fact. Buildings with off-center cores generally use space less efficiently, except when open-space planning is used for a full-floor tenant.

MODULES AND MULLIONS

Every commercial building is divided into imaginary sections. The length of a side of one of these sections varies, but is generally from three to five feet. You will find some that are three feet, eight inches, and some that are four feet, six inches. Whatever the measurement, it is usually consistent. These imaginary squares are called *modules;* they are given actual physical significance by the existence of devices called *mullions.* Mullions are metal strips placed at regular intervals along a window line. They are designed to receive wall partitions in a manner ensuring a smooth, soundproof connection. The distance between mullions is the length of one side of a module. A module size is also governed by interior supports.

Note the squares in the floor plan in figure 1–4. They are defined by mullions (not shown). This floor plan is of a building with five-foot modules. The building can easily accommodate ten-foot by ten-foot or five-foot by ten-foot offices, both of which are popular sizes. It can accommodate offices measuring any multiple of five. Basing office measurements on module size is the most efficient way to divide space, particularly in buildings with a lot of exterior glass.

Exercise A

Your tenant is interested in a certain office space laid out in five-foot modules. He is content to have ten-foot-long offices along the window area, except at one end. Here he wants three nine-foot-long offices. Why is this a problem? Check your answer with the one given at the end of this exercise.

Answer A

Three nine-foot offices laid end-to-end would total 27 feet. If the tenant wants offices of this size instead of three ten-foot modules totaling 30 feet, substantial carpentry work will have to be done to place walls at intervals that are not multiples of five. Also, building three nine-foot offices would leave an undesirable (and probably useless) area at the end of one floor.

Buildings with five-foot modules are desirable for tenants who seek a maximum of private office space, because most such companies consider a ten-foot by ten-foot office the minimum acceptable size. Module size is less important for businesses that do not place a premium on individual offices with windows.

FIGURE 1.4   Central-Core Floor Plan Divided for Multitenant Use

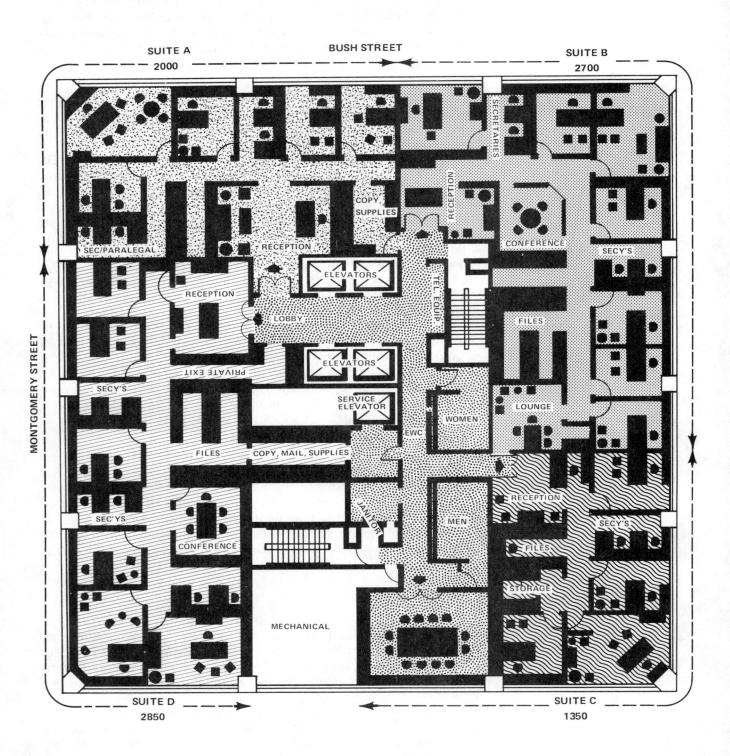

Exercise B _____

You are showing a prospect a building with five-foot modules. You happen to know that she is considering space in a competitor's building, which has four-foot modules. The prospect says to you, "I need offices at least ten feet by ten feet. Some will be larger, but none smaller." What do you tell her?

Answer B _____

Tell her your building has a big advantage over the other one she is considering. In order to have offices at least ten feet square in the competing building, she would have to make them 12 feet square, since the lower alternative is eight feet. Point out that this would waste space—space she would still be paying for.

You can check out module size by obtaining a set of building plans from the owner or architect. Modules and mullions are important to office marketing salespeople. They can make or break a deal.

HVAC

A building's heating, ventilating and air-conditioning system is usually referred to simply as its HVAC. Get used to the term—you'll be hearing it often. Especially, become familiar with your building's air-conditioning specifications.

Until about ten years ago, the design of a 40-story building's and a two-story building's air-conditioning equipment varied little. Both usually had a single unit located on the roof. Today, one tendency is for a building of 40 stories to have four or more separate units, each controlling the temperatures of different floors. The other alternative is for each individual floor in a high-rise building to have its own air-conditioning system. This enables tenants on any floor to control inexpensively their own air conditioning regardless of the time of day or night. This can be particularly important for tenants with special HVAC requirements, for example, tenants with an extensive computer system. It could also be important to a tenant whose office has nonstandard working hours or flex hours. Another advantage is that the failure of one floor's HVAC system does not affect the rest of the building.

Exercise C _____

What are two advantages to operating ten separate air-conditioning systems, one for every four floors of a 40-story building?

Answer C _____

1. *If one unit breaks down, the entire building is not left without service.*

2. *Such a building might be attractive to a tenant with a large computer installation that requires 24-hour air conditioning, or to a*

company whose employees sometimes work weekends or work flexible hours. Whether the cost of running the equipment is borne by the owner or the tenant, air conditioning four floors for the benefit of one is certainly preferable to air conditioning the entire building.

Always ask building owners for specifications on their HVAC systems. Your question may surprise them, but the information will be invaluable.

FLOOR LOAD CAPACITY

Floor load capacity is a factor often overlooked by office marketing salespeople. Yet it can be critical when the potential lessee is, for example, a law firm with a large library. A library of heavy law books may require a floor load capacity even higher than that of the average printing operation. Such firms have sometimes been barred from the space of their choice simply because its floor load capacity was not high enough.

The floor load capacity of an office building normally varies from 75 to 100 pounds per square foot. The latter figure will support most heavy floor loads, even law libraries. If the floor load capacity is under 75 pounds per square foot, problems may arise, even with normal types of business operations. Load capacities can be increased for certain areas, but alterations can be costly. Floor load capacities of low-rise and garden-type buildings vary enormously. As you can see, it's important to check this feature with the building owner.

FLOOR DUCTING

Some modern buildings have what are called electrified floors. An electrified floor is one in which the concrete is poured over and around ducts containing both telephone and power lines. Wires encased in metal boxes emerge from these channels, usually at six-foot intervals.

Electrified floors are particularly appealing to people-intensive businesses—banks, stockbrokerage firms, insurance companies—that require many desks, each with its own telephone. Telephone and power lines can be run through new points in floors and walls with conventional flooring, but the process is more than three times more expensive, and cost is a real consideration when many such installations are required. Electrified floors also may have a safety advantage. In space with large open areas, there is less chance of people tripping over wiring.

Flat wiring and carpet tiles have been used to substitute for electrified floors in some recent construction. This system provides better flexibility in changing office designs.

ELEVATORS

The speed of the elevator service in any high rise is extremely important. Elevator speeds vary a great deal, and very slow elevators can be frustrating, especially to the people who rely on them eight or nine hours a day. You should know the speed of the elevators, the number of elevators per 1,000 square feet and the guaranteed longest waiting period for elevators in any building you handle. A general rule of thumb is that one elevator is needed for every 25,000 to 40,000 square feet above the ground floor. A number of factors affect this. In some cases, for example, large multifloor tenants may use elevators extensively to go back and forth between floors, which significantly impedes overall elevator service efficiency. So be familiar with actual elevator service in a given building.

Find out if the owner or developer has a specification sheet or brochure—anything in writing that you can show to a tenant or file for future reference—that describes the elevator service.

CEILING HEIGHTS

People are unconsciously influenced by the "feel" of a ceiling height. The difference between the feel of an eight-foot ceiling or even an eight-foot six-inch one and a nine-foot ceiling is dramatic. A mere linear six inches added to the height of a room results in many extra cubic inches of room space. Such space gives more light as well as a much more expansive feeling. Some firms, too, need high ceilings for equipment such as computers. So if you are marketing space with a nine-foot ceiling, don't overlook it as a selling point.

PLUMBING

At least a few columns will be located in any tenant space, and one of these will always be a wet column. A vertical plumbing pipe that can be tapped to add additional plumbing facilities runs through a wet column. If your prospective tenant wants an extra bathroom, a wet bar or a kitchenette, the wet column will allow the addition of such amenities at the least extra cost.

LIFE SAFETY FEATURES

An entire category of building improvements that are becoming increasingly important to tenants can be grouped under "life safety features."

Most life safety features are devised to guard occupants against fire and earthquake. Here are some of the more common such features found in modern buildings.

Automatic Sprinkler Systems.   When the temperature reaches a certain critical heat in any given area, the sprinklers turn on and pumps supply water to the system. In some installations, the water flow will cause a fire alarm to sound.

Manual Fire Alarms.   Activation of these alarms alerts both a central control station and the occupants of the floor on which the alarm is sounded.

Smoke Detection Systems.   Like manual fire alarms, these alert a central control station and warn the occupants of the floor in immediate danger.

Smoke Evacuation Systems.   These can be either manual or automatic. They work as exhaust equipment, removing smoke from occupied areas.

Automatic Door-Release Systems.   These systems automatically close certain doors critical to the isolation of fire and/or smoke. They can be operated by smoke detectors.

Elevator Recall Service.   Elevators are dangerous places to be during a fire. Elevators respond to heat and will often automatically go to the floor where a fire is. Special smoke detectors can cause elevators to close their doors and descend automatically to the first floor when smoke is detected.

Emergency Stair Towers.   These specially constructed stairwells resist fire for a certain period of time, usually two to four hours. The stipulated time is designed to be long enough to permit complete evacuation of the building via the stairwells.

Remote Stairway Unlocking.   For security reasons, stairways are often locked from the outside to restrict passage from floor to floor. These systems permit doors to be automatically unlocked from a central control location in case of fire.

Firefighters' Phone Service.   In this portable communication system, phone jacks are installed in stairway vestibules and elevator lobbies on each floor. The firefighters pick up handsets for these jacks at the building control center.

Emergency Power.   Continued operation of the lighting system, as well as of all the systems listed here that need power to function, is provided by an emergency generator in case of power failure.

Central Control Console.   This type of center is located on the ground floor and is equipped for emergency use. It includes multiple telephones and telephone lines, elevator location indicators, a loudspeaker paging system and a panel that receives messages from all building fire alarms and smoke detectors.

Security Alarms.   Activation alerts either a central control station, the police department, or both.

OFFICE-SPACE MEASUREMENT

Space is the product the owner has to sell, and he or she wants top dollar for it. The lessee, on the other hand, is looking for the lowest price possible. Often neither of them knows the real value of the building under consideration. You, the office-marketing sales representative, will be expected to ascertain this real value. Standards for measuring vary from market to market, but the standard most often used is the one set by the Building Owners and Managers Association International (BOMA). (The BOMA standard is approved by the American National Standards Institute and is widely used, but other standards do exist. Don't assume that a particular method of measurement is used in a particular building—check with the owner to be sure.) A BOMA brochure, *Standard Method of Floor Measurement,* details the association's measuring procedure. Highlights of the brochure follow, but you may want to obtain your own copy from BOMA.

Office Space Measuring Standards: Physical Aspects

The two types of space measurement of office buildings are: (1) rentable area and (2) usable area. According to BOMA, the definitions of these terms are as follows:

1. *Rentable area.* This method measures the tenant's pro rata portion of the entire office floor, excluding elements of the building that penetrate through the floor to areas below. The rentable area of a floor is fixed for the life of a building and is not affected by changes in corridor sizes or configuration. This method is, therefore, recommended for measuring the total income-producing area of a building and for use in computing the tenant's pro rata share of a building for purposes of rent escalation.

2. *Usable area.* This method measures the actual occupiable area of a floor or an office suite and is of prime interest to a tenant in evaluating the space offered by a landlord and in allocating the space required for personnel and furniture.
    The amount of usable area on a multitenant floor can vary over the life of a building as corridors expand and contract and as floors are remodeled. Usable area on a floor can be converted to rentable area by using a conversion factor.

Figures 1–5 and 1–6 illustrate rentable space versus usable space. Note that a building floor's rentable space does not change: It is the entire floor less major vertical penetrations of the floor. Usable space (i.e., rentable space less common areas) can change as offices and corridors are moved or remodeled.

FIGURE 1.5   Rentable Area

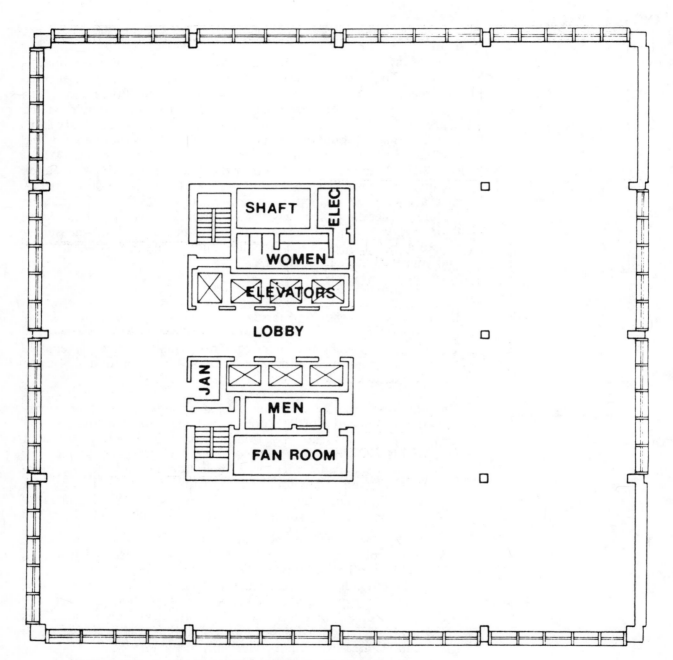

*Note: Assumes glass line as illustrated is the dominant portion.

FIGURE 1.6   Usable Area

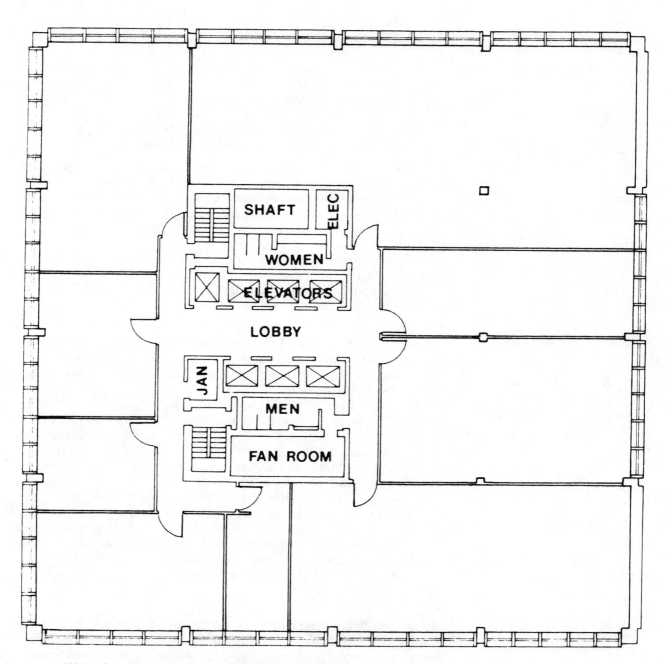

*Note: Assumes glass line as illustrated is the dominant portion.

When space costs are quoted, they are usually quoted on a *rentable* basis. As such, it is very important to understand rentable versus usable space and how the two measurements are derived. Below are BOMA's official standards.

1. *Rentable Area.* The rentable area of a floor shall be computed by measuring to the inside finished surface of the dominant portion of the permanent outer building walls, excluding any major vertical penetration of the floor.

    No deductions shall be made for columns and projections necessary to the building.

    The rentable area of an office on the floor shall be computed by multiplying the usable area of that office by the quotient of the division of the rentable area of the floor by the usable area of the floor resulting in the "R/U Ratio" described herein.

2. *Usable Area.* The usable area of an office shall be computed by measuring to the finished surface of the office side of corridor and other permanent walls, to the center of partitions that separate the office from adjoining usable areas, and to the inside finished surface of the dominant portion of the permanent outer building walls.

    No deductions shall be made for columns and projections necessary to the building.

    The usable area of a floor shall be equal to the sum of all usable areas on that floor.

3. *Where:*
    a) "Finished surface" shall mean a wall, ceiling or floor surface, including glass, as prepared for tenant use, excluding the thickness of any special surfacing materials such as paneling, furring strips and carpet.
    b) "Dominant portion" shall mean that portion of the inside finished surface of the permanent outer building wall which is 50 percent or more of the vertical floor-to-ceiling dimension measured at the dominant portion. If there is no dominant portion, or if the dominant portion is not vertical, the measurement for area shall be to the inside finished surface of the permanent outer building wall where it intersects the finished floor.
    c) "Major vertical penetrations" shall mean stairs, elevator shafts, flues, pipe shafts, vertical ducts and the like, and their enclosing walls, which serve more than one floor of the building, but shall not include stairs, dumbwaiters, lifts and the like, exclusively serving a tenant occupying offices on more than one floor.

In every building there will be a ratio between rentable space and usable space, since rentable space will almost always exceed usable space. This ratio or percentage of rentable space over and above usable space is called the *R/U ratio.* This factor is a key index for the floor's efficiency—the greater the R/U ratio, the less efficient the space. A related efficiency index is known as the load factor or loss factor. This is the percent of space on the floor that is not usable, expressed as a percent of usable space.

These various relationships can be expressed in formulas, as shown below:

1. $\dfrac{\text{Rentable area}}{\text{Usable area}} = $ Rentable/Usable ratio (R/U) ratio

2. Usable area $\times$ R/U Ratio = Rentable area

3. $\dfrac{\text{Rentable area}}{\text{R/U ratio}} = $ Usable area

4. R/U ratio $-1. = $ Load factor

Note that with the R/U ratio and load factor formulas, a tenant's rentable area can be quickly derived by either multiplying the usable area needed by the R/U ratio or by adding needed area plus the load factor.

The rentable area of an office on a multitenant floor is measured from the inside finish of permanent outer building walls to the office side of permanent partitions and to the center of partitions that separate the premises from adjoining rentable areas. No deductions are made for columns and projections necessary to the building.

Compare figure 1–7, which shows a multitenant floor, with figure 1–6. Such shared areas as restrooms, corridors, elevator lobbies and nonexclusive supply areas are not shaded. They are considered rentable space, but their costs are prorated to the various tenants based on the ratio of each tenant's rentable space to the total rentable space.

An Example. A prospective tenant decided he would need 20,000 square feet in a particular building. The space is offered at $20 per rentable square foot per year, with a load factor of nine percent. The effective annual rent is computed as follows:

20,000 square feet usable + 9 percent load factor
= 21,800 square feet needed
21,800 square feet rentable $\times$ $20 per rentable square foot per year
= $436,000
$436,000 $\div$ 20,000 usable square feet = $21.80 per usable square foot,
or $21.80 effective rent per square foot per year.

You can see why the load factor and the cost per usable square foot can be very important to the prospective tenant. Also note that usable footage on a multitenant floor will have a higher load factor and R/U ratio than on a single-tenant floor because shared areas are added to the load, and multitenant floors usually have more nonusable space than single-tenant ones.

Exercise D

A tenant wants to rent 10,000 square feet of usable space. One building is offered at $20 per square foot and has a load factor of nine percent. Another building rents for $19.50 per square foot, with a load factor of 14 percent. Which building offers the tenant the best deal, and what will be the effective rent in each case?

FIGURE 1.7   Multiple-Tenant Floor

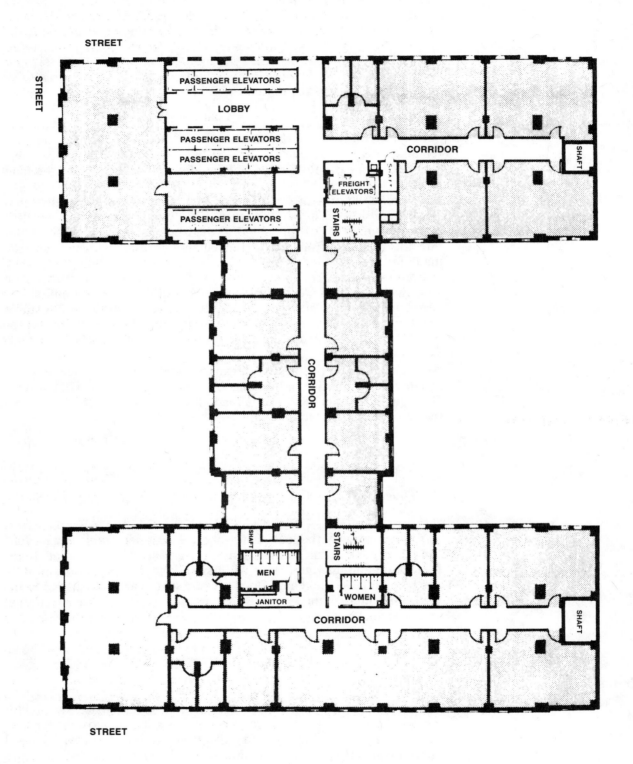

Answer D

> *With the first building's nine percent load factor, the tenant will need 10,900 square feet of rentable space (10,000 + 9 percent). At $20 per square foot, that totals $218,000 per year, or $21.80 per usable square foot. The rentable space needed in the second building would be 10,000 plus 14 percent, or 11,400 square feet. At $19.50 per square foot, that totals $222,300 per year, or $22.23 per usable square foot. The first building is the better buy because its effective rent is $21.80 as opposed to the second building's effective rent of $22.23.*

The method of calculation owners use to arrive at a rental figure can vary. Always ask whether the quoted price is for rentable space or usable space. And after you have done that, get the owner's definition of the terms "rentable" and "usable." Sometimes the answers will surprise you—the terms can mean different things to different people. Don't even rely on the owner to be able to tell you the load factor on a particular space. Bear in mind also that a building seldom has a load factor lower than nine percent.

You can see from this discussion that informing your prospective tenant of the cost of usable space is important in evaluating alternative solutions to the tenant's problems. Your careful analysis of the figures involved can save the tenant many dollars and assure you a long-term relationship.

TENANT IMPROVEMENTS

At the beginning of this chapter, when the terms "shell" and "skin" were defined, tenant improvements were mentioned. These are improvements the owner will pay for in filling in the building's skin. Tenant improvements usually include such features as ceilings, walls, paint, lighting and telephone and electrical outlets. They are a major part of any lease negotiation. The agreed-upon improvements are always spelled out in considerable detail in a *work letter* that is attached to the lease as a separate exhibit. A typical work letter is shown in figure 1–8.

"Gypsum board, ⅝ in. thick," for example, is not an adequate description of the partitions that are to be installed. The description should read, "⅝ in. gypsum board (finished, painted, and with rubber base) on both sides of 2½ in. metal studs."

Other features typically covered are the exact type of ceiling to be installed, the number and placement of electrical and telephone outlets, the exact kind and number of coats of paint to be applied and any limitation on the number of colors permitted. If the building is furnishing floor covering and draperies, these too should be described in detail.

The owner usually will provide a *preliminary space plan*, particularly in the case of new buildings. This is merely a rough layout, not a set of final working drawings. A tenant who requires working drawings must pay for them—a not inconsiderable cost, since working drawings cost from seven to eight times as much as a preliminary space plan.

The owner has figured out how much money to allow for tenant improvements for the entire building long before a tenant moves in. This amount is included in the owner's overall budget. The tenant's improvements allowance will usually be quoted to the tenant as a dollar amount per square foot of rentable or usable area. Such an allowance, for example $18 per square foot usable, is subject to negotiations between owner and tenant. Thereafter, any desired improvements costing more than the allowance or work letter provisions must be borne by the tenant.

CONCLUSION

At the beginning of this chapter, you were told that we would begin by analyzing your product, leaving the subject of selling skills for a later chapter. This turns out not to be entirely true. It has probably occurred to you by now that modules, mullions, core areas, tenant improvements and the other features discussed here are more than mere physical attributes. They are also powerful selling tools when you present them to the client as benefits.

One fact is constant in all office-marketing negotiations: tenants want to obtain the exact space that will best meet their requirements, plus other features that vary from tenant to tenant, at the smallest possible cost. Owners, on the other hand, want to maximize the return on their investment. In the hands of a skilled office marketing sales representative, any one of the features discussed here is a potential opportunity to turn a seemingly hopeless negotiation into an attractive commission and a tentative relationship into a long and rewarding association.

So, in one sense at least, this chapter has really been about selling after all.

FIGURE 1.8   Work Letter Agreement

Grubb&Ellis

_____   Date:_____

_____

Ladies and Gentlemen:

You (hereinafter called "Tenant") and we (hereinafter called "Landlord") are executing simultaneously with this Work Letter Agreement the written lease of certain premises in the building known as _____ to which this Work Letter Agreement is attached. Said premises are described in said lease and are hereinafter called "the premises".

To induce Tenant to enter into said lease (which is hereby incorporated by reference to the extent that the provisions of this agreement may apply thereto) and in consideration of the mutual covenants hereinafter contained, Landlord and Tenant mutually agree as follows:

1. Plans and Specifications

(a) Landlord agrees to furnish at its sole cost and expense, all architectural, mechanical, and electrical engineering plans and specifications required for the performance of the "Building Standard Work" hereinbelow described (including complete detailed plans and specifications for Tenant's partition layout, reflected ceiling, heating and air conditioning, electrical outlets and switches and telephone outlets).

(b) It is understood and agreed that any interior decorating services, such as selection of special wall coverings, fixtures, carpeting, and any or all other decorator items required by Tenant in the performance of said work referred to in subparagraph (a) hereinabove shall be at the Tenant's sole cost and expense.

(c) Tenant agrees (i) to furnish to Landlord on or before_____, 19_____, all information respecting Tenant's requirements necessary for the preparation of the plans and specifications to be furnished by Landlord pursuant to subparagraph (a) above and (ii) that said plans and specifications will be approved by Tenant within _____ days after submittal of same to Tenant.

Grubb & Ellis Company   One Montgomery Street, Telesis Tower, San Francisco, CA 94104 (415) 956-1990

FIGURE 1.8   Work Letter Agreement (continued)

2. Building Standard Work at Landlord's Cost and Expense

Landlord agrees, at its sole cost and expense, to furnish and install all
of the following "Building Standard Work" limited to the quantities
specified by the Landlord and as indicated on final plans furnished by
Landlord.

(a) PARTITIONS
Landlord shall provide one (1) lineal foot of full-height partitioning
per 15 square feet of usable area. An acceptable standard would be
$5/8$ inch thick drywall, taped, painted with metal studs on 16"
centers, with top set base, both sides. Vinyl wrapped demountable
systems will be acceptable in lieu thereof, and, in fact, would be
preferable. Colors as selected by Tenant from Landlord's building
standard color chart.

(b) DOORS
(Excluding entry & exterior)—Landlord shall provide one
full-height interior door—solid-core walnut veneer or stain—frames
and hardware, per 35 lineal feet of interior partitions. Two rated
entry/exit doors including frames and hardware shall be provided
by Landlord for every 5,000 usable square feet. Landlord to furnish
Tenant six (6) sets of suite & building entrance keys.

(c) CEILING TILE
Landlord shall provide a suspended fissured mineral fiber
acoustical ceiling with an acoustical STC minimum rating of 40–45.
If no building standard system is available, a minimum
requirement of exposed T-bar and Lay-in tile is expected.

(d) LIGHT FIXTURES
Landlord shall provide sufficient fixtures so as to allow a
maintained maximum at desk height of 70–75 footcandles. Warm
white tubes to be used throughout work area.

(e) SWITCHES
Landlord shall provide one (1) electrical wall switch for every 250
usable square feet.

(f) FLOOR COVERING
Vinyl asbestos floor covering in all noncarpeted area including vinyl
or rubber base (coved or carpet base) in colors selected by Tenant
from a color range and type as specified by the Landlord. At

FIGURE 1.8   Work Letter Agreement (continued)

Tenant's election carpeting will be furnished and installed in lieu of furnishing and installing vinyl asbestos floor covering, in which event, Landlord will bear the first $4.50 per square yard of the cost of such carpet installation and any and all cost in excess of $4.50 per square yard shall be paid for by Tenant promptly upon being billed.

(g) ELECTRICAL OUTLETS/TELEPHONE OUTLETS

Landlord shall provide one (1) standard convenience duplex outlet and one (1) telephone for every 150 usable square feet. Landlord shall locate outlets according to Tenant layout.

(h) HEATING, VENTILATING AND AIR CONDITIONING

Systems to be designed to meet the requirements of applicable codes and regulations. Exhaust systems shall be provided in toilets, staff rooms, conference rooms. All systems to be in accordance with sound engineering practices.

(i) WINDOW COVERING AND TREATMENT

Landlord to provide building standard window treatment. If no building standard is established, an acceptable standard would be partial-open-weave casement. In either event, drapes will be hung from top of frame to within two (2) inches of finished floor with two-way traverse pull.

(j) PERIMETER AND DRYWALL PARTITION FINISHES

Landlord shall provide one (1) sealer coat, two (2) coats of finish paint, or vinyl. User to select from Landlord standard colors.

(k) DRINKING FOUNTAIN

One (1) chilled-water drinking fountain shall be installed on each floor in core walls as designated by Landlord's architect.

(l) LIFE SAFETY SYSTEM

The premises will be provided a life safety support system as established by code.

NOTE: Tenant to review all plans and specifications—including HVAC— prior to construction.

FIGURE 1.8   Work Letter Agreement (continued)

3. Substitution and Credits

Tenant may select different new materials in place of "Building Standard Work" materials that would otherwise be initially furnished and installed by Landlord for the interior of the premises under the provisions of this Work Letter Agreement, provided such selection is indicated on the plans and specifications approved by Tenant. If Tenant shall make any such selection and if the cost of such different new materials of Tenant's selection shall exceed Landlord's cost of Landlord's "Building Standard Work" materials thereby replaced, Tenant shall pay to Landlord, as hereinafter provided, the difference between Landlord's cost of such different new materials and Landlord's cost of the materials thereby replaced. Credit shall be granted for use of less than stated quantities of "Building Standard Work" and may be applied toward substitutions other than in kind.

No such different new materials shall be furnished or installed in replacement of any of Landlord's "Building Standard Work" materials until Landlord and Tenant have mutually agreed in writing on the amount by which Landlord's cost of such different new materials exceeds Landlord's cost of such replaced "Building Standard Work" materials. Conditional upon the aforesaid prior mutual agreement of the parties, Tenant agrees to promptly pay to Landlord the amount of such excess.

All amounts payable by Tenant to Landlord pursuant to this Paragraph 3 shall be paid by Tenant promptly after the rendering of bills therefor by Landlord to Tenant, it being understood that such bills may be rendered during the progress of the performance of the work and/or the furnishing and installation of the materials substituted for "Building Standard Work" materials shall at once become a part of the realty and belong to Landlord.

4. Completion and Rental Commencement Date

It is agreed that, notwithstanding anything set forth in the lease to the contrary, Tenant's obligation for the payment of rental thereunder shall not commence until Landlord has substantially completed all work to be performed by Landlord as hereinabove set forth; provided, however, that if Landlord shall be delayed in substantially completing said work as a result of:

(i)   Tenant's failure to furnish, within the applicable times set forth in this agreement, any information or approvals to be furnished by Tenant pursuant to the provisions hereof; or

FIGURE 1.8   Work Letter Agreement (concluded)

(ii)   Tenant's request for materials, finishes, or installations other than Landlord's "Building Standard Work"; or

(iii) Changes by Tenant in the plans and specifications after approval by Tenant of same;

then the commencement of Tenant's obligation to pay rent shall be accelerated by the number of days of such delay.

If the foregoing correctly sets forth our understanding, kindly sign copies of this Work Letter Agreement where indicated.

Accepted:
Very Truly Yours,

By: _____   By: _____
              (Tenant)   (Landlord)

Exercise E

Answer the following questions.

1. Name the three basic types of office buildings.

2. Wall partitions connect to the window wall by means of _____ .

3. HVAC stands for _____ .

4. a. Define rentable space.
   b. Define usable space.

5. You want to find out the floor load capacity of a certain building. The owner doesn't know the answer. What do you do?

6. How should tenant improvements be listed in the lease?

7. Define the term *load factor*.

8. You have secured an exclusive listing on 10,000 square feet in a brand-new building with which you are unfamiliar. When examining the space for the first time, what three things should you immediately establish about it?

9. Name the two basic structural components into which all buildings are divided.

10. What type of core location is best suited to the needs of a multitenant floor?

Answer E

1. *The three types are high-rise, low-rise and garden type.*

2. *Mullions*

3. *Heating, ventilating and air-conditioning equipment*

4. a. *Rentable space is the total space on which the tenant is charged rent, whether or not all the area charged for can actually be used as office space.*
   b. *Usable space is the area within the rentable space that the tenant can use as office space.*

5. *Ask the architect.*

6. *List tenant improvements in a separate work letter.*

7. *The load factor is the percentage of rentable space not actually available to the tenant to use as office space.*

8. *Establish (a) the location of the core, (b) the overall amount of floor space, and (c) the distance from the outer core wall to the windows.*

9. *A shell and a skin comprise the structure of all buildings.*

10. *A central-core location is best for a multitenant floor.*

2

Economics of Office Buildings

INTRODUCTION

Why should you, positioned as you are at the selling and leasing end of real estate transactions, need to know anything about building pro formas, financing and operating expenses? The answer is simple: If you are to do a good, professional job, you must be able to look at a point of negotiation from the developer's or owner's perspective. Fortunately, the information you need to master to do this is also simple.

In the field, you will deal with many owners and developers. You will find that they are almost always willing to at least hear you out on any concession you may request for a prospective tenant, but will flatly turn you down at the suggestion that they lower their rent. A sound economic reason for this exists, as you will learn.

BUILDING EVALUATION

Study the seven-item formula that follows. It shows what deductions building owners must make from gross income to determine how much is actually spendable income. You should memorize this formula.

1.   Gross Income
2. – Vacancy Factor =
3.   Adjusted Gross Income
4. – Expenses =
5.   Net Income
6. – Debt Service =
7.   Cash Flow

Every property that you will deal with will have a *gross income*. This is the total amount of money collected from rented space. No property remains 100 percent leased all the time, so provision must be made for a *vacancy factor*. The gross income minus the vacancy factor is the *adjusted gross income*. Now subtract all the *expenses* of operating the building—maintenance, utilities, taxes, insurance and so on. This leaves the *net operating income* (often referred to as the NOI). From the net, subtract the *debt service*, the amount needed to pay off the building mortgage(s). The debt service includes both principal and interest. What is left is the *cash flow*, or spendable income.

Investors considering developing or buying a specific piece of property must arrive at a gross income figure even before negotiating with a bank for a loan. First, they decide what their average rent per square foot will be. Then they work through the formula, figuring in a vacancy rate estimate, derived as a function of current economic conditions. Then, expenses and loan payments are projected. The net income thus arrived at is an extremely important figure. It helps determine how much the lending bank will advance an investor.

Developers and owners then *capitalize* the net income figure. This means they use the net income as a base from which to project the value of the building. They take a *capitalization rate* of, say, nine percent, and ask themselves, "This net income represents nine percent of what amount of money?" The answer is the building's estimated value.

For example, the net income on a proposed building has been figured by the developer, Mark Weston, at $100,000. The capitalization rate ("cap" rate) is ten percent. Weston divides his $100,000 by .10 to arrive at the estimated value of the property, $1 million. Reversing the process, if a building has a value of $1 million, it will generate a net income of $100,000 at a cap rate of ten percent.

The cap rate is not a figure the investor pulls out of the air. It is determined largely by the cost of money (interest rate) prevailing in that particular market at that particular time. The current market demand for the particular type of property in question and the investment risk are also factors.

In another example, the property has a net income of $90,000. If the cap rate is still ten percent, the property's estimated value is $900,000 ($90,000 ÷ .10). This is called the *income approach* to appraisal.

Now compare the two examples.

1. $100,000 capped at ten percent yields a value of $1 million.

2. $90,000 capped at ten percent yields a value of $900,000.

This comparison demonstrates why building owners and developers would rather make almost any concession than lower the rent. Lowering the rent lowers their net income; lowering their net income lowers the value of their property, and their property is their asset.

Exercise A

A building has an annual gross income of $460,000 and operating expenses of $175,000. At a capitalization rate of ten percent, what is the value of the building? (Allow for a five percent vacancy rate.) Check your answer with the one below.

Answer A

Gross Income	$460,000
5% Vacancy Factor	– 23,000
Adjusted Gross Income	437,000
Expenses	– 175,000
Net Income	$262,000

$262,000 capped at 10% = $2,620,000.

Exercise B

Now perform the same valuation using a cap rate of eight percent.

Answer B

$262,000 capped at 8% = $3,275,000.

The second exercise was not intended merely for extra practice. It illustrates what a tremendous difference in value a two-point spread in the cap rate can make. Look at the figures again.

OBTAINING FINANCING

Weston, the hypothetical developer who wants to construct a $1-million building from which he plans to generate an annual net income of $100,000, approached a bank for a 75 percent loan. He would, in other words, be borrowing $750,000 and putting up $250,000 in cash. The bank officer agreed to a 75 percent loan—with a condition.

"Mr. Weston," said the banker, "I think a 75 percent loan on a $1-million property reasonable. But I can make this loan only if your building is *still* worth at least $1 million when its vacancy rate is ten percent."

What does that mean to Weston? Study the figures that led him to arrive at the net income of $100,000 from which he made his $1-million building valuation. They are the first five points of the seven-point formula.

Gross Income	$174,800
Vacancy Factor	− 8,740
Adjusted Gross Income	166,060
Expenses	− 66,000
Net Income	$100,060

But now Weston must raise the vacancy factor to ten percent while retaining a building valuation of $1 million. He can do this only by increasing his net income—by raising the rent on a building that hasn't even been constructed yet.

	So this:	*Becomes this:*
Gross Income	$174,800	$184,500
Vacancy Factor	− 8,740	− 18,450
Adjusted Gross Income	166,060	166,050
Expenses	− 66,000	− 66,000
Net Income	$100,060	$100,050

You needn't understand the mathematics Weston used to change his analysis, but you should understand this: the overall projected annual rent must be raised by $9,700 for Weston to keep a $1-million building assessment and qualify for this 75 percent loan.

If you see how lowering the office-space rental basis lowers the value of a property, you know why brokers run into such stiff resistance whenever they suggest it.

THE PRO FORMA

An investor applying for a loan on a proposed new building takes a cost and income projection known as a pro forma to the bank. Figures 2–1 and 2–2 show the cost and income portions of the pro forma. Review the cost items briefly.

Section one is the cost of the land on which the building is to be constructed.

Section two covers expenditures known as hard costs or direct costs. These are the costs of constructing the building's shell and skin, landscaping and making tenant improvements. An estimated cost of $16,741,800 is projected for the building's total of 418,545 square feet. This equals $40 per square foot. Note the $4,762,380 for tenant improvements. The figure to the left on that line, 317,492 square feet, represents the portion of the total square footage that can be considered rentable space. The developer has allowed $15.00 per square foot for tenant improvements. The final item under hard costs is landscaping.

Section three is composed of soft costs, also known as indirect costs, most of which are self-explanatory. They represent the total amount of fees, interest and related costs of the project.

FIGURE 2.1   Pro Forma Project Costs

PRO FORMA PROJECT COSTS

1. Land, at cost

   $ 4,500,000

2. Building:

31 floors at 12,695 sq. ft.	393,545 sq. ft.
basement	15,000 sq. ft.
penthouse (mechanical)	10,000 sq. ft.
	418,545 sq. ft.

   418,545 sq. ft. at $40

   $16,741,800

   Tenant improvements: 317,492 sq. ft. at $15.00

   4,762,380

   Landscaping, etc.

   374,450

   $21,878,630

3. Indirect costs:

Bonds and insurance at 1% of construction (rounded)	$ 218,800
Architecture and engineering at 5% of construction	1,093,900
Taxes during construction	600,000
Legal, escrow and consulting at 1% of land and construction	263,800
Advertising and miscellaneous at 1% of land and construction	263,800
Tenant inducements: 326,111 sq. ft. at $2	652,000
Leasing fees: 326,112 sq. ft. at $4	1,304,400
Contingency at 5% of construction	1,093,900
Developer's Equity Opportunity Cost: $8,100,000 × 11⅜% × 21 months	1,610,000
Permanent loan fees at 1% × $31,000,000	310,000
Construction loan fees at 2% × $31,000,000	620,000
Construction loan interest: $31,000,000 × 13% × 45% × 21 months (rounded)	3,174,000
	$11,204,600

4. Developer's management fees: $37,583,230

   $ 1,503,300

$ 4,500,000
21,878,630
11,204,600
1,503,300

   Total project costs $39,086,530

   Round figure $39,100,000

FIGURE 2.2 Pro Forma Income Projection

Scheduled gross income		$7,222,900
Less 5% vacancy factor		361,100
Effective gross income		$6,861,800
Operating expenses:		
317,492 sq. ft. at $5.00 × 95%	$1,508,100	
Property taxes (1)	827,000	$2,335,100
Net annual income		$4,526,700
Annual debt service on permanent 30-year take-out loan @ 12%		
$31,000,000 at 12.34 constant		$3,825,400
Cash flow		$ 701,300

A few items, however, should be emphasized. The $652,000 projected for tenant inducements is the amount the developer can offer in concessions without cutting into income. Leasing fees should be of special interest to you—they are your commission. You may also see them referred to as "commission expense" or "marketing expense." This cost has already been provided for and will ultimately be paid as rent by the tenants you acquire. The contingency fund is intended to cover emergencies such as unexpected costs and construction errors. In this case, the contingency fund is five percent of total construction costs.

The pro forma income projection (figure 2–2) is an elaboration of the seven-point formula introduced earlier. The construction loan interest included in soft costs shows that the loan on the property is figured at $31 million. This means the developer is putting up $8.1 million in cash on this $39.1 million project.

Exercise C

Using the pro forma, evaluate the property using a cap rate of nine percent.

Answer C

$50,300,000 is a rounded answer.

Earlier in the chapter you were introduced to the term *cash flow,* but until now little has been said about it. The cash flow is used to figure a building's *cash-on-cash return* (this, too, is a common term). The cash-on-cash return is the ratio of annual cash flow to the actual cash invested in the project.

For example, a developer obtains a $750,000 loan on a building valued at $1 million. That means she puts up $250,000 cash. Her cash flow at the end of the first year is $30,000. The cash-on-cash return is the ratio of $30,000 to $250,000; $30,000 divided by $250,000 is .12. So 12 percent is the cash-on-cash return.

Exercise D

Using the figures from the pro forma, calculate the cash-on-cash return on the property.

Answer D

The pro forma income projection tells you the annual cash flow is ~~$681,800~~. #701,300 *The pro forma project cost shows a loan of $24 million. Since the project costs $29 million altogether, the investor put up $5 million. $701,300 divided by $8.1 million gives a cash-on-cash return of 8.66 percent.*

Exercise E

Use the pro forma to figure the average annual rent per square foot.

Answer E

The pro forma income projection shows a scheduled gross income of $7,222,900. The pro forma project cost reveals that the building will have 317,492 square feet of rentable space. Dividing annual income by rentable space gives an annual rental of $22.75 per square foot.

On a high-rise project like this, the square-foot rental rate would, of course, vary throughout the building. Penthouse space would cost perhaps $28 per square foot; ground-floor space, perhaps $32; and a low floor other than the ground floor might be only $17.

WHERE TO GET HELP

As you work with building owners and developers, you will begin to acquire a sense of the various construction and operating costs. Don't try to memorize this information—it will come naturally as you become familiar with the field. Remember that the Building Owners and Managers Association can help you here. BOMA releases an annual tabulation of office building operating costs for each area of the country called the *Building Owners and Managers Experience Exchange Report*. It analyzes various operating costs by building type: modern steel high rises, older steel high rises in good locations and older buildings not constructed of steel. The files of your local office are another source of current construction and operating costs.

CONCLUSION

This chapter has equipped you with many of the terms needed to understand the area of building valuation and financing. It also has prepared you for the section on concessions in the office lease. Now that you know why owners and developers cannot afford to lower their rent once it has been established, you have an understanding of the principal reason for concessions. A concession is a means for investors to reduce tenants' **effective rent**—through shouldering parking costs, lending the money for improvements the tenants are to pay for, or extending a month's free rent, for example—while protecting the value of their property by not tampering with the **quoted rent.**

Exercise F

Define the following terms.

1. debt service
2. cash flow
3. cash-on-cash return
4. adjusted gross income
5. hard construction costs
6. soft construction costs
7. cap rate
8. pro forma
9. contingency fund
10. effective rental rate

Answer F

1. *The debt service is the combined cost of interest and principal paid on a mortgage, usually quoted on an annual basis.*

2. *Cash flow is the actual, spendable income remaining when debt service has been subtracted from net income.*

3. *The cash-on-cash return is the ratio of annual cash flow to cash invested. (The percentage is arrived at by dividing cash flow by cash invested.)*

4. *Adjusted gross income is the income remaining when the basic gross income has been reduced by the vacancy factor.*

5. *Hard construction costs are the costs of land acquisition and the actual physical product in constructing a building.*

6. *Soft costs are all indirect, intangible costs.*

7. The cap rate is a variable rate, dictated by the prevailing money market, that (together with net income) is used to determine the value of a building.

8. A pro forma is a basic cost-and-income projection used by a developer as the basis for planning a building project and negotiating a loan.

9. A contingency fund is a fund set aside by a developer as a cushion to cover the cost of oversights in cost estimating or errors in the construction itself.

10. The effective rental rate is the rent a tenant actually pays when the monetary value of concessions is subtracted from the quoted rate.

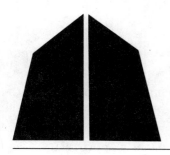

3

Legal Aspects of Office Marketing

INTRODUCTION

As a marketer of office space, you will be filling out many real estate forms. This chapter will familiarize you with the most useful ones.

A major pitfall for salespeople when they first begin to use real estate forms is that they may inadvertently find themselves practicing law without authorization. In many states, creating or even modifying legal documents is illegal for brokers and their sales personnel, who are permitted only to fill out standard forms.

In your day-to-day work, however, it will often be necessary to alter a contract. Be aware of potential problems, and take the precaution of getting your manager's approval on every contract you alter. Your manager will know when it's safe to make changes in a contract.

If you follow these rules, you are not likely to slip into any legal booby traps.

1. Never rely on oral agreements. Put everything in writing.

2. Keep a log of contacts with owners and tenants. Record and date all information obtained from these sources.

3. Never permit your company's approved forms to pass from your control. If you give a blank contract to prospects, you run the risk that they may modify it or use it for another transaction. In such a case, your firm might be held legally liable for the consequences.

4. Choose your cooperating brokers carefully, and put all agreements with them in writing.

5. Consult your manager whenever you find yourself in an ambiguous legal or ethical question.

6. Remember that all written agreements must be signed by both principals to the agreement in order to be enforceable, and each signer must receive a copy of the agreement.

7. Never alter a contract without your manager's approval.

As an office marketing salesperson, you will soon become familiar with the following documents:

1. exclusive authorization of lease

2. exclusive marketing agreement

3. nonexclusive authorization of lease

4. commission agreement

5. offer to lease

6. tenant representation agreement

7. office lease

The office lease is so important that an entire section will be devoted to it. This chapter will examine the other legal forms listed above and consider some problems in real estate sales.

EXCLUSIVE AUTHORIZATION OF LEASE

The exclusive authorization of lease states that you and your company have an exclusive right to lease a certain space and that no matter who performs the negotiations—you, the owner or an outside broker—you have earned a commission. It is obviously to your advantage to try to secure an exclusive on any property you handle.

Grubb & Ellis's exclusive-authorization-of-lease form is reproduced in figure 3–1. Note that the second line has a space for the date of the listing period. This information is vital. If you don't fill in a specific termination date, your exclusive is merely a piece of paper.

The terms of the lease come next. Be as specific as possible here. If the owner wants $1.10 per square foot, a five-year lease, an escalation clause covering taxes and insurance, the rent per square foot tied to the consumer price index beginning with the third year...all of that information goes right here. You may have to attach the terms in the form of an addendum. When you deliver a tenant willing to meet all the specified terms but the owner decides not to go through with the deal, you are still entitled to your commission if you have listed the terms in detail. But if the terms are vague, the owner might try to take advantage of that loophole to avoid paying your commission.

Include details in specifying the location of the property, too. Don't describe a property simply as being located at "1542 Main Street in the City of Los Angeles, County of Los Angeles." A better description is "the southeast corner of Main and Kookamunga streets, further described as that certain five-story office building consisting of approxi-

FIGURE 3.1   Exclusive Authorization of Lease

OWNER hereby grants to GRUBB AND ELLIS COMMERCIAL BROKERAGE COMPANY ("Broker") the exclusive right to negotiate a lease or leases on the subject property (the "Property") for a period commencing on _____ , 19_____, and ending at midnight on _____ , 19_____. The Property is located in the City of _____ , County of _____ , State of _____ , located at _____ , and further described as _____
_____
_____

The price and terms of the lease(s) shall be as follows: _____
_____
_____

In consideration of this Authorization and Broker's agreement diligently to pursue the procurement of a tenant or tenants for the Property, Owner agrees to pay Broker a commission or commissions as set forth in the attached SCHEDULE OF COMMISSIONS.

Owner shall pay said commission(s) to Broker if: (a) the Property is leased to tenant(s) by or through Broker, Owner or any other party prior to the expiration of this Authorization or any extension hereof; or (b) a tenant is procured by or through Broker, Owner or any other party who is ready, willing and able to lease the Property on the terms above stated or other terms reasonably acceptable to Owner prior to the expiration of this Authorization or any extension hereof; or (c) any contract for the lease of the Property is made directly or indirectly by Owner prior to the expiration of this Authorization or any extension hereof; or (d) the Property is withdrawn from lease without the written consent of Broker or made unmarketable by Owner's voluntary act during the term of this Authorization or any extension hereof; or (e) within one hundred eighty (180) days after the expiration of this Authorization or any extension hereof, the Property is leased to any person or entity with whom Broker has negotiated or to whom Broker has submitted the Property prior to such expiration in an effort to effect a transaction and whose name appears on any list of such persons or entities which Broker shall have mailed to Owner at the address below stated within thirty (30) days following such expiration, provided that if Broker has submitted a written offer to lease or purchase, it shall not be necessary to include the offeror's name on such list.

If a sale or other transfer or conveyance is made by Broker, Owner or any other party prior to the expiration of this Authorization or any extension hereof, or during the one hundred eighty (180)-day period thereafter, Owner shall pay Broker a commission as set forth in the attached SCHEDULE OF COMMISSIONS.

If during the term of this Authorization or any extension hereof an escrow is opened or negotiations involving the sale, transfer, conveyance or leasing of the Property have commenced and are continuing, then the term of this Authorization shall be extended for a period through the closing of such escrow, the termination of such negotiations or the consummation of such transaction, provided this Authorization would otherwise have expired during such period.

Owner agrees to cooperate with Broker in effecting a lease or leases of the Property and immediately to refer to Broker all inquiries of any party interested in the Property. All negotiations are to be through Broker. Broker is authorized to accept a deposit from any prospective tenant. Broker is further authorized to advertise the Property and shall have the exclusive right to place a sign or signs on the Property if, in Broker's opinion, such would facilitate the leasing thereof.

It is understood that it is illegal for either Owner or Broker to refuse to present, lease or sell to any person because of race, color, religion, national origin, sex, marital status or physical disability.

Owner warrants that he is the owner of record of the Property or has the legal authority to execute this Authorization. Owner agrees to hold Broker harmless from any liability or damages arising from any incorrect information supplied by Owner or any information which Owner fails to supply. Owner acknowledges receipt of a copy of this Authorization and the attached SCHEDULE OF COMMISSIONS, which Owner has read and understands.

If either Owner or Broker commences any litigation to enforce the terms of this Authorization, the prevailing party shall be entitled to receive a reasonable attorney's fee from the other party hereto.

No amendments or alterations in the terms hereof or withdrawal of this Authorization shall be valid or binding unless made in writing and signed by both Owner and Broker.

The heirs, transferees, successors and assigns of the parties hereto are duly bound by the provisions hereof.

DATED: _____ , 19_____   OWNER: _____

ACCEPTED: GRUBB AND ELLIS COMMERCIAL   By _____
               BROKERAGE COMPANY
                                                                   By _____

                                                                   Address: _____

                                                                   _____

By _____   Telephone: _____

mately 50,000 rentable square feet, more commonly known and designated as 1542 Main Street." This demonstrates your professionalism.

The paragraph following the terms states that in return for your delivery of a satisfactory tenant, the owner will pay you the appropriate commission (as set forth in your company's commission schedule) within five days of the lease's execution. Always attach a letter to the authorization form that quotes the commission schedule, and be sure the owner signs *both* the authorization form and the attachment. The owner's signature on the commission schedule is the only proof that he or she actually examined it, and the contract is not binding without this signature. Attaching the commission schedule itself to the authorization form would ensure a binding contract, but most schedules are long and complicated-looking. Building owners tend to think they should have their lawyers examine such schedules before signing. A simple letter quoting only the relevant portions of the commission schedule is more effective. Be sure to learn the schedule thoroughly. You won't look very professional if you have to refer to the form each time an owner asks a question about your commission rates.

The next paragraph guarantees your commission if someone to whom you have shown the property becomes a tenant within 180 days after the expiration of the agreement, as long as you mail a list of all prospects with whom you have negotiated to the owner within 30 days of the expiration date. This means, in effect, that a six-month exclusive is really a 12-month exclusive—if you register the names of all your prospects with the owner.

The rest of the exclusive-authorization form is self-explanatory.

In addition to protecting your commission no matter who produces the tenant, the exclusive listing has another advantage for you: It commits your firm to supporting your efforts. The company will regard your exclusive as worth investing its time, money and energy to help you complete the deal.

In regard to the entire matter of signatures, always make certain when working with large corporations that the person signing a contract is authorized to do so. Otherwise, your signed contract is just a worthless piece of paper. If the person tells you he or she is authorized but you still have doubts, ask to see the corporate resolution that confirms this fact. Don't be hesitant about asking—you have a right to know.

EXCLUSIVE MARKETING AGREEMENT

Like the exclusive authorization of lease, the exclusive marketing agreement states that you and your company have an exclusive right to represent a certain space.

The exclusive marketing agreement is reproduced in figure 3–2. As with any other agreement the date of the listing period (section 2) must be completed.

The duties of the broker are listed next. These clearly state the functions that the broker will fulfill. Included are a reporting schedule and an overview of the marketing plan. Listed next are the obligations of the lessor-owner with a time frame for completion.

FIGURE 3.2   Exclusive Marketing Agreement

This Agreement made this _____ day of _____ , 19_____ , by and between _____ _____ hereinafter referred to as "Lessor/Owner" and SMITH AND JONES COMMERCIAL BROKERAGE COMPANY, a California corporation, hereinafter referred to as "Broker."

WITNESSETH:

WHEREAS, Lessor/Owner is the owner of record of that certain real property, more specifically identified in Exhibit "A," attached hereto, and hereinafter referred to as the "Project"; and

WHEREAS, Broker is a licensed real estate brokerage company experienced in handling the planning and execution of the marketing of the type of property constituting the Project;

NOW THEREFORE, in consideration of the mutual covenants herein contained, the parties hereto do hereby agree as follows:

1. APPOINTMENT AS AGENT:

Lessor/Owner retains Broker to act as its sole and exclusive agent hereunder to lease and/or sell those portions of the Project which are available for leasing and/or sale subject to the terms and conditions hereinafter set forth.

2. TERM OF AGREEMENT:

The term of this Agreement shall commence on the date of this Agreement as set forth above and, subject to the termination provisions set forth hereinafter in Section 6, shall terminate automatically at midnight on _____ 19_____ ; unless prior thereto the parties hereto agree in writing to an extension of the term. If during the term of this Agreement or any extension hereof an escrow is opened or negotiations involving the sale, transfer, conveyance, or leasing of the Project have commenced and are continuing, then the term of this Agreement shall be extended for a period through the closing of such escrow, the termination of such negotiations, or the consummation of such transactions, provided this Agreement would otherwise have expired during such period.

3. DUTIES OF BROKER:

3.1 Broker shall plan and administer all activities related to the marketing of the Project, subject to the direction and approval of Lessor/Owner. These activities shall include, among others, cooperating with all organizations and individuals performing functions for the Project so as to coordinate marketing requirements with all applicable planning considerations.

3.2 Broker shall consult with Lessor/Owner regarding all facets of the Project, including tenant categorization and orientation in the Project, tenant construction requirements, market rental conditions, and the overall decor and design of the Project.

3.3 Broker shall coordinate with Lessor/Owner in order that the advertising and public relations campaigns for the Project are planned and executed in a professional, effective manner. Any brochures that are specifically prepared in order to market the Project shall be prepared at the sole cost and expense of Lessor/Owner, provided that such costs and expenses have been previously approved.

3.4 Broker shall assist in the origination and preparation of a standard form of Proposal to Lease or Letter of Intent, and a standard form of tenant lease, including those provisions or exhibits governing landlord/tenant construction responsibilities. Broker shall also develop a package for presentation to Lessor/Owner, including any financial statements or operating projections which may be required by Lessor/Owner.

3.5 Broker shall use its best efforts in order to obtain and present to Lessor/Owner lease proposals from qualified prospective lessees. In performing this phase of the marketing program, Broker shall conduct a canvassing campaign and supervise a direct mailing campaign in order to solicit and follow through on any and all prospects.

3.6 Broker shall report periodically to Lessor/Owner and deliver monthly written reports regarding the status of its performance under this Agreement. Broker shall furnish whatever other reports of its activities on the Project that Lessor/Owner may from time to time reasonably request.

3.7 Broker shall solicit and encourage the cooperative support of other real estate organizations qualified in the field of commercial (retail) real estate in _____ County in order to maximize the number of potential leases that can be consummated with prospective tenants. Broker shall from time to time keep the other real estate firms informed regarding the status of said Project.

3.8 Broker shall designate one individual from its staff as Project Coordinator and another as the Leasing Representative:

A. The Project Coordinator shall be directly responsible for interfacing with Lessor/Owner. Duties shall include but not necessarily be limited to the following:

    I. Organization of overall leasing program

    II. Daily consultation with individual leasing agents

    III. Coordination of leasing efforts with outside brokers

FIGURE 3.2   Exclusive Marketing Agreement (continued)

    IV. Scheduling periodic meetings with Lessor/Owner, the contractor, the architect and any third party agents of Lessor/Owner if appropriate

    V. Preparation and Presentation of the Monthly status report to Lessor/Owner

    VI. Submission of the financial operating statements and leasing documents to Lessor/Owner for its approval

    VII. Evaluation of Performance of Broker's personnel to achieve maximum leasing results

B. The Leasing Representative shall be responsible for day-to-day contact with tenants and their interfacing with the architect, the contractor, and the Project Coordinator as required, including activities such as:

    1. Solicitation of tenants

    2. Physical inspection of current tenant operations

    3. Review of the financial operating statements and presentation of reports to the Project Coordinator

    4. Submission of Proposals to Lease or Letters of Intent to the Project Coordinator

    5. Participation in the review of the lease form with tenants and their attorneys

    6. Assisting in the preparation of the final lease documents and exhibits and addenda thereto

    7. Securing tenant's execution of the lease, and

    8. Presentation of the final package to the Project Coordinator

4. OBLIGATIONS OF LESSOR/OWNER:

4.1 Lessor/Owner agrees to provide at its expense the following material to Broker no later than sixty (60) days after the commencement of the term.

A.   Leasing plans, plot plans, elevation and renderings

B.   Leasing Brochures

C.   Tenant improvement schedules, including tenant construction allowances, if any

D.   Estimates of "additional rent," such as property taxes, insurance premiums, common area expenses and merchants' association dues, etc.

E.   Approval of the standard leasing documents and exhibits thereto

F.   Rental schedules and acceptable parameters of terms and conditions of tenant leases, and

G.   Project sign(s) designating Broker as the exclusive marketing agent, if other than Broker's standard sign(s) are required.

5. COMPENSATION OF BROKER:

5.1 Lessor/Owner shall pay a commission to Broker if:

A.   During the term of this Agreement or any extension hereof, Lessor/Owner and any lessee execute a lease covering any part of the Project, whether said lease is procured by Broker, by Lessor/Owner, or by any other party; or

B.   During the term of this Agreement or any extension hereof, a lease is executed by a ready, willing, and able lessee covering any part of the Project, whether said lease is procured by Broker, by Lessor/Owner, or by any other party, on terms acceptable to Lessor/Owner and any contingencies regarding the lessee's or lessor's obligations under such lease are not removed or waived (and such lease does not become fully effective) due to the default of Lessor/Owner; or

C.   During the term of this Agreement or any extension hereof, Lessor/Owner sells or agrees to sell all or any portion of the Project or executes an Agreement to construct a building on the Project for the use of a long-term lessee (a "build to suit") or executes a ground lease covering any part of the Project, whether any of the above is procured by Broker, by Lessor/Owner, or by any other party; or

D.   During the term of this Agreement or any extension hereof, an Agreement of sale, build to suit or ground lease is executed by a ready, willing, and able purchaser or lessee covering any part of the Project whether said lease is procured by Broker, by Lessor/Owner, or by any other party on terms reasonably acceptable to Lessor/Owner and any contingencies regarding the lessee's or lessor's obligations under such sale or lease are not removed or waived (and such sale or lease does not become fully effective or finally consummated) due to the default of Lessor/Owner; or

E.   Within six (6) months after the expiration of this Agreement or any extension hereof, all or any portion of the Project is leased or sold to any person or entity with whom Broker has negotiated or to whom the Project has been submitted by Broker prior to the expiration of this Agreement or any extension hereof and whose name appears on any list of such persons or entities which Broker shall have delivered to Lessor/Owner no later than thirty (30) days after such expiration.

5.2 Commission rates payable to Broker and the time of payment are as follows:

A.   (Rates from your company's schedule of commissions will be listed here)

B.   Time of Payment:

FIGURE 3.2   Exclusive Marketing Agreement (continued)

One-half (½) of each commission shall be due Broker at the time the lease is executed and the remaining one-half (½) upon the occupancy of the lessee in the Project and in each instance such to be paid within ten (10) days after submission of invoice provided that:

1. Any leasing commission earned by Broker pursuant to subparagraphs 5.1B or 5.1D above shall be paid to Broker in its entirety at the time of the default of Lessor/Owner, and

2. In the event a lessee does not take occupancy of its premises in the Project, then the remaining one-half (½) of Broker's commission shall be paid to Broker when the notice of completion is filed on the Project or six (6) months following the execution of the lease, whichever first occurs, and

3. If a lessee does not take occupancy of its premises in the Project or vacates such premises (for any reason except for the default by Lessor/Owner under its lease) within three (3) months after taking occupancy, then Broker will use its best efforts to secure a replacement lessee, and if secured then no additional commission shall be payable to Broker except only to the extent that there may be an increase in the minimum rental payable under the replacement lease, in which case, Lessor/Owner shall pay to Broker a sum equal to the difference by which the commission payable under the replacement lease exceeds that which was paid to Broker under the prior lease.

4. Broker is hereby authorized to deduct its commission pursuant to the preceding schedule from funds held in its trust account.

C. Should the term of any lease for which a commission is payable hereunder be extended or the lessee under such lease occupy any additional space, then Lessor/Owner shall pay a commission to Broker at such time as said term is extended or such additional space is occupied computed in accordance with the provisions of this Section 5 as if the initial term of the subject lease had included said extension period or the premises initially demised had included such additional space.

D. In the event Lessor/Owner sells the Project, Broker shall be paid a sales commission at close of escrow, provided that any sales commission earned by Broker pursuant to Subparagraphs 5.1C or 5.1D above shall be paid to Broker in its entirety at the time of the default of Lessor/Owner.

5.3 In the event a prospective lessee or purchaser fails to consummate a lease or sale and Lessor/Owner thus receives a defaulted deposit from said lessee or purchaser, then Lessor/Owner shall first deduct from such defaulted deposit its out-of-pocket costs (limited to legal fees, title fees, escrow fees, and expenses of collection) incurred in connection with such transaction, and Broker shall receive one-half (½) of the remainder of such defaulted deposit not to exceed the amount of any commission payable to Broker under this Agreement.

6. TERMINATION:

6.1 Either party hereto shall have the right to terminate this Agreement in the event of any material default by the other party hereto in the performance of any covenant, condition, or other provision of this Agreement to be performed by such other party by giving at least sixty (60) days' prior written notice of such termination to the other party.

6.2 Each of the parties hereto shall perform all of its respective obligations under this Agreement to the date of termination, and thereafter Lessor/Owner shall continue to make payments on earned commissions on the schedule set forth in Section 5 above. No termination of this Agreement shall relieve either of the parties hereto of the responsibility for obligations incurred prior to termination.

7. INDEMNIFICATION:

7.1 Provided that Lessor/Owner complies with all of the provisions of this Agreement, Broker shall indemnify, defend, and hold Lessor/Owner harmless from any liability arising out of the claim of any broker, agent, or finder for a commission pursuant to a lease allegedly procured by any such third party, except only as to any party with whom Lessor/Owner has dealt without the knowledge and consent of Broker. Lessor/Owner agrees to advise any broker, agent, or finder who contacts Lessor/Owner of the fact that Broker has exclusive right to lease the Project and that all negotiations must be conducted through Broker.

7.2 Lessor/Owner agrees to indemnify, defend, and hold Broker harmless, except in instances where Broker has acted in a grossly negligent or willfully fraudulent manner, from all claims, lawsuits, and causes of action which may arise, directly or indirectly, from the execution of or performance under this Agreement by either party hereto or in any way related to or connected therewith. For the purposes of this Subparagraph, the term Broker shall include all of Broker's affiliates and successor and all officers, directors, agents and employees of each.

8. NOTICES:

Any and all notices provided for herein shall be in writing and shall be delivered personally or deposited as certified United States mail, return receipt requested, in an envelope with postage prepaid, addressed to Lessor/Owner or to Broker with a copy to Broker's general counsel.

FIGURE 3.2 Exclusive Marketing Agreement (concluded)

9. MISCELLANEOUS:
   9.1 In the event either party hereto institutes legal action to enforce the provisions of this Agreement, the prevailing party therein shall receive reasonable attorney's fee incurred in said action and all costs and expenses of such action.
   9.2 Neither party to this Agreement shall assign its right or delegate its duties hereunder without the prior written consent of the other party.
   9.3 Whenever possible, each provision of this Agreement shall be interpreted so as to be effective and valid under applicable law, but if any provision of this Agreement shall be prohibited or invalid under applicable law, the remainder of such provision and the remaining provisions of this Agreement shall continue in full force and effect. This Agreement shall be construed under the laws of the State of California.
   9.4 The provisions of this Agreement constitute the entire Agreement of the parties hereto. No terms, conditions, warranties, promises, or understandings of any nature whatsoever, expressed or implied, exist between the parties except as herein expressly set forth. This Agreement cannot be amended or modified except by instrument in writing signed by both parties to the Agreement.

IN WITNESS WHEREOF, the parties hereto have executed this Agreement as of the date first above written.

SMITH AND JONES COMMERCIAL BROKERAGE COMPANY

By _____

By _____

By _____

By _____

The fifth section states the terms under which you will receive compensation. Notice that your company's schedule of commissions is referenced in section 5.2A.

The remainder of the exclusive marketing agreement is self-explanatory.

NONEXCLUSIVE AUTHORIZATION OF LEASE

A Grubb & Ellis nonexclusive authorization of lease is shown in figure 3–3. With this form, you will get a commission only if you yourself produce a satisfactory tenant. However, you are still protected by the 180-days-after-expiration clause if you register your prospects with the owner within 30 days of the agreement's expiration. Attach commission schedules in the same way that you would attach them to the exclusive authorization of lease.

COMMISSION AGREEMENT

The Grubb & Ellis commission-agreement form appears in figure 3–4. This agreement is designed to be used in real estate sales more than in office leasing. But if you have not already reached a signed agreement

FIGURE 3.3   Nonexclusive Authorization of Lease

NONEXCLUSIVE AUTHORIZATION OF LEASE

OWNER hereby lists with GRUBB & ELLIS COMPANY ("Broker") on an open listing basis the right to negotiate a lease or leases on the subject property (the "Property") for a period commencing on _____ , 19 _____ , and ending at midnight on _____ , 19 _____ . The Property is located in the City of _____ , County of _____ , State of _____ , located at _____ , and further described as _____

_____

The price and terms of the lease(s) shall be as follows: _____

_____

In consideration of this Authorization and Broker's agreement diligently to pursue the procurement of a tenant or tenants for the Property, Owner agrees to pay Broker a commission or commissions as set forth in the attached SCHEDULE OF COMMISSIONS.

Owner shall pay said commission(s) to Broker if: (a) the Property is leased to tenant(s) by or through Broker prior to the expiration of this Authorization or any extension hereof; or (b) a tenant is procured by or through Broker who is ready, willing and able to lease the Property on the terms above stated or other terms reasonably acceptable to Owner prior to the expiration of this Authorization or any extension hereof; or (c) within one hundred eighty (180) days after the expiration of this Authorization or any extension hereof, the Property is leased to any person or entity with whom Broker has negotiated or to whom Broker has submitted the Property prior to such expiration in an effort to effect a transaction and whose name appears on any list of such persons or entities which Broker shall have mailed to Owner at the address below stated within thirty (30) days following such expiration, provided that if Broker has submitted a written offer to lease or purchase, it shall not be necessary to include the offeror's name on such list.

If a sale or other transfer or conveyance is made by Broker prior to the expiration of this Authorization or any extension hereof, or during the one hundred eighty (180)-day period thereafter, Owner shall pay Broker a commission as set forth in the attached SCHEDULE OF COMMISSIONS.

If during the term of this Authorization or any extension hereof an escrow is opened or negotiations involving the sale, transfer, conveyance or leasing of the Property have commenced and are continuing, in either event with a client of Broker, then the term of this Authorization shall be extended for a period through the closing of such escrow, the termination of such negotiations or the consummation of such transaction, provided this Authorization would otherwise have expired during such period.

Owner agrees to cooperate with Broker in effecting a lease or leases of the Property. Broker is authorized to accept a deposit from any prospective tenant. Broker is further authorized to advertise the Property and shall have the exclusive right to place a sign or signs on the Property if, in Broker's opinion, such would facilitate the leasing thereof.

It is understood that it is illegal for either Owner or Broker to refuse to present, lease or sell to any person because of race, color, religion, national origin, sex, marital status or physical disability.

Owner warrants that he is the owner of record of the Property or has the legal authority to execute this Authorization. Owner agrees to hold Broker harmless from any liability or damages arising from any incorrect information supplied by Owner or any information which Owner fails to supply. Owner acknowledges receipt of a copy of this Authorization and the attached SCHEDULE OF COMMISSIONS, which Owner has read and understands.

If either Owner or Broker commences any litigation to enforce the terms of this Authorization, the prevailing party shall be entitled to receive a reasonable attorney's fee from the other party hereto.

No amendments or alterations in the terms hereof or withdrawal of this Authorization shall be valid or binding unless made in writing and signed by both Owner and Broker.

The heirs, transferees, successors and assigns of the parties hereto are duly bound by the provisions hereof.

DATED: _____ , 19 _____   OWNER: _____

ACCEPTED: GRUBB & ELLIS COMPANY   By _____

By _____   By _____

Address: _____

_____

Telephone: _____

FIGURE 3.4   Commission Agreement

COMMISSION AGREEMENT

For and in consideration of the efforts and services rendered by Grubb and Ellis Commercial Brokerage Company in connection with the lease of that certain property described as:

_____

_____

_____

_____

from _____

_____

_____ as Landlord

to _____

_____

_____ as Tenant, the undersigned

agrees hereby to pay to Grubb and Ellis Commercial Brokerage Company the sum of $_____ in lawful money of the United States to be payable when both parties have signed an appropriate lease agreement, and all contingencies set forth in said lease agreement have been satisfied or waived by the party for whose benefit such contingency has been included. Grubb and Ellis Commercial Brokerage Company is hereby authorized to deduct the foregoing sums from funds held in its trust account, if any, and the undersigned agrees to pay any difference in cash in accordance herewith.

In the event an action is commenced to enforce the right of Grubb and Ellis Commercial Brokerage Company to payment, the undersigned hereby agrees to pay to Grubb and Ellis Commercial Brokerage Company reasonable attorney's fees and expenses, whether said action is prosecuted to judgment or not.

Receipt of a copy of this Agreement is hereby acknowledged.

DATED: _____ , 19_____   LANDLORD _____

GRUBB AND ELLIS COMMERCIAL BROKERAGE   By _____
COMPANY
                                              By _____
By _____

Address: _____   Address: _____

City _____ , State _____   City _____ , State _____

Telephone: _____   Telephone: _____

with an owner, you may find this form useful when you have a qualified tenant who is interested in the space. It should not be difficult to secure a signature, since you have exactly the client the owner is looking for.

Never reveal the tenant's identity before the owner signs a contract. Many real estate salespeople have learned this lesson the hard way. Some building owners will forget that you exist the moment they learn the name of a qualified space-seeker. And once you have revealed a tenant to a lessor, you are under a legal obligation to show that space to that tenant—even though you have let your commission position deteriorate!

Your commission is *not* usually a matter for negotiation. Present the commission rate suggested by your firm to the owner, and defend it if necessary by explaining that services as a professional are worth that amount. If the owner still will not accept your commission rate, you should probably bid him or her goodbye. Only under extremely rare circumstances should you cut a commission.

Sometimes a lessor is reluctant to pay the entire commission up front for a long-term lease if the lessor thinks the tenant may be unable to keep up the rent payments. This is not your problem. You must bring in qualified tenants, but the owner decides whether to accept them. In such a case, rather than accept a partial commission, suggest that the owner reject the deal.

OFFER TO LEASE

The offer to lease can be a very important tool when used with an open listing for an office property. Assume you have found a tenant, perhaps a major bank, for a large space in a building with an open listing. You have obtained a signed commission agreement from the owner. You bring in the tenant. Everything is going smoothly. But the lease negotiations may go on for a month or more. It is now that you should attempt to persuade the tenant and the owner to sign the offer to lease.

Why bother nailing down a signed offer to lease? Wouldn't it be simpler to just begin negotiating the lease itself, since both parties seem satisfied so far?

The danger is that another broker may come along tomorrow with a tenant the building owner likes even better. A signed offer to lease will prevent the owner from beginning negotiations with the other broker. This document, in effect, takes the property off the market while your negotiations are being carried out. It does not bind owner and tenant to the lease itself, but it does bind the owner to continued negotiations. He or she must continue to negotiate in good faith until all points have been covered. So if another broker does turn up tomorrow with tenants willing to pay 20 percent more rent, the owner must turn them down, or at least put them off. An offer to lease binds an owner to completing negotiations with your tenant before the owner can either execute a lease or put the property back on the market.

The Grubb and Ellis offer to lease in figure 3–5 spells out the description of the premises, monthly rent, term of the lease, use, security deposit, prepaid rent, taxes, insurance, improvements and other terms.

Offers to lease have often held up in court against building owners who found out too late that they could have gotten a better deal.

FIGURE 3.5   Offer to Lease

The undersigned (hereinafter "Tenant") hereby offers to lease the Premises described below on the following terms and conditions:

1. Premises. Located in the City of _____ , County of _____ , State of _____ , described as follows: _____

2. Monthly Rent. _____

3. Term of Lease and Commencement Date. _____

4. Use of Premises. _____

5. Security Deposit; Prepaid Rent. _____

6. Taxes. _____

7. Insurance. _____

8. Utilities. _____

9. Improvements to Premises. _____

10. Other Terms and Conditions. _____

If this Offer to Lease is not accepted by the Landlord on or before _____ , 19____ the Offer shall terminate, and all sums deposited herewith shall be promptly returned to Tenant upon receipt of a written request therefor. Upon acceptance of this Offer to Lease, Landlord is to proceed with the preparation of a Lease, it being expressly understood that this proposal is not binding on either of the parties and that the Lease, when executed by the parties, shall contain their full agreement. In the event the Landlord accepts this Offer to Lease and the parties are for any reason unable to consummate a Lease, all sums deposited herewith shall be promptly returned to Tenant upon receipt of a written request therefor. In consideration of Grubb and Ellis Commercial Brokerage Company presenting this proposal to Landlord, Tenant agrees to conduct all negotiations through Grubb and Ellis Commercial Brokerage Company in the event Tenant commences negotiation to lease or purchase the Premises during the one-year period following the date hereof. Tenant acknowledges receipt of a copy hereof.

Date _____   Tenant _____

_____ , _____   By _____
City   State

Receipt is hereby acknowledged of cash ☐ check ☐ in the sum of _____
_____ dollars, to be delivered in accordance with the terms hereof.

Date: _____   Grubb and Ellis Commercial Brokerage Company

_____ , _____   By _____
City   State

Landlord hereby accepts the foregoing Offer to Lease and appoints Grubb and Ellis Commercial Brokerage Company its agent in connection with the lease of the Premises. Landlord agrees to pay a commission to Grubb and Ellis Commercial Brokerage Company in accordance with the attached Schedule of Commissions. Landlord acknowledges receipt of a copy hereof.

Date: _____   Landlord _____

_____ , _____   By _____
City   State

NOTICE TO LANDLORD AND TENANT: GRUBB AND ELLIS COMMERCIAL BROKERAGE COMPANY IS NOT AUTHORIZED TO GIVE LEGAL OR TAX ADVICE, NO REPRESENTATION OR RECOMMENDATION IS MADE BY GRUBB AND ELLIS COMMERCIAL BROKERAGE COMPANY OR ITS AGENTS OR EMPLOYEES AS TO THE LEGAL SUFFICIENCY, LEGAL EFFECT OR TAX CONSEQUENCES OF THIS DOCUMENT OR ANY TRANSACTION RELATING THERETO, SINCE THESE ARE MATTERS WHICH SHOULD BE DISCUSSED WITH YOUR ATTORNEY.

TENANT REPRESENTATION AGREEMENT

The tenant representation agreement (figure 3–6) is to a tenant what the exclusive listing is to a property owner. A tenant who signs this form agrees to work exclusively through you in searching for office space. Although this form is seldom used, it can be extremely helpful.

A tenant representation agreement is easiest to secure when a tenant doesn't have time to deal with a number of brokers. If you can inspire confidence in your ability, you can probably persuade a tenant to sign this form.

The agreement works to your advantage in two ways. First, you have an exclusive right to represent the client. Second, this right implies to an owner that you must have special abilities.

Most of the forms presented so far in this module are designed to be used for inventory control. Having full control of the space being marketed is the best way to ensure a sale, which is why you are reminded again and again always to try for an exclusive. But if you can't control the inventory, the next best thing is to control the tenant. This is where the much underused tenant representation agreement can help you. Tenant representation raises agency issues that are discussed further in the tenant representation chapter.

ETHICS

Real estate ethics is often a gray area, unlike the legal sphere of real estate where rules are spelled out in black and white. An action that is ethically wrong is not necessarily illegal, but it can still cost you a great deal in reputation, respect and ultimately in commissions.

Cooperating with Outside Brokers

Ethically, you should cooperate with all brokerage firms that operate according to high standards. You cannot honestly claim to represent the best interests of the building owner who is going to pay your commission unless you make every effort to deliver all qualified tenants. Top producers usually engage in a higher percentage of cooperative transactions than do the less productive salespeople.

The commercial, industrial and investment sectors of the brokerage business employ a relatively small percentage of all real estate sales representatives, but the people in these sectors usually make a lifetime career of their work. As a result, these people get to know each other personally or at least by reputation. Your reputation will be placed on the line time and again. You will find that it pays handsomely on all levels to protect that reputation.

When working with an outside broker who is unknown or whose reputation is questionable, you and your company should be protected by a broker cooperation agreement. A Grubb & Ellis version of this form is reproduced in figure 3–7. Three things about the execution of this document must be made clear.

FIGURE 3.6   Tenant Representation Agreement

TENANT REPRESENTATION AGREEMENT

TENANT hereby appoints GRUBB & ELLIS COMPANY ("Broker") as its exclusive agent with the exclusive right to select property and negotiate for its lease on behalf of Tenant, subject to the following provisions:

1. *Time.* The period of this agency shall commence on _____, 19_____, and terminate at midnight on
_____, 19_____.

2. *Property and Authority.* Broker is authorized only: (a) to select properties that substantially meet the requirements set forth below, as modified from time to time in writing by Tenant; (b) to present those properties to Tenant; and (c) on Tenant's approval to negotiate for their lease, but not to commit Tenant to the lease of any premises or to sign any instruments on behalf of Tenant without Tenant's express written consent.

3. The requirements for the property are:
   A. Type of Property: _____
   _____
   _____

   B. Rent; Other Charges: _____
   _____
   _____

   C. Location: _____
   _____
   _____

4. *Compensation.* The Owner of the property shall pay Broker's commissions in accordance with the attached Schedule of Lease Commissions. If the Owner does not agree to pay a commission which is acceptable to Broker, but a lease of the property is consummated, then Tenant shall pay a commission in accordance with said Schedule of Lease Commissions, payment to be made upon execution of the lease by both parties. Broker shall also be entitled to receive the aforesaid commission from Tenant in the event of Tenant's default on an executed lease. Tenant agrees that in the event of a purchase of the property presented to Tenant during the term of this agency or any extension thereof, or during the one hundred fifty (150) day period referred to in Section 5 hereof, Broker shall be entitled to be paid a commission based upon _____% of the sales price to be paid through escrow.

5. If within one hundred fifty (150) days after the expiration of the period of the agency described above or any extension of it, Buyer shall enter into an agreement to lease property from any person with whom Broker has communicated in pursuit of the objectives of the agency before its expiration, Buyer shall pay compensation as though the transaction were procured during the agency period provided Broker notifies Buyer of the communication in writing during the agency period or within ten (10) days after the expiration thereof, identifying the Owner and the property.

6. In consideration of this Agreement, Broker agrees to utilize reasonable effort and diligence to achieve the purpose of this Agreement.

7. Tenant acknowledges receipt of a copy of this Agreement.

DATED: _____, 19_____   TENANT: _____

GRUBB & ELLIS COMPANY   By _____

By _____   By _____

Address: _____   Address: _____

City _____ State _____   City _____ State _____

Telephone: _____   Telephone: _____

FIGURE 3.7   Broker Cooperation Agreement

BROKER COOPERATION AGREEMENT

BROKER hereby agrees to conduct all negotiations for the purchase, sale, lease or other transfer of all or any interest in the below described property(s), whether for the account of BROKER or a third party, through GRUBB AND ELLIS COMMERCIAL BROKERAGE COMPANY (hereinafter ''G&E''). BROKER shall in no manner deal with the owner of the property(s) nor any agent of the owner other than G&E.

The property(s) to which the Agreement pertains is described as follows:

_____

_____

_____

_____

The undersigned hereby registers with G&E the following prospective Buyers or Tenants for the above property(s).

_____

_____

_____

_____

In the event BROKER or any salesman or other broker working in cooperation with BROKER desires to negotiate for the sale, lease or transfer of the property(s), all negotiations shall be conducted through G&E. If such negotiations are successful and a transaction is consummated, fifty percent (50%) of the total commission paid by the Seller or Landlord shall be payable to G&E. Except for those prospects registered above, G&E may sell, lease, transfer or otherwise deal with the property without incurring any obligation to divide any commission or pay any portion thereof to BROKER.

For and in consideration of the execution of this Agreement and the supplying of valuable information concerning the property, BROKER agrees to be bound by this Agreement for a period of twelve (12) months from the date hereof. BROKER agrees not to divulge any information concerning the above property(s) to anyone excepting prospects, salesmen engaged by BROKER and other brokers who agree to be bound by the terms hereof.

Receipt of a copy of this Agreement is hereby acknowledged.

DATED: _____ , 19_____

GRUBB AND ELLIS COMMERCIAL BROKERAGE COMPANY   BROKER: _____

By_____   By _____

Address: _____   Address: _____

City _____ State _____   City _____ State _____

Telephone: _____   Telephone: _____

1. The agreement must be signed for both parties by the managers, not the salespeople, from the two cooperating companies. Because when you agree to cooperate with an outside broker, you have no way of knowing whether another salesperson at your own office is working on this particular space. By signing away part of your own commission, you may be inadvertently signing away part of a colleague's compensation as well. Your manager will spot-check other lease listings to eliminate this possibility before signing the agreement.

2. The term of the agreement must not extend beyond one year.

3. The agreement covers only the cooperating office. It does not apply to any other office without the prior written consent of the manager of that office.

All of the ethical questions you will run into as a salesperson cannot possibly be covered here. Some of the typical situations you're likely to encounter will be introduced in question-and-answer form. As you read the questions, respond in the space provided. This is not a test. It is simply presenting new material in a way designed to get you involved and to make you think. Don't worry if you don't get most of the answers right. Some have no one right answer. That's another difference between legal and ethical. In problems of ethics, you will sometimes have to play it by ear.

Exercise A

Consider the following questions. Write down your answers and compare them with those given at the end of this exercise.

1. An outside broker calls you for information on a specific listing. He also wants to know the termination date. Which of this information, if any, are you obligated to give him?

2. You know an outside broker has an exclusive listing for a sublease. You have a qualified prospect. Must you work through the other broker, or can you contact the property owner directly?

3. You have an oral agreement with an outside broker to cooperate with her on a certain property, and you know she does not have an exclusive listing. Must you negotiate through her as long as the property is still available?

4. Should you place an advertisement soliciting "principals only"?

5. Another broker's client has decided you are a better contact than her own and asks you to complete a transaction started by the other broker. Should you do it?

6. Are there any circumstances under which you can ethically introduce yourself into a transaction initiated by another broker?

7. You are cooperating with another broker. You have procured a tenant, and the lease has been signed. How soon should you supply a copy of the lease to the cooperating broker?

8. You have an offer. You have tried to locate the listing broker, but she seems to have disappeared. Should you contact the seller directly?

9. You have delivered your offer to the listing broker, but to the best of your knowledge he hasn't yet presented it to the seller. How long should you wait before applying pressure?

10. You have developed an offer on your own exclusive listing, but simultaneously two other brokers have each developed an offer on the same listing. To further complicate matters, they don't trust you to present their offers impartially—they want to present them in person. What should you do?

11. Which broker's registration rules govern a cooperative situation?

12. An outside broker mentions the name of a tenant to you in a situation in which you are the listing broker. Does that constitute registration?

13. An outside broker asks you to sign a broker cooperation agreement in return for information on a property. Should you do it?

14. You have a listing that stipulates that the commission will be paid in several payments over time. An outside broker makes a co-op deal on the space and finds a tenant. You forgot to inform her of the delayed commission arrangement. Under what terms, immediate or delayed, do you share the commission with her?

15. You have a sign on a property that has just been leased. How long should you leave your sign up without putting a "leased" rider on it?

16. You have just leased another broker's listing. Should you install your sign on the property indicating that it has been leased?

Answer A

1. *You are obligated to reveal whether or not the listing is an exclusive. You need not give the other broker the termination date.*

2. *You can contact the owner directly. There is no ethical conflict here, because the other broker's contract is with the tenant. You are not violating a contractual relationship with the owner, because the outside broker has none. When you are the salesperson involved in a sublease, always try to begin negotiations with the owner immediately, before some other broker beats you to it.*

3. *This is a perfect example of one of those gray areas of ethics. Legally, the oral agreement is not binding. But if this is a broker you have worked with before and whose respect you value, you will probably honor it. However, suppose that after you entered into the oral agreement the owner put up his own sign, throwing the listing open to the whole world? This changes the situation; what was at most a moral obligation is no longer even that. (If you have executed a broker cooperation agreement, then you are legally bound, and even the owner's putting up his own sign does not release you from the agreement.)*

4. *Such ads mean only one thing: the advertising broker does not want to split the commission. This type of advertising would not only inform the world that you did not extend the cooperation you'd like to receive, but it would also inform the owner that you had his or her best interests at heart only if it didn't cost you any money.*

5. *No.*

6. *Only if the other broker dies, is fired or quits can you become involved in his or her transaction.*

7. *The cooperating broker must receive a copy as soon as possible, within two days at most.*

8. *If you have honestly attempted to locate the listing broker and cannot reach her, you can contact the seller directly. In fact, you have an obligation to the lessee to submit his offer within a reasonable period. Suppose you keep tenants waiting while you try to contact the other broker, and meanwhile the other broker slips a tenant in to see the owner. This may have been her intention all along. Not only would such an action be unethical on her part, but it would leave you with a very angry tenant on your hands. A 24-hour waiting period is long enough under these circumstances.*

9. *Apply pressure immediately.*

10. *Let them present their offers to your owner. You have a right to refuse, but you may want to make the same request of them someday. Arrange to present your own offer last, so you can spot any weak points in the other offers and emphasize parallel strengths in your own. Ask your manager to accompany you on offer presentations.*

11. *The listing broker's rules govern.*

12. *No. To effect a registration, the other broker must deliver a letter to you from the company he or she is registering that says the broker has been appointed as the company's exclusive agent.*

13. *Have your manager sign for the protection of other sales representatives in your office who may be working on the listing. You should also make it clear to the outside broker that only your own office is covered by the agreement.*

14. *The broker is entitled to the immediate full payment that she had every reason to assume she would get in the absence of any information to the contrary.*

15. *Always keep signs up as long as possible. It's great advertising. Also, even though the advertised space has been taken, the sign may attract a tenant for whom space is available in another building.*

16. *No.*

Cooperating with Other Brokers in Your Company

Many of your problems with business ethics will crop up much nearer home than the ones we have just outlined. As you develop new leads, you will often find yourself cooperating with other brokers in your own firm. Some may even be close personal friends. You can preserve many friendships—and commissions—by following one simple rule: All deals must be put in writing. In the case of simple referrals, where the referring broker is traditionally entitled to ten percent of the commission, written agreements are still advisable. And in particular, have the other salesperson sign such an agreement whenever you enter into a special arrangement about splitting a commission. Remember, you may be talking about a large sum of money when you discuss commission splits with a colleague.

All listings, including exclusives, should go into the company listing system. If you obtain an exclusive and can immediately think of several tenants who might want this space, develop these sources before your listing goes into the system. But any listing held back more than four or five days will be suspected of being a listing that you have consciously decided to keep for yourself. Truly professional brokers don't play the game that way. It does an injustice to themselves as well as to their tenant. The chapter on marketing will discuss these "pocket listings" at greater length.

Exercise B

The next exercise asks you to think about some of the ethical problems that you will confront in your own office. Strive for objectivity and try to put yourself in the other salesperson's shoes. Back up your answers with reasons whenever possible.

1. A man calls your company from a phone booth. He has just seen one of your firm's signs and he wants information on the space. The salesperson who put up the sign is not in, but the man insists on getting immediate information. The call comes to you and you give him as much information as you can. Is this your deal now, or does it still belong to your colleague?

2. You receive a call from an outside broker who is a stranger to you. She asks if you have any exclusives on a 25,000-square-foot office space. You don't have such an exclusive, but you know of someone in your office who has one. How do you handle the situation?

3. A prospect calls the office to inquire about a newspaper ad that says your company has an exclusive on an office building. It is not your exclusive, but for some reason the operator gives you the call. What should you do?

4. You make a cold call on a company and the person you talk to says, "I'm working with Chris Williams from your office." What should you do?

5. A colleague has placed an open listing on a property in your company's property-listing system. You receive a call from an outside

broker, a friend of yours, requesting information on buildings similar to the one in question. Should you give out the open-listing information, or should you check first with the person who put up the building in the system?

6. A salesperson from your investment division says to you, "I have a tenant who wants to lease 5,000 square feet of office space. I expect to share the deal with you 50–50." Is this an equitable position?

7. A friend of yours, who happens also to be a tenant, sees one of your firm's signs on a rental office building and calls you about it, even though the sign was put up by a salesperson in another office. Your friend says, "Get me the information on that property." Should you do this? If you did, would you have a position in any deal that might result?

8. You are in your office, and the operator gives you an incoming call. You discover that the woman placing the call is looking for an industrial building. What do you do?

9. During your weekly sales meeting you mention that you are looking for a particular space. One of the other sales reps says, "I've got the perfect building for you." He gives you the information on the spot. You find that this building is not listed in any of your firm's listing systems and is probably a pocket listing. What should you do?

Answer B

1. *The person who put up the sign should get the full commission. Help the caller as much as you can, then take his name and telephone number and relay it to your colleague.*

2. *Never divulge information on another salesperson's listing without checking with that person first. The minute you bring another broker into it, you have introduced a three-way commission split. The listing salesperson has the right to decide on any such split.*

3. *The reasoning here is similar to that in the first question. The salesperson who brought in the exclusive deserves the commission. Help the caller if pressed to do so (provided you have the information). Then pass the name and number on to your colleague.*

4. *This is another gray area. You may have to probe a little to find out what the outsider's relationship to Chris Williams is. If the person you talk to has to thumb through a file of business cards to come up with Williams's name, you might suspect that the relationship took place a long time ago or at least is not very firm. This would give you the right to make a case for your own services. If, however, you get the impression that Williams has some control over the potential tenant, put in a good word for her and make a friendly exit.*

5. *First, check with the lister and see if she objects to your handling the deal yourself. If not, ask the outside broker to come in and sign (or have his manager sign, depending upon his status) a bro-*

ker cooperation agreement in return for the information. Your manager must agree to the broker cooperation agreement. Don't give out the information before you get the signature. There are two keys to this situation. First, any time you are dealing with someone else's listing, check first, with the lister. Second, never give the outside broker an opportunity to take an open listing away from you. The broker might, of course, find out from some other source that this is an open listing. But you needn't make it easier by telling him the location of the space.

6. *This is another situation in which the exact relationship between the other salesperson and the prospect determines the answer. The tenant could be the salesperson's brother, for instance, and the company president to boot. In that case the investment division salesperson would have real control, and a 50–50 split would be reasonable. But if the client is just some random person over whom the investment sales representative seems to have little control, this is merely a referral and only a ten percent split would be justified.*

7. *This situation is similar to question six, but the shoe is on the other foot. If you know the caller well enough to have real control and if you are willing to work hard to close this deal, you have a right to ask for a 50–50 split. If not, let your conscience be your guide, and adjust your request to something between ten and 50 percent. In either case, don't give out any information without getting the other salesperson's approval.*

8. *You are not a specialist in industrial real estate. Transfer the call to someone in that division. (Always get the name and number of the caller in case the call is accidentally disconnected.)*

9. *Find out immediately why your colleague didn't put the listing into the system. If the answer sounds legitimate (perhaps the listing was received only the previous day, for instance), a 50–50 split is in order. But if the other salesperson has had the information for a week and simply wants to share it only on his own terms, either refuse to get involved or take the problem to your manager.*

Ethics of Client Relationships

As you become more and more familiar with your field, not all the ethical minefields you walk through will involve other sales representatives, either inside or outside. Tenants can pose ethical problems, too. Walk away from the would-be tenant who offers to write you a $15,000 personal check as compensation for some information or advice. On the other hand, nonmonetary gifts given in appreciation for diligent work or special services are perfectly acceptable. They can range from a bottle of Scotch to a Hawaiian vacation. But monetary compensation for your real estate services comes to you only through your brokerage firm. To sell those services any other way guarantees the loss of your license.

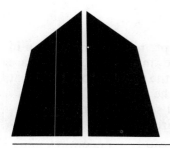

4

The Office Lease

INTRODUCTION

The forms examined in the previous chapter were all primarily designed to protect your interests. Their purpose was either to guarantee your commission or to extend your inventory (or at least tenant) control. But the office lease, instead of being a contract between you and a principal, is between the principals themselves. The purpose of the office lease is to spell out a relationship that satisfactorily resolves the conflicting needs and desires of tenant and owner. Your job is to facilitate that resolution, and to do this you must have a thorough understanding of basic lease clauses.

TYPES OF LEASES

There are three main types of leases: gross, net and percentage. They differ in the manner in which rents are computed and paid.

1. *Gross lease.* Under a gross lease, the tenant pays only a base rent. The owner pays all other expenses involved in the building's operation.

2. *Net lease.* Under the terms of a strictly net lease, the tenant pays some or all of the real estate taxes in addition to the base rent. A *net-net lease* requires the tenant to pay all items included under

the net lease terms, plus any insurance premiums agreed upon in the contract. Agreed-upon repair and maintenance costs are added to the net-net payments to derive the tenant's total payment under a *net-net-net (triple-net) lease*. The triple-net lease is unusual in office space rental, but you will see it occasionally, especially when one tenant occupies an entire building.

3. *Percentage lease.* A percentage lease requires the tenant to pay a fixed rent, plus a percentage of the tenant's gross income in excess of a predetermined minimum. This arrangement is typical of retail operations, but rarely used in office leasing.

Because the differences among kinds of net leases are a matter of degree—how many extra expenses the tenant pays—you probably could not get three people out of any ten to agree on the definitions of these terms. To eliminate confusion, make sure the owner and the tenant know exactly what net, net-net and triple-net mean in their particular situation.

Tenants have been known to sign a triple-net lease thinking they have assumed maintenance costs, only to find themselves responsible for repairs to a caved-in roof or a floor flooded by a burst pipe. Even when the owner states explicitly that the tenant is assuming *all* costs, spell it out to your prospect. Tenants are often surprised to find that the phrase "all costs" includes the expense of repairing roofs and sidewalks, for instance. (At one time these items were exceptions, but that is no longer the case in most leases.)

Don't let tenants be fooled by bargain-basement rents in triple-net lease situations. Of course owners offering such leases can provide low rental rates—they're walking away from practically all of their building expenses. Explain these distinctions.

Exercise A

A building owner says to you, "I'm willing to lease my building on either a gross or a net basis. On a gross lease, I need to charge $20 per square foot per year. It costs $6.00 per square foot per year to run this building." What must the owner charge per year on a triple-net lease to generate the same net income as a gross lease? Check your answer with the one below.

Answer A

She must charge $14.00 per year on a triple-net basis to generate the same net income.

DOING YOUR LEASE HOMEWORK

Start now to read office leases. You may not find them exciting reading, but the more leases you read, the more familiar you will become with the typical lease clauses. And the more familiar you are with the various clauses, the more professionally you will perform in the field.

Occasionally, you will be dealing with leases of 80 pages or more. Master the basic clauses now, and you won't find an 80-page lease intimidating.

Whenever possible, use the lease form the building owner suggests. Use your company's standard form as a second choice. As you read in the previous chapter, you will be called upon from time to time to modify clauses in a standard lease. For your legal protection, ask your manager for a book of approved standard lease clauses. These clauses can often be safely inserted into a lease, as long as they are used intact. Remember to get your manager's approval before making such a change. And never draft a lease clause yourself.

THE STANDARD OFFICE LEASE

Figure 4–1 is a standard Grubb & Ellis office lease. Note that it contains three alternate second pages, each with different tax provisions. It also has two alternate fourth pages with different provisions for insurance and damage to premises. Attached to the lease are figure 4–2 dealing with construction of tenant premises and figure 4–3 pertaining to tenant rules and regulations.

Several clauses in the standard office lease are reproduced in this chapter. A grasp of their meaning is only the beginning of a thorough understanding of this entire form. Read the lease during free moments until you have absorbed it word for word. As you read, take notes on anything that is not clear. Ask your sales manager questions while they are still fresh in your mind. Your tenant and, often, the building owner may not understand a particular lease clause, but they will expect you to. Explaining lease clauses is part of your job, and the deal you have so carefully nurtured can be in big trouble if you can't answer the principals' questions.

Study on your own those parts of the lease that deal with legalities. Several paragraphs that you are likely to be unfamiliar with and that may become negotiating points in your transactions are reviewed here. Items 4 and 5 in figure 4–1 show two key lease clauses and items 18 and 33 in figure 4–4 illustrate two others.

SECURITY DEPOSIT

A security deposit is an amount of money the tenant deposits with the property owner, who holds it for the period of the lease. It is pledged as security in case the tenant does not honor all the lease conditions. After the tenant has vacated the property, any damage to the premises beyond normal wear is paid for out of the security deposit. The balance is refunded to the tenant. Don't fall victim to the popular misconception that a security deposit is the last month's rent. The tenant must pay the last month's rent and vacate. Then the owner ascertains the condition of the premises and determines whether to refund the security deposit. The "last month's rent" idea grew up in the area of residential leases (and even there a true security deposit is usually required).

FIGURE 4.1   Standard Grubb & Ellis Office Lease

LEASE-GENERAL FORM

THIS LEASE is made and entered into this_____day of _____ , 19___, by and between _____ _____ (hereinafter "Landlord") and _____ _____ (hereinafter "Tenant").

For and in consideration of the rental and of the covenants and agreements hereinafter set forth to be kept and performed by the Tenant, Landlord hereby leases to Tenant and Tenant hereby leases from Landlord the Premises herein described for the term, at the rental and subject to and upon all of the terms. covenants and agreements hereinafter set forth.

1. PREMISES

1.1   Description. Landlord hereby leases to Tenant and Tenant hereby hires from Landlord those certain Premises (hereinafter "Premises") crosshatched on Exhibit A, together with appurtenances, situated in the City of_____, County of_____,State of California, commonly known as_____ _____ more particularly described as follows:

1.2   Work of Improvement. The obligations of Landlord and Tenant to perform the work and supply the necessary materials and labor to prepare the Premises for occupancy are set forth in detail in Exhibit B. Landlord and Tenant shall expend all funds and do all acts required of them in Exhibit B and shall have the work performed promptly and diligently in a first class workmanlike manner.

2. TERM

2.1   Term. The term of this lease shall be for a period of_____ commencing on the ____ day of _____ , 19__, and ending on the ____ day of _____ ,19__, unless sooner ter-minated pursuant to this Lease.

2.2   Delay in Commencement. Tenant agrees that in the event of the inability of Landlord for any reason to deliver possession of the Prem-ises to Tenant on the commencement date set forth in Section 2.1, Landlord shall not be liable for any damage thereby nor shall such inability affect the validity of this Lease or the obligations of Tenant hereunder. but in such case Tenant shall not be obligated to pay rent or other mone-tary sums until possession of the Premises is tendered to Tenant. If Tenant with Landlord's consent takes possession prior to the commencement of the term, Tenant shall do so subject to all of the terms and conditions hereof and shall pay rent for the period ending with the commencement of the term at the same rental.

2.3   Acknowledgement of Commencement Date. In the event the commencement date of the term of the Lease is other than as provided in Section 2.1, then Landlord and Tenant shall execute a written acknowledgement of the date of commencement and shall attach it to the Lease as Exhibit C.

3.   RENT.
Tenant shall pay to Landlord as rent for the Premises in advance on the first day of each calendar month of the term of this Lease without deduction, offset, prior notice or demand, in lawful money of the United States, the sum of _____ _____ ($_____).

If the commencement date is not the first day of a month, or if the Lease termination date is not the last day of a month, a prorated monthly install-ment shall be paid at the then current rate for the fractional month during which the Lease commences and/or terminates.

Concurrently with Tenant's execution of this Lease, Tenant shall pay to Landlord the sum of _____ _____($_____) as rent for the month(s) of

4.   SECURITY DEPOSIT.
Concurrently with Tenant's execution of this Lease, Tenant shall deposit with Landlord the sum of_____

($_____). Said sum shall be held by Landlord as a Security Deposit for the faithful performance by Tenant of all of the terms, covenants, and conditions of this Lease to be kept and performed by Tenant during the term hereof. If Tenant defaults with respect to any provision of this Lease, including but not limited to the provisions relating to the payment of rent and any of the monetary sums due herewith Landlord may (but shall not be required to) use, apply or retain all or any part of this Security Deposit for the payment of any other amount which Landlord may spend by reason of Tenant's default or to compensate Landlord for any other loss or damage which Landlord may suffer by reason of Tenant's default. If any portion of said Deposit is so used or applied, Tenant shall, within ten (10) days after written demand therefore deposit cash with Landlord in an amount sufficient to restore the Security Deposit to its original amount; Tenant's failure to do so shall be a material breach of this Lease. Landlord shall not be required to keep this Security Deposit separate from its general funds, and Tenant shall not be entitled to interest on such deposit. If Tenant shall fully and faithfully perform every provision of this Lease to be performed by it, the Security Deposit or any balance thereof shall be returned to Tenant (or, at Landlord's option, to the last assignee of Tenant's interests hereunder) at the expiration of the Lease term and after Tenant has vacated the Premises. In the event of termination of Landlord's interest in this Lease, Landlord shall trans-fer said Deposit to Landlord's successor in interest whereupon Tenant agrees to release Landlord from liability for the return of such Deposit or the accounting therefor.

FIGURE 4.1 (continued)

5. TAXES

5.1 Personal Property Taxes. During the term hereof Tenant shall pay prior to delinquency all taxes assessed against and levied upon fixtures, furnishings, equipment and all other personal property of Tenant contained in the Premises, and when possible, Tenant shall cause said fixtures, furnishings, equipment and other personal property to be assessed and billed separately from the real property of Landlord. In the event any or all of Tenant's fixtures, furnishings, equipment and other personal property shall be assessed and taxed with Landlord's real property, the Tenant shall pay to Landlord its share of such taxes within ten (10) days after delivery to Tenant by Landlord of a statement in writing setting forth the amount of such taxes applicable to Tenant's property. For the purpose of determining said amount, figures supplied by the County Assessor as to the amount so assessed shall be conclusive. Tenant shall comply with the provisions of any law, ordinance or rule of taxing authorities which requires Tenant to file a report of Tenant's property located in the Premises.

5.2 Real Property Taxes. Tenant agrees to pay all real estate taxes, levies, assessments and all other charges in the nature of taxes or assessments upon the Premises, general and special, ordinary and extraordinary of any kind and nature which during the term of this Lease are laid, levied, assessed or imposed or become a lien upon or chargeable against the Premises. Tenant shall pay said taxes quarterly upon receipt from Landlord of a statement delineating Tenant's share of said taxes; said share to be paid within ten (10) days after receipt of said statement. In the event the Premises are not separately assessed for tax purposes, then the taxes and assessments on the Premises shall be apportioned according to the floor area of the Premises (including mezzanine, if any) as it relates to the total floor area (including mezzanines, if any) of the Buildings including the Premises or the Building and Land underlying said Building with which such assessment is concerned. All taxes for the year in which the Lease commences shall be apportioned and adjusted. With respect to any assessment (other than those delineated in the tax bill) which may be levied against or upon the Premises and which under the laws then in force may be evidenced by improvement or other bonds, or which may be paid in annual installments, Landlord shall cause such bonds to be issued or cause such assessments to be paid in the maximum permissible number of annual installments, and in such event Tenant shall only be required to pay such installment payments with interest thereon as each thereof matures and Tenant shall have no obligation to continue such payments after the termination of this Lease. The term real estate taxes shall include all taxes imposed upon the real property and permanent improvements and all assessments levied against said Premises, but shall not include personal income taxes, personal property taxes, inheritance taxes or franchise taxes levied against Landlord, even though such taxes may become a lien against the Premises.

5.3 New Taxes. In addition to rent and other charges to be paid by Tenant hereunder, Tenant shall reimburse to Landlord, within thirty (30) days of receipt of a demand therefore, any and all taxes payable by Landlord (other than net income taxes, estate and inheritance taxes and taxes excluded in Section 5.2 hereof) whether or not now customary or within the contemplation of the parties hereto; (a) upon, allocable to, or measured by the area of the Premises or on the rent payable hereunder, including without limitation any gross income tax or excise tax levied by the State, any political subdivision thereof, City or Federal Government with respect to the receipt of such rent; or (b) upon or with respect to the possession, leasing, operation, management, maintenance, alteration, repair, use or occupancy by Tenant of the Premises or any portion thereof; or (c) upon or measured by the value of Tenant's personal property, equipment or fixtures located in the Premises; or (d) upon this transaction or any document to which Tenant is a party creating or transferring an interest or an estate in the Premises.

6. USE

6.1 Use. The Premises shall be used and occupied by Tenant for_____

_____

_____

_____

_____and for no other purpose without the prior written consent of Landlord.

6.2 Suitability. Tenant acknowledges that neither Landlord nor any agent of Landlord has made any representation or warranty with respect to the Premises or the Building (if any) of which the Premises may be a part or with respect to the suitability of either for the conduct of Tenant's business, nor has Landlord agreed to undertake any modification, alteration or improvement to the Premises except as provided in this Lease. The taking of possession of the Premises by Tenant shall conclusively establish that the Premises and said Building were at such time in satisfactory condition unless within fifteen (15) days after such date Tenant shall give Landlord written notice specifying in reasonable detail the respects in which the Premises or the Building were not in satisfactory condition.

6.3 Uses Prohibited.

(a) Tenant shall not do or permit anything to be done in or about the Premises nor bring or keep anything therein which will in any way increase the existing rate or affect any fire or other insurance upon the Premises or the Building (if any) of which the Premises may be a part or any of its contents (unless Tenant shall pay any increased premium as a result of such use or acts), or cause a cancellation of any insurance policy covering said Premises or said Building or any part thereof or any of its contents, nor shall Tenant sell or permit to be kept, used or sold in or about said Premises any articles which may be prohibited by a standard form policy of fire insurance.

(b) Tenant shall not do or permit anything to be done in or about the Premises which will in any way obstruct or interfere with the rights of other tenants or occupants of the Building (if any) or injure or annoy them or use or allow the Premises to be used for any unlawful or objectionable purpose, nor shall Tenant cause, maintain or permit any nuisance in, on or about the Premises. Tenant shall not commit or suffer to be committed any waste in or upon the Premises.

(c) Tenant shall not use the Premises or permit anything to be done in or about the Premises which will in any way conflict with any law, statute, ordinance or governmental rule or regulation or requirement of duly constituted public authorities now in force or which may hereafter be enacted or promulgated. Tenant shall at its sole cost and expense promptly comply with all laws, statutes, ordinances and governmental rules, regulations or requirements now in force or which may hereafter be in force and with the requirements of any board of fire underwriters or other similar body now or hereafter constituted relating to or affecting the condition, use or occupancy of the Premises, excluding structural changes not relating to or affecting the condition, use or occupancy of the Premises, or not related or afforded by Tenant's improvements or acts. The judgment of any court of competent jurisdiction or the admission of Tenant in any action against Tenant, whether Landlord be a party thereto or not, that Tenant has violated any law, statute, ordinance or governmental rule, regulation or requirement, shall be conclusive of the fact as between Landlord and Tenant.

7. UTILITIES.
Tenant shall during the term hereof pay prior to delinquency all charges for water, gas, heat, light, power, telephone and janitorial services and all other materials and services supplied to the Premises and shall hold Landlord harmless from any liability therefrom. If the Premises are not served by a separate water meter, then Tenant shall pay to Landlord the sum of $_____ per month in advance for water in said Premises.

FIGURE 4.1   (continued)

8.   MAINTENANCE AND REPAIRS; ALTERATIONS AND ADDITIONS

8.1   Maintenance and Repairs.

(a) Landlord's Obligations. Landlord, at its sole cost and expense, shall maintain in a good state of repair the exterior of the roof and walls, and all structural portions of the roof, walls, floors and foundations except for any repairs caused by the wrongful act of Tenant and its agents.

(b)   Tenant's Obligations.

(i)   Tenant at Tenant's sole cost and expense shall maintain the Premises and appurtances and every part thereof (excepting those items which Landlord is obligated to repair pursuant to Section 8.1(a)) in good order, condition and repair, including but not limited to the interior surfaces of the ceilings, walls and floors, all doors, windows, all plumbing pipes, electrical wiring, switches, fixtures, signs and equipment installed by or at the expense of Tenant. Tenant expressly waives the benefits of any statute now or hereafter in effect which would otherwise afford Tenant the right to make repairs at Landlord's expense or to terminate this Lease because of Landlord's failure to keep the Premises in good order, condition and repair.

(ii)   Upon the expiration or earlier termination of this Lease, Tenant shall surrender the Premises in the same condition as received, ordinary wear and tear and damage by fire, earthquake, act of God or the elements alone excepted, and shall promptly remove or cause to be removed at Tenant's expense from the Premises any signs, notices and displays placed by Tenant.

(iii)   Tenant agrees to repair any damage to the Premises caused by or in connection with the removal of any articles of personal property, business or trade fixtures, machinery, equipment, cabinetwork, furniture, moveable partition or permanent improvements or additions, including without limitation thereto, repairing the floor and patching and painting the walls where required by Landlord to Landlord's reasonable satisfaction, all at Tenant's sole cost and expense. Tenant shall indemnify the Landlord against any loss or liability resulting from delay by Tenant in so surrendering the Premises, including without limitation any claims made by any succeeding Tenant founded on such delay.

(iv)   In the event Tenant fails to maintain the Premises in good order, condition and repair, Landlord shall give Tenant notice to do such acts as are reasonably required to so maintain the Premises. In the event Tenant fails to promptly commence such work and diligently prosecute it to completion, then Landlord shall have the right to do such acts and expend such funds at the expense of Tenant as are reasonably required to perform such work. Any amount so expended by Landlord shall be paid by Tenant promptly after demand with interest at ten percent (10%) per annum from the date of such work. Landlord shall have no liability to Tenant for any damage, inconvenience or interference with the use of the Premises by Tenant as a result of performing any such work.

(c)   Compliance with Law. Landlord and Tenant shall each do all acts required to comply with all applicable laws, ordinances, regulations and rules of any public authority relating to their respective maintenance obligation as set forth herein.

8.2   Alterations and Additions.

(a)   Tenant shall make no alterations, additions or improvements to the Premises or any part thereof without first obtaining the prior written consent of Landlord.

(b)   Landlord may impose as a condition to the aforesaid consent such requirements as Landlord may deem necessary in its sole discretion, including without limitation thereto, the manner in which the work is done, a right of approval of the contractor by whom the work is to be performed, the times during which it is to be accomplished, and the requirement that upon written request of Landlord prior to the expiration or earlier termination of the Lease, Tenant will remove any and all permanent improvements or additions to the Premises installed at Tenant's expense.

(c)   All such alterations, additions or improvements shall at the expiration or earlier termination of the Lease become the property of Landlord and remain upon and be surrendered with the Premises unless specified pursuant to Section 8.2(b) above.

(d)   All articles of personal property and all business and trade fixtures, machinery and equipment, cabinetwork, furniture and moveable partitions owned by Tenant or installed by Tenant at its expense in the Premises shall be and remain the property of Tenant and may be removed by Tenant at any time during the Lease term when Tenant is not in default hereunder.

9.   ENTRY BY LANDLORD.   Landlord reserves and shall at any and all times have the right to enter the Premises to inspect the same, to submit said Premises to prospective purchasers or tenants, to post notices of non-responsibility and "for lease" signs, and to alter, improve or repair the Premises and any portion of the Building without abatement of rent, and may for that purpose erect scaffolding and other necessary structures where reasonably required by the character of the work to be performed, always providing the entrance to the Premises shall not be blocked thereby, and further providing that the business of Tenant shall not be interfered with unreasonably. Tenant hereby waives any claim for damages for any injury or inconvenience to or interference with Tenant's business, any loss of occupancy or quiet enjoyment of the Premises, and any other loss occasioned thereby. For each of the aforesaid purposes, Landlord shall at all times have and retain a key with which to unlock all of the doors in, upon and about the Premises, excluding Tenant's vaults and safes, and Landlord shall have the right to use any and all means which Landlord may deem proper to open said doors in an emergency, in order to obtain entry to the Premises, and any entry to the Premises obtained by Landlord by any of said means, or otherwise, shall not under any circumstances be construed or deemed to be a forcible or unlawful entry into, or a detainer of, the Premises, or an eviction of Tenant from the Premises or any portion thereof.

10.   LIENS.   Tenant shall keep the Premises and any Building of which the Premises are a part free from any liens out of work performed, materials furnished, or obligations incurred by Tenant and shall indemnify, hold harmless and defend Landlord from any liens and encumbrances arising out of any work performed or materials furnished by or at the direction of Tenant. In the event that Tenant shall not, within twenty (20) days following the imposition of any such lien, cause such lien to be released of record by payment or posting of a proper bond, Landlord shall have, in addition to all other remedies provided herein and by law, the right, but no obligation, to cause the same to be released by such means as it shall deem proper, including payment of the claim giving rise to such lien. All such sums paid by Landlord and all expenses incurred by it in connection therewith including attorney's fees and costs shall be payable to Landlord by Tenant on demand with interest at the rate of ten percent (10%) per annum. Landlord shall have the right at all times to post and keep posted on the Premises any notices permitted or required by law, or which Landlord shall deem proper, for the protection of Landlord and the Premises, and any other party having an interest therein, from mechanics' and materialmen's liens, and Tenant shall give to Landlord at least ten (10) business days prior written notice of the expected date of commencement of any work relating to alterations or additions to the Premises.

FIGURE 4.1   (continued)

11. INDEMNITY

11.1   Indemnity. Tenant shall indemnify and hold harmless Landlord from and against any and all claims arising from Tenant's use of the Premises or the conduct of its business or from any activity, work, or thing done, permitted or suffered by Tenant in or about the Premises and shall further indemnify and hold Landlord harmless from and against any and all claims arising from any breach or default in the performance of any obligation on Tenant's part to be performed under the terms of this Lease, or arising from any act or negligence of Tenant, or any of its agents, contractors or employees, and from and against any and all costs, attorney's fees, expenses and liabilities incurred in connection with such claim or any action or proceeding brought thereon; and in case any action or proceeding be brought against Landlord by reason of any such claim, Tenant upon notice from Landlord shall defend the same at Tenant's expense by counsel reasonably satisfactory to Landlord, provided, however, that Tenant shall not be liable for damage or injury occasioned by the negligent or intentional acts of Landlord and its designated agents or employees unless covered by insurance Tenant is required to provide.

11.2   Exemption of Landlord from Liability. Landlord shall not be liable for injury or damage which may be sustained by the person, goods, wares, merchandise or property of Tenant, its employees, invitees or customers, or any other person in or about the Premises caused by or resulting from fire, steam, electricity, gas, water or rain, which may leak or flow from or into any part of the Premises, or from breakage, leakage, obstruction or other defects of the pipes, sprinklers, wires, appliances, plumbing, air conditioning or lighting fixtures of the same, whether the said damage or injury results from conditions arising upon the Premises or upon other portions of the Building of which the Premises are a part, or from other sources. Landlord shall not be liable for any damages arising from any act or neglect of any other Tenant (if any) of such Building.

12. INSURANCE

12.1   Public Liability. Tenant shall, at Tenant's sole cost and expense, but for the mutual benefit of Landlord and Tenant, maintain throughout the term of this Lease general public liability insurance against claims for personal injury, death or property damage occurring in, or about the Premises, and in, on, or about the sidewalks directly adjacent to the Premises and such other areas as Tenant, its officers, agents, employees, contractors and invitees shall have the right to use pursuant to this Lease. Such insurance shall have a combined single limit of not less than $500,000.

12.2   Fire and Extended Coverage. Landlord shall take out and keep in force during the term of this Lease at the expense of _____, fire and extended coverage insurance, including vandalism and malicious mischief coverage in an amount equal to the full replacement value of the Premises, exclusive of Tenant's fixtures, personal property and equipment.

12.3   Form of the Policies. The policies required by 12.1 and 12.2 shall be in a form reasonably satisfactory to Landlord. A certificate as to such insurance shall be presented to Landlord. Tenant shall have the right to provide insurance coverage which it is obligated to provide for pursuant to blanket policies obtained by Tenant, provided such blanket policies expressly afford coverage to the Premises and to Tenant as required by this Lease. Tenant shall obtain a written obligation on the part of any such insurance company to notify Landlord in writing of any delinquency in premium payments and at least fifteen (15) days prior thereto of any cancellation of any such policy. Tenant agrees if Tenant does not take out such insurance or keep the same in full force and effect, Landlord may take out the necessary insurance and pay the premium therefor, and Tenant shall repay to Landlord the amount so paid promptly after demand.

12.4   Waiver of Subrogation. Landlord and Tenant each hereby waive any and all rights of recovery against the other or against the officers, employees, agents and representatives of the other, on account of loss or damage occasioned to such waiving party or its property or the property of others under its control to the extent that such loss or damage is insured against under any fire and extended coverage insurance policy which either may have in force at the time of such loss or damage.

13. DAMAGE TO PREMISES

13.1   Partial Damage — Insurance Available. In the event of damage causing a partial destruction of the Premises during the term of this Lease and there is made available to Landlord pursuant to 12.2 insurance proceeds for such damage paying eighty percent (80%) or more of the cost of repairing such damage, Landlord shall utilize all such insurance proceeds and pay any additional cost and cause the Premises to be repaired promptly to a condition existing immediately prior to such damage, with this Lease to continue in full force and effect.

13.2   Partial Damage — Insurance Not Available. In the event of damage causing a partial destruction of the Premises during the term of this Lease and there are no insurance proceeds available, or the insurance proceeds available are less than eighty percent (80%) of the cost of repairing such damage, then Landlord shall have the option for a period of sixty (60) days after the unavailability or amount of insurance proceeds is determined to elect to terminate this Lease and to retain all insurance proceeds or to repair the damage at Landlord's expense. The failure of Landlord to take any actions within the sixty (60) day period shall be deemed to be an election to terminate the Lease. In the event Landlord elects to repair such damage, such work shall be completed promptly restoring the Premises to the condition existing immediately prior to such damage, and this Lease shall continue in full force and effect. In the event Landlord elects to terminate the Lease, Tenant shall have thirty (30) days thereafter to elect to pay for the cost of such repairs to the extent insurance proceeds are not available. In the event Tenant elects to do so, coincidentally therewith Tenant shall deposit with Landlord or make available to Landlord on terms acceptable to Landlord, the amount required in addition to any available insurance proceeds to complete the repairs. Landlord shall cause such repair work to be completed promptly thereafter restoring the Premises to the condition existing immediately prior to such damage, and this Lease shall continue in full force and effect.

13.3   Destruction. In the event the Premises are totally destroyed or the Premises cannot be repaired as required herein under applicable laws and regulations, notwithstanding the availability of insurance proceeds or contributions from Tenant, this Lease shall be terminated effective the date of the damage.

13.4   Damage to Building or Damage During Last Six Months of Term. In the event of any partial destruction to the building in which the Premises are located representing thirty percent (30%) or more of the replacement cost of the building even though the Premises are not damaged, or any partial destruction to the Premises occurring during the last six (6) months of the term or any extension thereof, notwithstanding the provisions of Sections 13.1 and 13.2, Landlord shall have the right for a period of thirty (30) days after the determination of the availability of insurance proceeds to retain all insurance proceeds and to terminate this Lease.

13.5   Abatement of Rent. In the event of any partial destruction which is repaired by Landlord, for the period between the date of damage until the repairs are completed, and in the event of the termination of this Lease, for the period between the date of the damage and the date of termination, the rent payable by Tenant shall be reduced in the proportion which the area of the Premises with improvements that are not useable bears to the total area of the Premises containing improvements. This right to a partial abatement of rent shall be Tenant's sole remedy as a result of any such damage and repair. Landlord shall not be required to make any repair or restoration of injury or damage to any improvement or property installed on the Premises by or at the expense of Tenant; such items shall be replaced by Tenant at Tenant's sole cost and expense.

FIGURE 4.1   (continued)

14. CONDEMNATION. If all or any part of the Premises shall be taken or appropriated for public or quasi-public use by right of eminent domain, with or without litigation or transferred by agreement in connection with such public or quasi-public use, either party hereto shall have the right at its option exercisable within thirty (30) days of receipt of notice of such taking to terminate this Lease as of the date possession is taken by the condemning authority, provided, however, that before Tenant may terminate this Lease by reason of taking or appropriation as provided herein-above, such taking or appropriation shall be of such an extent and nature as to substantially handicap, impede or impair Tenant's use of the Prem-ises. If any part of the Building other than the Premises shall be so taken or appropriated, Landlord shall have the right at its option to terminate this Lease. No award for any partial or entire taking shall be apportioned, and Tenant hereby assigns to Landlord any award which may be made in such taking or condemnation, together with any and all rights of Tenant now or hereafter arising in or to the same or any part thereof; provided, however, that nothing contained herein shall be deemed to give Landlord any interest in or to require Tenant to assign to Landlord any award made to Tenant for the taking of personal property and fixtures belonging to Tenant and/or for the interruption of or damage to Tenant's business and/or for Tenant's unamortized cost of leasehold improvements. In the event of a partial taking which does not result in a termination of this Lease, rent shall be abated in the proportion which the part of the Premises so made unusable bears to the rented area of the Premises immediately prior to the taking. No temporary taking of the Premises and/or of Tenant's rights therein or under this Lease shall terminate this Lease or give Tenant any right to any abatement of rent thereunder; any award made to Tenant by reason of any such temporary taking shall belong entirely to Tenant and Landlord shall not be entitled to share therein.

15. ASSIGNMENT AND SUBLETTING
  15.1   Landlord's Consent Required. Tenant shall not assign, transfer, mortgage, pledge, hypothecate or encumber this Lease or any interest therein, and shall not sublet the Premises or any part thereof, without the prior written consent of Landlord and any attempt to do so without such consent being first had and obtained shall be wholly void and shall constitute a breach of this Lease.
  15.2   Reasonable Consent. If Tenant complies with the following conditions, Landlord shall not unreasonably withhold its consent to the subletting of the Premises or any portion thereof or the assignment of this Lease. Tenant shall submit in writing to Landlord (a) the name and legal composition of the proposed subtenant or assignee; (b) the nature of the business proposed to be carried on in the Premises; (c) the terms and pro-visions of the proposed sublease; (d) such reasonable financial information as Landlord may request concerning the proposed subtenant or assignee.
  15.3   No Release of Tenant. No consent by Landlord to any assignment or subletting by Tenant shall relieve Tenant of any obligation to be performed by Tenant under this Lease, whether occurring before or after such consent, assignment or subletting. The consent by Landlord to any assignment or subletting shall not relieve Tenant from the obligation to obtain Landlord's express written consent to any other assignment or subletting. The acceptance of rent by Landlord from any other person shall not be deemed to be a waiver by Landlord of any provision of this Lease or to be a consent to any assignment, subletting or other transfer. Consent to one assignment, subletting or other transfer shall not be deemed to constitute consent to any subsequent assignment, subletting or other transfer.
  15.4   Attorney's Fees. In the event Landlord shall consent to a sublease or assignment under this Section 15, Tenant shall pay Landlord's reasonable attorney's fees not to exceed $500 incurred in connection with giving such consent.

16. SUBORDINATION
  16.1   Subordination. This Lease at Landlord's option shall be subject and subordinate to all ground or underlying leases which now exist or may hereafter be executed affecting the Premises or the land upon which the Premises are situated or both, and to the lien of any mortgages or deeds of trust in any amount or amounts whatsoever now or hereafter placed on or against the land or improvements or either thereof, of which the Premises are a part, or on or against Landlord's interest or estate therein, or on or against any ground or underlying lease without the necessity of the execution and delivery of any further instruments on the part of Tenant to effectuate such subordination. If any mortgagee, trustee or ground lessor shall elect to have this Lease prior to the lien of its mortgage, deed of trust or ground lease, and shall give written notice thereof to Tenant, this Lease shall be deemed prior to such mortgage, deed of trust or ground lease, whether this Lease is dated prior or subsequent to the date of said mortgage, deed of trust, or ground lease or the date of the recording thereof.
  16.2   Subordination Agreements. Tenant covenants and agrees to execute and deliver upon demand without charge therefore, such further instruments evidencing such subordination of this Lease to such ground or underlying leases and to the lien of any such mortgages or deeds of trust as may be required by Landlord. Tenant hereby appoints Landlord as Tenant's attorney-in-fact, irrevocably, to execute and deliver any such agree-ments, instruments, releases or other documents.
  16.3   Quiet Enjoyment. Landlord covenants and agrees with Tenant that upon Tenant paying rent and other monetary sums due under the Lease, performing its covenants and conditions under the Lease and upon recognizing purchaser as Landlord pursuant hereto, Tenant shall and may peaceably and quietly have, hold and enjoy the Premises for the term, subject, however, to the terms of the Lease and of any of the aforesaid ground leases, mortgages or deeds of trust described above.
  16.4   Attornment. In the event any proceedings are brought for default under any ground or underlying lease or in the event of foreclosure or the exercise of the power of sale under any mortgage or deed of trust made by the Landlord covering the Premises, the Tenant shall attorn to the purchaser upon any such foreclosure or sale and recognize such purchaser as the Landlord under this Lease, provided said purchaser expressly agrees in writing to be bound by the terms of the Lease.

17. DEFAULT, REMEDIES
  17.1   Default. The occurrence of any of the following shall constitute a material default and breach of this Lease by Tenant:
      (a) Any failure by Tenant to pay the rent or any other monetary sums required to be paid hereunder (where such failure continues for five (5) days after written notice by Landlord to Tenant);
      (b) The abandonment or vacation of the Premises by Tenant;
      (c) A failure by Tenant to observe and perform any other provision of this Lease to be observed or performed by Tenant, where such failure continues for twenty (20) days after written notice thereof by Landlord to Tenant; provided, however, that if the nature of the default is such that the same cannot reasonably be cured within said twenty (20) day period, Tenant shall not be deemed to be in default if Tenant shall within such period commence such cure and thereafter diligently prosecute the same to completion;
      (d) The making by Tenant of any general assignment or general arrangement for the benefit of creditors; the filing by or against Tenant of a petition to have Tenant adjudged a bankrupt or of a petition for reorganization or arrangement under any law relating to bankruptcy (unless, in the case of a petition filed against Tenant, the same is dismissed within sixty (60) days); the appointment of a trustee or receiver to take possession of substantially all of Tenant's assets located at the Premises or of Tenant's interest in this Lease, where possession is not restored to Tenant within thirty (30) days; or the attachment, execution or other judicial seizure of substantially all of Tenant's assets located at the Premises or of Tenant's interest in this Lease, where such seizure is not discharged within thirty (30) days.

FIGURE 4.1 (continued)

17.2 Remedies. In the event of any such material default or breach by Tenant, Landlord may, at any time thereafter without limiting Landlord in the exercise of any right or remedy at law or in equity which Landlord may have by reason of such default or breach:

(a) Maintain this Lease in full force and effect and recover the rent and other monetary charges as they become due, without terminating Tenant's right to possession irrespective of whether Tenant shall have abandoned the Premises. In the event Landlord elects not to terminate the Lease, Landlord shall have the right to attempt to re-let the Premises at such rent and upon such conditions and for such a term, and to do all acts necessary to maintain or preserve the Premises as Landlord deems reasonable and necessary without being deemed to have elected to terminate the Lease, including removal of all persons and property from the Premises; such property may be removed and stored in a public warehouse or elsewhere at the cost of and for the account of Tenant. In the event any such re-letting occurs, this Lease shall terminate automatically upon the new Tenant taking possession of the Premises. Notwithstanding that Landlord fails to elect to terminate the Lease initially, Landlord at any time during the term of this Lease may elect to terminate this Lease by virtue of such previous default of Tenant.

(b) Terminate Tenant's right to possession by any lawful means, in which case this Lease shall terminate and Tenant shall immediately surrender possession of the Premises to Landlord. In such event Landlord shall be entitled to recover from Tenant all damages incurred by Landlord by reason of Tenant's default, including without limitation thereto, the following: (i) the worth at the time of award of any unpaid rent which had been earned at the time of such termination; plus (ii) the worth at the time of award of the amount by which the unpaid rent which would have been earned after termination until the time of award exceeds the amount of such rental loss that is proved could have been reasonably avoided; plus (iii) the worth at the time of award of the amount by which the unpaid rent for the balance of the term after the time of award exceeds the amount of such rental loss that is proved could be reasonably avoided; plus (iv) any other amount necessary to compensate Landlord for all the detriment proximately caused by Tenant's failure to perform its obligations under this Lease or which in the ordinary course of events would be likely to result therefrom; plus (v) at Landlord's election, such other amounts in addition to or in lieu of the foregoing as may be permitted from time to time by applicable State law. Upon any such re-entry Landlord shall have the right to make any reasonable repairs, alterations or modifications to the Premises, which Landlord in its sole discretion deems reasonable and necessary. As used in (i) above, the "worth at the time of award" is computed by allowing interest at the rate of ten percent (10%) per annum from the date of default. As used in (ii) and (iii) the "worth at the time of award" is computed by discounting such amount at the discount date of the U.S. Federal Reserve Bank at the time of award plus one percent (1%). The term "rent", as used in this Section 17, shall be deemed to be and to mean the rent to be paid pursuant to Section 3 and all other monetary sums required to be paid by Tenant pursuant to the terms of this Lease.

17.3 Late Charges. Tenant hereby acknowledges that late payment by Tenant to Landlord of rent and other sums due hereunder will cause Landlord to incur costs not contemplated by this Lease, the exact amount of which will be extremely difficult to ascertain. Such costs include, but are not limited to, processing and accounting charges, and late charges which may be imposed on Landlord by the terms of any mortgage or trust deed covering the Premises. Accordingly, if any installment of rent or any other sum due from Tenant shall not be received by Landlord or Landlord's designee within ten (10) days after such amount shall be due, Tenant shall pay to Landlord a late charge equal to ten percent (10%) of such overdue amount. The parties hereby agree that such late charge represents a fair and reasonable estimate of the costs Landlord will incur by reason of late payment by Tenant. Acceptance of such late charge by Landlord shall in no event constitute a waiver of Tenant's default with respect to such overdue amount, nor prevent Landlord from exercising any of the other rights and remedies granted hereunder.

17.4 Default by Landlord. Landlord shall not be in default unless Landlord fails to perform obligations required of Landlord within a reasonable time, but in no event later than thirty (30) days after written notice by Tenant to Landlord and to the holder of any first mortgage or deed of trust covering the Premises whose name and address shall have theretofore been furnished to Tenant in writing, specifying wherein Landlord has failed to perform such obligations; provided, however, that if the nature of Landlord's obligation is such that more than thirty (30) days are required for performance then Landlord shall not be in default if Landlord commences performance within such thirty-day period and thereafter diligently prosecutes the same to completion.

18. BROKER'S FEE

18.1 Broker's Fee. Upon execution of this Lease by both parties, Landlord shall pay to Grubb and Ellis Commercial Brokerage Company, a licensed real estate broker, a fee of _____ ($_____) for brokerage services heretofore rendered. Landlord further agrees that if Tenant exercises any option granted herein or any option substantially similar thereto, either to extend the term of this Lease, to renew this Lease, to purchase said Premises or any part thereof and/or any adjacent property which Landlord may own or in which Landlord has an interest, or any other option granted herein, or if said Broker is the procuring cause of any other lease or sale entered into between the parties pertaining to the Premises and/or any adjacent property in which Landlord has an interest, then as to any of said transactions, Landlord shall pay Broker a fee in accordance with the commission schedule of Broker in effect at the time of execution of this Lease. Landlord agrees to pay said fee not only on behalf of Landlord but also on behalf of any person, corporation, association, or other entity having an ownership interest in said real property or any part thereof, when such fee is due hereunder. Any transferee of Landlord's interests in this Lease, by accepting an assignment of such interest, shall be deemed to have assumed Landlord's obligation under this Section 18. Said Broker shall be a third party beneficiary of the provisions of this Section.

19. MISCELLANEOUS

19.1 Estoppel Certificate.

(a) Tenant shall at any time upon not less than ten (10) day's prior written notice from Landlord execute, acknowledge and deliver to Landlord a statement in writing (i) certifying that this Lease is unmodified and in full force and effect (or, if modified, stating the nature of such modification and certifying that this Lease, as so modified, is in full force and effect) and the date to which the rent and other charges are paid in advance, if any, and (ii) acknowledging that there are not, to Tenant's knowledge, any uncured defaults on the part of Landlord hereunder, or specifying such defaults if any are claimed. Any such statement may be conclusively relied upon by any prospective purchaser or encumbrancer of the Premises.

(b) Tenant's failure to deliver such statement within such time shall be conclusive upon Tenant (i) that this Lease is in full force and effect, without modification except as may be represented by Landlord, (ii) that there are no uncured defaults in Landlord's performance, and (iii) that not more than one month's rent has been paid in advance.

(c) If Landlord desires to finance or refinance said Premises, or any part thereof, or any building of which the Premises may be a part, Tenant hereby agrees to deliver to any lender designated by Landlord such financial statements of Tenant as may be reasonably required by such lender. Such statements shall include the past three years' financial statements of Tenant. All such financial statements shall be received by Landlord in confidence and shall be used only for the purposes herein set forth.

FIGURE 4.1   (continued)

19.2   Transfer of Landlord's Interest. In the event of a sale or conveyance by Landlord of Landlord's interest in the Premises or in any building of which the Premises may be a part other than a transfer for security purposes only, Landlord shall be relieved from and after the date specified in any such notice of transfer of all obligations and liabilities accruing thereafter on the part of Landlord, provided that any funds in the hands of Landlord at the time of transfer in which Tenant has an interest, shall be delivered to the successor of Landlord. This Lease shall not be affected by any such sale and Tenant agrees to attorn to the purchaser or assignee provided all Landlord's obligations hereunder are assumed in writing by the transferee.

19.3   Captions; Attachments; Defined Terms.

(a)   The captions of the paragraphs of this Lease are for convenience only and shall not be deemed to be relevant in resolving any question of interpretation or construction of any section of this Lease.

(b)   Exhbits attached hereto, and addendums and schedules initialed by the parties, are deemed by attachment to constitute part of this Lease and are incorporated herein.

(c)   The words "Landlord" and "Tenant", as used herein, shall include the plural as well as the singular. Words used in neuter gender include the masculine and feminine and words in the masculine or feminine gender include the neuter. If there be more than one Landlord or Tenant, the obligations hereunder imposed upon Landlord or Tenant shall be joint and several; as to a Tenant which consists of husband and wife, the obligations shall extend individually to their sole and separate property as well as community property. The term "Landlord" shall mean only the owner or owners at the time in question of the fee title or a tenant's interest in a ground lease of the Premises. The obligations contained in this Lease to be performed by Landlord shall be binding on Landlord's successor's and assigns only during their respective periods of ownership.

19.4   Entire Agreement. This instrument along with any exhibits and attachments hereto constitutes the entire agreement between Landlord and Tenant relative to the Premises and this Agreement and the exhibits and attachments may be altered, amended or revoked only by an instrument in writing signed by both Landlord and Tenant. Landlord and Tenant agree hereby that all prior or contemporaneous oral agreements between and among themselves and their agents or representatives relative to the leasing of the Premises are merged in or revoked by this Agreement.

19.5   Severability. If any term or provision of this Lease shall, to any extent, be determined by a court of competent jurisdiction to be invalid or unenforceable, the remainder of this Lease shall not be affected thereby, and each term and provision of this Lease shall be valid and be enforceable to the fullest extent permitted by law.

19.6   Costs of Suit.

(a)   If Tenant or Landlord shall bring any action for any relief against the other, declaratory or otherwise, arising out of this Lease, including any suit by Landlord for the recovery of rent or possession of the Premises, the losing party shall pay the successful party a reasonable sum for attorneys' fees which shall be deemed to have accrued on the commencement of such action and shall be paid whether or not such action is prosecuted to judgment.

(b)   Should Landlord, without fault on Landlord's part, be made a party to any litigation instituted by Tenant or by any third party against Tenant, or by or against any person holding under or using the Premises by license of Tenant, or for the foreclosure of any lien for labor or material furnished to or for Tenant or any such other person or otherwise arising out of or resulting from any act or transaction of Tenant or of any such person, Tenant covenants to save and hold Landlord harmless from any judgment rendered against Landlord or the Premises or any part thereof, and all costs and expenses, including reasonable attorneys' fees, incurred by Landlord in or in connection with such litigation.

(c)   If Tenant or Landlord or their successors or assigns shall bring an action against Broker or make Broker a party to litigation arising out of this Lease, Broker shall be entitled to recover reasonable attorney's fees and court costs from either Landlord or Tenant if Broker is adjudged by a court of competent jurisdiction to be without fault in such matter.

19.7   Time; Joint and Several Liability. Time is of the essence of this Lease and each and every provision hereof, except as to the conditions relating to the delivery of possession of the Premises to Tenant. All the terms, covenants and conditions contained in this Lease to be performed by either party, if such party shall consist of more than one person or organization, shall be deemed to be joint and several, and all rights and remedies of the parties shall be cumulative and nonexclusive of any other remedy at law or in equity.

19.8   Binding Effect; Choice of Law. The parties hereto agree that all provisions hereof are to be construed as both covenants and conditions as though the words importing such covenants and conditions were used in each separate paragraph hereof. Subject to any provisions hereof restricting assignment or subletting by Tenant and subject to Section 19.2, all of the provisions hereof shall bind and inure to the benefit of the parties hereto and their respective heirs, legal representatives, successors and assigns. This Lease shall be governed by the laws of the State of California.

19.9   Waiver. No covenant, term or condition or the breach thereof shall be deemed waived, except by written consent of the party against whom the waiver is claimed, and any waiver or the breach of any covenant, term or condition shall not be deemed to be a waiver of any preceeding or succeeding breach of the same or any other covenant, term or condition. Acceptance by Landlord of any performance by Tenant after the time the same shall have become due shall not constitute a waiver by Landlord of the breach or default of any covenant, term or condition unless otherwise expressly agreed to by Landlord in writing.

19.10   Surrender of Premises. The voluntary or other surrender of this Lease by Tenant, or a mutual cancellation thereof, shall not work a merger, and shall, at the option of the Landlord, terminate all or any existing subleases or subtenancies, or may, at the option of Landlord, operate as an assignment to it of any or all such subleases or subtenancies.

19.11   Holding Over. If Tenant remains in possession of all or any part of the Premises after the expiration of the term hereof, with or without the express or implied consent of Landlord, such tenancy shall be from month to month only, and not a renewal hereof or an extension for any further term, and in such case, rent and other monetary sums due hereunder shall be payable in the amount and at the time specified in this Lease and such month to month tenancy shall be subject to every other term, covenant and agreement contained herein.

19.12   Signs.

(a)   Tenant shall not inscribe, paint, affix, place or permit to be placed any projecting sign, marquee, awning, advertisement, sign, notice or placard on the exterior or roof of the Premises or upon or about the entrance doors, windows, sidewalks or areas adjacent to the Premises without Landlord's prior written consent. Landlord reserves the right in Landlord's sole discretion to place and locate on the roof, exterior sidewalls and rear wall of said Premises or any portion of the Building of which the Premises may constitute a part but which are not leased to Tenant, such notices, signs, marquees and advertisements as Landlord may deem appropriate in the operation of Landlord's affairs.

(b)   Any such signs or other items described above installed by Tenant with Landlord's consent shall be removed at the expiration or earlier termination of the Lease at Tenant's expense and Tenant shall repair any damage caused to the Premises resulting from such removal. If Tenant fails to do so, Landlord may cause such removal and repair on Tenant's behalf at Tenant's expense. If Tenant installs such items without

FIGURE 4.1 (concluded)

Landlord's consent, Tenant shall remove same promptly upon receipt of a request by Landlord to do so and shall repair the Premises accordingly. If Tenant fails to do so, Landlord may cause such removal and repair to be performed on Tenant's behalf at Tenant's expense. Tenant shall not be allowed to use the name of the building in which the Premises are located (if any) or of the owner of such building or of the Premises or words to such effect in connection with any business carried on in said Premises (except as the address of the Tenant) without the prior written consent of Landlord. Landlord reserves the right to change the name and title of the building at any time during the term of said Lease. Tenant hereby expressly agrees to such change at the option of Landlord and waives any and all damage occasioned thereby.

19.13 Reasonable Consent. Except as limited elsewhere in this Lease, wherever in this Lease Landlord or Tenant is required to give its consent or approval to any action on the part of the other, such consent or approval shall not be unreasonably withheld. In the event of failure to give any such consent, the other party shall be entitled to specific performance at law and shall have such other remedies as are reserved to it under this Lease, but in no event shall Landlord or Tenant be responsible in monetary damages for failure to give consent unless said consent is withheld maliciously or in bad faith.

19.14 Interest on Past Due Obligations. Except as expressly herein provided, any amount due to Landlord not paid when due shall bear interest at ten percent (10%) per annum from the due date. Payment of such interest shall not excuse or cure any default by Tenant under this Lease.

19.15 Arbitration. Any question, dispute, or controversy arising under the provisions of Sections 13 and 14 of this Lease, at the option of Landlord, shall be determined by arbitration. Such arbitration shall be conducted pursuant to the provisions of the laws of the State of California then in force, with the rules of procedure to be those of the American Arbitration Association or its successor insofar as said rules of procedure do not conflict with the laws of the State of California then in force. Any award entered as a result of arbitration shall be entered as a judgment, with the costs of arbitration to be paid as ordered by the arbitrator.

19.16 Notices. All notices or demands of any kind required or desired to be given by Landlord or Tenant hereunder shall be in writing and shall be deemed delivered forty-eight (48) hours after depositing the notice or demand in the United States mail, certified or registered, postage prepaid, addressed to the Landlord or Tenant respectively at the addresses set forth after their signatures at the end of this Lease.

19.17 Corporate Authority. If Tenant is a corporation, each individual executing this Lease on behalf of said corporation represents and warrants that he is duly authorized to execute and deliver this Lease on behalf of said corporation in accordance with a duly adopted resolution of the Board of Directors of said corporation or in accordance with the By-laws of said corporation, and that this Lease is binding upon said corporation in accordance with its terms. If Tenant is a corporaton Tenant shall, within thirty (30) days after execution of this Lease, deliver to Landlord a certified copy of a resolution of the Board of Directors of said corporation authorizing or ratifying the execution of this Lease.

In Witness Whereof, Landlord and Tenant have executed this Lease the date and year first above written.

Landlord: Tenant:

_____   _____

_____   _____

Address: Address:

_____   _____

_____   _____

_____   _____

(If Landlord or Tenant is a corporation, the corporate seal must be affixed and the authorized officers must sign on behalf of the corporation. The Lease must be executed by the President or a Vice President and the Secretary or Assistant Secretary unless the By-laws or a Resolution of the Board of Directors shall otherwise provide, in which event the By-laws or a certified copy of the Resolution, as the case may be, must be furnished.)

THIS LEASE HAS BEEN PREPARED FOR SUBMISSION TO YOUR ATTORNEY WHO WILL REVIEW THE DOCUMENT AND ASSIST YOU TO DETERMINE WHETHER YOUR LEGAL RIGHTS ARE ADEQUATELY PROTECTED. GRUBB AND ELLIS COMMERCIAL BROKERAGE COMPANY IS NOT AUTHORIZED TO GIVE LEGAL OR TAX ADVICE; NO REPRESENTATION OR RECOMMENDATION IS MADE BY GRUBB AND ELLIS COMMERCIAL BROKERAGE COMPANY OR ITS AGENTS OR EMPLOYEES AS TO THE LEGAL SUFFICIENCY, LEGAL EFFECT OR TAX CONSEQUENCES OF THIS DOCUMENT OR ANY TRANSACTION RELATING THERETO. THESE ARE QUESTIONS FOR YOUR ATTORNEY WITH WHOM YOU SHOULD CONSULT BEFORE SIGNING THIS DOCUMENT.

FIGURE 4.2   Lease Provisions Relating to Construction of Tenant's Premises

---

EXHIBIT B

PROVISIONS RELATING TO CONSTRUCTION
OF TENANT'S PREMISES

A. GENERAL PROVISIONS RELATING TO PREPARATION OF PLANS AND SPECIFICATIONS

1. Promptly upon execution of this Lease, Landlord shall deliver to Tenant its standard floor plan showing Tenant's Premises and the column spacing and overall dimensions and setting forth Landlord's requirements for information needed to prepare preliminary plans and specifications for the Building Standard Work as described in Section C of this Exhibit.

2. Within ten (10) days of receipt thereof, Tenant shall prepare and deliver at its sole cost and expense all of the aforesaid information needed by Landlord to prepare said preliminary plans and specifications.

3. Tenant shall cause to be prepared at its sole cost and expense and delivered simultaneously with the information required in (2) above, plans and specifications prepared by an architect approved by Landlord for any work which varies or is in addition to Building Standard Work including without limitation thereto, the number and types of offices, conference rooms, public areas, desk locations, (such work being hereafter referred to as "Building Non-Standard Work").

4. Tenant shall cause to be prepared at its sole cost and expense and delivered simultaneously with the items required under (2) and (3) above, Tenant's finish schedule for interior decoration of the Premises, (including without limitation thereto, any special wall coverings, lighting or other fixtures, carpets or floor coverings, painting, finish hardware and detailed drawings of all shelving and cabinet work).

5. Wherever Tenant utilizes architects, designers or engineers other than those utilized by Landlord, Tenant shall pay all costs in connection therewith and shall cause any plans and specifications which Tenant is obliged to provide hereunder to be prepared promptly and in coordination with the preparation of any plans and specifications which Landlord is required to prepare.

6. As to Building Standard Work, upon receipt of the information required in (2) above, Landlord shall promptly have prepared preliminary plans and specifications for the work and shall deliver a copy thereof to Tenant. Tenant shall have ten (10) days to review and approve said preliminary plans and specifications in writing by initialing each page thereof, provided, however, that the Tenant shall be obliged to approve said preliminary plans and specifications if they reflect the information provided by Tenant pursuant to (2) above. Failure to approve or disapprove in writing specifying the reasons of such disapproval within said ten (10) days shall be conclusively deemed an approval thereof.

7. As to Building Non-Standard Work, Landlord shall have ten (10) days to approve the plans and specification referred to in (3) above in writing by initialing each page thereof, which approval shall not be unreasonably withheld. Within ten (10) days of receipt of any reasonable written objection of Landlord, Tenant shall cause said plans and specifications to be corrected and shall redeliver the corrected portion thereof to Landlord for Landlord's approval. This procedure shall be followed until all reasonable objections have been resolved and the plans and specifications for Building Non-Standard Work approved.

8. Upon the approval of preliminary plans and specifications for Building Standard Work, the approval of plans and specifications for Building Non-Standard Work, the receipt of Tenant's Finish Schedule, Landlord shall have promptly prepared and delivered to Tenant final plans and specifications for the work on the Premises. Tenant shall pay for that portion of the cost of preparation of final plans and specifications attributable to the incorporation of Building Non-Standard Work therein. Tenant shall have ten (10) days from receipt of said final plans and specifications within which to approve said final plans and specification by initialing each page thereof, provided, however, that Tenant shall be obligated to approve said final plans and specifications if they reflect the information provided in (2), (3) and (4) above. Failure to approve or disapprove in writing specifying the reasons for such disapproval within ten (10) days shall be conclusively deemed an approval thereof. Within ten (10) days of receipt of any reasonable written objection of Tenant, Landlord shall cause said final plans and specifications to be corrected and shall redeliver the corrected portion thereof to Tenant for Tenant's approval. This procedure shall be followed until all reasonable objections have been resolved and the final plans and specifications have been approved.

9. When the final plans and specifications have been approved and accepted by Tenant, Landlord shall supply Tenant with _____ sets of final working, plans and specifications to permit Tenant to be familiar with the course of construction of the Premises.

10. In the event said final plans and specifications for all work in the Premises have not been completed within _____ days from the date of execution of the Lease, then the Landlord shall have the right to cancel this Lease, but in such event Tenants shall pay one half (1/2) of Landlord's cost of having said final plans and specifications prepared.

11. Once any portion of the preliminary or final plans and specifications have been approved by Landlord and Tenant, there may be no material changes in the approved portion thereof without the prior written consent of Landlord and Tenant. Any additional charges, expenses or costs arising by reason of any subsequent change, modification or alteration in said approved plans and specifications made at the request of Tenant shall be at the sole cost and expense of Tenant. Should Tenant change its space use requirements at any time after design work has commenced based on information supplied by Tenant to Landlord pursuant hereto, the cost of design changes, including architects fees shall be at Tenant's expense.

B. GENERAL PROVISIONS RELATING TO CONSTRUCTION

1. Landlord shall cause Tenant's Building Non-Standard Work to be installed by Landlord's Contractor pursuant to the approved final plans and specifications at Tenant's sole cost and expense. Prior to commencing any such work, Landlord, its Contractor, or its Office Planning Architects shall submit to Tenant for Tenant's approval a written estimate of the cost thereof. Landlord's Contractor shall not proceed with any work to be paid for by Tenant without first obtaining Tenant's approval of the cost thereof. Tenant agrees to pay Landlord or its Contractor promptly upon being billed therefor the cost of all such Building Non-Standard Work.

Landlord shall cause its Contractor to perform the work and supply the materials in compliance with the approved plans and to have such work performed diligently and in a first class workmanlike manner in compliance with applicable laws and codes and with applicable standards of the local Building Code, National Board of Fire Underwriters, the local Electric Code, the American Gas Association and the American Society of Heating, Refrigerating and Air Conditioning Engineers. Such work shall be completed at the earliest possible date, subject to delays beyond the control of Landlord.

FIGURE 4.2 (concluded)

2. All amounts payable by Tenant to Landlord pursuant to this Exhibit B shall be paid by Tenant promptly after the delivery of bills therefor by Landlord or its Contractor to Tenant, it being understood that such bills may be delivered during the progress of the performance of the work and/or the furnishing and installation of the materials to which such bills related, for work that has been performed and materials that have been supplied.

3. Tenant may select different new materials (except exterior window draperies) in place of Building Standard Work materials which would otherwise be initially furnished and installed by Landlord for or in the interior of the Premises under the provisions of this Exhibit B, provided such selection is indicated on Tenant's final plans and specifications. If Tenant shall make any such selection and if the cost of such different new materials of Tenant's selection shall exceed the Landlord's cost of Landlord's Building Standard Work materials thereby replaced (as established by the price at which Landlord's Contractor will perform the work), Tenant shall pay to Landlord, as hereinafter provided, the difference between the work cost of such different new materials and the work cost to Landlord for the materials thereby replaced. No credit shall be granted for the ommission of materials where no replacement in kind is made. There shall be credits only for substitutions in kind, e.g., a lighting fixture credit may be applied only against the cost of another type of lighting fixture.

No such different new materials shall be furnished and installed in replacement for any of Landlord's Building Standard materials until Landlord, or its Contractor and/or its Architects shall have advised Tenant in writing, and Tenant or its Contractor and/or its Office Planning Architects have agreed in writing to the work cost of such different new materials and the Landlord's cost of such different new materials and the Landlord's cost of such replaced Landlord's Building Standard Work materials.

4. Landlord agrees at Landlord's expense to obtain and maintain public liability and workmen's compensation insurance adequate to fully protect Tenant as well as Landlord from and against any and all liability for death or injury to person or damage to property caused in or about or by reason of the construction of any work which is Landlord's obligation hereunder. Tenant agrees at Tenant's expense to obtain and maintain public liability and workmen's compensation insurance adequate to fully protect Landlord as well as Tenant from and against any and all liability for death or injury to person or damage to property caused in or about or by reason of the construction of any work which is Tenant's obligation hereunder.

5. In the event of any delay caused by Tenant in providing information and approvals in the preparation of plans to be prepared by Landlord or Tenant in excess of the time periods provided, or in the event of any delay caused by revisions or changes to approved plans requested by Tenant, or in the event of any delay in preparation of plans or construction of the tenant improvements caused by Tenant, Tenant at the time it accepts possession of the Premises shall pay to Landlord an amount equal to the amount of rent payable under this Lease for the period of time equal to the period of delay.

6. Tenant agrees that upon substantial completion of the work in the Premises as set forth in the final plans and specifications and upon delivery of possession to Tenant, Tenant will accept the Premises in the condition which it may then be. The fact that Tenant may enter into possession prior to substantial completion for the purpose of installing equipment or fixtures shall not be deemed an acceptance by Tenant of completion by Landlord, but in such event Tenant shall hold Landlord harmless and indemnify Landlord for any loss or damage to Tenant's equipment, fixtures or merchandise and for injury to any persons unless caused by the active negligence of Landlord or its agents.

Tenant, recognizing that the Landlord may deliver the Premises to Tenant prior to the date on which the term of the Lease is scheduled to commence pursuant to Article 2 of the Lease, agrees to pay rent and other monetary sums due under the Lease commencing upon the date of delivery of possession of the Premises to the Tenant pursuant to the terms of this Exhibit.

FIGURE 4.3 Rules and Regulations

EXHIBIT C
RULES AND REGULATIONS

1.   No sign, placard, picture, advertisement, name or notice shall be inscribed, displayed or printed or affixed on or to any part of the outside o inside of the Building or the Premises without the written consent of Landlord first had and obtained and Landlord shall have the right to remove an such sign, placard, picture, advertisement, name or notice without notice to and at the expense of Tenant.

All approved signs or lettering on doors shall be printed, painted, affixed or inscribed at the expense of Tenant by a person approved b Landlord.

Landlord shall not place anything or allow anything to be placed near the glass of any window, door, partition or wall which may appea unsightly from outside the Premises; provided, however, that Landlord is to furnish and install a building standard window drapery at all exterio windows.

2.   No Tenant shall obtain for use upon the Premises, ice, drinking or bottled water, towel or other similar service or accept barbering o bootblacking services on the Premises, except from persons authorized by the Landlord and at the hours and under regulations fixed by the Landlorc

3.   The bulletin board or directory of the Building will be provided exclusively for the display of the name and location of Tenant only an Landlord reserves the right to exclude any other names therefrom.

4.   The sidewalks, halls, passages, exits, entrances, elevators and stairways shall not be obstructed by any of the tenants or used by them for an purpose other than for ingress to and egress from their respective Premises. The halls, passages, exits, entrances, elevators, stairways, balconies an roof are not for the use of the general public and the Landlord shall in all cases retain the right to control and prevent access thereto by all person whose presence in the judgment of the Landlord shall be prejudicial to the safety, character, reputation and interests of the Building and its tenant: provided that nothing herein contained shall be construed to prevent such access to persons with whom the Tenants normally deals in the ordinar course of Tenant's business unless such persons are engaged in illegal activities. No tenant and no employees or invitees of any tenant shall go upo the roof of the Building.

5.   Tenant shall not alter any lock or install any new or additional locks or any bolts on any door of the Premises without the written consent Landlord.

6.   The toilet rooms, urinals, wash bowls and other apparatus shall not be used for any purpose other than that for which they were constructe and no foreign substance of any kind whatsoever shall be thrown therein and the expense of any breakage, stoppage or damage resulting from th violation of this rule shall be borne by the Tenant who, or whose employees or invitees shall have caused it.

7.   Tenant shall not overload the floor of the Premises or mark, drive nails, screw or drill into the partitions, woodwork or plaster or in any wa deface the Premises or any part thereof. No boring, cutting or stringing of wires or laying of linoleum or other similar floor coverings shall b permitted except with the prior written consent of the Landlord and as the Landlord may direct.

8.   No furniture, freight or equipment of any kind shall be brought into the Building without the consent of Landlord and all moving of the san into or out of the Building shall be done at such time and in such manner as Landlord shall designate. Landlord shall have the right to prescribe th weight, size and position of all safes and other heavy equipment brought into the Building and also the times and manner of moving the same in an out of the Building. Safes or other heavy objects shall, if considered necessary by Landlord, stand on wood strips of such thickness as is necessary properly distribute the weight. Landlord will not be responsible for loss of or damage to any such safe or property from any cause and all damai done to the Building by moving or maintaining any such safe or other property shall be repaired at the expense of Tenant. There shall not be used any space, or in the public halls of the Building, either by any tenant or others, any hand trucks except those equipped with rubber tires and si guards.

9.   Tenant shall not employ any person or persons other than the janitor of Landlord for the purpose of cleaning the Premises unless otherwi agreed to by Landlord. Except with the written consent of Landlord, no person or persons other than those approved by Landlord shall be permitti to enter the Building for the purpose of cleaning the same. Tenant shall not cause any unnecessary labor by reason of Tenant's carelessness indifference in the preservation of good order and cleanliness. Landlord shall in no way be responsible to any Tenant for any loss of property on t Premises, however occurring, or for any damage done to the effects of any Tenant by the janitor or any other employee or any other person. Janit service shall include ordinary dusting and cleaning by the janitor assigned to such work and shall not include cleaning of carpets or rugs, except norm vacuuming, or moving of furniture and other special services. Janitor service will not be furnished on nights when rooms are occupied after 9:30 P. Window cleaning shall be done only by Landlord, and only between 6:00 A.M. and 5:00 P.M.

10.   Tenant shall not use, keep or permit to be used or kept any food or noxious gas or substance in the Premises, or permit or suffer the Premises be occupied or used in a manner offensive or objectionable to the Landlord or other occupants of the Building by reason of noise, odors and/ vibrations, or interfere in any way with other tenants or those having business therein, nor shall any animals or birds be brought in or kept in or abc the Premises or the Building. No Tenant shall make or permit to be made any unseemly or disturbing noises or disturb or interfere with occupants this or neighboring Buildings or Premises or those having business with them whether by the use of any musical instrument, radio, phonogra[unusual noise, or in any other way. No Tenant shall throw anything out of doors or down the passageways.

11.   The Premises shall not be used for manufacturing or for the storage of merchandise except as such storage may be incidental to the use of t Premises for general office purposes. No Tenant shall occupy or permit any portion of his Premises to be occupied as an office for a pub stenographer or typist, or for the manufacture or sale of liquor, narcotics, or tobacco in any form, or as a medical office, or as a barber shop manicure shop. No Tenant shall advertise for laborers giving an address at the Premises. The Premises shall not be used for lodging or sleeping for any illegal purposes.

FIGURE 4.3 (concluded)

12.   Tenant shall not use or keep in the Premises or the Building any kerosene, gasoline or inflammable or combustible fluid or material, or use any method of heating or air conditioning other than that supplied by Landlord.

13.   Landlord will direct electricians as to where and how telephone and telegraph wires are to be introduced. No boring or cutting for wires will be allowed without the consent of Landlord. The location of telephones, call boxes and other office equipment affixed to the Premises shall be subject to the approval of Landlord.

14.   All keys to offices, rooms and toilet rooms shall be obtained from Landlord's Building Management Office and Tenant shall not from any other source duplicate, obtain keys or have keys made. The Tenant, upon termination of the tenancy, shall deliver to the Landlord the keys of the offices, rooms and toilet rooms which shall have been furnished or shall pay the Landlord the cost of replacing same or of changing the lock or locks opened by such lost key if Landlord deems it necessary to make such change.

15.   No Tenant shall lay linoleum, tile, carpet or other similar floor covering so that the same shall be affixed to the floor of the Premises in any manner except as approved by the Landlord. The expense of repairing any damage resulting from a violation of this rule or removal of any floor covering shall be borne by the Tenant by whom, or by whose contractors employees or invitees, the damage shall have been caused.

16.   No furniture, packages, supplies, equipment or merchandise will be received in the Building or carried up or down in the elevators, except between such hours and in such elevators as shall be designated by Landlord.

17.   On Sundays, legal holidays and on Saturday commencing at 12:00 noon, and on other days between the hours of 7:00 P.M. and 7:00 A.M. the following day, access to the Building, or to the halls, corridors, elevators or stairways in the Building, or to the Premises may be refused unless the person seeking access is known to the person or employee of the Building in charge and has a pass or is properly identified. The Landlord shall in no case be liable for damages for any error with regard to the admission to or exclusion from the Building of any person. In case of invasion, mob, riot public excitement, or other commotion, the Landlord reserves the right to prevent access to the Building during the continuance of the same by closing the doors or otherwise, for the safety of the Tenants and protection of property in the Building and the Building. Landlord reserves the right to close and keep locked all entrance and exit doors of the Building on Sundays, legal holidays, and on Saturdays commencing at 12:00 noon, and on other days between the hours of 7:00 P.M. and 7:00 A.M., and during such further hours as Landlord may deem advisable for the adequate protection of said Building and the property of its tenants.

18.   Tenant shall see that the doors of the Premises are closed and securely locked before leaving the Building and must observe strict care and caution that all water faucets or water apparatus are entirely shut off before Tenant or Tenant's employees leave the Building, and that all electricity shall likewise be carefully shut off, so as to prevent waste or damage, and for any default or carelessness Tenant shall make good all injuries sustained by other tenants or occupants of the Building or Tenant.

19.   Landlord reserves the right to exclude or expel from the Building any person who, in the judgment of Landlord, is intoxicated or under the inflluence of liquor or drugs, or who shall in any manner do any act in violation of any of the rules and regulations of the Building.

20.   The requirements of Tenant will be attended to only upon application at the Office of the Building. Employees of Landlord shall not perform any work or do anything outside of their regular duties unless under special instructions from the Landlord, and no employee will admit any person (Tenant or otherwise) to any office without specific instructions from the Landlord.

21.   No vending machine or machines of any description shall be installed, maintained or operated upon the Premises without the written consent of the Landlord.

22.   Landlord shall have the right, exercisable without notice and without liability to Tenant, to change the name and the street address of the Building of which the Premises are a part.

23.   Tenant agrees that it shall comply with all fire and security regulations that may be issued from time to time by Landlord and Tenant also shall provide Landlord with the name of a designated responsible employee to represent Tenant in all matters pertaining to such fire or security regulations.

24.   Landlord reserves the right by written notice to Tenant, to rescind, alter or waive any rule or regulation at any time prescribed for the Building when, in Landlord's judgment, it is necessary, desirable or proper for the best interest of the Buildng and its tenants.

25.   Tenants shall not disturb, solicit, or canvass any occupant of the Building and shall cooperate to prevent same.

26.   Without the written consent of Landlord, Tenant shall not use the name of the Building in connection with or in promoting or advertising the business of Tenant except as Tenant's address.

27.   Landlord shall furnish heating and air conditioning during the hours of 7:00 A.M. to 9:00 P.M. Monday through Friday, and 7:00 A.M. to 12:00 P.M. on Saturday, except for holidays. In the event Tenant requires heating and air conditioning during off hours, Sundays or holidays, Landlord shall on notice provide such services at the rate of $17.50 per hour.

FIGURE 4.4 Lease Clauses

13. RELOCATION OF PREMISES

18.1 Conditions. For the purpose of maintaining an economical and proper distribution of Tenants throughout the Building acceptable to Landlord, Landlord shall have the right from time to time during the term of this Lease to relocate the Premises in the Building on the following terms and conditions:

(a) The rented and usable areas of the new location in the Building are of equal size to the existing location (subject to a variation of up to ten percent (10%) provided the amount of rent payable under this Lease is not increased;

(b) If the then prevailing rental rate for the new location is less than the amount being paid for the existing location, the rent shall be reduced to equal the then prevailing rent for the new location;

(c) Landlord shall pay the cost of providing tenant improvements in the new location comparable to the tenant improvements in the existing location;

(d) Landlord shall pay the expenses reasonably incurred by Tenant in connection with such substitution of Premises, including but not limited to costs of moving, door lettering, telephone relocation and reasonable quantities of new stationery;

18.2 Notice. Landlord shall deliver to Tenant written notice of Landlord's election to relocate the Premises, specifying the new location and the amount of rent payable therefore at least thirty (30) days prior to the date the relocation is to be effective. If the relocation of the Premises is not acceptable to Tenant, Tenant for a period of ten (10) days after receipt of Landlord's notice to relocate shall have the right (by delivering written notice to Landlord) to terminate this Lease effective thirty (30) days after delivery of written notice to Landlord.

33. COST OF LIVING

The fixed monthly rentals stated in paragraph 6 herein shall be adjusted to reflect any change in the cost of living at the anniversary date of each successive year of the lease term. The adjustment, if any, shall be calculated upon the basis of the United States Department of Labor, Bureau of Labor Statistics Consumer Price Index for Urban Wage Earners and Clerical Workers (subgroup "all items") for the San Francisco-Oakland Area (1967-100) (the "Index"). The index published nearest the commencement date of the lease term shall be considered the "base". The monthly fixed rent shall be adjusted by 100% of the percentage increase or decrease, if any, in the Index published nearest the anniversary date of each successive year of the lease term over the "base" Index; provided, however, that in no event shall the monthly fixed rent be less than the amount specified in paragraph 6 above, notwithstanding the fact that the Index may, as of some adjustment date, be less than the "base" Index. When the monthly fixed rent for each applicable period of the lease term is determined, Lessor shall give Lessee written notice to that effect indicating how the new monthly fixed rent figure was computed. If at any time or from time to time during the lease term the Bureau of Labor Statistics, Department of Labor, shall change its method of computing such Index, or shall discontinue computing such Index, and shall establish one or more alternate or substitute indices, Lessor shall determine upon the most appropriate successor to be used in determining the adjustment to be made to the basic monthly rental, and such substitute Index and base figure applicable thereto shall thereafter be used to compute the adjustment to be made to base monthly rental payable under the terms of the Lease. Should the Bureau of Labor Statistics discontinue the publication applicable to the increase to the base monthly rental, thereby making it impossible for Lessor to determine upon an appropriate Bureau of Labor Statistics index to be used, then some other generally used and recognized index of cost shall be selected by mutual agreement of Lessor and Lessee as a substitute index. In the event the parties are unable to agree upon such an index it shall be selected by the Presiding Judge of the Superior Court of the State of California, County of San Francisco or the person holding such equivalent position if the form of courts or if the Government shall be then changed. Pending such substitution of index, rental shall continue to be paid at the same total monthly rent as previously paid and shall, within ten (10) days, pay to the other the amount of additional sum determined, retroactive to the beginning of the period involved.

Informing building owners that they have the right to ask for a security deposit may win you points. Keep in mind that, although owners have a right to request a security deposit, tenants also have a right to refuse. In some states, tenants can insist that the security deposit be put into a separate account and that interest be paid to them during the term of the lease. Be sure to inform your tenants of this right if it applies in your area.

TAX AND BUILDING OPERATING COST INCREASES

This clause will probably be an issue in all of your major transactions. It can almost always be turned into a negotiating point, so you must understand it thoroughly. It provides that the rental rate will increase at a predetermined time, often beginning with the third year of the lease. The amount of the increase is based on the rise in the building's operating expenses over the base (initial) period.

Since tenants usually think of the rental rate as something that remains unchanged over the term of the lease, they often look at this clause as an attempt to cheat them. But such a clause is essential in maintaining the building's net income, which, as you learned in the previous chapter, cannot be lowered without lowering its value.

For example, consider a five-year gross lease in which the owner pays all building expenses. Each year over the five-year period, the costs of janitorial services, energy and probably taxes will increase. If the building's gross income remains steady over the five years, its net income will decline drastically. Without the escalating costs clause, the value of the building will shrink as the net income deteriorates. This clause permits the building owner to raise rents just enough to cover increased expenses. Such flexibility is vital in an inflationary period.

The tenant in this example has a five-year lease with an escalator clause and occupies ten percent of a 100,000-square-foot building. The first year of the tenant's occupancy is called the base year. (The actual dates of the base year can be negotiated.) The second year of occupancy is the comparison year. During the base year, the owner's expenses run at $3.00 per square foot, or $300,000. During the comparison year, expenses go up ten percent, so the owner's annual expenses for that year are $330,000—a $30,000 increase. Since the tenant occupies ten percent of the space, she will be charged ten percent of $30,000 or an additional $3,000, during the third year of occupancy unless an expense stop has been established. This $3,000 may be payable in a lump sum, or it may be added to the monthly rent over the year.

RELOCATION OF PREMISES

This clause is not common and is most often used for smaller tenants. It gives the developer the right, within a stipulated time, to move the tenant to another, similar-size area of the building. The owner bears all moving expenses, but the tenant may have to pay additional rent, depending on the size and/or desirability of the new space.

This clause is especially useful to owners of a brand-new building just beginning to fill with tenants. The owners do not know how to apportion the space economically because they have no idea who the next tenants will be or what space they will want. Suppose the owners have a tenant occupying 20,000 square feet on the fifteenth floor, and is looking for a tenant to fill the other 30,000 square feet of that floor. Instead, a prospective tenant wants to rent the entire fifteenth floor. The relocation clause gives the developer the right to move the first tenant to similar space, perhaps the corresponding 20,000 square feet on the floor below.

COST-OF-LIVING ESCALATION

The now common cost-of-living escalator clause is similar to the tax and building operating cost increases clause. Whereas the tax and operating cost clause compensates an owner for increased expenses, the cost-of-living escalator compensates the owner for the shrinking value of the dollar. Suppose, for example, an owner's expenses rise five percent during the calendar year 1988. She passes on a prorated increase of five percent to all her tenants. If the value of the building was $1 million in 1987, this increase will maintain its value at $1 million in 1988. But $1 million is not as much money in 1988.

One million dollars is not as much money in 1988 as it was in 1987 because it will not buy as many goods and services. The cost-of-living escalator clause protects the owner from the lower value of the inflated dollar. This clause can be tied to one of several indexes that measure the rate of inflation. The Consumer Price Index for the particular market involved is often used.

A common method of protecting owners from increasing costs is an *expense and tax stop* clause. Such a clause provides that the owner will pay a flat fixed amount per leased foot for tenant expenses and taxes every year. Any expenses or taxes above that amount are borne by the tenant. For example, an owner might "stop" his expense and tax outflows at $5.00 and $1.50 per square foot, respectively, for a given tenant. Then, in successive years the tenant would pay all expenses in excess of $5.00 per square foot and all taxes in excess of $1.50 per square foot. Such a simplified cost control clause assures the owner that his or her cash flow will be known and predictable.

One point to consider in your negotiations is that expenses and taxes borne by the tenant can be *capped,* that is, limited. For example, the landlord can be responsible for the first $5.00 of expenses and $1.50 of taxes per square foot. The tenant is then responsible for any balance, unless there is a cap. In this case, if we had a cap of $5.00 and $2.00, respectively, the landlord would pay the first $5.00 and $1.50, the tenant would pay the next $5.00 and $2.00, and the additional expenses would then be the responsibility of the landlord.

These lease clauses, plus the work letter discussed earlier, are the basis for many negotiating points in the office lease.

Exercise B

A tenant moves into a building where the initial payment is $18 annual rent on 20,000 square feet. The area represents five percent of the building's rentable space. The owner's building costs are $450,000 that year. At the end of the second year of the lease, the building costs rise ten percent. Costs rise another ten percent the third year. What is the annual rent at the beginning of the third year? What is it at the beginning of the fourth year?

The tenant's initial annual rent is $360,000 ($18 × 20,000 sq. ft.).

The owner's initial annual expenses are $450,000.

The second year, the owner's annual expenses are up $45,000 to $495,000 ($450,000 + ten percent).

At the beginning of the third year, the tenant pays $362,250 ($360,000 + five percent of the additional $45,000).

The third year, the owner's annual expenses go up $49,500 (ten percent of $495,000).

At the beginning of the fourth year, the tenant pays $364,725 (the third year's $362,250 + five percent of the additional $49,500).

THE SUBLEASE

The standard Grubb & Ellis sublease is reproduced in figure 4–4. On the face of it, negotiating a sublease may seem like a simple operation. Most owners will permit a tenant to sublease as long as they have the right to approve the sublease. (A clause to that effect appears in most standard lease forms.) You will usually become involved in a sublease when a tenant wants to get out of a lease and asks you to find a sublessee. This seems a simple matter of locating a sublessee, getting the owner's approval, obtaining signatures on the sublease and collecting your commission. Unfortunately, a number of things can go wrong during any of these steps.

When a tenant approaches you to find a sublessee, you should immediately do three things.

1. Have the tenant sign a commission agreement.

2. Ask to see a copy of the lease.

3. Contact the lessor.

In a sublease situation, the tenant is responsible for your commission. Obtaining a signed commission agreement ensures that you will receive that commission. Also, warn the tenant that any tenant improvements necessary to prepare the premises for subleasing must be paid for by him or her.

Examine the lease immediately, because the subtenant will take over the exact terms and conditions of the existing lease. Don't rely on the tenant's description of those terms and conditions. Tenants leasing under an escalator clause, for example, often cannot tell you what rent they

FIGURE 4.5   Standard Grubb & Ellis Sublease

SUBLEASE

1.   PARTIES

This Sublease is entered into by and between _____ ,
Sublessor, and _____ , Sublessee,
as a Sublease under the Master Lease dated _____ , 19_____ , entered into by _____
_____ as lessor, and Sublessor under this Sublease as Lessee; a copy of the

Master Lease is attached hereto as Exhibit A.

2.   PROVISIONS CONSTITUTING SUBLEASE

(a)   This Sublease is subject to all of the terms and conditions of the Master Lease in Exhibit A and Sublessee shall assume and perform the obligations of Sublessor and Lessee in said Master Lease, to the extent said terms and conditions are applicable to the Premises subleased pursuant to this Sublease. Sublessee shall not commit or permit to be commited on the Premises any act or omission which shall violate any term or condition of the Master Lease. In the event of the termination of Sublessor's interest as Lessee under the Master Lease for any reason, then this Sublease shall terminate coincidently therewith without any liability of Sublessor to Sublessee.

(b)   All of the terms and conditions contained in the Exhibit A Master Lease are incorporated herein, except for Sections _____
_____
_____ , as

terms and conditions of this Sublease (with each reference therein to Lessor and Lessee to be deemed to refer to Sublessor and Sublessee) and, along with all of the following Sections set out in this Sublease, shall be the complete terms and conditions of this Sublease.

3.   PREMISES

Sublessor leases to Sublessee and Sublessee hires from Sublessor the following described Premises together with the appurtenances, situated in
the City of _____ , County of _____ ,
State of _____ , _____
_____
_____
_____

4.   RENTAL

Sublessee shall pay to Sublessor as rent for the Premises in advance on the first day of each calendar month of the term of this Sublease without deduction, offset, prior notice or demand, in lawful money of the United States, the sum of _____
_____ ($ _____). If the commencement date is not the first day of the month, or if the
Sublease termination date is not the last day of the month, a prorated monthly installment shall be paid at the then current rate for the fractional month during which the Sublease commences and/or terminates.
Receipt of $ _____ is hereby acknowledged for rental for the
first month, and the additional amount of $ _____ as non-
interest bearing security for performance under this Sublease. In the event Sublessee has performed all of the terms and conditions of this Sublease throughout the term, upon Sublessee vacating the Premises, the amount paid as a security deposit shall be returned to Sublessee after first deducting any sums owing to Sublessor.

5.   TERM

(a)   The term of this Sublease shall be for a period of _____ commencing on _____ , 19_____ ,
and ending on _____ , 19_____ .

(b)   In the event Sublessor is unable to deliver possession of the Premises at the commencement of the term, Sublessor shall not be liable for any damage caused thereby, nor shall this Sublease be void or voidable but Sublessee shall not be liable for rent until such time as Sublessor offers to deliver possession of the Premises to Sublessee, but the term hereof shall not be extended by such delay. If Sublessee, with Sublessor's consent, takes possession prior to the commencement of the term, Sublessee shall do so subject to all of the covenants and conditions hereof and shall pay rent for the period ending with the commencement of the term at the same rental as that prescribed for the first month of the term, prorated at the rate of 1/30th thereof per day.

6.   USE

Sublessee shall use the Premises for _____
_____

and for no other purpose without the prior written consent of Sublessor.
Sublessee's business shall be established and conducted throughout the term hereof in a first class manner. Sublessee shall not use the Premises for, or carry on, or permit to be carried on, any offensive, noisy or dangerous trade, business, manufacture or occupation nor permit any

FIGURE 4.5   (concluded)

auction sale to be held or conducted on or about the Premises. Sublessee shall not do or suffer anything to be done upon the Premises which will cause structural injury to the Premises or the building of which the Premises form a part. The Premises shall not be overloaded and no machinery, apparatus or other appliance shall be used or operated in or upon the Premises which will in any manner injure, vibrate or shake the Premises or the building of which it is a part. No use shall be made of the Premises which will in any way impair the efficient operation of the sprinkler system (if any) within the building containing the Premises. Sublessee shall not leave the Premises unoccupied or vacant during the term. No musical instrument of any sort, or any noise making device will be operated or allowed upon the Premises for the purpose of attracting trade or otherwise. Sublessee shall not use or permit the use of the Premises or any part thereof for any purpose which will increase the existing rate of insurance upon the building in which the Premises are located, or cause a cancellation of any insurance policy covering the building or any part thereof. If any act on the part of Sublessee or use of the Premises by Sublessee shall cause, directly or indirectly, any increase of Sublessor's insurance expense, said additional expense shall be paid by Sublessee to Sublessor upon demand. No such payment by Sublessee shall limit Sublessor in the exercise of any other rights or remedies, or constitute a waiver of Sublessor's right to require Sublessee to discontinue such act or use.

7.   NOTICES

All notices or demands of any kind required or desired to be given by Sublessor or Sublessee hereunder shall be in writing and shall be deemed delivered forty-eight (48) hours after depositing the notice or demand in the United States mail, certified or registered, postage prepaid, addressed to the Landlord or Tenant respectively at the addresses set forth after their signatures at the end of this Sublease. All rent and other payments due under this Sublease or the Master Lease shall be made by Sublessee to Sublessor at the same address.

DATED: _____ , 19 _____

SUBLESSOR: SUBLESSEE:

By _____   By _____

By _____   By _____

Address _____   Address _____

City _____ State _____   City _____ State _____

Telephone _____   Telephone _____

The undersigned, Lessor under the Master Lease attached as Exhibit A, hereby consents to the subletting of the Premises described herein on the terms and conditions contained in this Sublease. This consent shall apply only to this Sublease and shall not be deemed to be a consent to any other Sublease.

DATED: _____ , 19 _____   LESSOR: _____

                                                    By _____

                                                    By _____

                                                    Address _____

                                                    City _____ State _____

                                                    Telephone _____

(If Sublessor or Sublessee is a corporation, the corporate seal must be affixed and the authorized officers must sign on behalf of the corporation. The Sublease must be executed by the President or a Vice President and the Secretary or Assistant Secretary unless the Bylaws or a Resolution of the Board of Directors shall otherwise provide, in which event the Bylaws or a certified copy of the Resolution, as the case may be, must be furnished.)

This Sublease has been prepared for submission to your attorney who will review the document and assist you to determine whether your legal rights are adequately protected. Grubb & Ellis Commercial Brokerage Company is not authorized to give legal or tax advice; no representation or recommendation is made by Grubb & Ellis Commercial Brokerage Company or its agents or employees as to the legal sufficiency, legal effect or tax consequences of this document or any transaction relating thereto. These are questions for your attorney with whom you should consult before signing this document.

FIGURE 4.6   Grubb & Ellis Exclusive Right to Sublease

In consideration of the following agreements and of the efforts of GRUBB & ELLIS ("G&E") to secure sublet tenants for the property and improvements described below ("Property"), the undersigned ("Sublessor") hereby grants G&E the Exclusive Right to Sublease the Property for a period beginning on _____ _____ and ending on _____
upon the following terms:

Address and/or legal description of Property:

_____
_____
_____
_____
_____

RENTAL RATES: _____
_____ , or such lesser amount Sublessor may agree to accept.

POSSESSION DATE: _____

AGENCY TERMS

I.   **SUBLESSOR WARRANTS:** That Sublessor leases the Property and has authority to execute this Agreement and grant to G&E the exclusive right to sublease the Property for the period provided herein.

II. **SUBLESSOR AGREES:** To cooperate fully with G&E and refer all inquiries to it, to conduct all negotiations through G&E, to pay G&E a real estate brokerage commission in the amount stipulated on and in accordance with the Schedule of Commissions included herein if (1) should a sublease agreement be consummated between the Sublessor and another party during the term of this Agreement of its extensions for all or a portion of the space described herein; (2) G&E or Sublessor or any other persons during the term of this appointment, produces a sublet tenant ready, willing and able to sublease the Property on the terms herein provided, or (3) a sublease is executed within six months after termination hereof to a prospect submitted by G&E during the term hereof, or to anyone on behalf thereof, whose name was disclosed to Sublessor. (4) Sublessor is relieved of their obligations under the original lease by the Landlord of the building or any other party through recapture, direct lease, etc. Sublessor also agrees to pay the cost of advertising the Property.

Sublessor also agrees, only in the event that G&E does not receive any commission(s) pursuant to or in connection with the terms of this Brokerage Agreement, that it will pay the cost of advertising the Property; provided, further, however, in such event, the costs of advertising shall not exceed _____ without the prior written authorization of the Sublessor.

III. **G&E AGREES:** To perform marketing efforts for the Property, take prospective tenants through the property at convenient times; to make a continued effort to sublease the property; and to direct the advertising for the property under the approval of the Sublessor. G&E is not charged hereunder with the custody of the Property, nor its management, upkeep or repair.

G&E shall enlist the services of other real estate brokers and agents ("Cooperating Brokers") in connection with the subleasing of the Property, and G&E agrees to act as coordinator of such Cooperating Brokers. Sublessor agrees to deliver to G&E a standard form of cooperating broker letter agreement to be used in connection with Cooperating Brokers.

IV. **ARBITRATION OF DISPUTES:** Any controversy or claim arising out of or relating to this Agreement or the breach thereof, shall be settled by arbitration in Chicago, Illinois, in accordance with the rules of the American Arbitration Association, and judgment upon the award rendered by the arbitrators may be entered in any court having jurisdiction thereof.

V.   **NONDISCRIMINATION:** The parties hereto acknowledge that it is illegal for either Sublessor or G&E to refuse to display or to sell the Property to any person because of race, color, religion, national origin, sex or physical disability.

VI. **MISCELLANEOUS:** No amendment or alterations in the terms hereof with respect to the amount of commission or to the time of payment of commission shall be valid or binding unless made in writing and agreed to by Sublessor and G&E. Notices shall be given in writing by United States Registered Mail to the address indicated under the signature lines of this Agreement or as directed by either party from time to time. Notices are deemed to be given on the date deposited at an authorized United States mail receptacle. Sublessor agrees to indemnify and save harmless G&E, its officers and agents, against any and all actions, claims, damages and liabilities relating to damage or injury to person or property resulting from or occurring on or about the Property. If more than one Sublessor or sublet tenant is involved, the pronouns and grammatical structure shall be understood to conform. This Agreement shall be binding upon and inure to the benefit of their heirs, personal representatives, successors and assigns of the parties hereto.

FIGURE 4.6   (concluded)

COMMISSION

SUBLEASE COMMISSION

A. ON GROSS LEASES (subleases wherein the Sublessor is responsible for paying all or a major portion of the costs of maintaining and operating the Property).

Commission is seven percent of the average annual rent, plus two percent of the remaining term rental. For gross leases less than one year, commissions shall be calculated as eight percent of the total rental reserved in the sublease.

B. On *NET LEASES* (leases wherein the sublet tenant is responsible for paying all or a major portion of the costs of maintaining and operating the Property other than by way of tax and operating expense stops).

Initial commissions are calculated as eight percent of the average annual rent, plus three percent of the remaining term rental reserved in the sublease. For subleases one year or less in term, commissions shall be calculated as ten percent of the total rent reserved in the lease.

Notes: Average annual rental in A and B above is defined as the aggregate rental reserved in the sublease divided by the number of months defined by the term of that sublease multiplied by twelve (12).

Remaining term rental is the total rent reserved under the sublease less the amount of average annual rental. Rental shall exclude the rent reserved for any period which is subject to a Subtenant's option to cancel, unless cancellation fees are included in a sublet tenant's cancellation fee.

If a Cooperating Broker procures the sublet tenant, G&E will receive a commission equal to one and one-half (1.5) times the amounts of the commissions, as defined herein, with the outside broker receiving one full commission distributed by G&E and G&E retaining one-half of a full commission as its compensation.

RENEWAL OPTION

If a sublease or separate instrument or agreement gives the sublet tenant an option of renewal or extension, the commission is due for the term of the sublease exclusive of the period covered by the renewal or extension period. In the event the sublet tenant exercises the option of renewal or extension, an additional commission will be due on the extended or additional period. In the event the sublet tenant remains in the premises under a new sublease or an amendment to the original lease, a commission shall be due equal to two percent of the rent for the entire renewal term. Any such commissions shall be due and payable at the time of the renewal or extension of the new sublease or amendment to the original lease.

ADDITIONAL SPACE OPTION

If a sublease or separate instrument or agreement gives the sublet tenant an option to lease additional space and the sublet tenant exercises such option, or at any time during the original term, whether or not the sublease or agreement for said additional space shall be upon the same terms and conditions as set forth in the original lease, then an additional commission is due equal to the amounts defined under A and B of this Commission Schedule shall apply. The additional commission shall be due and payable at the time the option is exercised or the new sublease is consummated.

PAYMENT

Initial commissions are payable in full upon the consummation of the sublease. Nothing herein, however, shall preclude the broker from pursuing claims for a commission where the legal right to collect such commissions exists. Time is of the essence with respect to payment of all commissions.

By: G&E _____

Title: _____

Grubb & Ellis Company

Dated: _____
_____

By: Sublessor _____

Title: _____

_____
_____
_____
_____

Dated: _____
_____

are currently paying. When the sublease is executed, attach a copy of the original lease to it and note any modifications specifically on the sublease.

Contact the lessor after talking with the lessee, even if the lessee has already informed the owner of his or her desire to sublease the property. The owner can give you a clearer idea of the alternatives than can the tenant. You may discover, for instance, that the owner will cancel the lease entirely if you provide a tenant who will lease for a longer period than the unexpired term of the lease. The owner could raise the rent immediately in such a case, and all parties would get what they wanted.

Explain to the tenant the distinction between *subleasing* and *assigning a lease*. A tenant who subleases retains all responsibility for carrying out the terms of the lease. A tenant who assigns a lease passes the obligation on to the sublessee—up to a point. If the sublessee defaults, the obligation goes right back to the original tenant. There is no way the original tenant can entirely escape responsibility for fulfilling a lease once it has been signed.

INDUCEMENTS

In chapter two, you studied the pro forma, learned the formula for figuring net income and learned how net income is capitalized to arrive at a property evaluation. So far in this chapter, you have begun to understand the office lease and its importance as an effective tool in performing your job. Now you will put all this information together in a way that will give you an in-depth understanding of what inducements (concessions) are all about.

Consider the example of Susan Emerson, a developer who is beginning to fill her building with tenants. You bring her a client, David Walden, who wants 50,000 square feet on a five-year lease. Walden likes the building, but he does not like the $22.50 per-square-foot rent. By now you know you won't get anywhere asking the owner to lower her rent. To lower it by $1 per square foot would cost Emerson $50,000 in net income, and assuming she has capitalized at a rate of ten percent, that would lower the value of her building by $500,000. (If you can't follow these figures, review the Building Evaluation section of chapter two.)

You want to lower the *effective rent* for your client while maintaining a quoted rent of $22.50. This can be done in several ways. You can, for example, suggest that Emerson give two months' free rent as a concession. At an annual rate of $22.50, Walden would pay $3.75 for two months. On 50,000 square feet, this amounts to $187,500. Because this is a five-year lease, divide $187,500 by five to get the annual saving in rent. Divide that number, $37,500, by 50,000 to arrive at the annual saving per square foot, $0.75. Instead of the quoted rent of $22.50, Walden's effective rent would be $21.75.

Emerson would reduce her cash flow for the first year if she offered this inducement, but she would not lower the value of her property because she did not lower the quoted rent. But wouldn't two months' free rent lower her net income in addition to her cash flow? If you refer to page 30 in the economics chapter, you will note that the developer allowed $652,000 for tenant inducements and figured the amount into his building costs. Emerson would have done the same thing, and that is where the $125,000 would come from, so it would not lower her net income.

Exercise C _____

You have brought in a client who is interested in leasing 20,000 square feet in a new building. He is willing to sign a five-year lease, but he doesn't want to pay the $18 rent. You do some fast calculating and decide that, if you can induce the owner to give your client ten months' free rent, the effective rent will be lowered considerably. Exactly what would the effective rent be?

Answer C _____

At $18 per year, annual rent would be $360,000 ($18 × 20,000 square feet).
$18 per year is $1.50 per month, or $15 for ten months.
The total saving is $300,000 ($15 × 20,000 square feet).
The annual saving is $60,000 ($300,000 ÷ 5, since this is a five-year lease).
The effective annual rent is $300,000 ($360,000 − $60,000).
The effective annual rent per square foot is $15 per year ($300,000 ÷ 20,000 square feet).

Probably ten months' free rent seems like an astronomically large giveaway. Such deals have been made, however, particularly in the case of new buildings, by smart real estate sales representatives who have reminded owners that, since the building is new and tenants are just beginning to move in, that space might stand idle for at least ten months anyway! It's called "creative leasing."

TYPES OF INDUCEMENTS

Free rent was discussed at some length to show you how an inducement is used as a negotiating point. Similar techniques can be applied with equal effectiveness to any number of inducements. Following are some typical inducements and the main points to keep in mind when negotiating them.

1. *Free rent.* This inducement has already been discussed in detail.

2. *Tenant improvements above standard.* Often the standard tenant improvement allowance is too small to cover all the changes a tenant wants. In such cases, the owner can sometimes be persuaded to absorb some or all of the excess cost.

For example, a corporate branch manager is looking for 20,000 square feet. She likes the space you show her at $22 per square foot, but she knows that the person who makes the rent decision back in New York won't go over $20. The tenant improvements the branch manager wants will run $5 per square foot over this particular owner's tenant allowance. This is an opportunity for you to arrange a mutually beneficial deal. If the tenant is desirable enough, the owner may be willing to extend an additional $200,000 for tenant improvements. Then you can explain to the tenant that the $100,000 saving applied over the period of a five-year lease will lower the effective rent to $20, a figure the New York office will approve.

Sometimes an owner will agree to raise a tenant's improvement allowance just to acquire a prestigious tenant. A law firm, for example, that wants expensive wall paneling and plush carpeting, might by its very presence lend prestige to the building in which it is located.

Tenant improvements above the standard allowance can often be negotiated another way. Sometimes the owner will not give away additional improvements, but will lend the tenant money for them. The cost to the tenant can then be amortized over the term of the lease by adding it to the rent. The owner may even lend the money interest-free. If there is no provision for this inducement in a tenant improvement fund, the owner might borrow the money, charging tenants a point more interest than they are paying the original lender.

3. *Relocation expenses.* An owner can sometimes be induced to pay all or part of a tenant's moving expenses, such as movement of physical possessions, cost of telephone installation and furniture acquisition. The owner's willingness to grant this or any other inducement depends, of course, on the client's overall negotiating position.

4. *Parking costs.* If the owner controls a garage or a parking lot, parking costs are a natural negotiating point. The inducement might stipulate the reservation of a certain number of spaces for the tenant at a reduced rate. Or it might call for the reservation of spaces for the tenant's clients. A bank, for example, would probably be eager for an inducement allowing free parking spaces, which could be passed on to customers.

5. *Unexpired lease.* Sometimes an owner will take over the unexpired lease in the tenant's old building. Frequently such inducements take the form of an exchange of rent. Perhaps the tenant is paying $1,000 per month in the new building and $500 in the old. The owner may agree to forego $500 in rent in his or her own building until lease obligations in the other building are fulfilled. In effect, the owner is paying the rent in the old building.

The owner, however, should *not* assume the responsibilities of the prior lease in reimbursing the tenant for rent paid to a third party. If the new tenant should default on the new lease, the landlord could be liable for the new lease and the old lease.

Assuming a few months of a lease is, of course, hardly the same thing as taking on one that has a year or more to run. The latter can be an expensive proposition for an owner, and the tradeoff would have to be very attractive. Negotiations over lease assumption can become long and involved. They can be a key factor in ruining a deal if not skillfully handled. But don't discount this concession—simply be aware that it is a tricky area.

6. *Options.* An option is a promise made by one party to enter into a contract at a later date at a specified price and terms if so desired by the other party, who pays a fee for that promise. Options can be designed to cover many situations, including lease renewal, lease cancellation and space expansion. Tenant options on lease renewal have become less attractive to owners in a time of rapidly rising inflation and changing markets.

Cancellation options can be difficult to negotiate. Take the example of a company that wants a ten-year lease with a five-year cancellation clause. The company might want such a lease because it foresees a merger or acquisition or a move to another city within the next few years. But such an arrangement is unattractive from the owner's point of view because of the increased risk of tenant turnover and lack of security. Or if the owner is carrying a mortgage, the lending institution may not approve of leases containing cancellation options.

Options on additional space are attractive to young, growing companies, and you will probably be asked to try for such an option at some point. But expansion options are not popular with owners. Consider a company that is ready to move into 30,000 square feet and wants a six-month option on an adjoining 10,000-square-foot space that now stands empty. The option would give the tenant an absolute right to that space within that period. What does this mean from an owner's point of view? It effectively takes the 10,000 square feet off the market for six months, with no benefits to the owner and a distinct possibility that, at the end of that time, the tenant will refuse the space. The owner might even be approached by another company willing to take the space the day after the option agreement is signed. You see why you are not likely to find a sophisticated owner willing to grant an option of this kind.

7. *First right of refusal.* A much better solution to the problem of the company with future expansion plans is the first right of refusal. First right of refusal is often incorrectly regarded as the same thing as a cancellation option. Actually it works quite differently and is much more attractive to building owners. In the case of the tenant who agrees to take 30,000 square feet and wants an option on an additional 10,000, a smart salesperson would suggest a first-right-of-refusal clause on the additional space. This clause means that if Tenant A is given first right of refusal and two months later Tenant B wants to lease the space, Tenant A is given first choice—provided Tenant A meets Tenant B's offer in every detail. Tenant A will be required to consider making an offer whenever a new prospect shows interest in the space, but the owner will not chance losing a tenant by tying up the space in an option. Tenant A may even be given a continuing right of refusal, in case Tenant B moves in and then vacates after two or three years. These details are matters for negotiation.

In granting a right of refusal, specify in the lease the time Tenant A is given to make a decision. One week is a reasonable period, depending on the tenant firm's circumstances. Otherwise, if Tenant A procrastinates, Tenant B may tire of waiting for a decision and decide to look elsewhere. And the owner may end up with no tenant at all for the 10,000 square feet.

You should now have an understanding of the many tools at your disposal in negotiating a deal. What these tools really do is lower the tenant's effective rent while retaining the owner's quoted rent to help the owner maintain the value of this investment. A big part of your job will be to convince the tenant that the effective rent is the figure that counts, because it is the amount that will actually exchange hands. It is to the tenant's advantage to ignore the quoted rent and look instead at the effective rent that you have managed to negotiate. Tenant education will be a challenging task at times, but you will find it well worth the trouble.

DIFFERENT INDUCEMENTS FIT DIFFERENT TENANTS

You will develop a sense of which inducements appeal to different types of businesses as you gain confidence and a knowledge of your field. Since law firms tend to be interested in elaborate quarters, tenant improvement allowances will probably be high on their list. A young and growing computer leasing company, on the other hand, might prefer a first right of refusal on additional space. Just the opposite might be true of an advertising agency. Ad agency business fluctuates widely and the loss of a single large client can mean the layoff of employees and the sudden need for substantially less space. The right to sublease part of its space under a generous subleasing arrangement might be the most attractive concession you could secure for such a company.

Inducements have a psychological value as well as an economic one. They remind both parties to the transaction that the situation has open ends, that there can be give and take and that both sides are free to try to make the most advantageous bargain possible.

KNOW YOUR PRINCIPALS' NEEDS

Although the granting of inducements is a commonly accepted practice in the office-marketing field, take nothing for granted. Discuss inducements openly with owners or developers before a transaction gets under way. Find out what their practices have been and how far they might go, indeed can go, given the economics of the situations. Nowhere are frankness and openness more important to a mutually satisfactory transaction than in the area of inducements.

Almost every deal involves at least one inducement. Successful negotiation involves give and take, so you must know what is most important to both client and owner. Then you can evaluate various inducements and assign priorities. You will know which can be sacrificed in return for others that the principals deem more important in each particular deal.

CHAPTER 4 / The Office Lease   87

The most important consideration in negotiating inducements is the bottom-line figure that client and owner look at. You must keep the economic limits of both parties in mind during such negotiations.

Exercise D

Answer the following questions.

1. Name the three basic types of leases.

2. In which type of lease does the owner assume all costs and collect only the rent?

3. A tenant who finds herself (perhaps to her surprise) having to pay the cost of a leaking roof has probably signed which type of net lease?

4. What is the purpose of a security deposit?

5. What is the purpose of the tax-and-building-operating-cost clause?

6. Why would a building owner rather grant an inducement than lower the rent?

7. What is the difference between an option to lease additional space and a first right of refusal on additional space?

8. When you locate a new tenant to fulfill a sublease situation, who usually pays your commission?

9. What is the difference between subleasing and assigning a lease?

Answer D

1. *The three types are gross, net and percentage leases.*

2. *The owner assumes all costs in the gross lease.*

3. *She has probably signed a net-net-net lease.*

4. *A security deposit ensures compensation for any damage to property at the termination of the lease period.*

5. *The clause maintains the level of net income by passing on rising tax and maintenance costs to the tenant.*

6. *Granting inducements will not lower the owner's net income.*

7. *An option takes the space off the market for the period of the option. A first right of refusal keeps the space on the market, but gives the tenant the right to lease it by matching any other prospective tenant's offer.*

8. *The original tenant pays the commission.*

9. *In a sublease, the original tenant is held directly responsible for fulfilling all obligations of the lease. In a lease assignment the sublessee is held responsible, although in the case of default, responsibility reverts to the original tenant.*

5

Marketing

INTRODUCTION

In commercial brokerage, the term "marketing" can refer to numerous activities: selling property, getting listings, locating tenants for specific properties or simply cold calling tenants in a territory. In practice, all these activities can be described as marketing or selling. In addition, these activities will overlap and even occur simultaneously in actual practice; for example, a salesperson can be working on a particular exclusive *and* cold calling area users at the same time.

In an altogether different sense, marketing in commercial brokerage can be defined as acquiring, managing and using market information. If the salesperson's product is viewed as timely, accurate information, then the term *marketing* for that individual becomes the processes of uncovering such market information, maintaining it within company information systems and ultimately delivering it to the broker's customers, be they owner, developer, tenant or landlord. Whether the product is viewed as information or physical office space itself, marketing for the salesperson is assimilating, maintaining and delivering that product to the owner and user.

Our presentation in this chapter will describe the process of marketing office space—what this process entails as well as ways to go about performing this central task. For convenience, the subject will be divided into two principal sections: marketing listings and marketing users. The first section will summarize how to market the owners of office properties in what is called the listing process. The next section, Marketing Users, will examine the flip side of owner marketing, that is, how to generate and control the users of office space in your territory. A final section discusses corporate support of the salesperson's marketing responsibility and how this support can be utilized to the salesperson's advantage.

Note that the discussion of marketing in this chapter is a general presentation of marketing as an overall process rather than specific selling procedures and tactics. Refer to chapter six, "Selling Skills," for the many selling situations encountered in the process of marketing users and owners.

MARKETING LISTINGS

In this section we will describe the listing process as a three-phase activity: getting the listing, servicing the listing and keeping the listing.

As a backdrop to the process of listing properties for sale or lease, there is a very important axiom for salespeople to learn and remember:

> CONTROL = DOLLARS

The salesperson who controls the properties and tenants in his or her territory is the person who will be making the deals and the money. Equally true, the person who cannot control property and user will not make the deal or the money.

Given that axiom, the question for the salesperson now becomes "How do I gain control?" "What do I do to achieve control?"

In the context of listing property, a second axiom points the way toward answering the control question. That axiom is:

> ALL PROPERTY MOVES

Sooner or later, all property in a given territory will turn over, either through leasing or through selling. Except under severe market conditions, an owner's leasing or selling is a function of how long that owner wants to hold the space at a given price. If the property doesn't move within a time frame at a given price level, our axiom states that the owner need only lower the price, and it will move. Only when market circumstances are extreme will this axiom fail.

Keeping this and the first rule in mind, let's take a closer look at what is entailed to controlling and listing the office space owner.

Prerequisites to the Listing Process

The first thing you need before selling your product is obviously the product itself. *If you have no information, you have no product to sell.*

As an office brokerage specialist, your product is market intelligence about office properties and your ability to provide a variety of services. The first step in listing is to go into your territory and develop that intelligence. In short, learn everything about your territory—what's in it, who's in it, what is happening, what will be happening, where, when and even why. You can directly correlate the amount of money in your pocket with the amount of market information in your head.

Specifically, you can break down prerequisite market intelligence into the following imperatives.

Know the Owners. Thorough market knowledge entails knowing who owns the buildings *and* the land in the territory. The salesperson should generate ownership data on *every* tract of land, either improved or unimproved, for sale or not for sale, in the market area. You can accumulate this data through person-to-person contacts, researching microfiche records and researching chain-of-title records of local title companies. Title companies may or may not charge a fee for this service.

Know the Tenants. A thorough salesperson will learn every tenant in a market area, particularly major tenants or high-potential tenants. Tenant intelligence, however, goes beyond knowing names to knowing *why* the tenant is there. Why did a tenant sign the lease on Main Street as opposed to Market Street? When does that lease expire? What is the critical location and site criterion for the tenant? Does the tenant rely heavily on street patterns? Demographics? Signage? Labor pool? In the listing process the "why are you here" data is critical to understanding how you are going to market a property and how you are going to convince the owner that you understand specific types of tenants and their respective needs.

For example, if an owner has a free-standing property near an airport, you may be able to cite four types of tenants in your market that need airport proximity. In the same conversation you can also assure the owner that your marketing focus would give only second priority to tenant prospects A, B and C, since they've told you they rely on central business-district sites, not airports.

The tenant data is of twofold importance. First, the data is usable for helping the tenant with his or her space needs. In listing, however, a good knowledge of area tenants is a most impressive tool when talking to owners and developers. The person who goes into an owner's office to get a listing on the building is well past first base if he or she knows every tenant in the area. Second, a salesperson who doesn't know any tenants will be hard-pressed to convince an owner that he or she is the right person for the exclusive listing.

Tenant intelligence is primarily generated by the cold call (as will be discussed in upcoming sections) and, secondarily, by researching office files.

Know the Deals. The sharp salesperson will know about deals transpiring in the territory as if they were his or her own. Such deals define the economic character of the market. They determine current leasing and selling values. When a vacant parcel is sold, one should know who bought it, who brokered it, the price per foot and what will be done with it. Also, what are other owners asking for their properties? What kind of deals do they have in the works? Where?

Information on current and recent deals is not so easy to uncover, because much of the key purchase or lease data is kept in relative confidentiality. However, associate brokers and salespeople, particularly those in your own firm, can be excellent sources of deal intelligence. Other sources include tenants in the area who have recently moved or renewed their leases. Less commonly, you can learn about transactions from press releases distributed by the brokerage community—but be aware that this information will often be very cursory and limited.

Know the Property.   Understanding the physical inventory in your territory is a cornerstone of your market knowledge. You should know your area's property types, how much footage exists of each type, what special feature each property has and what new projects are on the drawing boards. (For further details, review chapter one.)

Know the Competition.   Seasoned salespeople make a habit of knowing who else is in their market and just how big a piece of that market they are taking. It is also smart to know how your competition operates, its strengths and weaknesses and its marketing strategies.

Get to know your competition individually, on a person-to-person basis. Good competitive relations will yield commissions, because sooner or later you'll be sharing deals with them. In addition, you'll want them to help you market your exclusively listed space and their support when you bring your tenants to their buildings.

Finally, knowing your competition can boost your confidence. Once you know that your competitors are not "knights on white horses" but normal human beings just like yourself, you know your chances of success are just as good as anybody's.

Getting the Listing

Armed with the five components of market knowledge—owners, tenants, deals, property and competition—the salesperson can begin intelligently the process of obtaining the property listing for a specific property.

Note that generally getting to know owners in the marketplace is different from approaching a specific owner for a listing on a specific property. When you first get to know owners in the territory, such an encounter is superficial: you introduce yourself, your company, say that you're working in the area, etc. At the beginning of our listing process, however, it is assumed that the owner has already been singled out as a target for an exclusive listing on one of his or her properties.

The critical path to obtaining the listing consists of four steps: the initial contact, support and follow-up, formal presentation and response.

Initial Contact.   Like other selling situations that use the classic two-call approach, the salesperson's initial call on the owner or developer is for the purpose of gathering information—not closing the sale. Since the objective is to procure an exclusive listing, a substantial amount of data must be uncovered by the salesperson, not to mention the information the owner will want from you before granting an exclusive. Thus, in the first meeting, the salesperson must know what questions to ask, what data to get and what information to give out. Have these things prepared, lest you waste the owner's time and lose the momentum this first call must set in motion.

Besides preparation, remember that, in general, you should not go after the listing on the first call. You're feeling the owner out and vice versa. During this meeting, you may even decide you don't want the listing. Seldom will the owner have everything in order—such as pricing—and be ready to sign the exclusive with you. If that is the case, go ahead and take the listing—but know what you're doing.

The data you need from the first meeting can cover a wide range, depending on the situation. Common to most meetings, however, is a "critical mass" of data you should have, as follows:

- *Essential property data.* You must know the property inside out, including physical details, how the building is managed, rent levels and any special characteristics. You have enough property data when you're confident there won't be any surprises at the showing. Be prepared with building and lot size, parking, floor plans, age of the building and improvement allowances.

  Don't be reticent about asking for this data. Typical owners *want* to talk about their buildings. They have a problem that you can solve, called a vacancy, and if they're serious about leasing, they know you need the data.

- *Essential owner data.* You need a host of information about the owner and other people involved, including tenants and other brokers. Most important here is the motivation of the owner. What does he or she want or need to do? Is there a critical time frame? Is there a cash problem? What rent is being quoted? When you're getting this data, begin to develop in your mind how *serious* and how *realistic* the owner is. If an owner is way off base on rent levels, you can begin to formulate (a) whether the owner can be persuaded to become realistic and (b) how you can bring that about. If the owner's market perceptions are somewhat realistic, you can in the course of the meeting offer to provide a survey of comparables. In some cases you may have the good fortune of telling an owner he's *below* the market. Whatever the case, as you're talking about the market, you can move into the next critical data area, namely, what's been done to date to market the property.

- *Essential marketing data.* Owners' attitudes about you and about the market are strongly influenced by prior marketing efforts that succeeded or failed. Your task is to find out what in fact has happened up to the present. Did they try to sell or lease without a broker? If so, how did it go? Did they fail? Why? Was another brokerage company involved? Under what relationship? Open? Exclusive? What happened? Are other brokers presently working the listing?

  While pursuing this line of analysis, you need to uncover how owners feel about exclusive versus open listings. If the owners refuse exclusives, you might offer this third axiom:

> WITH AN EXCLUSIVE, YOU HAVE AT LEAST
> ONE BROKER WORKING THE LISTING.
> WITH AN OPEN, YOU HAVE NO BROKER
> WORKING THE LISTING.

This truth may hurt a little, but it may also be the reason why prior marketing efforts under an open listing failed. Many owners still

don't understand that commissions require extensive work and that the exclusive is the only assurance that such work will be performed.
- *Data to give the owners.* Give the owners a profile of yourself and a strong picture of your company. Owners gravitate toward the successful broker or salesperson who seems to be making all the deals in town. Your tactic is to make them perceive you as that person. Just how you do that depends on your personal skills, but remember to reinforce the perception whenever possible. In addition, lay out the strengths of the company in terms of *how those strengths will benefit them.* Owners don't care if your company has 2,000 employees; they want their space leased. But if you say that you have a pool of prospective tenants that is generated by a unified effort of 2,000 salespeople, you're offering a lot of prospects.
- *Set the next meeting.* After you've gotten your data and delivered the story about yourself and the company, think about the prospective listing. If the listing looks good, you've got a considerable amount of research to do on the property. Thank owners for their time and tell them you'd like to assimilate the information you've gathered and get back in touch in three to five days. (Don't wait longer than a week.) Suggest to owners that they reflect a bit on what you and your company can do for them and, if possible, pin down a meeting time.

Initial Meeting Follow-up.   The second step in the critical path to getting the listing is the follow-up from the initial meeting and the set-up of the second meeting, the formal presentation.

Assuming you got all your data initially, first decide whether you want the listing and under what terms. To make this decision, validate your three categories of data. Check out the property and the tenants. Use the knowledge of your manager and associates on the property as well as internal property files. If the building is yet to be built, talk to architectural and engineering personnel about building costs and the floor plans or blueprints. Find out what other people in your company know about the owners. Has anyone worked with them before? If so, what was the experience like? Did they pay the commission? Were they reasonable? Formulate the best indirect-source picture you can of the owners. Research prior marketing efforts from the broker's standpoint. If there was a problem, what's the broker's story?

The outcome of this overall analysis is your decision on whether the property has the potential to move, and in turn, whether you want the listing.

Assuming the potential is there, you must now prepare for your second meeting with the owners—your formal presentation meeting. As the favorable outcome of the second encounter is a signed exclusive, you must work backward at this pre-presentation stage to get everything in order for that anticipated result. Make a checklist of items you need and things you must do. Align your strategies and agenda items with the issues and problems you uncovered in the first meeting. If pricing was a problem, for example, get a good comparables analysis together. If the type of listing was a problem, line up the reinforcing arguments for the exclusive. If a previous broker failed to move the property, strengthen your marketing proposal with how you plan to avoid whatever pitfall may have caused the failure. The following checklist, though not exhaustive, highlights the important areas for you to get organized:

- *The Product Fit.* From your analysis, you will get an idea of how an owner's property fits into the market. This fit includes rents, physical condition, parking, ceiling heights, amenities, allowances and so forth. Pull this data together and summarize it for presentation. You're the outside expert and your analysis of how the product fits into the market will make or break your pricing stance.

- *Pricing.* Set in your own mind a ceiling price per foot that will move the property—above which the property will not likely move within a desired time. Be prepared to refuse the listing if the owner won't come under such a ceiling.
- *Marketing.* Organize what you plan to do and outline it for your oral presentation. Assimilate written materials for reinforcement to give the owner, such as brochures and your company's (prepackaged) marketing proposals. Remember a good rule here:

DELIVER WHAT YOU PROMISE AND DON'T PROMISE WHAT YOU CAN'T DELIVER.

In short, it's easy to make a presentation that promises miracles—but when they don't happen, it all comes back to haunt you.

When you've compiled your data and organized the product analysis, pricing range and marketing plan, you're ready for the formal presentation. Call the owner to confirm your meeting and be there on time.

The Formal Presentation.   If you're well prepared, the third step in getting the listing—your presentation—will be off to the best possible start. Begin your meeting by reconnecting where you left off and summarizing what you did in the interim. Give your oral presentation to the owner before presenting your written marketing proposal. Few people can read and listen well at the same time. Here are a few other guidelines for your presentation:

- Describe how the owner's property fits in the market before recommending a price.
- Stress cold calling in describing your strengths.
- Cold calling is what makes deals happen—not advertising or sitting around the office. Ads and signs support marketing, they don't constitute it.
- Remember again that your marketing proposal should state exactly what you plan to do and should not include activities you do not plan to do. If you say advertising, you'd better advertise. Otherwise, you'll hear about it.
- A good proposal—especially for larger projects—should include a mailing campaign of sorts. Detail to the owner whom you plan to mail to and what the mailing will contain. Emphasize that your mailing is not scatter shot; that you only mail to certain user types or to users within a specific geographical area according to the type of property listed. You should also personally remember—and stress to the owner—that all mailings are addressed to individuals, not companies, and that all such individuals are followed up by a phone call.
- Always cover what your services are going to cost and the mechanics of how you are to be paid. If you leave that out, you pave the way for problems.

- Don't pull out the completed listing form until you've settled the pricing issue and the type of listing issue. It doesn't look good to pull out a contract only to have to put it back in your briefcase if you can't settle those issues.

A more complete discussion of marketing proposals appears at the end of this chapter. Carefully review this material when developing your own proposals.

The Response.   As your presentation winds down, you'll be getting feedback on pricing and the type of listing the owner will go for. In most cases, your decision on pricing and the open versus the exclusive will be a judgment call you'll have to make yourself.

Remember, all property will move if priced right in a typical market. By now you've weighed the product in relation to pricing within current market circumstances, and it is that weighing that should determine your decision. If the owner declines your final recommendation, find out why and use your ability to handle objections. You get the exclusive listing if all goes well. If there are any exclusions to the exclusive, get them in writing and negotiate a time limit after which such parties are no longer excludable.

When you've succeeded in getting an exclusive, follow up the meeting with a thank-you note that emphasizes that the owner now has the full force of the company behind the leasing or selling effort. It is also a good touch to have one's sales manager send the owner a similar letter.

Servicing the Listing

The next phase in the listing process is servicing the listing. Servicing in this sense means execution—execution of your marketing plan and doing everything you promised. This period is the proving ground of your original product and pricing analysis, the success of which will be measured by the results you get.

There is little else to be said about this phase of listing other than now is the time to get the job done. In implementing your marketing plan, however, there are a few things to keep in mind.

- *Any honeymoon between the owner and new salesperson will be short-lived.*   Immediately after an exclusive is secured, there are good feelings and a measure of optimism on the part of the owner. This honeymoon period will subside with every day the space remains unoccupied or unsold. Underlying this erosion of optimism is the fact that this is a stressful period for the owner. Whether this stress is emotional, rational or financial, the owner will be anxiously watching and waiting for results. If you're not doing something you said you would, you'll hear about it now.

    It takes professional finesse to handle owners during the marketing phase. Their stress can manifest itself in any number of ways, and one should be ready to deal with it and assuage it.
- *Stick to a high level of cold calling in the immediate area.*   The best tenant prospects are those closest to the property, and that is where to begin, if not within the subject building itself. One cold call strategy is to lay out ever-larger concentric circles around the property and "spiral" your way outward.

EXCLUSIVE LISTING CHECKLIST

1. contract signed

2. All property facts verified, including price, size, terms and extra charges, if any

3. lease form agreed upon

4. listing filled out (What type of tenant best fits this project?)

5. marketing plan completed

6. signs ordered and entered in sign log

7. brochure designed and ordered, reviewed by owner

8. newspaper ads entered, reviewed by owner

9. brochures mailed to other brokers

10. brochures mailed to prospect groups

11. on-site office established if necessary

12. project announced at all office sales meetings

13. daily number of cold calls determined and made

14. report mailed to property owner on weekly or biweekly basis

15. all nearby tenants canvassed

16. access to property/keys arranged

- *Keep organized records.* When you undertake a selling activity, it is very important to make a record of that activity. This keeps you organized and helps to keep the listing intact. Log every cold call in a newly created cold-call file. When you do your mailing, start a mailing file describing the mailing and a phone log for entering your follow-up calls. Enter specifics in each log. Who did you talk to? When did you call? What was the parties' response? When did the mailing go out? When was the ad placed? Record exactly what you do. Why? There will come a time when the owner asks what you've done—and it will all be there. You won't have to say "Well, let's see now, what did I do? I've been working real hard on this, Mr. Owner; I've really been busy." Owners won't believe a word of it.

  Aside from keeping records, if you follow the letter of a good marketing plan—and the property is properly priced—you will succeed in moving the property for the owner, notwithstanding a severe downturn in local market conditions.

Keeping the Listing

The third phase in the listing process is keeping the listing. Keeping the listing can be best understood as keeping the owner happy long enough to have a fair chance of earning your commission. Stated negatively: you don't want to get fired before your efforts have begun to sink into the marketplace.

Keeping the listing is a function of two simple determinants: hard work and good communication. Good communication with an owner is absolutely essential to the listing process. Good communication means telling the owner the news, good or bad. If there is only bad news, communicate the bad news. The only news worse than that is no news at all.

To sharpen discipline, assume that if an owner doesn't hear from you, he or she will automatically assume that you're not working on the property.

Set up a system of calling each of your exclusive listings once a week with a progress report. If you've worked the listing and done your job of recording, the weekly report is simple—read the owner your logs over the phone. Then announce your projected activities for the upcoming week. Finally, throw in some of your ideas and analysis. The owner doesn't want to do all the thinking—that's what you're being paid to do. You'd be surprised at how well an owner can tolerate a no-results time period if you're keeping him or her fully apprised of events.

In addition to the weekly phone call, give the owner a written monthly summary of your progress. Recap the major tactics and their results. Then project a marketing scenario for the coming month that corrects the shortcomings of previous strategies. Convey to the owner that you are doing your very best to move that property.

Finally, a good communications touch is to have your manager periodically call the owner with supportive commentary. Besides the encouragement that it provides, the manager call can be a means to elicit the owner's feelings and reactions to the progress being made. The manager can, in turn, feed those responses back to the salesperson so the latter can make any necessary adjustments.

The salesperson must, by law, report each and every offer to the owner. Seeing actual offers conditions the owner to the realities of the marketplace. If an owner, for example, wanted $16 per foot for her space, three independent offers for $13.25, $13.60 and $13.40 would begin to tell that owner the story. Don't try to do the thinking for an owner regarding offers. Submit them and get his or her reaction first.

A final aspect of good communication is addressing the issue of the listing's expiration date well in advance. Don't let that date even come close without discussing renewal. If you've worked hard, you will have substantial momentum built up. If your reporting was thorough and documents your hard work, the owner should appreciate your momentum and be as reluctant as you are to lose it. So raise the issue of the listing renewal straightforwardly and well in advance.

Exercise A

A salesperson has completed his first meeting with an owner and has succeeded in obtaining thorough data on the property and the owner's various motivations and attitudes. Did the salesperson get everything?

Answer A

Three categories of critical-mass data must be obtained in the first meeting: data on the property, the owner and previous marketing efforts. The agent forgot to learn about previous marketing efforts.

Exercise B

Critique the following face-to-face dialogue, an initial meeting.

OWNER: *Yes, I've had a little trouble leasing that space.*

AGENT: *Why?*

OWNER: *I don't think the last broker worked on it enough. I never heard from him.*

AGENT: *Well, Mr. Adams, at our company, we make it a practice to regularly communicate with our owners. And we work our listings hard. As we are a larger firm, we do large mailings, advertising and frequent office tours.*

OWNER: *Well, I'm glad you communicate and all that. But I've heard the other stuff before. And my property's still vacant.*

Answer B

Possible Valid Critiques

1. *The salesperson should continue to ask questions to find out the problem instead of prematurely selling the company.*

2. *The salesperson did okay to point out the communication policy of his company, but his comment about the company's marketing practices has the following shortcomings:*
   a. *The comment is stated as a feature, not a benefit to the owner.*
   b. *The salesperson shouldn't imply that the company will do "large mailings" or "advertising" for this owner before knowing what will* really *be done—which he can't know at the first meeting.*
   c. *The salesperson forgot to mention the two most important things: his tenant knowledge and that he will cold call.*

Exercise C

After the initial meeting, one must research data and prepare for the formal presentation. What are the three most important things to organize for the upcoming presentation and why?

Answer C

The first thing is the analysis of how the product fits into the market. This builds your case about pricing, which is the second issue to pin down. You must be clear about pricing, because that will determine whether you want the listing and/or how quickly the property will move. Third, you must organize your marketing plan, as that represents your entire plan of action. The plan also heavily influences the owner's listing decision.

Exercise D

Throughout the sections on the listing process, at least five axioms and key rules were presented. Without looking back, can you list four of them?

Answer D

1. *Control equals dollars.*

2. *All property moves.*

3. *An exclusive puts one broker on a property listing. An open puts no broker on a property.*

4. *Deliver what you promise; don't promise what you can't deliver.*

5. *An owner who doesn't hear from you will automatically assume that you're not working the property.*

MARKETING USERS: EXERCISING TENANT CONTROL

As in other types of real estate, the marketing of office space tends to cluster around "hot spots" in the community. Salespeople naturally gravitate toward such centers of activity. If appropriate steps are not taken, blank spots will develop in the company's information system, and other properties will fall through the cracks.

This section describes *total area coverage,* one method to combat this problem. Under this system, the entire geographic area serviced by a particular office is divided among the various salespeople. Each salesperson is responsible for a specific area. You become familiar with all the buildings and all the space users within your area through cold calling.

Canvass your area building by building. Begin by going from office to office and from floor to floor within each building. Seek out the office-space decision makers. Do they need additional space? Do they intend to relocate? Do they know that such-and-such building will be ready for occupancy soon? Suppose they answer "no," "no" and "no." Don't back off too easily. Do the companies or the individual decision makers have other real estate needs—industrial, rental, residential, investment? Do they know of any other companies that want to expand or move? Keep each decision maker's name on file, no matter how little information you get. Try again later. Circumstances change—the company might need office space in the future.

The information you gather is entered into your firm's central inventory system. Each salesperson is responsible for placing accurate information into the system and for seeing that it is kept as up to date as possible.

Such canvassing is seldom done by telephone. It can best be accomplished through personal visits. During or immediately after the office call, the salesperson fills out a lease survey form giving the company's "vital statistics." (See figure 5-1.) This includes such information as lease expiration date, square footage now occupied, future space needs and the name of the person who makes the company's office-space leasing decisions, plus other pertinent information.

The setup of a typical information system and the ways in which it works for you will be discussed in the next section of this text. Acquiring the information is less difficult than it sounds. Techniques for doing so will be the subject of the "Cold Calling" section of this chapter.

The area-coverage method is practical only for large real estate companies. Not only size but perseverance is needed to gather such complete information, to say nothing of continually updating it so that the company can maintain a true picture of the current market at all times. If your company has the sales power to apply to the task, the area-coverage concept can do much to tip the share-of-market balance in its favor.

Although most of your transactions will lie within your own territory, the area-coverage concept is not meant to restrict your activities. Because you can call on any company and bring in listings from any area, you will become familiar with not only your own territory but the entire area and the area inventory as well. The assigned territory, however, is your main responsibility.

Obviously, teamwork is an important element in this plan. You will share all information gathered by the area-coverage system with your office-marketing associates. Weekly sales meetings indicate the properties your colleagues are working and identify their clients. Salespersons share ideas on how to complete transactions and often cooperate formally, because the expertise of any company is no greater than the combined expertise of all the people who work there.

Cooperation can gain you material benefits as well. When you place a valid survey form into the system, you will usually receive a percentage of the commission earned if another salesperson in your company subsequently closes a deal.

THE INVENTORY SYSTEM

The inventory system is divided into two categories, an active inventory of office-space users and an active inventory of space available in your company's marketing area.

The inventory of office-space users is compiled from *lease survey forms,* which list questions for which you must seek answers from your clients. A sample lease survey form is shown in figure 5–2. It includes such information as type of business, current square footage used, current rent, estimated future space needs and a thumbnail profile of the company to help match it to new quarters. Note the lease expiration date. It is the most important information of all, because whatever else you discover, the company *will* move (or renew its lease) someday. That date, placed in the file, is a lead in itself. If you get no information beyond this, your call has been worthwhile.

The sales manager approves the completed form. Then it is either entered into a central card file or fed into a computer. The information is filed by building. The status of all tenants in each building will be grouped together. It is also placed in a lease expiration file by expiration

FIGURE 5.1   Office Space Inventory Card

OFFICE SPACE INVENTORY   Store ☐ Office ☒

Address _14201 Central_	Listed By _John Murphy_
Cross Streets _Central & 14th_	Date _1/8/88_
Building Name _Boyce Building_	No. of Stories _3_

SUBLESSEE NAME	CONTACT PHONE	WHEN AVAIL.	LEASE EXPIRES
	bldg. eng. 668-2323	_Now–See Below_	_See Below_

Basement Area _3500 sq. ft._	Parking _yes_	Elevators: No. of Freight _1_	No. of Passenger _3_

Full Service Yes ☒ No ☐	Air Cond. Yes ☒ No ☐	Subdividable Yes ☒ No ☐	Usable ☒ Rentable ☐

REMARKS: _New Building_
Space can be divided

Floor No.	Size	Rent/Sq. Ft.
3	75x100 approx.	$18.00
2	40x100 approx.	$18.00
Base-ment	3500 sq. ft.	$10.00–12.50

Owner _Earl Macklin, Property Investments_	Phone _332-7600_
Address _1824 Park Boulevard_	City
How Shown? _Contact bldg. engineer_	Key in File? _no_ Sign? _no_
Address _14201 Central_	SQ. FT. _11,500 approx._

date. In addition to its obvious uses, this file provides the best source of leads when you need to find space for a particular tenant.

The card file inventory of space available is derived from office-space worksheets (see figure 5–3). This is where you will record information about office space that has recently become available or will be available in the near future. The worksheet describes in detail the building itself as well as the space available within the building. This form must be complete and accurate. Your source of information will typically be the building manager or engineer or, in the case of smaller buildings, the management agency or owner. If you speak to the owner, find out whether he or she is interested in selling the building. (You might want to set yourself a goal of listing one building and selling one building each year.)

Like the lease survey form, the completed office-space worksheet is reviewed by the manager. If the system is not computerized, the information is then transcribed by a secretary into an office-space inventory card. Some brokerage offices have computerized systems that record all this information in central files and print it out for dissemination to all area offices.

Office-space inventory cards are kept in a central file, and copies are given to each salesperson. The cards are filed alphabetically by both city and street as well as by square footage. This allows you to zero in on

FIGURE 5.2   Sample Lease Survey Form

LEASE SURVEY

Denver
OFFICE

COMPANY _____ *Home Specialty Marketing, Inc.* _____

ADDRESS _____ *17321 Armeda Blvd.* _____

CITY _____ *Denver* _____ PHONE _____ *777-2600* _____

CONTACT _____ *Armond Herschberger* _____ TITLE _____ *President* _____

TYPE OF
BUSINESS _____ *Sales* _____ HEADQUARTERS
OR BRANCH _____ *HQ.* _____

EXISTING SPACE INFORMATION/FEATURES

TYPE _____

SQUARE FOOTAGE _____ *6,386* _____ PARKING _____

D/H _____ G/L _____ SPRINKLERED YES ☐ NO ☐ SPUR YES ☐ NO ☐ CLEARANCE _____

LEASE EXPIRATION: MONTH _____ *Aug.* _____ YEAR _____ *1988* _____ OWNS YES ☐ NO ☒

RENT: $ _____ *15.35 sq. ft.* _____ MONTH _____ NET _____ GROSS _____

OPTION TERMS *Have none now; want 5-yr. lease with 3-yr. option* _____ EXERCISE DATE _____

COMMENTS: _____ *Company growing rapidly. 15–20 salespeople in and out of*

office need parking and good access to customers mostly on outer edges of

city. Few customers in office, don't need prestige space.

Other branch sales offices in Fort Collins, Colorado Springs, Laramie,

Wyoming and Santa Fe, New Mexico.

_____

_____

_____

_____

_____

DATE _____ *3/8/88* _____ REPORT BY _____ *Elmer D. Austin* _____

FIGURE 5.3 Office Space Worksheet

OFFICE SPACE WORKSHEET

STORE ☐
OFFICE ☒

ADDRESS _____ *14201 Central* _____ LISTED BY _____ *John Murphy* _____

CROSS STREETS _____ *Central & 14th* _____ DATE _____ *1/8/88* _____

BUILDING NAME _____ *Boyce Building* _____ NO. OF STORIES _____ *3* _____

SUBLESSEE NAME	CONTACT PHONE	*building eng.: A. L. Sams 668-2323*	WHEN AVAIL. *Now–See Below*	LEASE EXPIRES *See Below*

Basement Area _____ *3500 sq. ft. available for tenant(s)* _____ Parking *48 stalls + neighborhood parking* _____ Elevators: No. of Freight *one passenger also used for freight* _____ No. of Passenger *3* _____

Full Service Yes ☑ No ☐   Air Cond. Yes ☑ No ☐   Subdividable See Below Yes ☐ No ☐   Usable ☑ Rentable ☐

REMARKS: *New Building*

First floor entirely rented to insurance company.

Second floor has three smaller tenants.

Third floor open. Space can be divided (rental rate may be higher if floor is divided).

Tenant storage or workspace available in basement or possible for small printer, etc.

Will take two-year lease up to ten years with escalator provisions.

Floor No.	Size	Rent/Sq. Ft.
3 (whole)	*75x100 approx.*	*$18.00*
2 (part)	*40x100 approx.*	*$18.00*
Basement	*3500 sq. ft.*	*$10.00–12.50*

Owner _____ *Earl Macklin of Property Investments is General Partner of Limited Partnership–Investment Group* _____ Phone _____ *332-7600* _____

Address _____ *1824 Park Boulevard* _____ City _____

How Shown? _____ *Contact bldg. engineer or Macklin* _____ Key in File? _____ *No* _____ Sign? _____ *Possible–will take to Macklin* _____

Address _____ *14201 Central* _____ SQ. FT. _____ *11,500 approx.* _____

areas of the proper size, which can save valuable hours when you're searching for space for a specific tenant.

The inventory card file system provides a complete record in one central location of all space available in a market area. Use the system constantly to keep up to date on all major lessors and space users throughout your market area. It should be obvious by now that the sooner you make contact with a particular office-space decision maker, the less likely you are to be preempted by your competition.

The inventory system is a valuable marketing tool in another way. With this information you can present a complete picture of an area to a tenant—a more complete picture than your competitors present. This is another reason to maintain the inventory system properly.

Be aware that, although the inventory system may be referred to as the listing system, these cards are not listings in a legal or contractual sense. They do not constitute an agreement from the owner to pay a commission or establish the other provisions of a listing agreement. If in the course of your canvassing, you discover a prospect with space needs or an owner with space for rent, ask this person to sign a listing agreement.

COLD CALLING

There are three reasons for making a cold call:

1. to find out all you can about a company's future space needs, so you can be there to generate a transaction at that future date

2. to uncover situations in which a company is about to make a move

3. to learn the physical details of a property through visual examination

You will be successful in the second endeavor only occasionally. When you realize that the purpose of the cold call is to gather information rather than to make an immediate sale, you will see that receiving any significant information constitutes a successful cold call. Indeed, the only unsuccessful cold call is one in which you receive no information at all. The objective of this section is to ensure that seldom, if ever, happens.

As mentioned earlier, all cold calling should be done in person. This is essential in order for you to obtain the information you need and establish rapport with the office-space decision maker. Walking into a company's office without an appointment, getting to see the appropriate person and gathering information about the company's office-space needs require the mastery of a series of learned techniques. No one is born with the ability to perform these tasks well. Cold calling is an acquired skill and must be perfected through practice.

In addition to its primary goal of gaining valuable information, cold calling is a very effective learning tool. It helps you learn your territory as no other method can. It also lets you practice the art of establishing

FIGURE 5.4   Diagram of a Cold Call

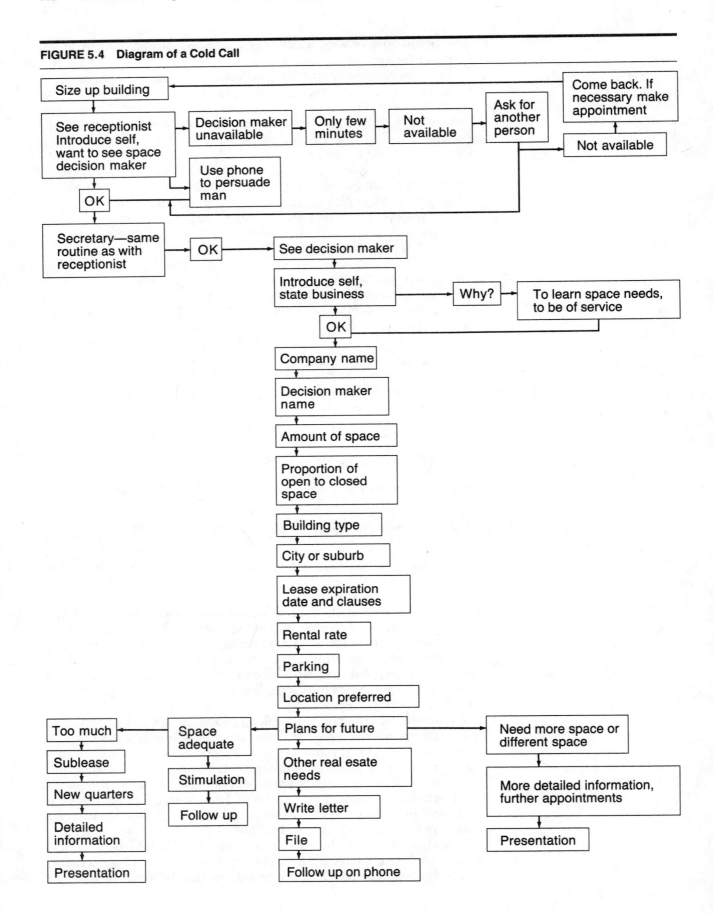

rapport and observe what techniques of prospect contact do and do not work.

The main ingredients in cold calling are:

1. confidence

2. imagination

3. assertiveness

4. persistence

Assertiveness need not mean pushiness, nor persistence mean becoming a pest. With practice you will soon learn to sense when going one more step would be going too far. Imagination allows you to switch tactics when the conversation takes sudden new twists. Confidence permits you to establish your credentials as a professional. Keep all four qualities in mind, for all are equally important.

No substitute for the real situation exists to develop your cold-calling skills. But certain guidelines can help you. This section will discuss some of those guidelines. It will tell you how to prepare for a cold call, overcome obstacles in trying to see the decision maker, ask the right questions and handle any contingencies that arise during a cold call.

The diagram in figure 5–4 shows some of the situations that can arise in the course of a cold call, and gives you step-by-step suggestions for alternative action. As you read through this section, refer to the diagram periodically.

Preparation

The wise salesperson does not begin cold calling completely cold. Prepare for the call by learning something about the type of business in question and its typical space needs. As you learned earlier, an insurance company will emphasize large amounts of open space as opposed to private offices. A law firm will reverse that emphasis and will probably want conference rooms and a library also. Know the general requirements that stem from the type of business a company operates; then learn specific needs from your cold call. Such knowledge will give you a starting point from which to launch a discussion. It will also make you look professional. Even better, it will give you confidence because it will make you *feel* professional.

You can further prepare yourself for a cold call by studying the particular company in advance. Look it up in Dun & Bradstreet or in a Chamber of Commerce or Association of Commerce and Industry publication. Find out the name of the office-space decision maker before you call in person. You can usually get this information by simply calling the company and asking the switchboard operator or a secretary. Make sure that, in the course of getting the decision maker's name, you don't find yourself speaking to that person on the phone. If the operator offers to connect you, decline the invitation. Reserve your information gathering for your face-to-face visit.

When you do make the cold call, there are some observations you should make before you ever enter the building. If there is a parking lot, is it full? Overcrowded? Half empty? Is the building old or modern?

What is the condition of the elevators? Is the building in a congested part of the city? These and other facts can tell you a great deal about the possible space needs of the company you are about to call on.

Getting In

The best approach to a receptionist and/or a secretary is to be concise, direct and courteous. The following is a sample opener.

"Hello, I'm Bob Jamieson, ABC Company, Office Space Division. I'm gathering information about real estate needs in this area. Who can give me this information about the XYZ Insurance Company? The office manager, perhaps?"

You have introduced yourself and stated your business briefly. The receptionist will give you the name of the decision maker and will probably let you see that person.

The person whose name you obtained may not be the one who actually makes the company's office-space decisions. Perhaps such decisions are made by a national manager in another city. But ordinarily the local person will at least recommend space, so you're not wasting your time talking to him or her. Of course, you won't be sure who the decision maker is until you talk with the person to whom you are directed, but qualify that person immediately as to position and influence in the company.

If the receptionist tells you the decision maker will be unavailable all day, make an appointment only as a last resort. You have spent time making a cold call. If an appointment were your objective, you could have made it by telephone. If possible, carry through on your real objective—gathering information. Ask the receptionist if there is someone else who can discuss space decisions with you.

What if you are told at 9:30 A.M. that the person you want to see will be available at 2:00 in the afternoon?

Again, go along if you must, but press a little. Without being pushy, indicate that returning would be inconvenient. Stress the fact that you need only a few minutes of the company representative's time. Agree to come back only if there is nothing else you can do.

What if the decision maker will talk with you, but only on the telephone?

Use the phone to press further for a personal interview. The whole idea of making the cold call is to see the company representative face to face. You want him or her to identify you with your company and with real estate. You want to be remembered. Apologize for dropping in unannounced—you realize how busy this person is. Explain that you are selling nothing. You simply want to ask a few questions and will need only five minutes. Few people are so busy that they can't spare five minutes. This argument will probably get you in the door.

Once past the receptionist, you still might have to deal with the decision maker's secretary. Use the same tactics that were successful with the receptionist. Don't offer the secretary any information beyond who you are and the general nature of your business. You want to discuss details with the decision maker, not with the secretary.

Getting the Information

Once you are in the company representative's office, shake hands and introduce yourself. State your business: information-gathering and service. Establish whether this person is the prime decision maker regarding office space. Next, establish the amount of time the interviewee can give you. It may be ten minutes, 20 minutes, a half hour. Use to the fullest whatever amount of time you are granted. You want to establish rapport in addition to gathering information, so that your name will leap to mind when your interviewee has office-space problems or needs.

Following is a list of the information you need. You already have the first two, of course.

1. name, address and telephone number of company

2. name of office-space decision maker

3. building type (high-rise, low-rise, garden) and location (city or suburb)

4. amount of space now leasing

5. proportion of closed to open space

6. lease expiration date plus any options or special clauses affecting the expiration date

7. parking facilities, if any

8. amenities—carpeting, draperies, etc.—now provided as tenant improvements

9. rental rate

10. location and building type preferred in the event of relocation

11. any changes in amenities desired in the event of relocation

12. future company plans that would affect office location

The form should be used as a checklist to ensure that you cover all the necessary points. Always take some office-space survey forms and lease survey forms on cold calls. However, do not complete them during the interview itself. This turns you into a "census taker," making rapport more difficult to establish. Take notes and transfer the information later.

In gathering data about the lease, don't assume the decision maker knows all the answers. Ask to see the lease to be sure your information is accurate. The person with whom you are talking may be new on the job and may have never looked at the lease. Or there may be clauses and stipulations in it that your interviewee does not remember or understand. Pay close attention to expiration date, rental rate and any special clauses, such as those related to subleasing or rent increases, as you examine the lease.

If the decision maker cannot tell you the precise number of square feet of space the company is leasing, remember the rule of thumb for estimating this yourself that you learned in the first chapter. Ask how many employees the company has, keeping in mind the difference in space needed by people-intensive and less people-intensive firms.

The company's future plans will provide the most important information you will gather. What are the growth expectations? How many people might be employed a year from now? Have company officers been thinking about a move to the suburbs? Is there a parking problem? Is the company contemplating opening additional offices? It is never foolish to discuss the future, even if a company seems happy where it is. Suggest that it is wise to begin long-range planning for future space needs rather than waiting until the last minute.

Suppose you discover that the company owns the building it is in and has provided for expansion of office space. Have you wasted your time? Not really. You are interested in the future. The company might well grow beyond its projected size. It might decide to open additional offices elsewhere. The important thing is that you have made a contact, one that may pay off in the future in unforeseen ways.

Suppose you discover that the company is completely happy with its present space, no space needs are anticipated for some time and there is no need for your office-marketing services. Is that the end of your call? No. If your firm is a multiservice company, it can take care of other real estate needs. Even if the company does not need office space right now, it may need industrial or warehousing space. Perhaps the company is transferring employees from other locations. They will need housing. Maybe the person you're dealing with owns an apartment building and wishes to sell. Perhaps the company has some retail interests. Keep in mind the other divisions of your company while conducting your interview, and forward any information you gather that is not within your sphere to the appropriate people.

What if the decision maker tells you the company has no space needs and refuses to discuss the matter? You have only one recourse: leave. But don't write off the company entirely. Complete the survey as completely as possible and make a note to follow up later. Remember, one of the cardinal elements of cold calling is persistence.

Reasons for Moving

There are many reasons besides an expiring lease that a company might wish to move or obtain more space in its present location.

1. The company may have grown more rapidly than expected and may be squeezed for space long before the anticipated date. Perhaps the company has been thinking about this problem—or has been trying to avoid thinking about it. In either case, you could find yourself at the right place at the right time, although you may need to do a little educating to make the decision maker appreciate the situation.

2. On the other hand, contraction might be the problem. Maybe the company has not grown as fast as expected or is looking for a way to curtail expenses. In either case, the company might be seeking less space or might consider subleasing some of the space it now has.

3. The area may have changed and may no longer suit the company's needs. Or perhaps it never was as suitable as the tenant expected.

For a downtown firm, for instance, the hassle of city life may have become too great and a move to the suburbs may be considered.

4. The present building may be in line for demolition.

5. Perhaps the company president has bought a new house and wants to relocate company offices closer to it. Superficial though this may sound, it happens often enough to be a factor.

6. The company may wish to consolidate office space. Perhaps it is scattered over several floors of a building, or maybe it has offices at several locations and wants to move everything to one central location.

You might bring up yet another reason for moving. Suppose the company's space is adequate and everyone is perfectly happy there. Besides, the company has a low rental rate and five years to go on its lease. What form of persuasion can you use?

You might agree that the company is in a good position now. But rates will almost certainly be higher in five years than they are now. A company can provide itself with a cushion by moving into new quarters at today's rental rates and subleasing the space it is now using at a higher rate than the company is currently paying. Point out that if the company moves now, it could cash in on an even more favorable rate over the long term. Before broaching the subject, of course, double-check the subleasing clause in the current lease.

Establishing Rapport

So far, the information-gathering aspect of cold calling has been stressed. The need to establish rapport will be examined separately now, although when you have actually done some cold calling, information gathering and establishing rapport will begin to blend into one smooth process.

As you gather information from the interviewee, present a rounded picture of yourself. You want to impress the decision maker as a professional, yet at the same time come across as a human being interested in other human beings, someone who enjoys being of service. Don't hesitate to put the conversation on a personal level if the occasion presents itself. If you see a photo of the company representative's family on the desk or a picture that indicates one of the person's hobbies, comment on it. If you can do so gracefully, find out where the decision maker lives— it could have a bearing on future relocation plans. Does this person travel to work by car or by public transportation? What about others in the company? Personal touches can go a long way toward establishing you as someone who genuinely wants to be of service, who is interested in the welfare of the company representative and the company itself. If you succeed in creating this impression, you may in time even become a small extension of the company, a sort of employee without salary, the custodian of the company's office-space needs.

Presenting yourself as eager to serve has another advantage. You might not get all the necessary information on the initial call. The person you speak to may be rushed or called away on an emergency, or may turn out not to have the power to make decisions. But if you make a good impression in the time you have, you'll probably be invited back for a more comprehensive interview.

Make sure, however, that the conversation does not get too far afield of your objective. Time is of great importance on a cold call. When you have the information you need and have established yourself in the interviewee's mind, leave. Don't waste time that could be more productively spent on another cold call or some other part of your daily routine. Also, don't force the interviewee to conclude the interview. Don't go beyond the time that was originally allotted to you unless the interviewee seems amenable and you sense that additional information is forthcoming.

Following Up

Always follow up a cold call with a letter. Summarize the conversation and thank the company representative for giving you his or her valuable time. If the company is not currently in the market for office space, ask that your letter be filed with the lease. When the time arrives for considering space needs, your name will then be in the most accessible place. Continue following up with phone calls from time to time as well.

File the information you have gathered in your company's inventory system. Keep a separate folder or computer record for yourself on each company you cold call. Treat these folders like the valuable leads they are, and check them regularly.

The crucial fact to retain from this section is that the main reason for cold calling is to get an indication of a company's future space needs, so you can be there to generate a transaction before anyone else does. This is why follow-up phone calls can be as important as the cold call itself. You want to keep a high profile with the decision maker. Get that person into the habit of thinking positively of you whenever the subject of real estate comes up. If you can accomplish this, no other salesperson will have a chance.

When to Cold Call

It is vital that you make cold calls regularly. Set aside certain times each day or each week, whichever works better for you. The important thing is to set a work pattern for yourself and stick to it. Many times you will be tempted to skip the cold calls on a scheduled day, especially as you become more involved in deals at various stages of development. But you must learn to assign priorities. Cold calling never becomes a second-class task. After all, its sole aim is to generate business for you. Yet once you let your cold calling pattern slip just a little, it is that much easier to let it slip a little more the next time you are tempted instead to pursue a deal with a shorter path between you and your commission.

In addition to your regular times for cold calling, you can sometimes work in a few calls at odd, unscheduled times. If someone breaks an appointment or if an appointment is completed more quickly than anticipated, that might leave a block of time for making cold calls.

Attitude Is Everything

The ingredients of successful cold calling are confidence, imagination, quiet aggressiveness and persistence. Pursue information with the expectation that people will respond favorably to your visit. You are a professional, an expert in your field. Convey that impression, and people will be pleased to deal with you.

In order to feel comfortable on cold calls, you must *practice*. Memorize the questions you want to ask. Role-play cold calling with anyone who will toss back responses. Try to cover every conceivable situation and reaction. Be as thoroughly prepared as you can be—and then be further prepared to shift gears, tactics or follow a new lead during the course of the interview.

Once you have perfected your techniques, the appropriate actions will become automatic. Try to obtain all the specific information discussed in this module. At the same time, regard calls where you secure any information at all as successful.

The following questions will help you to review what you have just read. In Exercises A through C, you have just entered an office to cold call. How will you respond to each of the following developments?

Exercise A _____

The receptionist tells you that the decision maker will not be available until 3 P.M. (It is now midmorning.) Check your answer with the one below.

Answer A _____

Agree to the appointment only as a last resort. Press a little. Make it clear that you need only a few minutes. If that doesn't work, find out if there is another qualified person you can talk with on the spot. Try, without being obnoxious, to be persistent enough that it's easier for the receptionist to give you what you want than to deny you.

Exercise B _____

The person you wish to see will talk with you immediately, but only by telephone.

Answer B _____

Agree to the phone call, but use it to your advantage. You have already accomplished one objective—you are talking directly with the person you wish to see. The next objective is to gain face-to-face access. Tell the interviewee that you need only a few minutes, that you are selling nothing, that you seek only information. Since you have gotten this far, you probably will be admitted.

Exercise C

You see the decision maker, but are told the company does not need additional space and refuses to discuss the matter further. In the meantime, note any applicable information on the survey form.

Answer C

You have no recourse here but to leave. But follow up on this company later.

Exercise D

Give five reasons why a company might want to move before its lease expires.

Answer D

Six common reasons were given in the text:

1. *The company has expanded and is squeezed for space.*

2. *The company has shrunk and needs less space.*

3. *The area has changed and no longer provides a suitable environment.*

4. *The building is scheduled for demolition.*

5. *The company president wants the company to move closer to his or her home.*

6. *The company may wish to consolidate two or more offices that are at different locations.*

GETTING LEADS

Leads come from an infinite number of sources. No list could possibly cover them all. Still, a detailed discussion of sources will help you to recognize a lead when you see one. The successful salesperson seeks out leads constantly. The mediocre salesperson often does not recognize a lead when one volunteers itself. And a lead is only as good as the follow-through you give it—you don't want to find competing brokers closing deals that you made only a halfhearted attempt to initiate.

In a sense, this entire chapter is about leads. What is office-space marketing if not a constant seeking out of new prospects? And how better to find new prospects than continually to search for—and follow up on—leads? Cold calling is your surest method of developing leads, but it is a long-range process. Although it will pay off handsomely year after year, it seldom has immediate effects. While you are initiating cold calls and waiting for these long-range deals to develop, there are other steps you can be taking to generate commissions. A list of some of the best sources of leads follows. Most are ways of stimulating other people to give you referrals.

1. *Friends and neighbors.* As a newcomer starting out in office-space sales, make it easy for yourself and start with the obvious. Use friends and neighbors, the people you feel comfortable with, to help you generate your first leads. Let them know what you do for a living. Explain that you would enjoy being of service to them. Don't overlook your business associates in other fields—your lawyer, stockbroker, banker, insurance salesperson. Make friends in other companies located near your office. Find out who is moving. Don't wait for the arrival of the moving van to tip you off that the company next door has been planning a move for some time. If nearby companies have no space needs, they may in a year or two. Or perhaps they know of companies that need space right now. *Ask.*

2. *Colleagues.* Become acquainted with the other salespeople in your office. Let them know you are interested in referrals and will cheerfully pay a referral fee or split a commission. Let your sales manager see that you can recognize a lead and follow through on it—he or she may begin rewarding you with leads from time to time.

3. *Inventory system.* The inventory system contains a wealth of information of value to you. Look through it on a regular basis. Consult the lease expiration file, which covers all firms contacted in the entire marketing area by expiration date. Remember that this system works both ways—you are expected to contribute to it as well as extract leads from it.

4. *Outside brokers.* Cooperate with outside brokers. Make deals to help them with their exclusives, but remember to protect yourself. Register your tenant with the other broker by securing a letter of representation from the tenant. When you are with competing brokers, keep your ears open. Some brokers make unintended revelations because they can't resist the temptation to brag. More than one lead has come from such a source.

5. *Satisfied clients.* Regard all of your satisfied clients as potential continuing sources of referrals. As soon as you have closed their transactions, ask these clients about companies they know that might need space or have excess space. Follow up on them periodically to see if their own or their acquaintances' space needs have changed.

6. *Publications.* Scan newspapers and trade magazines for certain types of local news. Find out who is moving, what buildings are being demolished, which companies are growing rapidly (as indicated by such achievements as a record third quarter or the acquisition of another firm). Make a note of such information and follow through—that day or the next if possible.

7. *Other brokers' signs.* Watch for owners' or other brokers' signs on buildings and try to find out if these listings are open or exclusive. Cooperate with other brokers when you can.

8. *Miscellaneous lead sources.* Meet salespeople and managers of moving companies. Try to make a friend in a bank's mortgage loan department or a title company office. Attend local chapter meetings of the Building Owners and Managers Association. Building managers whose space is 100 percent rented are usually

generous with referrals if you approach them properly. Attend meetings of the National Association of Industrial and Office Parks (N.A.I.O.P.) and the Society of Industrial and Office Realtors (S.I.O.R.). Team up with salespeople from other businesses who also make cold calls, such as insurance representatives and office-machine salespeople. They often hear of impending moves, so you and they may be able to trade useful information.

CORPORATE MARKETING SUPPORT

A large company can support your individual efforts in many ways, including the following.

1. *Mailing pieces.* When you sign an exclusive listing on a large office space or an entire building, your company may assist you by developing descriptive literature. Depending on the size and value of the property, this material can vary from a one-page flyer to an expensive six-page brochure. You can mail such pieces, with or without a cover letter, to a select list of local or statewide prospects. You can also hand them out in person to appropriate contacts. Such printed materials lend you credibility and prestige, but to turn them into commissions, always follow up with a telephone call. Discuss the literature with the person you call.

2. *Advertising.* Institutional advertising in newspapers and financial and trade periodicals can familiarize the market area with your company's name, thus easing your path as you work through your cold calls. Even if an ad merely states that your firm is a particular building's specific agent, it gives you instant identity. And it lets you begin a call by asking, "Did you see our ad in such-and-such newspaper yesterday?"

3. *Signs.* Like advertising, a company sign on a building does much to enhance the corporate image. A sign has a more immediate function as well—it serves as a direct source of leads. Try to get signs up as often as possible, even on nonexclusive buildings.

   It's also wise to give no information on a sign other than the company name and telephone number. A sign that says "to lease: 15,000 square feet" shuts out all prospective tenants except the very few who are at that moment in the market for 15,000 square feet. A sign that doesn't give this information will generate calls from potential tenants who want more or less space than that, or who want to buy the entire building. And each of these calls is a chance to sell a different property—to a prospect who would never have called had your sign been too specific.

   For the same reason, leave a sign up as long as possible after the space inside has been filled. Why discourage other prospects with space needs from calling when they see that sign, since you can find other space that would suit their needs just as well?

Always ask exclusive-listing clients if you can hang a sign. You will almost surely be allowed, because the sign adds to the owner's prestige. And try to obtain permission to hang signs next to those of other brokers on nonexclusive listings. Signs are an excellent form of advertising.

MARKETING PROPOSALS AND SITE PRESENTATION PACKETS

A crucial marketing skill for you to master is the preparation of quality marketing proposals. You'll want to cover certain points while not going beyond suggested commitments.

To assist you in writing these proposals, an outline that abstracts the best elements from successful presentations and explains how they can be used in various situations is included here. If you model your proposals on this outline, you can save yourself a great deal of time and still develop consistently effective marketing proposals.

The following standard format is suggested in regard to the mechanics of proposal presentation.

1. *Folder.* Use a legal-size folder to enclose the proposal and all other inserts. The proposal itself can be spiral-bound or vela-bound.

2. *Proposal.* The proposal should follow the outline presented below. It should be bound and placed in the flap on the inside front cover if the folder method is used.

3. *Inserts.* A company history and fact sheet, client reference list, salesperson's personal history, maps, brochures, etc., should all be bound with the rest of the material or, if a folder is used, placed in the inside back cover.

I. SCOPE OF EMPLOYMENT

(Pattern this after the following statement.)

The ABC Company proposes to assume an overall marketing responsibility for leasing the space in (name and address of property). This responsibility includes overseeing all direct sales efforts of ABC people and coordinating the efforts of the brokerage community. It further includes the coordination of ABC's expertise in planning and executing advertising and public relations programs with the expertise of persons charged with that responsibility by the (owner/developer).

II. MARKETING PROGRAM

A. Personal Canvassing

(Use an introduction similar to this.)

The most important part of the entire campaign will be a direct sales effort in the form of personally calling upon all the prospective tenants we are able to locate. Our wide network of regional offices, coupled with the operating concept of area coverage, ensures this contact over the broadest possible area. "Area coverage" means that we have assigned all geographic areas within each major market we serve to a specialist in office leasing. This geographic assignment ensures complete knowledge of inventory, both existing and planned, and tenant requirements, including lease expiration dates and other important information relating to existing tenants.

The program will be conducted in the manner and in the areas indicated below:

1. (Describe the canvassing program for the immediate locale of the project. Include information on sales staff, tenant information systems, etc.)

2. (Do the same here and in succeeding paragraphs for other geographic areas in which prospects for the project will be sought.)

B. Marketing Tools

(The following introductory comment is suggested.)

ABC Company has had extensive experience in planning and coordinating advertising and promotion campaigns for various types of real estate projects. We propose to make this experience available to you by consulting with you or your designated public communications representative on the preparation of the campaign and the ongoing evaluation of its effectiveness.

The following are some preliminary recommendations.

1. *Direct mail.* This program will be carefully coordinated with personal canvassing so that both components will have maximum effectiveness. Our experience has taught us that mailing campaigns are only as effective as the follow-up efforts in the form of personal calls made by our salespeople. (Describe further what the direct mail piece should be and to whom it should be mailed. Also be specific regarding who has the cost responsibility for this program.)

2. *Brochures.* (Comment on the brochure requirements covering general content, quantity, overall quality required for the project, etc. If the project already has a brochure, evaluate its effectiveness. The brochure cost is virtually always borne by the owner.)

3. *Signs.* (Describe appropriate signing and who has the cost responsibility.)

4. *Media advertising.* (Discuss any recommendations for newspaper, magazine, radio, etc., including cost responsibility.)

5. *Public relations.* ABC in-house and outside public relations representatives will prepare and distribute news releases relating to the project. (Point out here that if a major public relations campaign is appropriate, our representatives will work with the owner's staff in conceiving and coordinating major news releases and special events.)

6. *Multimedia presentation.* (In projects where it is appropriate and approved by management in coordination with our in-house advertising department, a multimedia presentation designed for the project can be prepared.)

C. Broker Cooperation

1. *Communication.* We believe in aggressively seeking the cooperation of that relatively small segment of the brokerage community that, along with the ABC Company, does the vast majority of the business. It will be the project manager's responsibility to keep the brokerage community informed on current leasing activity and the status of the project, attend the sales meetings of these brokers to promote the project, conduct monthly mailings and follow up by inviting the more productive brokers on personal tours to introduce the project to them.

2. *Outside broker commissions.* (Include a recommendation on the commission schedule for outside brokers.)

III. MARKETING ADMINISTRATION

A. Securing the Tenant

After prospects have been identified, the following steps will be taken by our leasing staff.

1. Qualifying the tenant financially
2. Selling tenant the project versus any competition
3. Determining space requirement
4. Coordinating with space planner or owner's architect
5. Assisting in analysis of pricing the improvements and comparing these costs to building allowances
6. Negotiating with tenant to resolve the overstandard improvements
7. Negotiating basic lease terms, including terms, escalations, rent, any concessions, etc.

8. Overseeing and coordinating preparation of lease documents with owner's and tenant's representatives

9. Providing liaison among tenant, owner, contractor and designers during planning and construction of tenant improvements

B. Organization

(Include a brief organization chart showing the relationships among client, district manager, project manager, sales staff and other offices. Refer to the sample chart in figure 5–5 below.)

FIGURE 5.5   Sample Organization Chart

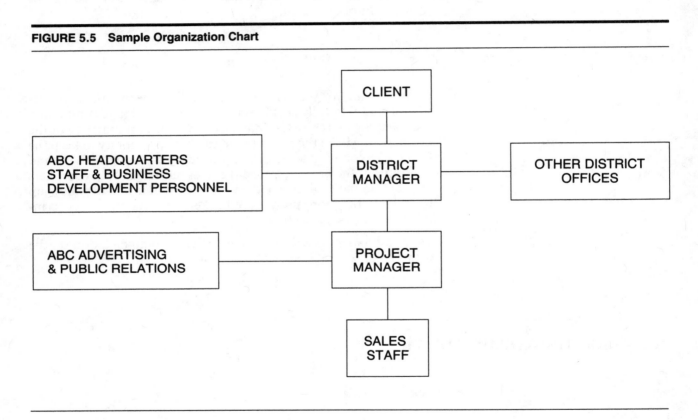

C. Staffing

(Name the project manager and salespeople to be assigned to the project. Include a brief resume on each, emphasizing the person's education, achievements in real estate and aptitude for the job. Sell our people; they are our best product. If the project manager has not yet been selected, state that the final choice will be subject to client approval.)

D. Reporting

(Specify the type and frequency of reports to the owner. Company policy is to submit written reports at least once a month. Weekly reporting may be appropriate in some cases. These reports must inform the owner of the number and results of prospect contacts, number of referrals from other offices, all efforts being made to promote the project and any trends that may affect the project's marketability.)

IV. MARKETING CONTRACT

(Attach to proposal.)

6

Selling Skills

INTRODUCTION

There was a time when an office-marketing representative did little more than simply introduce a tenant to an owner and leave the two principals to work out their own deal—after reminding the owner where to send the commission check. The service performed by the modern real estate salesperson goes far beyond this. The reason for this change is twofold. First, tenants and landlords today are more sophisticated. They expect more services than did their predecessors. Second, real estate marketing strategies also are more sophisticated. Service industries today must go far beyond fulfilling their basic obligations; they must compete on the basis of the extensiveness, quality and inclusiveness of the services they offer.

Consequently, the idea of *complete service* cannot be stressed too much. It is service that brings in commissions. If you are to succeed, you must offer better service than do the salespeople in other real estate companies.

As an office-marketing salesperson, you provide a specialized service based on real estate knowledge and experience that only you can offer. You are not an accountant, a lawyer or an architect, but you will need to know something about each of these fields. You are a real estate specialist who will perform a service tenants and owners cannot perform.

You will always be the person in the middle. On the one hand will be the owner, who wishes to charge the highest possible rent, spend a minimal amount for tenant improvements and have an ironclad lease that allows for no options or extensions. On the other hand will be the tenant, who wants the lowest possible rent, the maximum in tenant

123

improvements and services and an advantageous lease. You must find a way to bring these two opposing viewpoints together to the satisfaction of both parties. Only a professional can perform this task well.

Few people understand exactly what an office-marketing salesperson does besides collect a commission. Consequently, you must educate prospects while establishing a professional atmosphere of trust and respect. You can do so by explaining in detail what services you will render and how you will be compensated for your effort. Impress upon prospects the advantages of dealing with your company.

As you educate, you will also learn. You will learn about tenants' businesses—their services, products, objectives, marketing techniques, anticipated growth and other plans for the future. Probing for this information shows you are interested in their business and their welfare. Show prospects that you, like them, take pride in your work. Establish a feeling of mutual respect. Let them know that you will answer all questions candidly and openly and will find answers to the ones you can't handle yourself. Assure them that you will show all suitable available space, regardless of who holds the listing. As mutual trust and respect grow, so will your control of your tenants.

You will develop certain skills as you serve, educate and probe. The seven categories into which these skills fall are the subjects of the seven sections of this chapter.

First, you will learn to *qualify* prospects so you will not waste precious time on the ones who will never make a deal. You will learn the finer points of *showing space* and of *analyzing* various building features from the tenants' point of view. And, although you are not expected to be an expert on *space planning,* know enough about it to sense tenants' overall needs and to work intelligently with professional space planners.

As your deals progress, your skill at *negotiating* between tenant and owner will come into play. After completing negotiations, you will need a unique set of skills known as *closing techniques* when you present your tenants' offers to owners.

And throughout, like a thread woven through the entire fabric of your professional life, will run the ongoing improvement of your *time management* abilities.

QUALIFYING TENANTS

The first selling skill you must develop is that of qualifying prospects. Qualifying is the process of determining whether a company is seriously interested in leasing new space. Being serious means that the company:

1. wants to move or expand its facilities,

2. is financially able to acquire new space and

3. has provided you with a contact who has the authority to close the deal.

Qualifying is, in short, a probing process designed to find out whether what you have in hand is a potential transaction or a potential flop.

Qualify the potential tenant as soon as possible after getting a lead, ideally during the initial interview. Your time is too valuable to waste on companies that do not qualify on all three counts. Meeting two out of three criteria is not enough. The old adage "time is money" is nowhere more true than in the life of an office-marketing salesperson. You cannot afford to accept on faith a company's willingness or ability to perform. Insist that the tenant back up such promises with proof.

Now, consider in detail the three areas by which you will be qualifying prospects.

Qualifying by Need

To qualify a prospect by need, you must really do two things. First, make sure the company is serious about moving. If you suspect it is not, drop it tactfully. If you are convinced of the company's seriousness, ascertain whether the tenants perceive their space needs accurately. Many tenants, especially in small- and medium-sized firms, know they need more space but have not estimated correctly either the amount or the type of space required. Raise the question promptly if you think this may be a problem. Any delay could mean hours or days wasted looking at unsatisfactory premises while the client struggles toward a better perception of what he or she really wants. A company that isn't certain what it should be looking for is not necessarily an undesirable tenant, but it does need help in determining its space goals.

These problems are less likely to occur with large corporations, which usually have trained real estate professionals on staff who know exactly what they are looking for. But if a large company does not have such a staff member, you may find yourself dealing with a marketing vice president, for example, who would recognize the right space on sight but can't quantify the company's needs in such terms as square footage or the ratio of rentable to usable space. In this case, work out the exact specifications of the company's needs. If you must approach a higher authority for information, get your original contact's cooperation. Qualifying need is less likely to be your problem with large companies than qualifying your contact's authority.

Whatever the company, the best time to establish its space needs is during a tour of the premises. Ask the company representative a number of questions. How much space is currently occupied? What is the proportion of open to closed space? What is the traffic-flow pattern? Are any changes in space needs likely? What is the parking situation? What future parking needs are expected? What type of location does the company desire? Why? What is it willing to pay for new space? Is that amount realistic in terms of the current market? If the answer to the last question is "no," resolve the issue immediately—this discrepancy could ruin the entire transaction.

The combined building tour/qualifying interview will do more than clarify your perception of the company's space needs. It will also help the company refine its own thinking about its space needs and perhaps bring company thinking about what it wants into closer harmony with what it needs.

Your prior knowledge of the different space needs of different kinds of businesses will make your assessment of a particular tenant's needs considerably easier. When you begin to realize instinctively that an insurance company will need more storage space than a public relations company, or that a printing operation may require a large freight and materials handling area, you will be developing a skill for qualifying properties as well as tenants.

Financial Qualifying

You must find out exactly what its financial situation is early in your relationship with a company. Don't be afraid to ask probing financial questions. It is absolutely essential that you or at least the lessor has such information. The owner is being asked to give possession for a period of time. He or she has every right to know if the prospective lessee is financially able to honor the contract. If the tenant can't afford the space, the situation will eventually get very awkward for everyone concerned, and you may get your commission but lose a valuable referral source.

Your tactics for obtaining financial information will have to be flexible. Even the necessity for getting such information varies from company to company. Large companies and many medium-sized ones are listed in Dun & Bradstreet and can easily be checked. If they are really large—IBM for instance—their reputation may make it unnecessary to qualify them financially at all.

Small companies will probably be more of a problem. A company that is really on the way up is likely to be proud of the fact and more than happy to discuss financial capability. But a less successful small company may not want to make its financial information available. If you find yourself in such a situation, begin by explaining the right of the property owner to be protected against loss. If you still meet resistance, suggest that the tenant send the financial statement directly to the building owner without your seeing it. Or tenant and owner can meet on neutral ground, at one party's bank, to examine the tenant's financial statement.

If the company still refuses to disclose its financial status, a few options are still open to you. Find out how long the tenant has been in business. Get what information you can from its bank. Estimate from the present location what rent is affordable. Give these statistics to the owner, tell him or her the tenant refuses to divulge any information, and leave the decision entirely up to the owner. Do not give the owner any advice about whether to risk dealing with this tenant. If you don't have the necessary data, it is not up to you to give an opinion. Your intervention on a potential tenant's behalf won't make you any friends if the tenant ultimately defaults on the rent.

Qualifying Your Contact's Authority

More than one office-marketing salesperson has worked on a transaction for a large company right up to the lease signing, only to find that the company contact has no space decision-making authority and has suddenly been overruled by a superior. (When a company is small enough that you are dealing directly with the president or a close assistant, this is obviously not a problem.)

Although you should always try to work with the company's office-space decision maker, this is often not possible with large companies. If you find yourself dealing with a vice president of marketing or a regional manager, that person will probably search out space and get a deal started, then pass on the information to a superior who actually signs the lease. He or she may even pass the information on to someone who then passes the information on to someone else who signs the lease. And you may not meet the actual signer before the deal is closed.

The officer who has the responsibility for starting the deal, but not the authority to close it, may not be honest with you about his or her lack of decision-making power. But even if the original contact has no authority, he or she may have a great deal of influence over the final decision, so you'll want to maintain a harmonious working relationship. If you try to bypass this individual, you may get the deal or you may kill it outright. In either case, you'll probably never get a chance to work with that company again.

The best approach in a transaction in which you suspect you are not working with the decision maker is tactful probing. You might try this question: "After you and I agree on something, who else do we have to convince?" Or this: "When it gets to the point of putting something in writing, I'll send the information to you. To whom should I send the copy?" If the person you ask has the authority to sign, he or she will let you know. If that person can't sign, find out who can.

In dealing with a company contact who is not the decision maker, put all information in writing. When you transmit information orally to your contact who relays it orally to his or her superior, the message will inevitably be somewhat distorted by the relayer's perceptions. Unconsciously, the contact will hear partly what you really say and partly what the contact wants you to say. To retain control of the situation, give the company contact written information to pass along to the person in charge.

Someday you may find yourself simply unable to work with a particular prospect because a severe personality conflict exists. This is especially likely to happen with middle-management people who may resent the fact that they do not have final authority.

If the situation deteriorates beyond a certain point, the tenant will simply find another broker without saying anything to the salesperson. Your first clue will be when the tenant is suddenly unavailable for phone calls. When this happens, it's too late to remedy the problem.

Don't let an awkward situation deteriorate that far. If you sense that a personality problem is developing, act while you still can salvage something from the situation. Quickly try to substitute someone else from your office, someone whose personality will fit better. This will mean a split commission if your colleague closes the deal, but half a commission is infinitely better than none.

In unusual circumstances, it may be wise to circumvent the middle-management person you're having problems with. If the deal looks as though it's going nowhere, if the contact is indecisive and looks at many properties without appearing to be any closer to a decision, you stand a chance of losing the client anyway. If, at the same time, you are sure you have the right space package for this company, you may decide to go directly to the company representative's superior. But recognize that this is a one-shot deal. You win or you lose. It is only when you have reason to think you are going to lose anyway that you should risk it.

FIGURE 6.1   Qualifying Checklist

TENANT QUALIFYING QUESTIONS

A form to be used during the first call.

NEED

1. When does your lease expire? _____

2. When will you be ready to move? _____

3. If we find a building tomorrow that suits your needs, how long will it take for you to sign a lease? _____

4. Have you worked with any other brokers? _____

MONEY

1. How long have you been in business? _____

2. What are your annual sales? _____

3. What is the net worth of the company or person that will sign the lease? _____

4. Normally buildings of the type you have described to me rent in the range of _____ to _____ per square foot. Is this the kind of figure you had budgeted? _____

5. How much money do you have to spend on this purchase? _____

PERFORM

1. Who will sign the lease? _____

2. What is the process your company uses to approve matter of this type? _____

_____

3. Can we make an appointment to see the property for this afternoon? _____

4. Can I come by and visit your facility today? _____

Company name: _____

Address: _____ Phone: _____

Contact: _____

Person signing lease: _____ Phone: _____

Net worth: _____   Yrs. in business: _____

Following Up

In qualifying prospects, don't rely on memory. Ask all the important questions and get as much information as possible at the initial meeting. Use the checklist in figure 6–1. Once the prospect passes the checklist test and begins to look like a winner, get more detailed information, such as the following.

1. type of business
2. square footage in present building
3. current rent paid
4. how soon new space must be found
5. square footage required in the new space
6. access to public transportation desired
7. special space requirements, such as extra filing and storage space
8. special location requirements, such as availability of printing shops or other service businesses
9. parking requirements

Qualifying Sellers/Landlords

Qualifying sellers and landlords is easier, although equally important, as qualifying buyers and tenants. Prospects should be qualified by need and authority.

Determine a prospect's needs or motivation for selling or leasing. Do they need to complete a transaction within a certain time frame? Do they need to realize a certain rate of price? Factors such as these influence the rate, terms and conditions the prospect is willing to offer and accept. Having this information also enables you to provide prospects with the services that meet their needs.

Qualifying for authority must be done as early as possible in the selling process. Though it seems obvious that prospects indicating a desire to use your services would have authority to make decisions, this may not be the case. For example, in the case of a sale, a board of directors may be involved. Or restrictions may apply on the right to sell based on joint ownership or partnership. In the case of a lease, partners may be involved. Don't be afraid to ask the prospect. Try to do this subtly. Instead of "Are you the sole decision maker?", ask "What will be the process for making this decision?" or "I'm looking forward to working with you. Who else might be involved?"

Typically, you will have developed a list of perhaps two dozen people you consider prospects within a few months. When you analyze that list objectively, you will probably find only five or six people who have been thoroughly qualified and for whom you stand a good chance of consummating a transaction. You'll want to concentrate your efforts exclusively on them. Those people who do not look promising should quickly but tactfully be referred to someone who can manage the situation, or else they should be discouraged altogether. Time and talent are precious commodities that no salesperson should waste.

Exercise A

Check your answers with those given at the end of this exercise.

1. What is meant by the term *qualifying space*?

2. Why is qualifying important?

3. What are the three areas of tenant qualification? Explain briefly the importance of each.

4. What two broad areas must you consider when qualifying a prospect by need?

5. What must you discover in dealing with the company representative of a large company that is seeking space? Why?

6. Is it more important to put your information in writing when dealing with a large company or with a small one? Why?

7. Your attempt to pry financial information from a tenant has been completely unsuccessful. You have gathered some skimpy data from other sources. What should be your next move?

8. What should you do if you and your prospect do not get along?

9. Is there any circumstance in which you may have a legitimate reason for going around the company representative in the field? If so, name it.

Answer A

1. *Qualifying space is obtaining information that will indicate whether the tenant has real and immediate space needs and is likely to follow through to a completed transaction.*

2. *Qualifying protects the salesperson from investing many precious hours in trying to complete a deal that ultimately fails.*

3. *The areas of qualification are:*
   a. *real need and desire to move; qualifying protects the salesperson from the office-space window-shopper.*
   b. *financial ability to move; qualifying protects the salesperson from the tenant who has not yet faced the fact that the company really cannot afford the space it needs.*
   c. *ability of the tenant contact to perform; qualifying protects the salesperson from the contact who acts in the capacity of office-space decision maker without the authority to do so.*

4. *When qualifying by need, consider: (a) whether the tenant's space needs are great enough to motivate him or her to follow through on whatever steps you initiate, and (b) whether the tenant has correctly perceived what his or her space needs actually are.*

5. *Find out whether the representative has decision-making authority and, if not, who has. You cannot deal effectively with your contact unless you have an idea of how much weight his or her opinion carries and know who has the final decision-making power.*

6. *It is more important to put everything in writing when dealing with a large company, because you are more likely not to meet the real decision maker until the day the lease is signed. Oral information you give the original contact during the transaction might be garbled when it is relayed.*

7. *Give whatever information you have secured to the owner, explain the situation and make it clear that accepting the tenant is the owner's decision alone.*

8. *Find someone in your office who can better handle the situation to take over, and be prepared to split your commission if the deal is completed.*

9. *It may pay to circumvent the middle-management person if you feel that you have put together a package that really fits the company's space needs but, for one reason or another, your contact will probably not be interested.*

SHOWING SPACE

The actual showing of space to a tenant is a critical step in making a transaction. Here is where you demonstrate your expertise and professionalism and where you really do your selling.

This section is designed to acquaint you with the procedure of showing space. After you have completed the material, you should:

1. know why you must learn your tenants' needs in detail and establish rapport with them.

2. understand the process of developing a study to present to your tenants.

3. know the ingredients of a fruitful tour.

4. understand points to emphasize when showing space.

5. realize the value of cordial relationships.

In preparing to show space, learn your tenants' needs and desires. Then prepare a study of available space for them to examine. Finally, show them the locations.

Preparing the Tenant

Discuss space needs with your tenants. Find out whether they pinpointed a more or less specific location—suburb, financial district, high rise, low rise—or wish to review a broad cross section of available space. As you begin showing space and noting their reactions, you gain a deeper insight into their true needs and desires, a process that continues until they actually make a selection. As you prepare tenants for a space tour, be prepared to discover that showing space will be an education for all concerned.

In the beginning, don't get the tenants too excited about amenities. The amenities they like may be unavailable for the amount of money they can spend. When you tour the available space, let them develop a feeling for what amenities are suitable in terms of cost. Their budget is a governing factor in helping you determine what space you will show.

Never forget that your prospect is a person; you're not dealing simply with a position in a company. Establish rapport. Show that you have their interests and their company's interests at heart and will do all you can to be of service throughout the information-gathering process and beyond. Assure your client that, while you naturally want to promote your exclusives, you will show everything available that might be suitable. Your service will be full and complete; the client will have no need to consult another broker. If you establish rapport and provide good service, he or she will have no inclination to deal with anyone else.

As you gather information, you will find that many tenants prefer to keep it confidential. They may not even want their employees to know that a move is being considered. Some also wish not to divulge their companies' names to the owner whose space they are viewing. Respect such wishes and be discreet.

The Site Presentation Packet

Once you have the information you need, explain that you are going to prepare a site-presentation packet. You will do a preliminary study of space available, return at a time you specify with the completed presentation packet and then make an appointment to conduct them on a tour of the space discussed in the study.

The site-presentation packet will contain a number of items and may take some time to prepare. But it is important; spend as much time as is necessary to make it attractive and complete. A complete site-presentation packet, entitled *Current Review of Selected Peninsula Office Space Locations,* appears in figure 6–2. The basic ingredients of the site-presentation packet follow.

1. A cover letter summarizes previous conversations, thanks prospects for letting you serve them and explains briefly the presentation that is enclosed. In the letter, cite as references people and companies you have serviced in the past. The sample letter suggests a tour of suitable areas and lists some of the crucial points that must be considered in making a decision to relocate.

2. A map of the area in which the tour will take place shows, clearly numbered, the locations to be viewed. This could be a general map of the city or suburb or possibly an oil company map.

3. The review sheet describes each location numbered on the map, specifying the building's name, address, total square footage and footage available, projected rental rate, access to transportation and parking facilities, height, amenities, services, improvements the tenant will probably inherit and timing for occupancy.

4. Letters and brochures from owners and developers describe the properties in question and put them in the best possible light. Owners and developers will provide you with such statements because they can do the best job of selling their own space. They are

expected to promote their properties, while you are expected to be objective in providing information to the prospective tenant. Both of the properties used as examples here refer to projects that have not yet been completed. The brochures show the projects' general appearance, layout and both horizontal and vertical views. They also indicate parking facilities and show views of both first and second floors of two-story buildings.

5. Finally, your presentation will contain economic and demographic information about the areas in which the tour will be conducted. This will take the form of brochures and data gathered from the Building Owners and Managers Association, Chambers of Commerce, other business and civil groups and the Census Bureau. The hypothetical document shows growth in population, employment and retail sales in San Mateo and San Mateo County over a 20-year period. It also deals with transportation facilities, buying income and assessed valuations, and it indicates the number and names of shopping centers, the number of building permits and their value and the number of single, two-family and apartment dwellings in the city of San Mateo.

CONDUCTING THE SPACE TOUR

Once the tenant has examined your site-presentation packet, you are ready to conduct a tour of available space. This is the critical point. Whether you make a transaction depends largely on how the tour goes.

First, plan well. You are dealing with a busy person. You want the prospect to see everything suitable, but you do not want to waste time. So plan. Know where you'll begin the tour, where you'll end it and where you'll be at the halfway point. Make sure that all space is accessible. Do you need to obtain keys? Do you need to provide current tenants with advance notice of the tour? In addition, know what floors you'll be showing and make sure the space is as presentable as possible.

Drive the route you intend to follow before conducting your tenant over it. Make sure your car is clean and has plenty of gas. Look at the space ahead of time if possible. Make sure that keys and lights work. If the space is occupied, alert them in advance. Know the fastest route and where to find parking. If the showing infringes on the lunch hour, plan to take the tenant to lunch.

How many locations should you show in a normal tour? That depends on a number of things—the amount of time your prospect has, the number of available locations that might suit the tenant's needs and whether you're touring the city, the suburbs or both. Most tenants will not want to inspect more than six or eight locations on one tour.

Your purpose is to educate tenants about the areas you are going to show. (This is especially true for prospects from out of town.) So cover all the relevant information. If you begin telling tenants something they already know, they'll cut you off fairly quickly.

Bring a copy of the presentation packet with you to refer to as the tour progresses. Don't assume that the prospect has read the survey thoroughly.

FIGURE 6.2   A Site-Presentation Packet

CURRENT REVIEW

of

SELECTED PENINSULA
OFFICE SPACE LOCATIONS

Prepared for:

XYZ Insurance Company

Prepared by:

John Smith
Grubb & Ellis Company

January 1, 1988

FIGURE 6.2   **(continued)**

Grubb&Ellis

August 25, 1987

Mr. John Doe
President
XYZ Insurance Company
15 Market Street
San Francisco, CA 94305

Dear Mr. Doe:

To confirm our conversation of August 23rd, I would like to introduce
myself to you and to begin exposing the office-leasing market on the
mid-Peninsula to XYZ Insurance Company. I was especially pleased to hear
the nature of the information you requested. I feel I am well qualified to
assist you in determining the feasibility of a move to the mid-Peninsula. I
have been an office-leasing specialist with Grubb & Ellis Company for the
past four years and have assisted many fine companies with their space
requirements, especially in the area we discussed.

I offer as references of my service on similar projects:

  Mr. Tom Moore, ABC, Inc., San Francisco: 222-2222

  Mr. C.A. Jones, DEF Company, San Mateo 111-1111

  Mr. Donald Collins, HIJ Corporation, Burmingham: 333-3333

I also have had the pleasure of working with a number of XYZ people,
including Charlie Atlas, Bob Wayne and Pete May.

Now that I have introduced myself, the first important point is my
understanding, as thoroughly as possible, XYZ's real requirements. This is
critical in that there are naturally certain features some office locations
offer that others do not. Some of the points I refer to are:

  - most desirable location: suburban, industrially mixed, city, etc.
  - importance of access to airport, San Francisco, restaurants, retail
    shops, hotels, etc.
  - the reliance by your employees on public transportation
  - contrast of low-rise, garden-type projects to medium-rise, city
    (Burmingham, San Mateo) locations
  - exact footage to accommodate approximately 100 people, ten of whom
    would be in private offices, the remainder in open space
  - budget

Grubb & Ellis Company   One Montgomery Street, Telesis Tower, San Francisco, CA 94104 (415) 956-1990

FIGURE 6.2   (continued)

Mr. John Doe
August 25, 1987
Page Two

   – desire to be on one floor or split divisionally
   – amenities: view, landscaping, etc.

I know we don't have the answers to all of the above today. However, once
an in-depth study is under way and you have had the opportunity to
inspect personally a cross section of possibilities, answers to these and
other unknowns will quickly surface.

As a first step, I have chosen to include a coded map of the area of
concentration, a skeleton breakdown of the first group of possible locations
I hope to explore with you, brochures and descriptive material on each of
those locations and additional data on the San Mateo-Burmingham area.
After reviewing the enclosed, I would then propose that you join me for a
tour of the area and the projects that you feel will be of the most interest.

I look forward to continuing to serve XYZ Insurance Company.

Sincerely yours,

John Smith
Office Leasing Division

FIGURE 6.2   (continued)

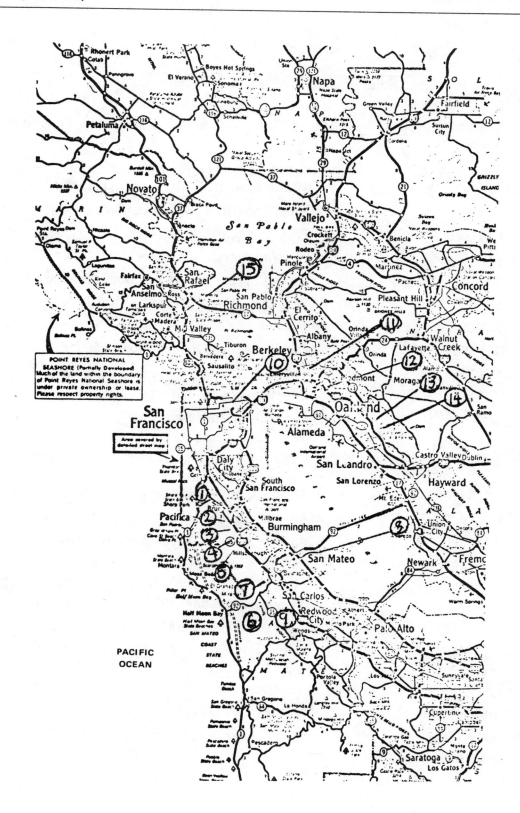

FIGURE 6.2   (continued)

CURRENT REVIEW
of
SELECTED PENINSULA OFFICE SPACE LOCATIONS

(1)   SAN FRANCISCO BAY OFFICE CENTER, a Crucial Commercial Construction Co.
Development

LOCATION:	Mailer and Galbraith Road, off of Old Bayside Highway on U.S. 1, Burmingham
FOOTAGE:	Approximately 54,000 square feet
PER FLOOR:	27,000 square feet
PARKING:	One (1) per 250 square feet
IMPROVEMENTS:	Carpets, drapes, air-conditioning, b-t-s
SERVICES:	Janitorial and utility, included
RENTAL RATE:	$19-20 per square foot
TIMING:	Completed and partially occupied
HEIGHT:	Two (2) stories
AMENITY:	Central courtyard, sauna
BROCHURE:	Available and enclosed

(2)   FINANCIAL CENTER, Smith Bros. Contractors

LOCATION:	Smith Road, Smithtown
FOOTAGE:	60,000 square feet
PER FLOOR:	Approximately 10,800 square feet
PARKING:	$40 per month--stall reserved
IMPROVEMENTS:	Carpets, drapes, air-conditioning, five (5) lineal feet per 100 sq. ft. partition
SERVICES:	Janitorial and utility, included
RENTAL RATE:	$20-21 per square foot
TIMING:	Building completed and ready for interior improvements
HEIGHT:	Six (6) stories
AMENITY:	City location, good public transportation
BROCHURE:	Available and enclosed

FIGURE 6.2   (continued)

CRUCIAL COMMERCIAL CONSTRUCTION COMPANY

January 16, 1988

Mr. John Smith
Grubb & Ellis Company
One Montgomery Street
San Francisco, CA 94104

Dear John:

To confirm our conversation of earlier this week, you will find enclosed
information on our new office project, located at the corner of Old Bayside
Highway and Space Road in Burmingham. The location of our new project
is within two blocks of our present office building, which leased out in six
months.

As you can see, the building will offer more than the normal number of
amenities for a suburban office building. The building will have a bank, a
restaurant and a number of other facilities that will benefit tenants in the
building. The project will be 110,000 square feet, three stories high with a
rustic redwood exterior. It was designed by one of San Francisco's leading
architects, Mark Hopkins, with whom I am sure you are familiar.
Extensive landscaping was designed by Jane Greenthumb. Two elevators
will service the building from two large lobby areas located off the interior
courtyard.

John, I know you are familiar with our present building and understand
the quality of the interior tenant improvements. The new building, if
anything, will be of a higher quality. It will continue to use the same bay
depths and office layouts with which we have had such great success.
Specifically with regard to a 10,000 sq. ft. requirement, we will be able to
offer them space in the low $20 range with the following improvements:
private offices designed and built to suit, full carpeting, drapes, air
conditioning and solid core walnut doors. The building was designed for
tenants in this approximate size range. Each floor contains 35,000 sq. ft.
separated into three equal sections. This will allow a 10,000 sq. ft. tenant
virtually its own floor with expansion room immediately adjacent to its
space.

As you know, we are about five minutes from public transportation in the
Burmingham area and are adjacent to the San Mateo International Airport.
Construction will start within a matter of days on our project. Occupancy
can be offered late in the third quarter of 1989.

I hope that we will be able to work together with your present prospect and
in the future.

Sincerely yours,

Ron Doss
Marketing Manager

FIGURE 6.2   (continued)

CRUCIAL COMMERCIAL CONSTRUCTION COMPANY
OFFICE PROJECT

The site of the project, as yet unnamed, is located at the southwest intersection of Space Road and Old Bayside Highway in the East Side Industrial Park in the City of Burmingham. The park is contiguous to the southern boundary of San Mateo International Airport. Bayside Freeway (U.S. 1) access is provided north to San Francisco via the Mill on-off ramp, and south to San Jose via the Broadway Avenue ramp. Located literally within easy walking distance of the site are some of the Peninsula's most popular restaurants and hotels. Additionally, many car leasing agencies and other services are immediately adjacent to the site.

The building will be the most generously amenitized building in the Burmingham area. Included in the building will be a ground-level restaurant with an open-air extension of the dining area into the Hiro Hito-designed fully landscaped courtyard. A conference room available on a reserved basis will be immediately adjacent to the restaurant and courtyard. The conference room will have its own fully concealable wet bar. On top of the building will be a sun deck with a beautiful view of the bay. Brown-baggers also will be able to observe from the sun deck activity at San Mateo International Airport just a few minutes away from the building. There will be a large lounge for tenants of the building. On the second floor will be a small gymnasium and sauna, further providing the working environment with complete rest and recreation facilities. The building is designed to accommodate a major commercial bank branch on the ground floor. Plans are to secure leases for a barber shop and travel agency to provide as many in-building services as needed. Free parking, telephone answering, stenographer and notary service also will be available. No other building in the area will offer so much in such an attractive package at competitive rentals.

Construction of the office center will consist of a wood-frame building with wood floors and wood roof. Suspended acoustical ceilings with sound insulation blankets will reduce sound transmissions. Partitioning will be standard wood studs and wall boards with three-and-one-half-inch-thick rock wool insulation blankets. Office partitions will be the fire-rated, vinyl-covered movable type with bronze anodized trim. Solid walnut, full-length doors will be used throughout the building. The layout of the building is perhaps the most unique feature of all. Almost all buildings in the park are designed for small tenants and have very limited flexibility. The Office Center will be flexible enough to handle very small tenants but is designed to accommodate up to a 35,000 square foot tenant on a single floor.

The office complex will be virtually three buildings joined together by lobbies. Air conditioning and heating will be provided with roof-mounted units with a maximum of 1,200 square feet of space per temperature zone. Anodized aluminum windows will be used which will be fully draped. The building will be fully carpeted, except for the lobbies which will have beautiful slate tile-like floors.

Mark Hopkins Associates, one of the Bay Area's most accomplished and respected project planners and architects, is designing the building. Hopkins's unique use of natural wood will provide both a rich interior and exterior environment. Public areas will receive special attention and the exterior will be handsomely integrated with the work of Jane Greenthumb, the professional landscape architect who designed the courtyard and exterior landscaping for the San Mateo Towers, a Crucial Commercial project in the same area.

FIGURE 6.2   (continued)

FIGURE 6.2 (continued)

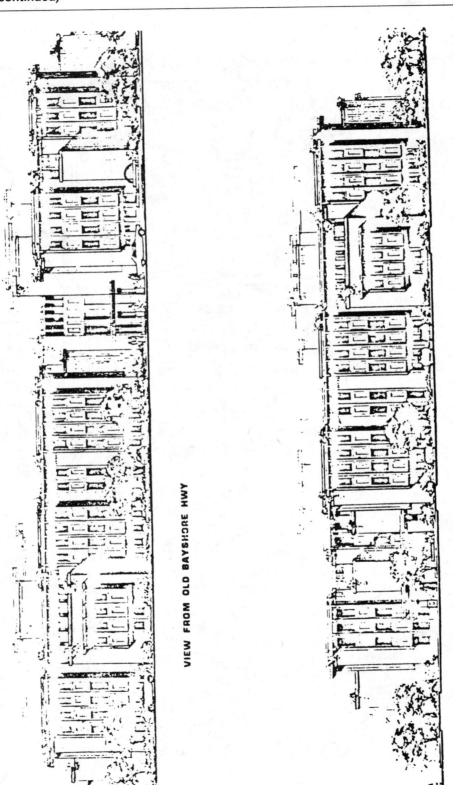

VIEW FROM OLD BAYSHORE HWY

VIEW FROM STANTON ROAD

FIGURE 6.2 (continued)

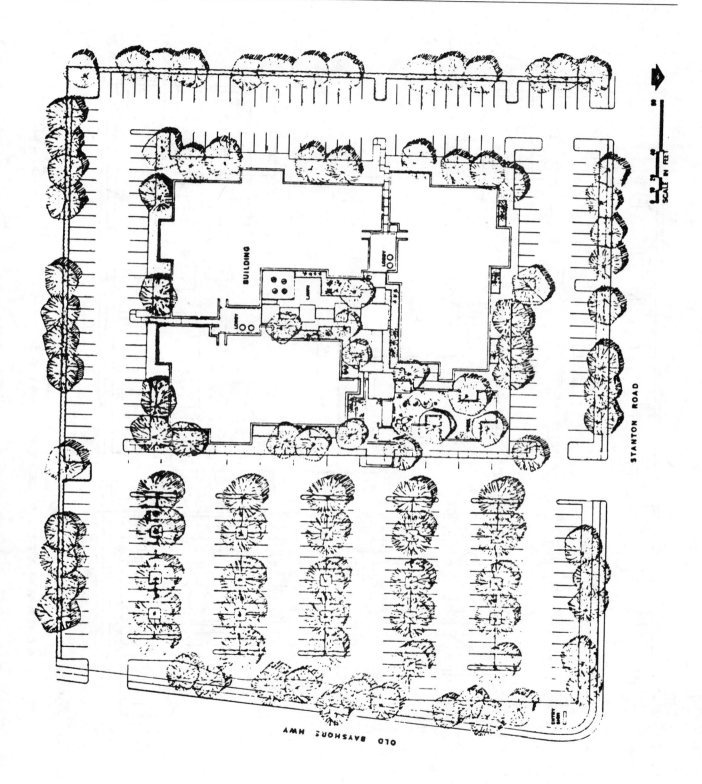

FIGURE 6.2   (continued)

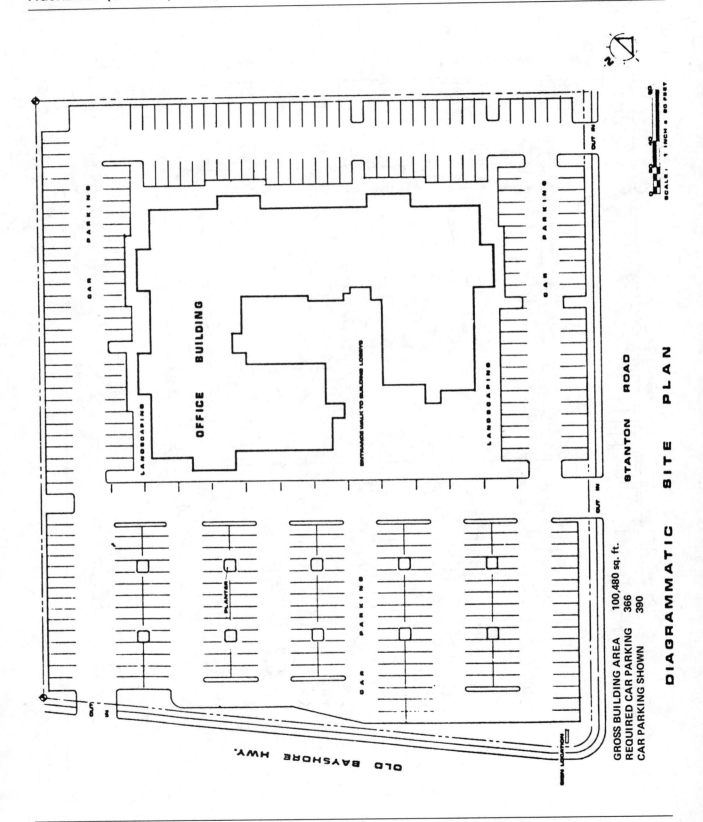

GROSS BUILDING AREA   100,480 sq. ft.
REQUIRED CAR PARKING   366
CAR PARKING SHOWN   390

DIAGRAMMATIC SITE PLAN

FIGURE 6.2   (continued)

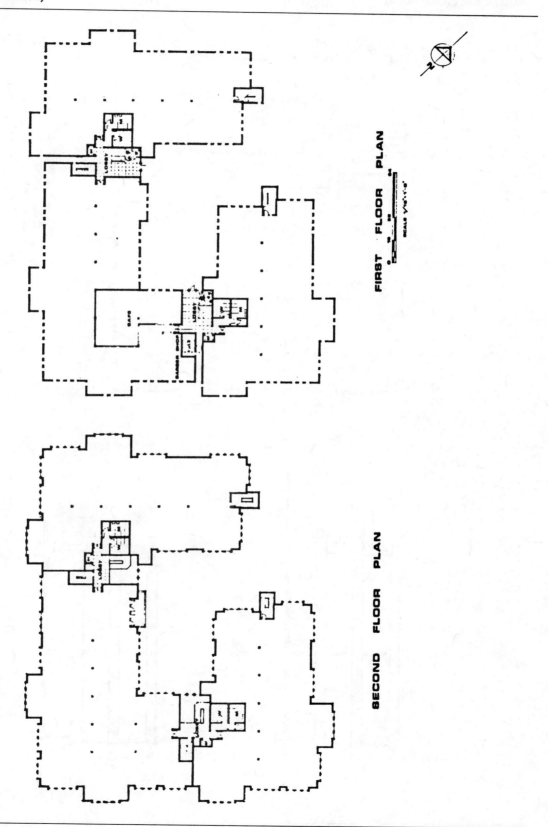

FIRST FLOOR PLAN

SECOND FLOOR PLAN

FIGURE 6.2 (continued)

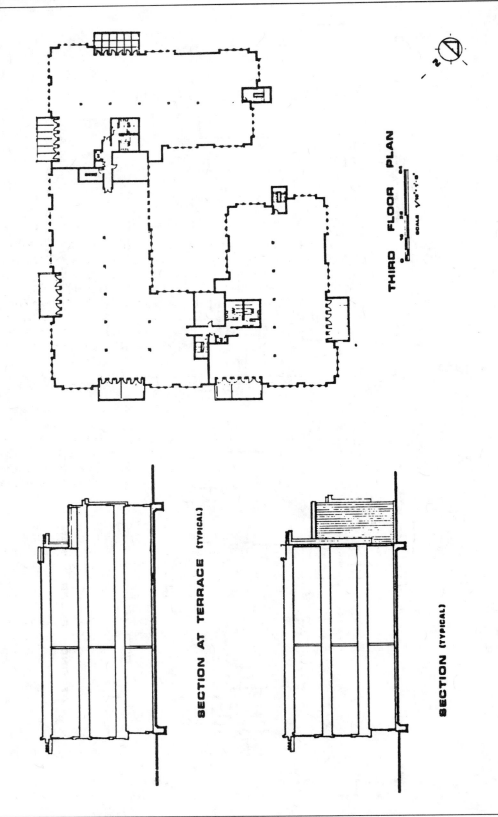

THIRD FLOOR PLAN

SECTION AT TERRACE (TYPICAL)

SECTION (TYPICAL)

FIGURE 6.2   (continued)

GENERAL OFFICE TENANCY CHARACTERISTICS IN MID-PENINSULA

TRANSPORTATION

1. *Automobile*

   An excellent Freeway System connects the mid-Peninsula area to either San Jose in 30 minutes or San Francisco in 25 minutes via Bayside Freeway (U.S. 101A), or the new Junipero Serra Freeway (U.S. 280). In addition, the mid-Peninsula is traversed by the El Camino Real (U.S. 101) which is the major commercial-retail free access highway linking all of the major communities between San Francisco and San Jose. The access to the East Bay is over the new 4-lane San Mateo Bridge making Oakland 25 minutes from San Mateo. The 19th Avenue Freeway, the most significant new State Freeway to be added in the area, is the main mid-Peninsula connection between the East Bay and the Pacific Ocean, thus enabling an employer to tap both of these rapidly expanding areas for personnel. The San Mateo International Airport is 10 minutes from Central San Mateo via the Bayside Freeway.

2. *Bus Service*

   The mid-Peninsula, is serviced by the Greyhound Bus Line connecting San Francisco and San Jose. The Bayside Transit is the local bus that services San Mateo and Burmingham.

   Greyhound Bus

   The Greyhound Bus provides several different routes from San Francisco to Redwood City and from San Jose to San Francisco, all of which stop in the San Mateo area. The "B" bus leaves San Francisco and Redwood City at convenient intervals from the early morning to late afternoon and travels along El Camino Real between Redwood City and Burmingham, stopping every two blocks and then travels between Burmingham and San Francisco express except for four or five stops.

   Inter-City Bus

   The Bayside Transit local bus has two routes, one of which connects Burmingham with Hillsdale Shopping Center and runs every hour, stopping on any corner where there is a waiting passenger, and an inter-San Mateo bus that extends from the most northerly city limit of San Mateo to the southerly city limits of San Mateo, stopping at corners where passengers are waiting.

3. *Train Service*

   The mid-Peninsula is serviced by a commuter train furnished by the Southern Pacific Railroad, and this train connects San Francisco to San Jose with stops at all of the major communities between these two cities. Most of these commuter trains stop at the Hillsdale Station and the San Mateo Station. Several of the trains stop at the Hayward Station, which is at the corner of 16th and South B Street in the center of San Mateo.

FIGURE 6.2   (concluded)

GENERAL ECONOMIC DATA ON SAN MATEO

Population:

San Mateo City*

1965	69,900
1969	79,000
1971	82,000
1975	79,000
1977	80,000
1981	78,200
1983	79,400

San Mateo County**

1965	439,200
1970	528,000
1975	557,400
1976	550,000
1977	561,200
1978	564,600
1979	570,100
1980	575,900
1981	581,400
1982	584,300
1983	584,400
1984	586,000

Employment:

San Mateo County**

1975	241,000
1982	225,000
1983	237,700

Retail Sales:

San Mateo City*

1965	$135,121,000
1970	183,123,000
1975	247,043,000
1980	342,531,000
1983	458,486,000

Median Income (per household):

San Mateo City*

1981	$ 24,827

Dwelling Units in San Mateo in 1979:

Single-family dwellings	18,000
Multifamily dwellings	12,000
Total	30,000

Shopping Centers in San Mateo (13):

Borel Square	Lauriedale
Conikar	Los Prados
College Plaza	Harvard Parkside
Crystal Lake	19th Avenue Parkside
Fashion Island	QFI
Hillside	Woodlake

Assessed Valuation:

San Mateo City*
1984-1985 net total $525,637,241

Building Permits (1984):

San Mateo City*

12 for construction of commercial buildings, totaling	$4,945,800
294 for remodeling of commercial buildings, totaling	4,092,433
	$9,038,233

  * Source: City of San Mateo
 ** Source: County of San Mateo

As you begin the trip, tell your tenant your plans for the day and continue to discuss the prospect's needs in light of the showings you have planned. During this discussion, some new need or requirement may arise that will automatically eliminate one or more of the locations you planned to show. Be flexible.

Point out to the space seeker that you know the properties and the areas. You know how far owners and developers might bend on rental rates, willingness to remodel and other factors that make a deal. Make it clear that you are the expert and that you will represent the tenant's best interests to the fullest extent possible. Reiterate that your presentation consists of the properties that in your opinion will come closest to meeting the space seeker's needs and that you will show all appropriate locations regardless of who has the listing.

At the outset, make no recommendations as to which property you think is best for the tenant. Stay neutral. Later, when the choice has narrowed to two or three, you might recommend the one you believe offers the best deal.

SHOWING THE LOCATION

From the minute you walk in the door, start pointing out features—building's appearance, air conditioning, lighting, carpeting and so on and stress how these features fulfill needs that the tenant has. Let the fact sheets on each building guide you. Observe what seems to please your tenant. It may be the way the elevators open onto the reception room, the window space and arrangement, the ease of access from elevator to offices or any number of things. Watching your tenant's reaction to various features will give you clues on how to bring him or her to a choice and a transaction. When the space seeker remarks favorably on an item, try to heighten that enthusiasm. Make notes on what seems to please the tenant and suggest that he or she take notes also. These notes will give you an idea of how quickly you should begin serious negotiations. Pay attention to negative comments as well. These also can be important clues. The tenant may, for example, notice immediately that a competitor is located down the hall and may register displeasure.

Don't hurry your tenant through a showing, but don't prolong it either. Let the tenant's interest in the particular space determine how much time you spend there.

If the tour cuts across the lunch hour, use the occasion to get better acquainted with the space seeker. Taking your tenant to lunch gives you an opportunity to further build rapport and develop his or her trust and confidence in you. It also lets you further define needs as you discuss the locations seen during the morning and touch on those that will be seen after lunch. Some tenants have difficulty visualizing their companies in a particular space. If a space seeker shows special interest in a location but has this problem, offer to demonstrate how such a space is used by a company similar to the tenant's own.

You should know your territory well enough to be able quickly to come up with an example, perhaps one in the same building. If possible, choose a building in which you have negotiated leases, for that is one you will know well.

BACK AT THE OFFICE

The tour is completed and you're back at your office or the tenant's office. What happens next? First of all, don't rush things. Give the space seeker time to digest what you've shown, time to reflect on the locations and his or her space needs. The tenant may have further questions. If so, answer them immediately. If you do not have ready answers, get them and call the tenant back at a specified time.

Set up an appointment to discuss the tour, go over the notes you have both made and begin to narrow choices. How quickly you get to final negotiations depends on how soon the tenant has to move, reaction to the space you've shown, the tenant's decision-making process and your reading of the situation. If the space seeker is making long-range plans, that point might not be reached for another year or so. The important thing is that by now you should have the tenant well in hand. If you have done your job well, you will be the salesperson who makes the transaction when the company is ready to move.

Now follow up with an appointment to discuss the properties you have shown. If your tenant is not moving immediately, then follow up periodically with phone calls to report changes in the market and to make sure that when the tenant is ready to relocate, you'll be the person who handles the deal.

Exercise B

Answer the following questions.

1. Why is it wise not to emphasize the subject of amenities at the beginning of the space showing period?

2. What five basic items will be included in your space and location study?

3. Why are statements from developers and owners desirable?

4. Name three possible sources of the information you gather for a tenant's site presentation packet.

5. What determines the number of locations you will show a tenant on one tour?

6. Why is it best not to make recommendations to the tenant until he or she has seen a selection of sites?

7. If a tenant has trouble visualizing his or her company in a particular space you are showing, what should you do?

8. After completing the tour, what should you do next?

9. What is the next step after that?

Answer B

1. *Naturally, the more amenities the happier the tenant will be. But there is a real danger that too much talk of amenities in the begin-*

ning will build hopes to heights that cannot be matched by the company's budget.

2. *The study should include (a) a cover letter, (b) a map of the area, (c) data on each property, (d) letters and statements from owners and developers and (e) demographic characteristics of the geographic area under consideration.*

3. *The developer knows the property better than anyone else and is expected to promote it. You, as the salesperson, should maintain an objective stance and protect the client's interests.*

4. *Sources of information are (a) owners and developers, (b) local chambers of commerce, (c) the U.S. Commerce Department and (d) local oil-company outlets (for maps).*

5. *If you are touring an area where a number of suitable spaces are available, let the tenants set the pace. Don't show more properties than they can view without becoming bored or tired. If you are touring an area where the properties are far apart (the suburbs, for instance), the distance between sites keeps the number of showings low.*

6. *You learn more about tenants' wishes by letting them make the comments on the spaces you show. When the space seeker narrows the appropriate sites down to a few, you can help with the final selection by guiding the choice on the basis of what you learned about the client's likes and dislikes.*

7. *If possible, show similar space being used by a company similar to the prospect's.*

8. *Return to the prospect's office and encourage questions about the space you just showed.*

9. *Set up an appointment to discuss the tour in detail and begin the selection process.*

SPACE ANALYSIS

Many things besides the rental rate are factors in tenants' decisions of which space best suits their company. No two tenants, even in the same business, have identical space needs. This uniqueness makes your job both difficult and challenging.

Make every effort at the first meeting to get all the necessary information regarding space requirements. Before ending the meeting, summarize those needs to double check that all essential points have been covered, and tell the prospect you will provide facts and figures on suitable buildings as quickly as possible.

The building economics comparison form, shown in figure 6–3, and the building quality comparison form in figure 6–4 will help you immeasurably in performing the promised task. Each form provides for the comparison of four buildings. Making clients' current building one of the four may help to clarify their thinking about building quality.

The first form compares buildings strictly on the basis of dollars-and-cents costs. The second, although certainly related to economics, lists features of building quality to be evaluated. Your ratings on the quality form will of necessity be somewhat subjective.

Building Economics Comparison Form

At the top of each column is a space for total square footage. Fill this in, then quantify the items listed here.

1. *Rent.* The annual rent is the rental rate times the number of square feet. The total rent is the annual rate times the number of years the lease will run.

2. *Improvements over standard.* If the improvements your tenant wants run higher than the building allowance, you need to figure the difference. If the owner pays for these extra improvements, the cost is amortized over the term of the lease.

3. *Lease deposit.* The deposit usually is not a crucial factor, but since this form considers all costs, it should be entered. Items three through seven are onetime costs, so the annual and total figures are the same.

4–7. *Moving, telephone, administrative and furniture costs.* Only the tenant can answer these questions. Try to persuade the tenant to fill these in, if only as a reminder that such costs must be taken into consideration at some point. You can help to estimate some of them by getting information from the telephone and moving companies. Bear in mind that all of these costs represent potential concessions, and, as such, may be adjusted later.

8. *Parking costs.* Two factors determine parking costs. One is the owner's policy—if parking is included in the rent, leave this space blank. The second is the tenant's policy toward employees. For example, if the owner charges extra for parking but the tenant passes on all parking costs to its employees, again leave this space blank. If the tenant passes on only some of its parking costs to employees, this figure must be adjusted.

9. *Rent escalation.* Lease escalator clauses were explained in the marketing section. If you expect a particular lease to contain a tax-and-building-maintenance or cost-of-living increase clause, provide for it here. You may have to estimate the amount.

The economics form is a valuable tool in helping the tenant make an intelligent choice.

Building Quality Comparison Form

The quality form will test your skill at judging many features of building quality, both tangible and intangible. You will need to know a great deal more about the buildings your tenant is considering than locations and rental rates in order to arrive at any rational decision. You will have to visit the properties and talk to a number of people to get all the information asked for here. But the time will be well spent. If the task seems overwhelming at first, remember that in addition to aiding your present

FIGURE 6.3   Building Economics Comparison Form

	BLDG. A sq. ft.		BLDG. B sq. ft.		BLDG. C sq. ft.		BLDG. D sq. ft.	
	ANNUAL	TOTAL	ANNUAL	TOTAL	ANNUAL	TOTAL	ANNUAL	TOTAL
1. Rent								
2. Est. costs—improvements over standard (amortized)								
3. Lease deposit								
4. Moving costs								
5. Telephones								
6. Admin. costs—stationery, etc.								
7. Furniture								
8. Parking costs								
9. Rent escalation								
GRAND TOTAL								

FIGURE 6.4   Building Quality Comparison Form

	BLDG. A	BLDG. B	BLDG. C	BLDG. D
DESIRABILITY OF LOCATION				
1. Suitability to tenant's needs				
2. Availability of restaurants				
3. Access to public transportation				
BUILDING QUALITY				
4. Construction				
5. Percentage of usable space				
6. Core location				
7. Core-to-window depth				
8. Module size				
9. Interior columns				
10. Space-planning service				
11. Air conditioning				
12. Elevators				
13. Floor ducting				
14. Life safety features/security				
15. Floor-load capacity				
16. Ceilings				
17. Storage				
18. Draperies				
19. Floor covering				
20. Parking				
21. Expansion capacity				
22. Quality of ownership				
23. Quality of management				
24. Quality of janitorial services				
TOTAL				

tenant, you will be broadening your professional capabilities, thus enhancing your value to future prospects. As you gather the information, take notes—don't rely on your memory.

On the form, check each feature that you think is above average quality in each building. You may want to total the checkmarks at the bottom of each column. But realize that totaling does not imply that all features can be weighed equally. Different tenants value different features to greater or lesser degrees. You may even wish to skip some items in some situations. A review of chapter one may be very helpful as you investigate some of these features.

1. *Suitability of location to tenant's needs.* Suitability can cover a host of factors. If the tenant considers prestige a high priority, a prestigious address may be warranted. Locating near or even in the same building as certain service industries may be most important to a particular tenant. A building in which competitors of the prospect are tenants may be unsuitable.

2. *Availability of restaurants.* In the selection of office space, the neighborhood restaurant situation is a vital consideration. Is there an outstanding restaurant nearby where company executives can take their clients to lunch or dinner? This is important if the company relies heavily on entertaining important people to secure their business. Are there inexpensive places nearby where the company's employees can eat lunch? Such factors influence a company's ability to hire good people?

3. *Access to public transportation.* The importance of such access will vary with the building's location. If a suburban site far from public transportation is desired, presumably the tenant is aware that only employees who own cars or live nearby will care to work there. But never assume that a prospect has faced any specific issue squarely—bring up the matter. In a city location, access to public transportation is a plus because it enlarges the pool of potential employees by including those who cannot or will not commute to work by car.

4. *Construction.* Investigate the soundness of the building's construction. A consideration here will be the age of the building, since that will be a factor in assessing its soundness. Make a habit of talking with building contractors and architects. They can educate you on the relative merits of different types of construction and the differences among various building materials. Don't be afraid to ask—most people enjoy talking about matters in which they are considered expert. Learn about the reputations of various builders in your area so that you can begin making your own judgments about building quality. Challenge building managers to sell you on the merits of their buildings. The more you learn about construction, the better you will be able to judge the merits of a manager's selling job.

5. *Percentage of usable space.* Tenants must know how much of the rentable space is actually usable in order to have a true picture of what they are getting for their money. Usable space, you will recall, is that part of the space on which the tenant is paying rent that can actually be used as working office space.

If you have forgotten how to measure it, how to arrive at the percentage figure or how to figure what amount of the rent goes to pay for the load factor—or what the load factor is—review the first chapter. Enter only the percentage of usable space, but explain to the tenant what this figure represents and how to compute how much of the rent will be absorbed by the load factor. The tenant may want to incorporate this information into the economics form since it is essentially an economic factor.

6. *Core location.* This item should be used at your discretion. It will not be an important consideration for all tenants. But, as discussed earlier, a central-core location can be crucial to certain types of businesses as well as to lessees on multitenant floors.

7. *Core to window depth.* In evaluating core location, the distance from core to window wall is important to efficient space use. Remember that the bay depth range is 30–45 feet depending on the tenant's needs. For some tenants, 30–35 feet is ideal, while larger tenants will want the 40–45 foot range for optimum efficiency.

8. *Module size.* The distance between mullions, you will recall, helps define the length of one side of a module, which is of vital importance in situations where walls are going to be moved. A tenant desiring a number of ten-foot by 15-foot private offices, for example, will find space with five-foot modules ideal. Ask the building owner or architect early about module size. Factoring it into the overall picture at the last minute can cause unnecessary headaches.

9. *Interior columns.* If the office space has too many interior columns, or if their locations inhibit efficient space planning, regard them as a negative factor in your evaluation.

10. *Space-planning services.* Most owners pay for at least a preliminary space plan, but many offer no space-planning services beyond that. Find out in advance if you can about each owner's policy. On this as on several other factors, you may have to make an educated guess at this stage. Space planning may later become a subject for negotiation and the picture may change.

11. *Air conditioning.* Is air conditioning provided only during normal office hours, or is there 24-hour service? Is it provided on weekends? Is it a double- or single-duct system? Is it operated by equipment on the roof or in the basement? Is there good air circulation? Tenant needs vary widely. A company using computer equipment or a flexible time schedule may need 24-hour, year-round air conditioning in its computer area. A client who wants numerous conference rooms will need a superior system with a good exhaust capability.

When constructing air-conditioning systems, designers establish zones and allow a ratio of so many square feet per zone. About 700 square feet per zone is as high as the ratio should go. Discuss what, if anything, the owner will do to improve the air-conditioning system if it is inadequate for your client's needs.

You can't tell much about an air-conditioning system simply by walking around a building or even by exploring the space to be rented. You must get specific information from the building manager. Again, educate yourself. Talk with air-conditioning designers, salespeople and contractors. Learn the qualities of various systems, their modes of operation, costs and relative merits. This homework will teach you how to ask the right questions.

12. *Elevators.* To judge the adequacy and quality of elevator service in a building, determine the ratio of the number of elevators to the total square footage. Find the square footage of a typical floor, measuring it yourself if necessary. Multiply it by the number of floors, then divide the total number of elevators into that. A ratio of one elevator to every 35,000 square feet is adequate. Anything lower is not.

Elevator speed is another consideration. Owners frequently cut back on service by reducing the speed at which doors open and close and the speed at which the elevators ascend and descend. Observe the door opening and closing times. Ride the elevators to find out how long it takes to go up or down a certain number of floors. Some elevators are programmed to go automatically to heavily trafficked floors.

Learn about elevators from people who manufacture, install and service them. Study the factors that govern elevator capacity in a given building, and learn what determines the speed of particular elevator installations. Acquire a working knowledge of how the products are manufactured. Have manufacturers and retailers try to persuade you that their products are better than their competitors'. Their comparisons will teach you a great deal about the various products.

13. *Floor ducting.* Newer buildings often have electrified floors in which telephone and power lines run through ducts and emerge at frequent intervals. Such construction permits the addition of telephones and power outlets at almost any point with relative ease of installation. Obviously, this consideration is important for a tenant who needs a number of outlet changes. Such tenants are usually people-intensive businesses in which many telephones or outlets for other types of power equipment must be added.

14. *Life safety features and security.* Life safety features were discussed in detail earlier. In large, new buildings, printed information outlining the sophisticated fire-safety measures will probably be available. In smaller or older buildings, you will probably have to investigate these features firsthand. Inspect for fire alarms, smoke-detection devices, automatic sprinkler systems and posted instructions telling tenants what to do in case of fire. Check to see if stairwells are clearly marked. Ask the building management about elevator recall service in case

of fire. See if there is a provision for emergency power or a contingency plan that specially trained personnel will follow in case of emergency.

Investigate the building's security system. Some building managements take a casual attitude toward security. Others have well-planned systems and maintain lobby guards and other security personnel. Find out whether stairwells are kept locked and whether provisions have been made for the security of employee restrooms. Ask what protection is offered to employees who work later than regular office hours, and what arrangements they must make for entering and leaving the building at night or on weekends.

15. *Floor-load capacity.* Floor-load capacity may or may not be important to a particular tenant, but even when it matters it is often overlooked. If your tenant has a library or a printing press, make sure the floor will support the load.

16. *Ceilings.* What about ceilings, their height and their relationship to sound control? Learn about the various types of ceiling construction and their insulation qualities from ceiling contractors.

The exposed-T ceiling system is the cheapest, but has poor sound control. Sound rises to the metal T and is dispersed across the tops of partitions. This kind of ceiling would not be favored by attorneys, accountants or other professionals who usually insist on soundproofing. The concealed-spine ceiling system, on the other hand, is particularly soundproof. Here the ceiling recesses on top of the partition and sound cannot escape over the top.

Between eight feet, four inches and eight feet, six inches is considered a more or less standard height. Anything higher adds light and a feeling of spaciousness to the office and can be used as a selling point.

17. *Storage.* Certain businesses—for example, ones that process many business forms—may require an unusual amount of storage space. If your tenant is one of these, a higher-than-average storage capacity may tip the scales in that building's favor.

18, 19. *Draperies and floor coverings.* Although owners often furnish such extras as draperies and carpeting, if the space under consideration already contains these items in good condition, that fact is worth consideration. Acceptance of the present curtains and carpeting may free money for other tenant improvements.

20. *Parking.* Parking costs were discussed in the economics form. The quality form is concerned with parking convenience. How far is the parking lot or garage from the building entrance? Park and time yourself. If it takes you ten or fifteen minutes to get from your car to the building, the client will probably consider the setup inconvenient.

Also investigate parking facilities for visiting clients or delivery people from businesses serving the tenant. Can they use the building's facilities? If not, is street parking available for delivery people? Is there a commercial parking lot nearby for visiting customers?

21. *Expansion capacity.* Most tenants are growth-oriented and will want a location with some expansion capabilities. Will the owner offer an option or a first right of refusal on additional space? Are neighboring tenants under long-term leases, effectively eliminating the likelihood of your tenant's acquiring additional space? Talk to the building tenants as well as the owner or manager to get this information.

22. *Quality of ownership.* Find out what you can about the building's owner or owners and their reputation. If the building has changed hands several times recently, something is probably wrong. The owners may regard it as a tax shelter, a tax write-off or a means of quick return, rather than an investment. If so, tenant services are probably minimal and tenant turnover high.

    On the other hand, if the building is owned by a company that treats it as a long-term investment, it should be considered for a high rating on this factor.

23. *Quality of management.* Discuss the management with the building tenants. Visit the manager's office and try to ascertain his or her attitude toward tenant services. If the manager's office is located in the mechanical part of the building and you find the manager dressed in overalls whose pockets are bulging with tools, you can surmise that the building has management problems. This kind of manager usually does little more than tap on gauges to see that equipment is operating. He or she is unlikely to anticipate problems, and when they are pointed out, is probably slow to respond. This building most likely has a high tenant turnover.

    If, on the other hand, the manager is a professional who has been successful in attracting major companies to the building, knows and is friendly with the tenants, tries to facilitate business between tenants and anticipates problems and handles them promptly, give the management a high rating. A good manager will try to sell you on the building because he or she is proud of it.

24. *Quality of janitorial services.* One sure way to get an indication of the quality of janitorial services is to talk with the building's tenants. They will probably be happy to answer your questions. How frequent is the cleaning? How thorough is it? What are the cleaning hours? Find out who supplies the janitorial service and check on the contractor's reputation. Read the cleaning contract yourself—the manager or the owner should not object to your seeing it.

    When you have finished the quality form, you will have a graphic depiction of which features of which buildings deserve a better-than-average rating. This is confidential information. Guard the form carefully. Don't let it fall into a competitor's hands. It is just as important that building owners and managers not see it either—they wouldn't be pleased to discover that you have given their building a poor rating.

When you have completed the building economics comparison form and the building quality comparison form, you are ready to present your tenant with facts and figures on which to base an intelligent decision. But don't discuss these forms with the tenant until you have shown all the buildings under consideration.

A Constant Learning Process

You have discovered by now that providing service to an office-space client is no slapdash, hit-or-miss procedure. Obtaining and preparing data on buildings takes time. But it is essential to your job, and it pays off handsomely. You are in competition every day with experienced brokers from other firms. You must prove that you are better at your job than they are and that you can give your prospects more and better service. Thorough building analysis is an important part of that service.

Everything you learn about office-space marketing makes the task of building analysis that much easier. In your new profession, you will be involved in a constant learning process. You will learn from contractors and architects, from business and real estate journals. You will learn by joining civic groups and developing contacts with people in commerce and industry, in manufacturing and marketing and in service companies. You also will learn a great deal from other office-marketing sales representatives. They will not discuss their clients' business with you any more than you would discuss yours with them, but they'll be eager to talk about their jobs in general. Don't overlook opportunities to talk shop—about buildings, rental rates, business trends and other related matters—with real estate salespeople you meet in the normal course of business and even in your social life.

Exercise C

Answer the following questions.

1. What two factors must you consider in determining whether a tenant will incur parking costs and, if so, how much they will be?

2. What are three factors to assess with respect to building location?

3. Name three sources from whom you can acquire information on the soundness of a building's construction.

4. Define rentable as opposed to usable space.

5. Name two types of tenants to whom a central-core location is very important.

6. What is the ideal core-to-window measurement range?

7. What is an acceptable number of square feet per air-conditioning zone?

8. What is an acceptable ratio of elevators to square feet of floor space?

9. Name four fire precautions to look for when you inspect a building.

10. Why would a building that has frequently changed hands warrant a low rating?

11. What are three characteristics of good building management?

12. What is the fastest way to find out the quality of a building's janitorial services?

Answer C

1. *Consider (a) whether the owner will pay the parking costs or pass them along and (b) whether the tenant will pay any parking costs the owner charges or pass them on to employees.*

2. *Assess (a) the general suitability of the location to a particular client's needs, (b) the availability of restaurants that will serve both executive and general employee needs and (c) the building's proximity to public transportation.*

3. *Ask (a) the owner, (b) the architect and (c) the building manager.*

4. *Rentable space is all space the tenant will be charged rent on. Usable space—usually a smaller area—is what the tenant can actually use as office space.*

5. *A central-core location is important to (a) tenants who need a proportionately large number of private offices with windows and (b) tenants who will be sharing a floor with other tenants.*

6. *The range is from 30–45 feet, depending on the tenant.*

7. *About 700 square feet per zone is acceptable.*

8. *One elevator for every 35,000 square feet of floor space is acceptable.*

9. *Look for (a) fire alarms, (b) smoke detectors, (c) automatic sprinklers, and (d) posted instructions telling tenants what to do in case of fire.*

10. *It is an indication that the owner is using the building for a short-term money-making scheme such as a tax write-off or tax shelter instead of as a long-term investment.*

11. *Here are five:*
    a. *The building has several major companies as tenants.*
    b. *The manager is friendly and knows the tenants.*
    c. *The manager tries to promote business among the tenants.*
    d. *The manager anticipates problems and handles them promptly.*
    e. *The manager tries to sell you on the building because he or she is proud of it.*

12. *Ask the building tenants.*

SPACE PLANNING

In today's sophisticated and highly competitive office-marketing atmosphere, office-space planning must be closely geared to the type of business involved, and space layout must take into consideration not only physical factors but such psychological factors as prestige and employee morale as well.

This section will present some of the specifics you should know about, both the quantitative and the qualitative aspects of space planning. It will offer guides for estimating square-footage needs for different types of office areas and will consider the evaluation of space in terms of nonphysical factors like location and the desirability of the other tenants. It will also discuss your role in working with a professional space planner.

You are not expected to be an expert in space planning, and much of this material is included merely to give you a feel for the space requirements of various office operations. Yet, you must have enough knowledge of the field to be able to work in harmony with a professional space planner if you are to be of maximum service to prospects. You also must know how to use space planning as a marketing tool in negotiations.

A Quantitative Guide

To understand a tenant's space needs, you must know not only the nature of the client's business, but something about the company hierarchy as well—how many people work at each level and the general nature of the tasks they perform.

You will need to know three categories of information about a company before you can determine its space needs.

1. *Business lifestyle.* A company wishing to project a prestige image or even one that wants to convey a casual image—an advertising agency—may be willing to assign space more liberally, even to lower-echelon employees.

2. *Hierarchical structure.* If the number of executives and supervisors in proportion to support personnel is high, a greater need exists for private offices and window areas and probably for greater space overall.

3. *Need for nonstandard space.* Some businesses rely on specialized equipment or personnel or both. Publishing companies, for example, may need one or more computer areas to service their circulation department and a microfilm storage area for their editorial operations. Certain other companies will require space for engineers and draftspeople and their bulky special equipment.

A Qualitative Guide

Don't restrict the discussion of your tenant's needs to the amount of space required. Tenants are often more comfortable talking about quantitative space needs, because these are tangible, measurable features. Tenants consider the quality of space important, but they may simply assume that you know they want a prestige location, a certain distance from their competition or some other intangible features, when you actually have no way of knowing about these qualitative requirements unless you ask. Here are some of the questions you should ask your tenants concerning the quality of space.

1. What image does the business wish to project? Some companies never ask themselves the question. Some will not think it important even after you bring it up. Your purpose is to uncover which tenants consider image important so you can factor their desires into your space search.

2. What about the other tenants on a multitenant floor or in the building? The company may not want to share a floor or building with certain types of tenants or with competitors. Or the tenant may not care what the other tenants' businesses are but may be very concerned that too high a density will cause congestion in elevators, hallways and rest rooms.

3. Is an attractive view or address important? A view or particular address are essential to some tenants who can afford a prestigious location.

You will acquire the ability to sense successful tenant combinations as you become more familiar with different types of business operations. Most tenants looking for prestigious quarters want to be in a building with other prestige tenants. Professionals like doctors, lawyers and public accountants may not object if the other prestige tenants are their competitors. On the other hand, some prestige customers may have reservations not only about the type of businesses with which they share a building but even about the kinds of customers who visit those businesses.

A company that supplies a specialty convenience service and counts on other tenants in the building or upon impulse buying for much of its trade will find competitors as neighbors especially objectionable. A flower shop is an example of such a tenant.

The presence of a particular company can make a building attractive to tenants who supply services to that company. A small printing operation, for example, might want to locate in the same building as a law firm that is a potential customer. The presence of a large advertising agency would appeal to suppliers such as commercial artists, music arrangers and recording studios. These smaller companies are not looking for prestige by association. They simply see the practical benefits of proximity to a potential source of new business.

In evaluating office space for single-tenant or multitenant floors, remember what you learned earlier about building cores. If you are seeking space for a tenant who plans to occupy only part of a floor, try to find a building with a centrally located core, where your client can obtain a maximum of window exposure and a minimum of hallway and other nonusable space. The corner areas of a building are generally the most desirable.

Remember, too, that such buildings are preferred for single-tenant-floor users who need many private offices and that 30–45 feet from outer core wall to window wall provides the most efficient space for such tenants. On the other hand, people-intensive companies—as well as those needing special facilities such as lunchrooms or lounge areas, storage areas or large filing and equipment areas—may be able to utilize large spaces away from windows very efficiently. Figure 6–5 presents an analysis of the importance of different building features to different kinds of tenants.

Working with Space Planners

Space planners are professionals, often specialized architects, who design floor layouts. They will draw preliminary space plans for clients, often at the owners' expense. If tenants want a space planner to develop the preliminary space plan into a set of working drawings, however, usually they must foot the bill. Working drawings indicate all the details of agreed-upon improvements, from electrical and power outlets to the type of wall construction. Contractors build in the tenant improvements from these drawings.

Smaller companies often think they cannot afford these extra space-planning services, but professional space planning may save them money in the end. When the cost per square foot of the new space is higher than that of the old (a situation that is almost automatic in inflationary times), a space planner can often show tenants how to use space more efficiently. This may enable them to acquire less space than originally needed, and they might end up paying no more, or only slightly more, rent in spite of the higher unit rate. Or a higher total rent may be more than offset by increased work efficiency. Use these advantages as selling points if you honestly believe that a particular tenant will benefit from space planning.

Often the owner or developer will pay for all space-planning services, particularly if you have an exclusive on the building and a thoroughly qualified tenant who is very serious about moving in. If you suspect the owner can be persuaded to provide such extra space planning, chalk this up as a possible concession. But before mentioning it to your tenant, know exactly how far the owner is likely to go. This is part of qualifying the owner.

The space planner for any given building will often be a person the owner has worked with before and will probably be familiar with the building. Meet the planner early, and make it clear that you control the situation and that contacts between the space planner and the tenant will be coordinated through you. You want to begin in control and remain in control throughout. Some companies will want to do their own space planning. The disadvantage of this is that a planner hired by a prospective tenant will not be familiar with the building you're promoting. He or she also may be more difficult to control. The advantage is that a tenant's space planner should understand thoroughly the tenant's wants and needs.

After you have made a preliminary survey of a qualified tenant's space needs and he or she has expressed strong interest, you are ready to consult a space planner and begin to develop more detailed specifications. Once the services of a space planner have been agreed upon, the next step is for the planner to survey on the spot the tenant's present location and use of space. The planner needs to know the tenant's operation and goals to determine how much open and enclosed space the tenant needs, the size of offices desired, special needs such as library space and conference rooms and access and circulation problems. Then the planner will match the tenant's needs to the configuration of the building under consideration. After completing the survey, the space

FIGURE 6.5   Importance of Building Features to Tenant Types

IMPORTANCE OF FEATURES TO TENANT TYPES

H – High A – Average L – Low	BUILDING IMAGE	CONFIGURATION	ELEVATOR	HVAC	LOCATION	MAINTENANCE	SECURITY	SERVICES	STANDARDS	UTILITY DISTRIBUTION
ACCOUNTING OFFICE	A	H	H	H	A	H	H	H	A	H
ADVERTISING AGENCY OFFICE	H	A	A	H	A	H	L	L	A	L
AIRLINE OR TRAVEL BUREAU	L	L	L	H	L	A	L	L	H	L
ARCHITECTURE OR ENGINEERING OFFICE	A	H	A	H	A	A	H	L	H	H
CORPORATE HEADQUARTERS	H	A	A	H	H	H	H	H	H	L
DESIGN OR GRAPHIC SERVICES	A	H	A	H	H	A	L	L	L	H
INSURANCE BROKER	A	A	L	H	A	A	L	L	A	L
INSURANCE CO. AGENCY	L	H	H	H	A	A	A	H	A	H
INVESTMENT BANKER'S BROKER	H	A	A	H	A	A	H	A	A	H
LAW OFFICE	H	H	A	H	H	H	H	A	H	A
PROFESSIONAL OR BUSINESS CONSULTANT	H	A	A	H	H	A	L	L	A	L
PUBLISHER'S OFFICE	H	A	A	H	L	H	L	L	A	L
REAL ESTATE RELATED COMPANY	A	L	L	H	A	A	L	L	A	L
REGIONAL OFFICE	A	L	A	H	H	A	L	A	L	L
SERVICE INDUSTRY OFFICE	A	L	A	H	L	A	L	L	L	H

FIGURE 6.5   (continued)

GUIDE TO INTENSITY OF SPACE USAGE

	ACTIVE FILING AREAS	CLERICAL SPACES	CONFERENCE AREAS	EMPLOYEE LUNCH OR LOUNGE AREAS	EQUIPMENT ORIENTED SPACES	SPECIAL FACILITIES	PRIVATE OFFICE	RECEPTION AREAS	SECRETARIAL SPACES	SUPPLIERS OR DEAD FILE STORAGE AREAS	TECHNICAL SUPERVISORY OFFICE
ACCOUNTING OFFICE	A	H	A	A	A	L	A	A	A	L	A
ADVERTISING AGENCY OFFICE	L	L	A	H	L	L	A	A	A	L	H
AIRLINE OR TRAVEL BUREAU	L	L	L	L	L	L	L	L	L	L	A
ARCHITECTURE OR ENGINEERING OFC.	A	L	A	L	A	L	L	A	L	L	H
CORPORATE HEADQUARTERS	H	A	H	A	L	L	H	H	H	L	L
DESIGN GRAPHIC SERVICES	L	L	A	L	A	L	A	A	A	L	H
INSURANCE BROKER	L	L	L	L	L	L	H	A	H	L	L
INSURANCE AGENCY	A	L	A	L	A	L	L	A	A	L	A
INVESTMENT BANKER'S BROKER	L	L	L	L	H	L	L	A	A	L	A
LAW OFFICE	H	L	H	H	L	H	H	H	H	A	L
PROFESSIONAL OR BUSINESS CONSULTANT	A	L	H	L	L	L	A	H	H	L	L
PUBLISHER'S OFFICE	A	L	A	L	L	L	A	H	A	L	H
REAL ESTATE RELATED COMPANY	L	L	A	L	L	L	A	L	A	L	A
REGIONAL OFFICE	A	L	L	L	L	L	H	A	H	A	A
SERVICE INDUSTRY OFFICE	L	H	L	L	H	A	A	L	A	L	L
TRADE OR PROFESSIONAL ORGANIZATION	A	A	L	L	L	L	H	A	H	L	L

FIGURE 6.5 **(concluded)**

GUIDE TO TENANT COMPATIBILITY CRITERIA

	BUSINESS IMAGE	CLERICAL EXECUTIVE RELATIONSHIP	CLIENT IMAGE	COMPETITION	FLOOR POPULATION	VIEW
ACCOUNTING OFFICE	A	L	A	H	H	A
ADVERTISING AGENCY OFFICE	H	L	A	H	A	A
AIRLINE OR TRAVEL BUREAU	A	L	A	H	L	L
ARCHITECTURE OR ENGINEERING OFC.	H	A	A	H	H	L
CORPORATE HEADQUARTERS	H	A	H	L	L	H
DESIGN OR GRAPHIC SERVICES	H	A	A	H	A	L
INSURANCE BROKER	A	L	A	H	L	A
INSURANCE COMPANY AGENCY	H	L	L	H	H	A
INVESTMENT BANKER'S BROKER	H	L	A	L	A	H
LAW OFFICE	H	H	H	H	A	H
PROFESSIONAL OR BUSINESS CONSULTANT	H	H	H	H	A	H
PUBLISHER'S OFFICE	H	H	H	L	L	H
REAL ESTATE RELATED COMPANY	A	A	H	H	L	A
REGIONAL OFFICE	A	L	H	H	L	A
SERVICE INDUSTRY OFFICE	L	L	L	H	L	L
TRADE OR PROFESSIONAL ORGANIZATION	H	A	L	L	L	A

planner will make working drawings, which usually must be revised several times before the tenant is satisfied.

Once the working drawings have been completed and the lease negotiated, the space planner may continue to work directly for the tenant, developing detailed plans for special purpose areas and dividers, paneling, carpeting, furnishings and so on. The extent to which this occurs is sometimes governed by the amount of money the owner will allow for improvements and the number of improvements over standard involved.

Space planners help you to sell tenants on your buildings. You have mastered the overall ideas and procedures involved in space planning. Planners help you get more specific and detailed information, matching the particular tenant's needs to the building under consideration.

Exercise D

Answer the following questions.

1. The _____ aspects of space planning are concerned with measurable space.

2. The _____ aspects of space planning are concerned with such intangibles as image, prestige and location.

3. What are the three categories of information you need to know before you can determine a business's space needs?

4. A professional space planner can help you sell a tenant on a building because:
   a. the planner helps you learn techniques of space planning.
   b. the planner helps you to know your tenant better.
   c. the planner helps you provide service.
   d. the planner gives you vital information to help sell the tenant.

5. Space planners always:
   a. submit layouts up to working drawings.
   b. are employed by the owner.
   c. survey the tenant's needs.
   d. are in your employ.

6. The astute office-leasing salesperson will:
   a. be able to do the required space planning.
   b. control the space-planning activity.
   c. avoid the space-planning issue whenever possible.
   d. let the prospective tenant and the space planner work out their own agreement.

Answer D

You should have answered: (1) quantitative, (2) qualitative, (3) the business's lifestyle, hierarchical structure and need for nonstandard space, (4) d, (5) c and (6) b.

Closing Techniques

You have worked on a particular transaction for many weeks ironing out all negotiating points between tenant and owner. It is now time to turn your weeks of negotiation into a signed lease to prepare and present the tenant's offer. Make sure the tenant is prepared for you to make the presentation, then call the owner for an appointment.

Follow these three rules in presenting offers:

1. Never present an offer until you are thoroughly prepared.

2. Present all offers as promptly as possible after preparing yourself.

3. Never present your offer or any part of it over the telephone. Facing the owner in person facilitates your control of the situation.

Preparation

First, make sure the listing has not expired. When you are in the midst of a complicated negotiation you can lose track of time, and a listing may expire before you realize it. If this happens, immediately ask the owner to sign a new exclusive or commission agreement before you reveal any information.

Next, run a last-minute check on all data relevant to the transaction. Review the listing file to see the number of times the property has been shown, how many ads have been run and the details of the other offers made. Include this information in your presentation. Reminding the owner of your interest and hard work on this deal may make him or her more receptive.

Then put in writing all the relevant facts that have come up during your conversations with tenant and owner. You will probably have approached the owner on several occasions with new negotiating points that have eventually been resolved. But this will be his or her first opportunity to hear all the information about the offer at one time. The picture can look quite different under these circumstances. Whether it appeals to the owner or not will depend in large part on your presentation.

Presentation

Approach the presentation appointment assuming that you are about to succeed in making a sale or lease. When you arrive, take whatever steps are necessary to make sure you will have the owner's full attention. Suggest that you go to a conference room or other quiet area. This will discourage the owner from receiving telephone calls or other interruptions during your presentation. Appear relaxed when presenting the offer. Make your presentation in terms of the owner's self-interest, but do not oversell. Under no circumstances should you mislead the owner.

Encourage the owner to interrupt you with questions, and answer them thoroughly. Begin your presentation with minor points on which you are sure you will get the owner's agreement. This will put you and the owner on the same side to start with. Introduce controversial items last, and always stress anything in the deal that will work to the owner's benefit.

When you have finished your presentation, say something like this: "Have I made everything clear, Mr. Jones, or do you have some more questions?"

If there are no questions, hand Jones the written offer and say, "As long as you have no further questions, please approve the offer by authorizing it here." Then be quiet until the owner either signs or speaks. If he signs, great! If he refuses, get him to be as explicit as possible about what his objections are. This will help you a great deal when you go back to the tenant, or, if necessary, look for a new tenant.

Don't hand the owner your written offer until the end of the presentation. If you bring it out too early, he or she may insist on reading it immediately, and you will have destroyed your presentation.

FOLLOW UP

You have now brought together two people who, if you play your cards right, will both become permanent sources of new leads—either by recommending your services to others or by seeking you out themselves at some future time. But don't wait for them to come to you with leads. Telephone both parties a few days after the lease has been signed and ask if all is going well. This is an ideal time to ask for leads.

Continue to follow up periodically when a suitable occasion presents itself, such as the anniversary of the tenant's moving day.

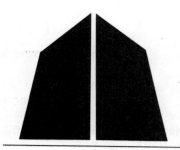

Telephone Techniques

INTRODUCTION

In recent years many companies have doubled and tripled their telephone bills. They have done so simply because the telephone has become an indispensable tool for conducting business. Thus, it is important that you develop the ability to use the telephone effectively. You have to know how to gather and present information by telephone as transactions develop. You should be able to use the telephone to initially qualify prospects and to make appointments with qualified individuals.

The one result you will not achieve on the telephone is the completion of a transaction or a sale. The complexities of the real estate business demand that such procedures be handled only on a direct, face-to-face basis.

If you make most initial contacts with businesses in person, you will use the telephone mostly to follow up after your initial contacts have been made and business has been generated. (For in-person cold-calling techniques, see chapter five.)

The telephone is the one tool of office real estate sales that we all think we know how to use correctly. And yet, the mere fact that you use the telephone many times each day for an assortment of purposes doesn't automatically equip you to use it effectively in the office marketplace.

The purpose of this chapter is to (1) familiarize you with effective telephone procedures for the general use of the telephone and (2) give you a strategy to use when it becomes necessary for you to use the telephone to make initial contacts or cold calls.

EFFECTIVE TELEPHONE PROCEDURES

Two salespeople in a real estate office have desks that look identical. The desks are cluttered with similar assortments of papers and files, and on each desk there is a worn-looking black telephone.

Smith, who sits at one of the two desks, is known around town as a powerful, productive salesperson. The other person, Hughes, isn't known very widely, and those who have done business with him consider him mediocre. Smith is prospering as an office salesperson. Hughes is just getting by.

For Hughes, using the telephone is a casual, impulsive activity that occurs when the mood hits him. Some of his telephone calls get good results, but many leave him feeling frustrated and leave the person he called feeling annoyed.

For Smith, telephoning is a highly organized, carefully planned part of her daily routine. Smith makes more calls than Hughes and a higher percentage of those calls get the results she wants. One reason is that Smith follows a set of effective calling procedures that govern her overall use of the telephone.

Your aim is to learn how salespeople like Smith handle overall telephone use, so that you can effectively use these methods for the many different kinds of calls you will make as an office salesperson. You should think about and develop a habit of using the procedures discussed in this chapter.

Plan Your Calls

Set your goal and know what you are going to say before you put through your call. Make a list of questions you are going to ask, the information you are going to convey and the agreements you want. Be sure to have any documents or reference materials at hand. Keep your plan simple and choose a single goal to achieve on each telephone call. Remember, a telephone conversation is almost always brief, and this means that complex plans with many goals are doomed to failure before they get off the ground.

Schedule Your Telephone Activity

Establish a specific time period (or perhaps two time periods) each day for making your calls. This should be a time when the people you are calling are likely to be available, and it should fit in well with the rest of your daily routine.

Determine how many calls you are able to make during that period if you do nothing else. Then, establish this number as the standard you will always expect to meet.

You may find it useful to group the persons or companies you plan to call according to the purpose of the call. That is, divide your list among potential prospects you are calling more or less blindly, those people you know have property to move, those who might need more space and other groups. Then stay with one group until you have exhausted that part of your list. You may, of course, devote the entire time to calling the numbers on one particular list. The important thing, in any case, is that your opening sentence or question vary, if necessary, from group to group. Categorizing the prospects by type of business, type of needs and so forth makes it easier for you to get your lead statement or question across. You will not need to shift gears with every call.

Clear away all other work and distractions for the period of time you will be making calls. Do not let yourself be interrupted. Effective calls are not made on a hit or miss basis or in an offhand manner. They require concentration. They must be the only business at hand at the time you set aside for them.

Make Each Call to the Point

Assume that the person you are calling is busy. You certainly are. Get immediately to the point of your call. Chitchat about personal things, the weather or the like simply wastes time. Idle conversation has nothing to do with the point of your call. Carry out your plan, make your point and say goodbye. Never force the other person to end the call because you are rambling on.

Use the Call-Back Technique

Do not try to interrupt a person in the midst of an important transaction or conference. If he or she is tied up, the secretary will say so. If the person you want is not available, you can either call back or have him or her call you.

If the prospect will be available in a short time or later in the day, identify yourself and tell the secretary that you will call back. Be sure to say when. Make a note of the time and follow up without fail at that time. If the prospect is not available until the next day or later, leave a message for him or her to call you, giving your number to the secretary. Do not, however, state your reason for calling. This is something you want to talk to the prospect about, not the secretary. It is a waste of time to go through the procedure twice.

In general, the record of call-backs, both for cold calls and follow-up calls, is excellent. Don't wait forever for the return call. Make a note as to when the person is supposed to call back. If he or she does not, call again.

Make Your Call Enthusiastic but Clear

Part of establishing good rapport is the tone of voice you use and the rate at which you speak. Speak confidently and courteously but with enthusiasm. Modulate your voice so you aren't speaking with a monotone. Adjust your speed to the other person's and to the complexity of the information you are presenting. If you speak quickly to a slow thinker, you will fail to communicate. If you speak slowly to a fast thinker, you will also fail to communicate because he or she will be thinking of other things while listening to you. Complicated ideas should be presented more slowly and carefully than simple ones if they are to be understood and accepted.

Learn to Listen

Among the four communication skills—reading, writing, speaking and listening—listening is the one most frequently neglected. Too often one concentrates so hard on what one is going to say next that he or she fails to pay attention to what the other person is saying. To insure proper understanding, restate questions or comments so that both parties understand and are talking about the same thing. Listening is a skill that can be learned. If you have not mastered it, your calls are not as effective as they could be. A salesperson who has honed listening skill to a fine point earns more appointments and more business than one who has not. As a start in learning how to listen, simply learn when to be quiet.

Don't interrupt your prospect and don't finish the prospect's sentences. Both types of behavior indicate that you are not listening and are not really interested in what the other party has to say. If the prospect gets this impression, the deal is dead. You have wasted the prospect's time and yours and the prospect will not forget it. You might as well cross that person off your list. If the person speaks slowly, be patient. If a party hesitates in choosing words, let him or her find them. Remember, you are after business, which means a commission for you. You do not earn it by showing how bright you are with words or how large your vocabulary is. You earn your commission by first listening for needs and then fulfilling them.

Control the Call

Some executives, judging from the length of time they will talk with you about nonessentials, give the impression that they have little else to do. Perhaps this is true of them, but it certainly is not the case with you. If the prospect wanders from the point of your call, bring him or her back. If, once the business is finished, the prospect prolongs the call with irrelevant discussion, find a way to bring it to a close quickly. Do not, of course, be offensive. Close the conversation firmly, but courteously. Time is money to you.

Confirm All Important Points Made in a Call

Confirm appointments as you close the conversation, repeating the time and day on which you will appear in the prospect's office. For example, you might say: "Very good. I'll see you at 11:00 o'clock tomorrow morning." Also confirm schedules, deadlines, places, names of people—anything that will directly affect your real estate deal.

Keep Score

Keep a record of the calls you make each week and the number of appointments resulting from them. Try to improve your score each week.

STRATEGY FOR COLD CALLS

The strategy for telephone cold calls differs somewhat from that of cold calling in person. The major difference is that a telephone cold call results in an appointment for an interview, and an in-person cold call results in an immediate interview.

There are seven major steps in the telephone cold call strategy.

1. Get to the decision maker as quickly as possible.

2. Identify yourself and your company before you are asked.

3. Explain why you are calling.

4. State a benefit of the meeting you wish to arrange.

5. Ask for an appointment.

6. Be ready to counter objections.

7. Follow up.

Get to the Decision Maker as Quickly as Possible

If your purpose is to move a particular listing or group of listings, call user companies that are most likely to be interested in the location and the type of building that you have available.

The person you want to talk with when you are promoting listings is the one who makes the company's real estate decisions. Your company should maintain a file listing the names of the real estate managers of all major corporations. If you are calling a large company, therefore, you will probably have the name of the right person to ask for.

If you are calling to obtain a listing on a vacant building or to inquire about a vacant piece of property, talk with the owner. Real estate ownership is a matter of public record, and your company may maintain a list of property owners. Names are also easily obtained from the office of the register of deeds.

If you do not have the name of a particular person and are calling the office of a large company, chances are you will be going through a switchboard. In this case, ask to be connected with the person in charge of real estate for the company. You will be put through, and the switchboard operator will probably give you the person's name. If not, ask for it. If you fail to ask or if the operator does not know the name but puts you through to the real estate department, you certainly will have a name when a secretary answers the telephone.

In a small company, the president usually makes real estate decisions. This is the person with whom you will want to talk. Your initial contact in a small company might be the receptionist rather than a switchboard operator. When cold calling in person, the receptionist is the first person you must get past. This is easier to accomplish on the telephone than in person. Whereas a receptionist might prove a roadblock to a call in person, he or she will usually put through a telephone call without question. If you have no specific name to ask for, simply ask to speak with the president, and then get the name from the receptionist.

Note that it is a good idea to master the pronunciation of a name before being put through to the person. Mispronouncing a person's name is no way to begin a conversation. Knowing the name (and being able to pronounce it properly) is of particular importance when dealing with executives who answer their own telephones, as some do. So, get the name from the switchboard operator or the receptionist. If it is unfamiliar, ask to have it spelled and pronounced, and write it down. If you are being put through to a woman, note if she prefers Miss, Mrs. or Ms. before her name.

Identify Yourself and Your Company before You Are Asked

Most secretaries will ask who is calling before putting a call through. Your best strategy is to take the initiative and identify yourself and your company before you are challenged.

Explain Why You Are Calling

When you are connected with the person you want to talk with, identify yourself again. The next step is vitally important, for here you get to the nub of your call. You want to establish rapport, but at the same time, you want to be brief and move immediately to the purpose of your call.

In office leasing, you are trying to find either space for a tenant, available space that you can list or a prospective tenant. Experienced office-leasing salespeople have found three openers to be very effective in getting to the point with a prospect:

1. "I am calling to inquire whether you have any space to sublease."

With this particular opening, if you receive a "yes," you move to present benefits. If you receive a "no," you ask, "Do you need additional space?" A "yes" would be the signal to move forward with the call. A "no" might trigger some questions tied to the in-person cold-calling approach such as "How long have you been in this place?" "How much longer does your lease run?" "Do you have other space requirements in another office?" "Are you paying market rents?"

This approach can be used when you don't know the needs of the prospect you are calling. It allows you to qualify the prospect either way—need space or fill space.

If the company has no space to sublease and does not need more space at the present time, your call still has accomplished some important goals: (1) You have gathered information, even though it might be negative; (2) you have made the person aware of your company and some of the services it offers; (3) you have an individual's name and that of a company that might be worth calling again some time in the future; (4) you have found out the lease expiration date and other important plans of the company.

2. "Congratulations on your increased revenue." (Comment on the news.) "Is this going to cause you to grow and need more space?"

With this particular opening, if you receive a "yes," you move on in the sales process. If you receive a "no," use the same procedure as above. This approach is obviously used to help you develop tenants who need space.

3. "I noticed the property at (address) was vacant. Were you planning to sell or lease it?"

A "yes" takes you on in the sales process, a "no" to "thank you, goodbye."

Your objective here is to gain an appointment for listing the property or having your company's sign put up. Before making a call of this type, you should check your company's property file to find out what other properties the person or company owns. They may be ripe for listing.

Perhaps you've seen a building with other realtors' signs on it. In that case, as above, your objective will be to get the listing for your company and erect your sign. Your lead sentence then will be related to the fact that the property is for lease.

State a Benefit of the Meeting You Wish to Arrange

So far, you have explained that you work for a real estate firm, and the prospect has explained that he or she has a real estate need. Now you have to give the prospect a reason for meeting you face to face. You have to promise a potential benefit, or the prospect will not grant the request you are about to make, which is to set up an appointment. Experienced office-leasing salespeople have found the following two benefit statements to be very effective.

1. "Ms. Prospect, I have some tenants who are looking for space in your general area."

2. "Mr. Prospect, my company has a large number of listings of properties available in this area."

Ask for an Appointment

Asking for an appointment is more than just saying you want to get together. You have to explain what you will do when you get together and also suggest a time. When suggesting a time be sure to give the prospect an alternative. This prevents the prospect from saying no. The prospect must explain, and it is usually easier to explain why one of the times is most convenient.

"What we should do is get together to discuss your space needs and look over our listings to find the ones that would fit your needs best. We could then go out to see them. Which would be a better time to get together, tomorrow morning at 11:30 or in the afternoon around 3:15?"

Giving such specific alternative times is a technique used by some salespeople to do two things: (1) immediately pin down the individual to a specific time, and (2) convey that you are efficient and organized, working on a highly programmed schedule and will be precise in getting the meeting completed quickly.

Be Ready to Counter Objections

By planning answers to standard objections you will be prepared to handle them fluently and effectively. Here are a few objections you might hear:

- "The company might need more space, but everyone is too busy to think about it right now."

Zero in on time. Stress the obvious need for long-range planning to save time. To get started on that planning with your help would take only a few minutes of the person's time. If a prospect remains adamantly opposed to considering specific future space needs, try to get the present square footage and configuration requirements and at least an estimate as to how much additional space might be needed. At the very least in a situation like this, you can send brochures on a property that might be suitable and get the person started thinking about you and your company. Later, follow up.

- "Cost is a real problem. I can't afford more space now."

This might lead you in one of several directions. First of all, it is essential that you know the market and know the specific area in which the company you are calling operates. It is up to you to demonstrate that a price represents the current market price for whatever type of building, business or location is under discussion. Do not offer to obtain space for less than the going rate in your eagerness to make a deal. And never be precise about rates. When you mention a range, your prospect will expect to get the minimum rate.

You may be promoting a new building in which space is going at a rate higher than an older building. In that case, stress the likely increased productivity of new facilities and their economies such as lower maintenance costs.

A company or a person with space to lease, sublease or sell, might have a price in mind higher than the market will bear. Here again, you must know the market. It is a foolish waste of time to take a listing at a price you know will prevent the property from moving. Never promise something you are not sure you can deliver. Never offer to obtain a price you know is too high. If a person will not accept the realities of the marketplace, you are much better off without the listing.

- "This space is perfect for us, but we can't wait four months to move in."

You might not be able to do anything about this. Yet, few things are impossible to change. Find out what possession time the prospective tenant has in mind. Find out if the present occupant is flexible. You can also represent the tenant in finding other properties that might suit him or her.

- "I do have space to lease, but I've been working with Oakleaf Real Estate."

Your question is, "Is that listing exclusive?" In all likelihood it is not. Your task then is to persuade the prospect that your company can do a better job of moving the property than any other company—although you should not go about this by downgrading the competition. Take a positive approach. Stress your company's reputation and performance record and the services it offers. Then work for an appointment to get the listing.

- "We're really looking for a very particular kind of space that you probably can't supply."

Assure the tenant that you have all kinds of listings. You can demonstrate this during the course of a brief appointment. At the least, you can mail brochures after getting specifications from the person to whom you are talking. Then follow up the mailings with another telephone call.

- "This building is just too big for our needs."

Here again, stress your many listings and knowledge of the marketplace. Ask the tenant what the specific requirements are. Get an appointment to go over those requirements in detail at the tenant's present location. It is not wise simply to take a person's word about space needs. It is quite possible that the tenant may be mistaken. You cannot tell, however, until you see what the tenant has and his or her methods of operation. You can do this only on the spot, through a personal inspection.

- "I don't have time to discuss real estate now. Call me later."

You want to know when. But you don't ask the prospect. Instead, you give him or her a choice of times that you might call. "Shall I call on Wednesday morning or Thursday afternoon?" The prospect will usually choose one. If neither time suits the prospect, offer two others.

- "I don't have time to discuss space now. I'll call you."

The prospect may or may not. Try to pin down a time that the call will be made. If this fails and the prospect does not call within a reasonable period of time, call the prospect back. You must judge what a reasonable time is.

The point with respect to objections, as with all other factors in a telephone call, is this: You stay in charge of the situation. Do not let control slip into the hands of the person you are calling. That is a sure avenue to wasted time and no business.

- "I've always worked with National Realty, and I'd just as soon continue with them."

You might not hear this objection frequently, but it will come up from time to time. Certainly, you will not want to knock the other firm. Simply point out the advantages of working with a company of the size, type and location of yours and with your company's reputation, record and services. Ask for an appointment to explain all this in more detail. Stress the value to the prospect of having access to your services in addition to the other firm's. If all else fails, send the prospect company brochures, then follow up.

Follow Up

How many follow-up calls you make during the course of a transaction and what their nature will be, depends entirely on the situation in question. You might make several follow-up calls as the need for additional information or appointments arises, as you progress toward closing a deal. The follow-up call, on the other hand, might be well in the future. A company with no unsatisfied real estate needs today might be the one interested in making a deal tomorrow. Many of the techniques and procedures involved in effective telephone cold calling apply equally to follow-up calls.

The following points summarize the effective procedures that pertain especially to telephone cold calls. Be sure you understand them clearly.

SUMMARY OF EFFECTIVE PROCEDURES

Planning

Make a list of persons or companies you are going to call during a certain period of time, and if possible group them. That is, divide your list among prospects you are calling blind, those whom you know have property to move, those who might need more space and other groups. Then, stay with one group until you have exhausted that part of your list. Your lead sentence or question will probably vary from group to group. Categorizing the prospects as to type of business, type of needs, and so forth, makes it easier for you to get your lead statement or questions across. You will not have to shift gears with every call.

Have your opener ready before you place each call. Prepare the questions you are going to ask. Be ready to counter objections. Plan to ask for an appointment. Know how you will lead up to that request, and set the time.

Naturally, you should have some idea of the geographic areas in which the companies you are calling operate. You also should have some idea about the types of businesses in which they are engaged and the general real estate situation and needs of such businesses.

Practice and Regularity for Perfection

Set aside a regular time for making calls. Decide how many you are going to make during each session. Then, during that time do nothing but make calls. Do not stop until you have completed all the calls you planned to make. When you stay with the task until it is finished, your telephone calling tends to be smoother and more productive.

Technicalities

Do not go deeply into technicalities on the telephone. Don't get bogged down in them. With an interested prospect, you will sometimes need to discuss amenities, location and so on. But these should only be touched on. The proper time for extended discussion about technical matters is during an appointment with the prospect. Dwelling on technicalities on the telephone is a waste of time.

Your Final Comment in Every Call

Thank the person you called. The prospect has taken the time to talk and listen to you and has given you a chance to present yourself, your company and your product. Thank the prospect for that.

Keeping Score

Keep a record of the calls you make each week and the number of appointments resulting from them. Try to improve your score each week.

Exercise A

1. What is the goal of a telephone cold call?
2. What are the three rules of effective telephone cold calling?
3. Why is it a good idea to group your calls by type of prospect?
4. Why is it important to keep chitchat to a minimum?
5. What is the final step of any telephone cold call?

Answer A

1. *The goal of a telephone cold call is to obtain an appointment to meet the prospect.*

2. *The three rules are: (1) schedule your telephone calling activities; (2) plan your calls; (3) keep score.*

3. *By grouping your calls, you can develop a smooth and effective opening without having to shift gears with each call.*

4. *Both your time and the prospect's time are valuable. You cannot afford to waste time on things that do not advance you toward your goal.*

5. *You must end each call by confirming the date, time and place of the appointment if you were successful in obtaining one. Thank the prospect for his or her time.*

8

Negotiation

INTRODUCTION

A real estate transaction begins when you find a potential tenant. It ends with a signed lease or sale agreement and a commission for you. The middle part of the transaction is the area of negotiation, that is, the area of bringing owner and lessee or buyer together to mutually satisfactory terms.

Negotiation is a complex art that can be mastered through study, practice and role playing. This chapter can only get you started down the path of understanding negotiation and developing your skill at it. Upon completing the chapter you should understand the importance of negotiation in developing a transaction, be aware of some negotiation techniques and appreciate some of the problems and pitfalls of the process.

Beyond this chapter it is up to you. Read books, role play negotiation situations with your fellow salespeople or sales manager and observe and learn from more experienced brokers in your company. Analyze each negotiation situation in which you participate to discover which techniques worked, which ones didn't and why. Build on the successful ones.

YOUR ROLE

As a salesperson you represent the best interests of both the seller/lessor and the buyer/lessee in a situation in which the parties' objectives appear to be mutually contradictory. One party wishes to obtain the highest rental rate or sale price, the other wishes to obtain the lowest price or rate. Your task is to bring these opposing points of view together to a conclusion that is mutually satisfactory and beneficial. It is, therefore, vitally important that you make sure both parties with whom you deal understand that you have the best interests of both in mind and that all discussion and negotiation will be conducted above board.

If you are an alert and skillful salesperson, you will make sure both the owner and tenant understand the steps of negotiation. You will sketch for each of them what will probably be accomplished at each stage. You will also set a timetable and will constantly check to see that you keep on schedule to the best of your ability.

In most instances settlement represents a compromise. It is toward that compromise that you work taking queries, proposals and responses back and forth between the owner and tenant until a transaction is agreed upon and the deal signed.

You, as negotiator, will generally keep the owner and tenant apart until the end. They might not even know each other's names until they get together to sign the final papers. Almost invariably if the parties meet earlier, negotiations are unnecessarily prolonged, simply because egos and emotions get in the way. A tenant may appear to be trying to push the owner into a nonprofit or loss situation, or the owner may seem to be gouging or cheating the tenant.

Also, both the owner's and the tenant's attorneys should be excluded from negotiations until the appropriate time. As a salesperson, you work with the owner and tenant to reach a business agreement. The lawyer's role is to put that agreement into the appropriate legal language after you have negotiated it. When lawyers are involved too soon in the process of negotiating, the process is usually prolonged, or matters become so complicated that the transaction is ruptured and a deal is never made. The lawyer generally has no motivation to see a transaction successfully completed, since his or her compensation, unlike yours, does not depend on a resolution. Therefore, the lawyer's task should be to tend to his or her client's best legal interests not to negotiate business points. That is your role.

TRUST, CONFIDENCE AND CONTROL

Your role as negotiator and the fact that lawyers should enter the picture only when their legal services are needed are two ground rules you must quickly establish in every negotiation. You must, at the same time, have thoroughly qualified both the owner and tenant, discovering what's really important to each and gaining a feeling for what they might like to have but would be willing to trade off for more important things.

In a leasing situation, make sure the owner understands that you will bring to him or her only thoroughly qualified tenants—those serious about the building, about making a deal, with the financial capability to uphold their end of an agreement and to allow the owner to continue to make a profit on his or her investment in the building. You must make sure the tenant understands the owner's need to make a profit and that only by doing so will the owner be able to keep the building in good repair and fulfill the agreement. You must also inform the tenant about the owner's feeling on rental rates and modifications. In every situation a number of items can be negotiated and some on which one or the other will not budge. It is necessary that the tenant know the areas in which the owner probably will be adamant and vice versa.

You must establish two points in each negotiation. First, you must present yourself as a professional—a person who knows his or her business and can really represent the interests of both parties. Second, you must control the situation at all times, for if control slips to either party, your deal is as good as lost. Keeping parties apart, seeing that lawyers stay out until negotiations are completed and explaining the steps in negotiating procedures are all means of taking and maintaining control. They also are part of the process of building confidence and trust in both the owner and tenant.

PROMISES

In every lease or sale, price is an important factor. When discussing price with a tenant, never assure him or her that you can arrange a sale or a lease for a certain price. If you do, you're taking a chance that might cost you the deal, the commission and a great deal of wasted time. If the owner is asking $15 a square foot to lease, do not tell your tenant that you can get the building for 15, or for any figure below the asking price. The price is on the listing. It cannot be raised. Whether or not it is lowered depends upon a number of things, principally whether price can be made a matter of negotiation. You must, however, remain noncommittal about what you think the owner will settle for, because you don't actually know. You will be doing your tenant an injustice and yourself a great disservice if you commit yourself.

If your tenant insists on making a bid below the asking price after you have reviewed the qualities of the building and their relationship to your tenant's needs, the current market, the building's location and other similar factors, you can only take his or her bid to the owner with the understanding that the owner may or may not accept it. You can always advise a tenant that the bid might be so low as to strike the owner as ridiculous and preclude a counteroffer. But you cannot and must not make up the tenant's mind. Above all, do not promise anything.

Some tenants will go into a market in which $15 a square foot is the going rate and insist that they will go no higher than $12. In this case, you might try to find the tenant a $12 building, but if the market is strong, your chances of success are slender. You might convince the tenant to be realistic, but if he or she remains adamant, you are probably better off not to waste time with that tenant.

Besides price, there are other items on which you must not commit yourself to a tenant. Building modification is such an item. Your tenant might want, and think the owner should pay for, extra doors, a sprinkler system where one does not exist and extra power. You don't know what the owner will concede in the way of modifications, regardless of how well you've qualified him or her. If a tenant's requests are unrealistic, say so, and persuade the tenant to modify or forego at least some of them. Tell the tenant that all you can do is try to negotiate a deal if he or she still wants you to, but you hold no real hope of success. Then, if you succeed, your tenant will be pleasantly surprised. On the other hand, tenant relations will surely suffer if you promise something and then are unable to make good on your commitment.

Further, make no promises about length of contract, escalator clauses or options. All these might be matters for negotiation, but commitments on them to your tenant might get you into difficulties.

In general, make no promises except to serve your tenant's best interests in a thorough and professional manner.

WHEN TO NEGOTIATE

A tenant will sometimes find a building suited to his or her needs as it stands. What then, if anything, is there to negotiate?

Several factors might be involved in negotiating the price, such as the amount of pressure on an owner to sell or lease, the owner's view of a tenant's suitability, the amount of pressure on the tenant to find suitable space within a given length of time and the state of the market. How these factors bear on a transaction depends entirely on the particular situation. How you persuasively nudge the owner and tenant together to a closing depends on your understanding of them and the prevailing circumstances. An offer, if not way out of line, may be greeted with counteroffers until a meeting of the minds occurs.

There is seldom an offer that cannot be sweetened. A longer lease period than originally contemplated might influence either, or both, the owner or tenant to move nearer to the price the other has in mind. Modification or escalation clauses in one or the other's favor might be influential, too. Option clauses, such as a renewal clause, might also be a factor in price negotiation.

Frequently, you must help tenants decide which building among those shown best suits their needs. You may want to arrange an inspection to highlight the buildings you previously concluded would be best. As you approach each building, state the features and benefits and how well they match the tenants' needs. In this event it is generally not difficult to get their agreement and move swiftly to an offer.

At other times tenants have difficulty deciding between two buildings, or sometimes three. List the pluses and minuses of each building and discuss them with the prospective tenants, relating each building to their needs. If you have properly done your job compiling a list of buildings to show them after qualifying them thoroughly, one of the buildings should satisfy their needs.

If your tenant leans toward a particular building but is not firm on it, suggest that he or she make a contingency offer, stipulating it within a certain period of time such as ten days, 30 days, or some other period of time. A contingency offer, as well as a firm, unfettered offer, takes a property off the market for the time stipulated for removing the contingencies. While such an offer can be advantageous to your tenant, it must be a serious one, and your tenant must understand this.

In the case of a sale, the buyer obtaining a certain amount of mortgage money at a certain interest rate within a particular time limit could be one contingency of the offer. However, avoid having the deal hung up over a half or quarter percentage point and a few years' difference in mortgage time. A tenant probably should not be in the market if a quarter of a percent interest makes too great a difference. Write the stipulation as broadly as possible. If the tenant wishes 12 percent mortgage money, make 13 the limit so as to allow for a fraction over what he or she would like to have. If the buyer wants an 18-year mortgage, make the limit 20 to allow some leeway. If your buyer does not get exactly what he or she wants in terms of interest rate and years, help to determine how much extra he or she will have to pay. Balance that against the advantages of having a building that well meets the needs.

In the case of either a sale or lease, a number of contingencies involving building modifications could be included in the offer. Among them might be the construction of special office space, installation of more air conditioning, increased power supply or installation of a different fire protection system.

Other contingencies might pertain to safety, power and drainage surveys. Such surveys would be completed within a certain time to determine the adequacy of these items for your tenant.

As to whether an owner will accept contingencies, and if so how many, there is no blanket answer. Much depends on the market, the attractiveness of the building, the amount of action there has been on it, the owner's estimate of how good a deal he or she can make and similar factors. It is up to you to know your area, the market and the owners with whom you deal in order to advise a tenant on the kinds and extent of possible contingencies.

PROCESS

It is important to remember that the primary objective of negotiation is to arrive at a meeting of the minds—a transaction that is mutually agreeable to both buyer and seller or lessor and lessee. To conduct a successful negotiation there are several phases that must be completed.

- planning
- preparation
- compromise
- agreement

Planning

In entering a negotiation, you must be clear on what each party hopes to accomplish. And always keep in mind that your objective is a completed transaction. Think through what information you will need to service both parties as professionally as possible. You must understand each person's viewpoint in order to assist in a meeting of the minds.

As part of the planning process, you must lay the rules for what is to follow in each phase of negotiations. Explain to both parties that you are the neutral intermediary. Also explain the appropriate role of lawyers. The tenant and landlord must understand that the negotiation is not a matter of win or lose, but should be a win-win situation. Your role is to facilitate this.

Preparation

Knowledge and planning are vital to a negotiation but are only helpful to the extent that you use them to prepare well. There are a number of questions you should ask yourself and do homework on if you don't know the answer.

1. What is each party trying to accomplish?

2. What are negotiable items for each party? To what extent are these negotiable?

3. What are the nonnegotiable points on each side? Why are these nonnegotiable?

4. What role does each party expect to play in the negotiation? What do they expect your role to be?

5. What outside factors (financing situation, marketplace, etc.) could have a bearing on the negotiation?

6. What deadline for completion is each side working with?

7. Have you qualified both parties completely (authority, financial ability and motivation)?

By answering these questions you should be able to begin the negotiation process informed and ready.

Compromise

Compromise is the process that keeps a negotiation progressing. Without compromise you would reach a deadlock. Your role in facilitating compromise is to balance the needs of each party with items that each would be willing to change or forfeit. Both sides must understand that they will have to make concessions. Your job is to maintain the credibility to realistically discuss each point. What is common or appropriate? Why or why not? The successful salesperson does not merely relay information between the two parties, he or she also provides market expertise to balance and evaluate each position.

All concessions should be relayed in person, not over the telephone. By meeting someone in person you will obtain more information, clues and feedback on what is or not acceptable and what pace and mood the negotiation is taking.

Sometimes negotiations reach a temporary deadlock. You must be able to judge if a time-out is needed. This could be time for additional reflection by either party, gathering information or just time to cool off. Your judgment of each party's needs and emotions will tell you when you should take a break rather than risk serious damage. If there is a lapse in negotiations, remember to do three things. First, remind both parties why it's in their best interests to successfully complete the transaction. Second, summarize for each side the items agreed upon.

Third, clarify the issues that still need to be resolved, and set a time to restart the negotiation process.

Agreement

When both parties have agreed upon a mutually satisfactory position and have put it in writing, you have successfully completed your role as negotiator. By using your market expertise, knowledge of each party and a level head, you should be able to facilitate a mutually satisfying transaction and provide a service that will encourage both landlord and tenant to use your services again in future transactions.

Negotiations: An Example

As an office-marketing salesperson, you must create a deal before the negotiation process comes into play. Here is an example of how you will do this.

Jane Studdock, a sales representative, has obtained an exclusive listing on a recently completed seven-story building containing 100,000 square feet. While obtaining the listing, she discussed some important points with developer Brian McAuliffe. First, she made it clear to McAuliffe that she, the sales representative, would represent his best interests. At the same time, however, she would represent the best interests of whatever client she brought to the building. No real conflict existed here. The objectives of both owner and tenant were basically economic. Studdock's task would be to bring the two parties together for the maximum mutual benefit. To achieve that objective, open and aboveboard negotiations would take place, with the best interests of both parties always foremost in mind.

Salesperson Studdock then questioned the developer about his attitude toward rental rates, tenant improvement allowances, various lease options and such concessions as parking costs, as well as space-planning costs. She pointed out the areas of possible flexibility, probing to find out what McAuliffe at this time considered too important to give in on.

Next, Studdock laid down certain ground rules. She would be the chief negotiator. She would act as the liaison between lessor and lessee and carry queries, proposals and responses back and forth. If the two parties insisted on meeting, she would be present every time. Studdock explained that the objective of negotiating is to obtain a signed lease satisfactory to both parties in the shortest possible time. If the parties met, especially on their own, it would only prolong negotiations. Egos and emotions might become involved. The developer might think the prospective tenant was trying to push him into a nonprofit situation. Or the tenant might think the developer was trying to overcharge. Such a situation could arise because of the seeming incompatibility of the two parties' objectives. Each party in a lease transaction wants a deal that gives him or her all possible advantages at the expense of the other party. Obviously, compromises must be made by both sides, and a fair and objective sales representative is the most qualified person to negotiate such compromises.

Studdock also told McAuliffe that she would prefer not to involve either his or the tenant's attorney in the negotiation phase if at all possible. The proper role of lawyers, she explained, is to cast the agreement in legal language after the salesperson has negotiated it. She pointed out that, in her experience, when lawyers were introduced into the lease negotiation process too early, the situation often became so entangled that negotiations were ruptured and an agreement was never reached. The lawyers' main task, she said, is to attend to the owner's and tenant's legal interest. Negotiating business points is the salesperson's job.

Finally, Studdock instructed McAuliffe on the path that negotiations would normally follow. She sketched briefly what would probably be accomplished by the end of stage A, then during stage B and finally during stage C. She told McAuliffe that she would establish a timetable for negotiation and schedule all meetings and that all information concerning negotiations would flow through her. After reminding McAuliffe that everyone's objective was to obtain a mutually satisfactory lease in the shortest time possible, Studdock departed.

In short, the sales representative showed the developer that she knew her business, that she intended to perform a service for him in a better way than anyone else and that she would leave him entirely satisfied and likely to return to her company later with any additional business. She established in the developer a feeling of trust and confidence in her as a professional.

Back at her office, Studdock wrote a summary of her conversation with McAuliffe, noting particularly his stand on rental rate, improvement allowances and concessions. Next, she reviewed similar buildings on the market and similar transactions that she and other people in her office had made. She compared them point by point to the exclusive listing she had just obtained.

Setting Up the Deal with the Tenant

When the groundwork had been laid with the developer, Studdock turned to the other important element in setting up a transaction—dealing with the tenant. While making a cold call a few days later, she discovered that the company she was calling on was in the market for 100,000 square feet of office space. Studdock immediately attempted to link the exclusive listing she had recently obtained with the company she had cold called. She met with the company's real estate representative, Ellis Cameron, to qualify the company thoroughly and discuss its office space needs in detail. She then told Cameron essentially what she had told McAuliffe.

The salesperson explained to the prospect that the developer needed to make a profit. If he did not, the building's services would inevitably deteriorate and it would eventually be sold. Consequently, it was in the tenant's best interest for the building to be a profit-making venture. Studdock explained the normal position of developers on rental rates, improvement allowances, option clauses and various other concessions. She then assured Cameron that she fully understood his company's goals. Her job was to bring the opposite viewpoints together in a mutually satisfactory and beneficial transaction. She emphasized that most areas could be negotiated, but that there might be items on which each side would not budge. She pointed out the problems that could arise if Cameron tried to deal directly with McAuliffe.

In addition, Studdock repeated to the tenant what she had told the developer concerning the role of lawyers in the transaction. She assured

Cameron that she would put all business points of the deal in order, thus making it easy and economical for the lawyer to provide the proper language. If Studdock overlooked anything, she said, or if anything was unclear, she would expect the lawyer to probe until all aspects of the agreement had been clarified.

As the salesperson outlined the steps the negotiation would follow, she brought up the subject of space planning. She wanted Cameron to understand that developers and owners frequently shoulder the costs of space planning up to a certain point but not beyond and that space-planning costs might be a point for negotiation. Studdock emphasized that she should be present at any meeting the tenant had with a space planner so there would be no misunderstanding about when and how the space planner would perform or about which party would assume which costs.

At this point, Studdock made an appointment to show the tenant the building. Cameron was very interested in the property, and negotiations began. They soon hit a snag—the rental rate. Neither side, it seemed, would yield. McAuliffe held out for his asking rate; Cameron insisted on a lower rate. Later, after considerable individual discussion with each side, Studdock suggested a compromise: one month's free rent, which amounted to $50,000. Both parties finally agreed to that, and the discussion went on to the improvement allowance.

Here a meeting of the minds was soon established. But then, just before an agreement was finally reached, McAuliffe realized that he had neglected to include certain costs when accommodating the tenant's wishes concerning improvements. Cameron had to be informed that he would either have to put some money into the improvements he wanted or forego the free month's rent. Which would he choose? After adding up some figures and doing some thinking, Cameron decided that having the developer pay for the improvements was of greater benefit to him than a month's free rent. So tenant and developer reached an agreement on the improvement allowance.

Next, Studdock began to negotiate concessions. She knew that the tenant wanted two concessions in particular. One was for the developer to pay relocation expenses, especially moving and telephone installation costs. The other was the term of the lease. Cameron wanted a ten-year lease containing a five-year cancellation option. He would also have liked a concession on parking costs, but this was not nearly as important to him as the other two concessions.

Studdock suspected that McAuliffe had more objections to the cancellation option than to paying the relocation expense. But instead of raising either of these issues, she first asked him about parking costs. She implied that this concession was most important to the tenant and that its denial might jeopardize the entire transaction. The developer turned down the parking cost concession cold. Studdock switched the discussion to other topics and returned later to parking costs. Again, McAuliffe refused. After discussing still other issues, the salesperson went back to the parking cost problem. But McAuliffe said no once more. At this point, Studdock halted the negotiations. She suggested that both sides let matters rest for a few days. She then set a time for negotiations to begin once again.

The next round of negotiations began with the tenant. Studdock probed him about relocation expenses and cancellation. Would he give up one or both of them? No, Cameron responded, he would not. Several times Studdock returned to the subject of these two concessions.

Finally she could see that Cameron was gradually coming around to choosing relocation expenses as more important than a cancellation option. At that point, Studdock reopened negotiations with the developer.

She laid out a proposition. Cameron would forego the cancellation clause and the parking cost concessions in return for relocation expense. After some discussion, McAuliffe agreed to go along with that.

After this, negotiations proceeded smoothly and swiftly. The whole deal was wrapped up within a few weeks. The developer and the tenant did not meet each other, and in fact did not even learn each other's names, until the transaction was about to be closed.

The Finer Points

Now analyze some of the finer points of the office-marketing salesperson's strategy in this situation. Studdock began her initial contacts with both developer and tenant by explaining the roles and interests of all three parties—McAuliffe, Cameron and herself. She did this for one reason: to establish control and maintain it from start to finish. If a sales representative loses control at any point in the course of a transaction, he or she risks losing control of the entire deal.

The first step toward establishing control is to create a feeling of trust and confidence in both owner and tenant. You accomplish this by showing that you're professional and by convincing tenant and owner that everything will be aboveboard, that nothing will be secret or hidden and that you will work in the best interests of both parties. Never assume that everyone knows the function of an office-marketing salesperson or how valuable such services are.

Studdock was determined to keep the tenant and the owner apart until negotiations were completed and was quite frank with both parties about why she wanted to do so. She explained that, if the two parties were to get together in her absence, egos might get involved. Since the goal of each party was to make a deal that was economically favorable to himself, each might suspect that the other was trying to push him into a no-win situation.

Studdock also quickly established the proper role of lawyers in an office-marketing negotiation. Once again the reason was control—not only of the tenant and owner but of the entire situation. To avoid trouble later on, spell out everything from the beginning and be able to give specific reasons for structuring the situations as you do.

Make sure that tenants are aware of the costs they will incur. A tenant may think, for example, that space planning will be included in the tenant-improvement allowance, when in reality the owner may be willing to pay only a certain portion of its cost. Don't let tenants or developers labor under false assumptions.

You cannot, of course, demand anything of either tenants or owners. You must be smooth and professional when structuring all aspects of the situation. You may not get your way about the lawyers' role, for instance, but you will have warned the parties of the difficulties that may arise if they do not follow your suggestions. Remember always that if you lose control you may well lose the deal—and your commission.

Upon returning to her office after meeting with the developer, Studdock analyzed other recent transactions made on similar buildings. This provided her with a yardstick by which to measure the competitiveness of the new listing's rental rate, improvement allowance and concessions. It is unlikely that the salesperson could get the developer to lower his rental rate, for the reasons given in the economics chapter. It is also unlikely that a smart developer would price his or her office space out of the market. When a developer does put an unrealistically high price on the property, be well advised not to get involved with it. You could spend a lot of time on the deal without finding a tenant willing to pay such a price. On the other hand, if the developer is charging less than the going rate, point out this fact. The developer may not realize how high the market rate is, or you may discover his reasons for being willing to charge less than the market.

Examining other transactions also can give you ideas about planning a strategy. How might you persuade the developer to raise the improvement allowance? Which concessions are customary in today's market? Which seem to be rare?

In dealing with both McAuliffe and Cameron, Studdock outlined the steps that would be followed in moving toward a transaction. She did this mainly to establish feelings of confidence, trust and mutual respect in both tenant and developer that are so essential in completing a deal satisfactorily. This technique also helped Studdock maintain control and demonstrated that no games would be played.

When you outline the negotiating procedure and establish a timetable, you show both parties what conditions must be satisfied at each stage before moving on to the next. Your job is to make the path toward completing the transaction as smooth and easy as possible. You assume accountability for the decisions being reached; you indicate objectives and specify the responsibilities of all parties concerned. Make it clear that you will help both tenant and owner in the decision-making process.

Outlining the procedure also will help you prepare your strategy. It will show you what homework you must do in order to be able to answer questions as they arise.

Your position is analogous to that of the salesperson you would deal with when making a major purchase. You want that person to advise you of the facts to help you make a decision. You do the same thing as a negotiator of office leases. You show both owner and tenant where the beginning and end of the transaction are and what lies between. Along the way, you suggest alternatives to consider and help each party examine them. You assist both tenant and owner to attain the big objectives: a mutually satisfactory transaction for them and a commission for you.

Studdock took great pains to find out which concessions the owner was absolutely going to hold out against and which he was likely to give in on. She then established the order of importance of the tenant's demands. There was no point in wasting her time trying to negotiate a concession the developer absolutely would not grant or one the tenant absolutely would insist on. Instead, she probed each party for weak spots and proceeded to negotiate from there.

Studdock kept returning to points on which the tenant and developer had negative feelings. She was following an important rule: never accept the first no. Don't accept the second or even, sometimes, the sixth or seventh. Persistence pays off. If your persistence annoys one or both parties enough that it might ruin the deal, back off from it. But you won't know until you try. If neither side will give in on a point, there will be no deal anyway. So push a little. If you maintain control of the situation at all times and if both parties bargain in good faith and work, with your aid, toward a mutually beneficial objective, you'll be able to achieve the necessary compromise.

Studdock made a horse trade to get around both the developer's and the tenant's refusals. People often say no as an automatic defense response. When the point comes up again you can, through discussion and persuasion, sometimes turn the no into a yes. Do all you can to prevent any door from being closed until you decide it should be. You might have to go through several refusals, depending on the negotiating capabilities of the parties involved, before obtaining the agreement you are seeking.

In negotiating with McAuliffe, Studdock spent a great deal of time on the parking concession, even though it was the least important to Cameron. She did this because every negotiating situation involves two groups of items: those that must be part of the final deal and those that will be used for bargaining purposes. You must have something to throw away, to exchange for something more important. Ideally, the things one party is willing to dispense with are those the other is not.

Structure every situation so that you are negotiating from a position of strength. The strongest position is one in which you have items that can be given up but the other side doesn't know what they are. Hold back an item or two so that it can be used at the appropriate time to obtain something more important.

Parking costs were important to McAuliffe. They were not especially important to Cameron. The cancellation option and relocation expenses were important to both. Studdock did not try to make a simple one for one trade-off of the cancellation option and parking costs in exchange for relocation expenses. The offer was reasonable, and the owner accepted it.

Negotiations can become extremely complicated. Many times parties will become so involved with details that they will forget what the main objective is. You will want to summarize the state of negotiations from time to time to, in effect, resell the deal to both parties. Review the intentions of both parties, the main objective, the positive aspects of the situation thus far, what remains to be accomplished and the items each party has indicated are important. Sometimes you might have to imply, without actually closing any doors, that if each does not obtain the points he or she considers extremely important, the deal will fall through.

At one point Studdock called a temporary halt to the discussion. Negotiations can become very intense, difficult and hard on everyone's nerves. A cooling-off period allows time for both parties to calm down and reconsider their positions. It also gives you an opportunity to do additional homework, rethink your strategy, discover why the situation bogged down and determine what to do about it. In time, you will be able to sense when a time to cool off is necessary.

When a Broker Brings You a Tenant

Sometimes a competing broker brings you a tenant interested in a building on which your company holds the exclusive listing. You should take the same attitude as when you are bringing a tenant and owner together. Assure your competitor that all commissions due will be fairly paid and that you will notify the broker of any meetings at which he or she should be present. Explain to the broker and the tenant that you will assume the central position in negotiations. You will inform the tenant of the ground rules, structure the situation, schedule meetings, set the timetable and lead the discussions. All information must be channeled through you and you will not allow the lines of communication to be clogged. Assure the broker and tenant that you have no intention of taking any shortcuts or doing anything counter to their best interests. Your objective is, as their's should be, to protect everyone's best interests by reaching a satisfactory agreement in the shortest possible time.

In other words, you define the role of the other broker and his or her tenant just as you define the roles of lawyers, space planners and anyone else involved in your transactions. Make it clear in the beginning that you will establish and maintain control.

The other broker may lack your experience or your skill in controlling situations, setting up timetables, spelling out all parties' roles and carrying out negotiations. He or she could jeopardize the deal if allowed to control the situation. In any case, the competing broker is bound to be involved in other transactions while this one is taking place and may welcome your taking the controlling, responsible position. Assume that if you do not control the situation throughout, you and your company may get hurt.

A Game of Chess

Successful negotiating demands a certain attitude. You are on the road to success if you convey to all parties a strong, positive, controlling attitude in the beginning. You take another step on that road if you do not get sidetracked into building your own ego or matching wits with other parties. And if you remind all parties what their objectives are, if you build in them a feeling of trust and confidence in you as a professional, you are almost certain to achieve your goal.

Office space negotiation bears definite resemblance to a game of chess, but much more is at stake than simply winning. As a chess game begins, you have in mind an overall strategy and alternative moves that might fit in with that strategy. As the game progresses, other choices are revealed as your opponent moves and countermoves. Your primary goal is to checkmate your opponent's king while protecting your own. You know which pieces are vital to you and which you can afford to sacrifice, and you never sacrifice a piece without gaining something in return. You are prepared to take advantage of unexpected opportunities as they occur at any point of the game.

In negotiating, you must study each situation on its own merits, thinking of moves you might make, knowing which items can be sacrificed to obtain more important ones. You might spend hours negotiating. You also must develop the ability to sense when calling a halt to allow the parties to cool off would be valuable. During the cooling-off period, you'll do additional homework and think of reasons why a give here and a take there might be beneficial to both tenant and owner and might facilitate the negotiations.

Innumerable considerations are involved in negotiating office leases and your skills will develop with more practice. Constantly analyze situations and think about effective moves and countermoves. Read books on the subject and learn from other salespeople. Discuss with them their failures as well as their successes.

Owners want maximum rents and minimum improvement allowances, concessions and tenant-favoring options. Tenants want just the opposite. You are in the middle, charged with bringing these opposing viewpoints together. This is where negotiating for office space differs from a chess game. In chess, you plan elaborate strategies in order to defeat your opponent. In office-space negotiations, your strategies are intended to bring opponents together so that both may win the game.

Exercise E

Answer the following questions.

1. What is the primary objective of the salesperson in explaining to both tenant and owner each other's roles and interests as well as those of the salesperson?

2. What is the salesperson's primary objective in defining the role of lawyers in the transaction?

3. Why did Jane Studdock analyze other transactions made on similar buildings?

4. Why is it important to know what items each party will refuse to compromise on?

5. Why did Studdock list the steps that would be followed in moving toward a transaction?

6. Why should a salesperson keep the tenant and owner apart until negotiations have been completed?

7. What important rule was Studdock following when she kept returning to points on which the parties gave negative responses?

8. Why did Studdock concentrate on the parking cost concession when negotiating with the developer?

9. Why did Studdock halt negotiations for a time?

Answer E

1. *You want to establish control over both parties to the transaction. You do this by inspiring confidence in your ability as a professional and your expertise in this area. And you inspire such confidence by convincing both parties you will work for their best interests and that, if both parties work strictly through you, the transaction can be brought to a swift and mutually satisfactory conclusion.*

2. *The objective here, too, is control. You want to control not only the tenant and the developer but the entire situation. That means controlling other parties to the deal. You cannot forbid another party to bring in a lawyer before the deal is closed, but you can point out the disadvantages of such a move.*

3. *She did this to ascertain whether her new listing was competitive with other buildings in the current market picture. She compared the new listing's rental rate and concessions to those typical for*

similar buildings. Examining other transactions also gave Stud-dock an opportunity to plan her strategy.

4. *Trying to negotiate points on which there is no chance whatsoever that one party will yield is a waste of time.*

5. *She did this to establish trust and confidence, ensure that there would be no surprises for either party and assure them that no games would be played.*

6. *When an owner and a tenant are permitted to negotiate directly, egos and emotions are likely to enter the picture and explode the deal. Each party is looking for a deal that gives him or her all possible advantages at the expense of the other party. These problems can be avoided when negotiations are handled by a disinterested third party who represents the interests of both principals.*

7. *She was following the rule of persistence, which states that a salesperson never takes no for an answer until convinced that it is unalterable.*

8. *When she discovered that this particular concession was not a vital issue from the tenant's point of view but was very important to the developer, she immediately saw it as a trading point—something to concede to the developer in exchange for a concession on which the tenant placed higher value.*

9. *At a point in any negotiation when there appears to be a deadlock and tempers are getting frayed, it usually pays to call off negotiations temporarily. This gives both tenant and owner a chance to rethink their priorities and gives the salesperson time to adjust his or her strategy.*

9

Time Management

Time is the office-marketing salesperson's most important resource. Unlike salaried employees, you suffer financially because commissions are lost if you plan your time badly. You must manage your time to achieve a maximum return. Each hour, each day, each week and each month must be planned in a way that reaps maximum reward for the energy invested.

If you find yourself unable to fit essential tasks into your daily routine, it is not because you don't have enough time, but because you are managing your time badly. If this happens to you, stop and reassess your priorities. Are you performing some tasks that could be handled just as well or better by your secretary? Are you unable to delegate small tasks for fear they won't be handled properly? Learn to make the hard choices between those tasks you must perform and those you can't possibly do without slighting more important things. Once you've delegated those unimportant chores, you'll find yourself with all the time you need.

Although efficient time management is essential, the best organizer in the world cannot plan a system for someone else to follow. You must devise your own system, suited to your temperament, your goals and your daily energy rhythm.

Don't try to plan every available minute, because many unanticipated situations will rise in the course of a day. But if you plan the activities that you can anticipate, you'll have time to deal with the unexpected when it occurs.

In this section you will find ideas, suggestions and examples. They should be used to help you develop your own personal time management system, the one that works for you.

Setting Your Goals

Time management begins with defining what you are working toward. This means setting both long- and short-range goals. Keep your goals practical and effective by making them conform to the following points.

1. Your goals must be *attainable.* Be realistic with yourself and establish goals in accordance with your own capabilities. You will never feel successful if your goals are always out of reach, and a feeling of success is of utmost importance in establishing a continued pattern of growth and development.

2. Your goals, on the other hand, must be *challenging.* If the goals you have set can be achieved too easily and require little or no effort, they are probably not meaningful.

3. Your goals must be *specific* and *measurable.* They should be stated in quantifiable terms—numbers, dollars, percentages and time. You must have a specific target date for attaining each objective.

4. Your goals must be *compatible* with those of your company. The successful accomplishment of your individual goals must contribute to the achievement of your firm's goals.

5. Your goals must be *in writing.* Compare them to your actual performance at regular intervals.

Begin by establishing broad, long-term goals for yourself. Work backward to the specific short-range goals—annual, monthly, daily and hourly—that will be steps toward achieving the large ones.

Your long-term goals should span a period of at least five to ten years. They should cover both business and nonbusiness areas—financial, family, recreation, travel, cultural, social, educational, retirement. For example, if you really want to spend the summer in Europe in five years, put that down as a long-range goal. When your long-range goals are down on paper, you will begin to see a certain interdependence among them.

List ten long-term goals for yourself here. Be sure to set specific target dates for each.

Priority	Long-term Goal	Target Date
1.	Achieve an income of $ _____ by _____ .	
2.		
3.		
4.		
5.		

6.

7.

8.

9.

10.

As you are no doubt beginning to discover, this is not an easy task. But it is the most important aspect of organizing your time, since it is the basis upon which you will build your system.

Now go back and organize your ten long-term goals in order of priority. How important is each goal? How much time have you allowed yourself in which to accomplish it?

Priority	*Long-term Goal*	*Target Date*
1.		
2.		
3.		
4.		
5.		
6.		
7.		
8.		
9.		
10.		

Your next task is to support the long-term goals with specific interim goals—steps that will lead to achieving them. Ask yourself these questions.

1. What is the most effective way of reaching my goal?

2. What knowledge and abilities do I already have that will assist me in reaching my goal?

3. What additional information and skills must I acquire to achieve my goal?

4. What specific steps must I take to attain goal success?

Using your five highest-priority long-term goals, establish three short-term goals for each. This is the third time you have listed these long-term goals. Has your list changed in any way? If you have given real thought to these exercises, your goals will probably have been modified with each writing. With the exercise below, you will complete your final statement of your long-term goals. Be sure you have established realistic target dates for both long- and short-term goals.

	Priority	*Goal*	*Target Date*

1.

   a.

   b.

   c.

2.

   a.

   b.

   c.

3.

   a.

   b.

   c.

4.

   a.

   b.

   c.

5.

   a.

   b.

   c.

You have just taken the first step toward effectively organizing your time—establishing your long-range objectives. Update them annually in writing, and analyze your progress toward meeting them at least every six months. In figure 9–1 you will find a suggested form to follow in listing your long-range objectives. Modify the form if necessary to suit your particular needs.

Once you have determined where you want to be financially, professionally, socially and educationally over the next five to ten years, lay out specific goals for yourself for the next year. Do not extend your short-term objectives beyond a one-year period. Review the rules for goal setting discussed earlier in this section—they apply to all plans that you set for yourself. These short-term goals will be more specific than the long-term ones you have already set. Figure 9–2 shows a sample form to follow in listing short-term objectives.

Building a Tickler File

Now add a prospect and call-control tickler file to your system. This file will be a primary source of input for your monthly, weekly and daily planners.

FIGURE 9.1   Goal-Organizing Form

Date Prepared _____

Long-Term Goals

Goal	Target Date	Completed Date

FIGURE 9.2   Short-Term Goal Form

Date Prepared _____

Short-Term Goals

Goal	Target Date	Completed Date

The hardware for the tickler file includes:

1. three-by-five cards

2. file for three-by-five cards

3. five weekly dividers

4. seven daily dividers

Arrange the monthly dividers in sequence beginning with the current month (e.g., April, May...March). Place the five weekly dividers in the current month (first through fifth). Place the seven daily dividers in the current week (Sunday through Saturday).

Each prospect, customer and follow-up is placed on a file card (figure 9–3). Record the name, address and telephone number in the upper left-hand corner. On the right-hand side, put the next contact date. The bottom portion of the card should contain brief notes regarding the contact. File the card in the appropriate month, week or day for follow-up. Figure 9–4 shows a typical tickler file.

FIGURE 9.3   Tickler File Card

Name _____ Dates _____

Address _____ _____

_____ _____

Telephone _____ _____

Comments:

Each month, sort and file the cards by the four or five weeks of that month. At the beginning of each week, sort and file the cards for that week by the appropriate day. When you have completed each contact, refile the card according to the next contact date.

This tickler-file system will automatically contribute to your success and profits. It will keep you aware of what day, date and time you are to call on or follow up on a contact. And most important, it permits you always to have at your fingertips all essential information regarding any given account. The system is most effective when you develop the habit of keeping full notes on what action you intend to take at the future date you have selected for contact.

Prepare the *monthly time planner* as shown in figure 9–5. First, enter all unavailable time periods, such as holidays and vacations. Note all scheduled events—sales meetings, seminars, meetings of civic organizations, etc. As you become aware of future events, enter them immediately on your monthly calendar.

Exercise F _____

Prepare your calendar for next month by completing the monthly planner in figure 9–5.

FIGURE 9.4   Tickler File

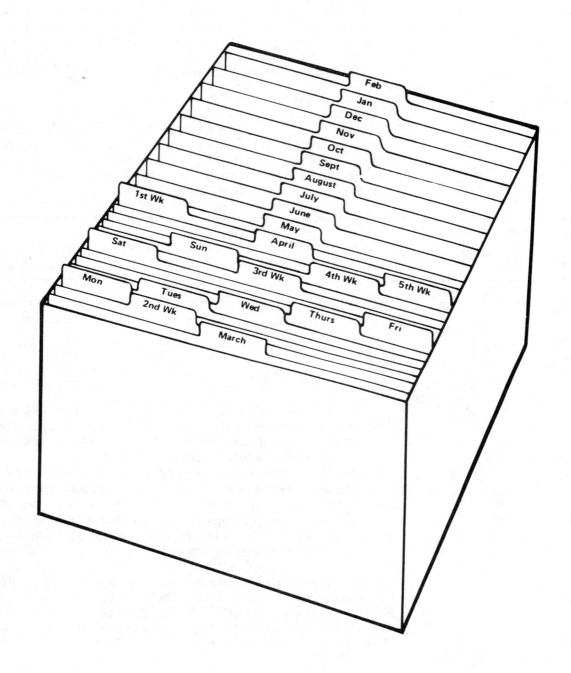

Using the monthly calendar, prepare your *weekly time planner*. Your tickler file will provide additional information for the specific details you will need when laying out this planner each week. Each week, write down the most pressing things that need to be done and the appointments you have scheduled. Set aside blocks of time for cold calling, working on specific transactions, researching new projects, answering correspondence and perhaps for reading important trade publications.

Exercise G

Using the form in figure 9–6, lay out your plan for the coming week.

Early each morning, or even the night before, fill out your *daily time planner*. Here are some suggestions for scheduling your activities.

1. Carry a notebook with you on your calls and write down everything you will need to know—notes, appointments, telephone numbers, leads.

2. Set aside parts of each day for specific tasks. For example, if you plan to cold call on Wednesday morning, block this out in your daily planner.

3. Once you have set a schedule, stick to it. If you plan to cold call Wednesday morning, don't make any appointments for that time. If you ignore your schedule, you will find that you are not allowing enough time for some important tasks.

4. Allow enough time to arrive promptly at appointments. You will often be calling on top-level executives who are too busy to wait for latecomers. Take into account the possibility of traffic jams and other delays. In fact, try to be ten minutes early—it gives the impression that you are serious, professional and eager to be of service.

5. Schedule appointments on a geographic basis. Allow plenty of time to get from one place to another—unrealistic estimates will upset your entire schedule. As the area in which you make appointments expands, be sure you don't schedule a meeting at 10:00 A.M. in a distant location and another at 5:00 P.M. in the same place.

6. Consider when making any appointment whether you actually must go to that meeting. Running around your territory for no purpose wastes much valuable time.

7. Develop self-discipline. Get out and cold call when your schedule says you should. Don't make a marginal appointment just to get out of doing something you don't feel like doing that day. The successful salesperson is the one who is out in the field knocking on doors as much as possible.

FIGURE 9.5 Monthly Time-Planner Form

Month _____ Year _____

SUNDAY	MONDAY	TUESDAY	WEDNESDAY	THURSDAY	FRIDAY	SATURDAY

FIGURE 9.6 Weekly Time-Planner Form

	MONDAY	TUESDAY	WEDNESDAY	THURSDAY	FRIDAY
	DATE _____	_____	_____	_____	_____
MORNING					
AFTERNOON					
EVENING					

8. Don't do the right thing at the wrong time. Don't catch up on your reading when you could be scheduling appointments or making cold calls. Write letters and do paperwork early in the morning or late in the evening, when doing other work is impractical.

9. Qualify each prospect to determine how much time you should spend with him or her. The people you deal with are often on salary and can afford to waste a little time. You cannot. When you are starting out, write down how long each appointment took. At the end of the day, total up the amount of time you spent with each prospect and consider how much you got out of it. How much closer did it put you to a deal?

    People who drop in off the street should be qualified immediately. If they are not qualified, be polite but don't waste your time. You have every right to measure people against the commission they are likely to generate. On the other hand, any time spent with potential major prospects is not time wasted. It is well worth your time to cultivate such people on a social as well as a business level.

10. Check your schedule hourly, or you'll find at the end of the day that you've missed things. After accomplishing a task, cross it off. At the end of the day check to see what you've missed, and plan to cover it later. The same thing is true for your accomplishments on a weekly or monthly basis. Transfer all important notes and phone numbers to their appropriate place.

Many new salespeople begin to feel disorganized and overwhelmed after a few weeks on the job. If they had begun by planning their days and weeks, they would never have had this problem. Talk to salespeople who have been in the business for some time. Ask them what their goals are and how they plan their time. If you don't know who would be a good source, ask your sales manager to recommend someone who is good at managing time.

Exercise H

On an hourly basis, plan a day from the weekly schedule you prepared. Use the form in figure 6–7.

Organizing Your Work

If you organize your work as well as your time, you will be able to make more deals more effectively. Three types of filing systems will help you to organize your work.

1. a pending file

2. the tickler file already mentioned

3. a file for completed transactions

FIGURE 9.7 Daily Time-Planner Form

Date _____   Activity   Comments

7:00 A.M.

7:30

8:00

8:30

9:00

9:30

10:00

10:30

11:00

11:30

12:00 noon

12:30

1:00

1:30

2:00

2:30

3:00

3:30

4:00

4:30

5:00

5:30

6:00

6:30

7:00

7:30

8:00

8:30

9:00

9:30

10:00 P.M.

For each transaction that is pending, prepare a file folder with a typed label listing the name of the deal. File these folders closest to you so they will be easily accessible. On the inside of each file folder, staple the business cards of the people involved in the deal or write in their names, addresses and telephone numbers. Keep all papers and correspondence with the prospect in chronological order in the file folder.

Jot down a brief summary of what you discussed every time you talk to someone connected with the deal. This is very important, especially if a dispute arises or a deal starts to fall through. If a prospect says you didn't discuss a particular point, you can pull out your notes and say, "Yes, Mr. Smith, we did discuss that—at 10:00 A.M. on June 15." This type of notation is admissible in a court of law or arbitration procedure.

You may want to design a form on which to enter all of the pertinent information about each transaction. The form should include the following items:

1. property involved
2. owner's name, address, phone number
3. prospective buyer or lessee's name
4. rent
5. taxes
6. maintenance
7. insurance
8. size of space
9. length of lease
10. landlord's improvements
11. tenant's improvements

Keep track on the form of all the developments in the deal—what was discussed, whether or not the tenant has agreed to pay the taxes, etc. The date and the item discussed should be noted. This information can eliminate disputes as lease negotiations progress.

Analyze and reassess each deal in the pending file once a month. Will you be able to make this deal? Be honest with yourself; don't waste your time on borderline situations.

Borderline transactions should be moved to the tickler file. Review this file every month or so to see if the picture has changed. If some deals in the tickler file begin to look more positive, put them in the pending file. Remove hopeless situations from your filing system altogether. If you are not sure into what category a particular deal should fall, discuss it with your sales manager.

Since timing is critical in office marketing, put all information on possible business moves or expansion into the tickler file. If you stay on top of things like this, you are bound to make an extra deal now and then. Other possible candidates for the tickler file are leases that will be expiring, whether in five months or five years. Information from the lease survey form (see the module *The Inventory System*) should be placed in the tickler file immediately.

When a deal is completed, move the information to a special file for completed transactions. But before doing so, abstract all information that could lead to new deals and put it in the tickler file.

Time Management Skills

Managing your time effectively so that you can reach your goals involves the development of certain skills. Practice them conscientiously and they will aid you in all aspects of your life. Some important ones are listed here.

1. *Increase your alertness.* It is easy to slip into comfortable habits and patterns that dull the mind, but there are tricks for getting out of them. Change your route for driving to work each morning. Start eating lunch in new places. Break out of any of your routines, and you will raise your level of awareness. Be careful not to let one routine be replaced by another. Keep your patterns changing.

    Make a hobby of studying the words, facial expressions and gestures of prospects. Become a student of body language. Soon you will be able to interpret certain pauses and gestures as clues to how clients are reacting and what they are thinking.

    Pay attention to the buildings in which you are cold calling and to their surroundings. Keep your eyes and ears open to new sights and sounds.

    Cultivate an interest centered around observation. A hobby like photography will sharpen your powers of observation. A camera picks up things that even a trained observer misses. Photograph the buildings in your area that interest you. This will help you to develop a feel for architecture, size and use. A photograph of a skyline can be not only attractive but revealing. It can show patterns in the development of a city that you were unaware of.

2. *Increase your energy level.* Keeping your energy up will help you make the most of your time. If you are not the athletic type, you may find it worthwhile to begin an exercise program. Although exercise requires energy, it creates even more energy than it takes.

3. *Become familiar with your own individual energy patterns.* Some people are morning people and do their most productive work before lunchtime. Others don't really wake up until afternoon. Learn to recognize your own peak energy periods and then schedule your activities around them as best you can. Arrange to handle routine tasks, such as correspondence and administrative duties, at times when you feel sluggish. Do your creative work during your peak times. You will not only accomplish more this way, but you will find yourself enjoying your work more as well.

4. *Learn to handle anxiety.* Letting your anxieties get the best of you drains your energy. Try to discover the true source of your worries. Real problems must be dealt with before they grow and destroy your energy sources. Imaginary problems must be recognized for the time wasters they are.

On the other hand, when puzzling out a seemingly hopeless problem, know when to stop and take a rest. Relentless pursuit of solutions can itself be a drain on energy. Put the problem aside for a while, then approach it again when you feel more up to the task. Problems sometimes work themselves out without conscious effort on your part when you put them on the back burner for a while.

5. *Delegate authority.* Doing all the work yourself is inefficient. If you feel you must construct an entire presentation package yourself, you are helping no one—not yourself, your prospect or the office staff that exists to assist you with precisely this type of activity. Don't overburden yourself with details. Allow your secretary and other assistants to develop their skills while you spend your time on the creative tasks for which you are best qualified.

6. *Don't waste time on regret.* Occasionally you will blow a deal. It is easy in retrospect to recognize exactly when you went wrong. But when you made the faulty decision, you did not have the benefit of hindsight. Reprimanding yourself will improve nothing. It may even make things worse if you let it sap the energy you should be applying to your next transaction.

7. *Anticipate down periods and learn to handle them.* Accept the fact that you will have slumps from time to time. Sometimes everything seems to be at a standstill, and no matter how hard you try, nothing happens. The important thing is how you handle slumps. If you feel you are on a treadmill, break your routine—go out and make cold calls for a few days. The self-discipline involved, plus the fact that you are bound to generate a few leads, will soon get you back on course. This is one of the few times it will pay you to break the rule of always sticking to your daily schedule.

8. *Learn how to manage your money.* One of the easiest ways to waste time is to become preoccupied with financial worries. While you are working on the larger, long-range deals, make certain you have some small bread-and-butter deals interspersed with the larger ones to offset feast-or-famine situations.

9. *Select your business reading carefully.* Keep up with what is going on in your field through newspapers and trade journals, but read with selectivity. Scan for articles and news releases that will increase your knowledge of your field, keep you up to date on the latest trends or produce leads. Then read those articles carefully.

Exercise I _____

Review your file and paperwork organization and answer the following questions.

1. Have you set up files for pending deals?

2. Are the pending files in alphabetical order?

3. How often should you review these files?

4. Have you set up a tickler file?

5. What kind of information goes into tickler files?

6. What do you do with the information in a file once a transaction is completed?

Exercise J

Think about the following questions.

1. As you progress through the day you scheduled in Exercise H, check off the things you have accomplished. Have you done everything you intended?

2. As you review your progress, what do you see as your greatest time-management problems?

3. How can you overcome the problems you have detected?

Exercise K

Respond to the following situations with comments on whether time is being used effectively and, if not, what is being done wrong.

1. Jack feels that nothing ever gets done right unless he does it.

2. Helen has been trying for four hours to figure out how to get the Smith Company and the Jones Corporation together on a lease and is coming up with nothing. But she's determined to sit there all night until she does.

3. George is always making comments like, "You should have done it the other day," or "I would have gotten that report in, but...."

4. Eleanor feels especially alive in the mornings, so she tries to plan her most important meetings then. In the afternoon her energy gradually drops off—at 5:00 she'll be reading trade publications and answering mail.

5. Carl feels secure in his lifestyle. He gets up at the same time every day, eats the same breakfast, drives Elm Street to Oak Street to Sycamore Street to work, eats lunch at the greasy spoon around the corner every day when he's in the neighborhood and goes home promptly at 5:00 every day via Sycamore to Oak to Elm.

Answer K

1. Jack has not learned how to delegate the small tasks to his assistants. Jack's life is undoubtedly one long, losing race against time.

2. If Helen has already spent four unproductive hours on the same problem, chances are she will be no closer to a solution the next morning, even if she does sit there all night. Helen needs to leave her problem alone for a while, turn to other tasks and come back to it later. She will probably be able to approach it from a fresh perspective then.

3.   George spends a lot of time pointing out errors in other people's decisions and defending past failures of his own. Neither is productive. George is a time waster.

4.   Eleanor wisely plans her daily routine around her own energy pattern, scheduling creative activities for the time of day she feels most energetic and routine tasks for her down period.

5.   Carl may feel secure, but chances are both he and his thinking are in a rut. Carl ought to get up one morning at 4:30 to go for an early drive, change his breakfast habits, find a new route to work, change his restaurant pattern and find still another route home in the evening.

10

Tenant Representation

INTRODUCTION

Exclusive tenant representation is an approach to office leasing in which the salesperson represents tenants exclusively in moving to new space or renegotiating a lease in their current location.

YOUR ROLE

As an exclusive representative of the tenant (as opposed to representing the property), your first responsibility is to qualify tenants and discover their requirements. Do this by visiting the current office, considering alternative layouts, determining their location preferences, determining financial parameters and understanding the business's long-term growth plans.

The second step in servicing tenants is to find the space(s) that matches the needs defined above. Since you already should be an expert in your market area and know of all available space, this involves getting up-to-date information on landlords' terms, doing an economic and functional analysis for the tenant and touring suitable locations.

After locating the right space for the tenants, you will, of course, be responsible for negotiating on their behalf. For more information on the negotiation process, refer to chapter eight.

Your role does not end with the successful negotiation of a transaction. Professional tenant representatives also should monitor the progress of the build-out for the tenant and keep in touch during the move itself. The service you offer includes being available to the tenant throughout the process of the relocation.

GETTING STARTED

The goal in practicing tenant representation is tenant control. A number of steps are involved in obtaining and retaining this control.

Market Knowledge

Before talking with prospects, you must know the marketplace. This includes the area in general, specific buildings, their benefits and drawbacks, typical tenants' needs, rates, common concessions and so on.

Planning

Before making your telephone or cold call, become thoroughly rehearsed. Plan your opening statement. How will you present the benefits of your company, yourself and tenant representation? What facts and figures should you have ready? If it is a face-to-face cold call, what materials should you bring with you? Thinking these things through will increase your professionalism and your confidence.

Cold Call Strategy

Once you have completed your planning, determine your strategy for cold calling. Generally, in the beginning you should personally visit every office tenant in your territory. This will increase your knowledge of the market and tenants' needs. As you progress, you may choose to specialize in a certain size or type of tenant. In either case, determine your strategy and stick to it.

The First Appointment

Prepare three objectives in the first appointment. First, establish a rapport with the prospect. Second, uncover tenant opportunities and needs. Third, start to qualify the tenant on authority, financial ability and motivation.

Often a prospect is unfamiliar with the concept of tenant representation and its benefits. You can use the information in figure 10–1 to review these with the prospect.

Remember in your presentation to stress benefits, remain confident and professional and, above all, to listen.

Your Presentation Package

As part of your presentation, you must organize a professional package. This should include the following items.

1. a tenant questionnaire, used to qualify the tenant and determine needs

2. information on your company, such as brochures or a fact sheet

3. a chart listing the steps in a relocation and the approximate amount of time needed to accomplish each step

4. samples of market information, a lease analysis or any other data illustrating your expertise and relevant to the tenant

5. a sheet reviewing the benefits of tenant representation

6. a reference list or reference letters from previous clients

The goal of the package is to inspire in tenants' minds confidence in your ability to service successfully their needs.

Gathering Data

The next step as a professional tenant representative is to gather data on space(s) that meets the tenants' needs and any additional market information that could have a bearing on their move. This information will be used either to make your pitch to be the exclusive representative or, if you have already obtained that agreement, to begin servicing the requirement.

Servicing the Listing

Eight basic steps are involved in servicing a tenant representation requirement.

1. defining the tenant's requirements

2. doing market research

3. completing an investigation of suitable sites

4. obtaining requests for proposals from landlords

5. completing lease negotiations

6. providing coordination as needed for phone, furniture, etc.

7. providing coordination as needed with a space planner

8. maintaining contact with the tenant throughout construction and occupancy

USING AN EXCLUSIVE REPRESENTATIVE

Tenants gain several advantages by using an exclusive broker. These include the following items.

1. management of the relocation process by the salesperson

2. market expertise

3. best utilization of the tenant's time and money

4. negotiating expertise on the tenant's behalf

5. a single point of contact

As we discussed before, the role of the salesperson who exclusively represents a tenant begins with gathering market information and continues until the tenant is successfully located in a new space or in an existing space with a new lease.

Your market expertise ensures that tenants see all sites that meet their needs. Tenants will also, through you, be provided with complete market information. Only by understanding the market and all alternatives will they be able to make the best possible decision.

A tenant's time is best spent on business. Your time is best spent in successfully completing the real estate transaction. By doing the "legwork" needed in a move, you can free the tenants' time.

In negotiations, knowledge is power. In this case, your expertise in the real estate market will give tenants a more powerful position in negotiations. Not only will this contribute to their peace of mind, but should enable them to receive the best possible lease, both functionally and economically. In addition, because you represent tenants and not the sites, they are assured that you have their best interest in mind. You will not be swayed by possible locations where you have a listing. Tenants will receive unbiased information.

Finally, by working with one broker, tenants save time and energy. Not only do they avoid having to speak with a number of different people, they also receive consistent, quality information. Each property will be considered without bias or duplication by a number of brokers. Tenants have one individual responsible for their successful move.

The Landlord's Perspective

A number of advantages accrue to the landlord as well as the tenant when tenants use an exclusive broker. These benefits include your expertise on and qualification of the tenants' requirements, less chance of commission disputes over who controls tenants and a single contact who will follow through on all aspects of the transaction.

THE TENANT REPRESENTATION AGREEMENT

In the chapter on Legal Aspects of Office Marketing, a tenant representation agreement is included. However, you may find it difficult to obtain a tenant's signature on a document such as this. An alternative is a tenant representation letter, a sample of which follows in figure 10–2. While this letter outlines the same responsibilities on the part of both you and the tenant, the tone is more informal than the agreement. Use your own judgment and knowledge of the tenant to determine which document is more acceptable. The most important thing is to obtain some commitment from the tenant in writing. Otherwise you may spend a substantial amount of time working with no commission to show in the end. You cannot afford to speculate time on a tenant who will not commit. For more information on how tenant representation affects agency duties, refer to the chapter on Negotiation and the section on ethics.

CONCLUSION

The opportunities to earn commissions from exclusive tenant representation may be very lucrative. This is particularly true in an overbuilt market where space is abundant and tenants more scarce. Try obtaining the exclusive right to represent on some cold calls. Then determine for yourself what mix of business—site representation versus tenant representation—is best for you in your marketplace.

FIGURE 10.1   Working Guidelines for Tenant Representation

WORKING GUIDELINES FOR TENANT REPRESENTATION

DEFINITION OF SPACE REQUIREMENTS

In order to assemble a meaningful survey of the alternatives, our first objective is to clarify and define the tenant's needs. These include: geographic location and proximity, square footage, special systems, budget, lease term, expansion areas, parking, transportation, storage areas, building amenities, corporate exposure, etc.

SURVEY OF THE ALTERNATIVES

A. Develop a comprehensive survey of all new and existing office buildings that are consistent with the tenant's requirements.
B. Make recommendations as to suitability of developers and ownerships of these buildings, with specific reference to their financial stability and reputation within the industry.
C. Make arrangements for our tenant's representatives to visit those properties that are of particular interest.

DESIGN AND LAYOUT OF INTERIOR SPACE

A. Review with the tenant the criteria for selecting a space planner.
B. Assist in the selection and negotiation of the space planner to work in establishing the most efficient and economical design of the available space.
C. Analyze and review the particular layout of the floors under consideration (core areas, perimeter exposure, access, etc.).
D. Once a lease is signed, coordinate with the space planner the conversion of preliminary plans to final working drawings satisfactory for constructing the interior space.

LEASE NEGOTIATIONS

Our method for eliciting preliminary and final proposals from building ownerships is through our preparation of a written request for proposal, typically covering all business points in the negotiation. This document is presented and reviewed with each landlord so each business point is understood and responded to accordingly.

A. rental rate
B. escalation clause, covering rental adjustments arising from increases in taxes and operating expenses
C. the size of the demised premises as determined by the preliminary layout
D. the floor location
E. the lease term required
F. occupancy date
G. parking, if available
H. options—where applicable, develop the following types of options with minimum contingent liability:
   –options for expansion over the term of the lease
   –options for renewal
I. subleasing and assignment rights
J. disposition of existing lease—if necessary, by subletting the existing space or making various arrangements with new and existing landlords
K. building services such as janitorial and electrical service
L. improvements—develop a work letter outlining those items to be installed and provided by the landlord, at his or her expense These include, but are not limited to:
   –construction materials
   –partitioning doors and frames
   –floor covering
   –ceiling systems, lights, etc.
   –telephone and electrical outlets
   –air conditioning and heating systems
   –window treatment
   –additional special improvements by landlord, if necessary

LEGAL COUNSEL

The above negotiations are necessary in establishing the business points of the lease. The legal points that must be considered are referred to and coordinated through your legal counsel.

SUPPLEMENTARY ITEMS

As necessary, we will enlist the assistance of property management and construction companies to review and make recommendations as to:

A. The quality of work and materials to be provided by landlord.
B. The construction costs.
C. The heating, ventilating and air-conditioning systems.
D. The landlord's proposed operating procedures and maintenance programs to be provided for the entire project.

FIGURE 10.2   Sample Tenant Representation Letter

February 17, 1988

John Doe
XYZ Company
123 Commercial Avenue
Hometown, St. 55555

Dear John:

This letter confirms our discussion today regarding your firm's desire to relocate your office from its present location.

Grubb & Ellis Company will serve as your exclusive representative for the purpose of locating new office space. While coordinating with you, Grubb & Ellis will be responsible for the following:

1. Locating suitable buildings per specifications as determined by XYZ Company.

2. Providing materials and consultations to aid in evaluating various buildings.

3. Negotiating the transaction on your behalf.

4. Following up to ensure that your move is successfully completed.

Unless we agree otherwise, Grubb & Ellis will be paid all brokerage fees by the seller/lessor. It is agreed that all solicitation, presentations or other direct contacts to you will be handled by Grubb & Ellis.

This agreement may be cancelled by either party upon twenty-four (24) hours' written notice of intent to cancel.

If the foregoing is acceptable, please indicate your acceptance where indicated below, keeping one copy for your files and returning the original to Grubb & Ellis Company.

I look forward to the opportunity to serve you and assure you that I will aggressively perform in order to meet your objectives.

Sincerely,

Jane Smith
Office Marketing Division

APPROVED AND ACCEPTED FOR XYZ COMPANY:

By: _____

Date: _____

11

Local Developers

INTRODUCTION

Developers create or manufacture the space that you market and tenants will occupy. Becoming acquainted with the developers in your area is one of your major priorities. Generally, developers will usually agree to meet with you, since, as a new salesperson, you will possess up-to-date information on the market area. Keep in mind that there are relatively few developers of large office buildings but many developers of small ones, particularly office/warehouses.

Leasing space in a new or existing project is crucial to developers. To establish working relationships with developers, you need experience with and a sound understanding of the leasing side of the business. It will give you an opportunity to be out among the tenants, to gain first-hand knowledge of available sites and changes in your area and to sharpen your skill in analyzing property and assessing real estate potential. In your first year as an office-marketing salesperson, most of your time will probably be devoted to leasing existing space. This percentage will undoubtedly change as you acquire more expertise with the development side or choose which side—the developer or tenant—you prefer to work with.

This chapter will outline the various types of developers and describe how they operate. In addition, the material will suggest ways of obtaining information on growth patterns and projections to help you anticipate the services required by developers.

TYPES OF DEVELOPERS

Developers can generally be classified into two categories: equity developers and nonequity developers. The primary difference between equity and nonequity developers is their investment stance in a project.

Equity developers enter into a project with the intention of holding and increasing their share of the ownership for long-term appreciation, equity build-up and increased cash flow. Because of their ownership role in a project, such developers are more concerned with the quality of a center's architectural treatment and the financial qualifications of tenants.

Nonequity developers build projects with the objective of selling them. In some cases, the cash flow on a project can yield more money to the owner than the developer because of the valuation of the land, the percentages of the cash flow each is to receive and because the owner's return is preferred. In a 50–50 joint venture, this is of course undesirable for the shorted party.

Take, for example, a project that yields $190,000 in cash flow. The partners agree that the owner's preferred return is based on ten percent of the land value and the developer's cut is the same, provided the funds are available. After the initial proceeds are distributed, both parties receive equal amounts of any remaining profits. Let's now assume the land is valued at $1 million. Notice that the owner's preferred return of ten percent would yield the owner an initial $100,000, leaving the developer with the remaining $90,000 of the $190,000 cash flow. Thus, in our example, the land value could (or would) be lowered to $900,000. Notice now that the owner gets his preferred return of ten percent, or $90,000. Likewise the developer gets $90,000, leaving $10,000 in cash flow remaining, which they split equally. Thus, by revaluing the land, each party receives $95,000.

Because their involvement is short-term, nonequity developers may have to provide tenants with some assurances on project quality.

JOINT VENTURE

Developers who cannot or do not wish to purchase land for development may choose to enter into a joint-venture transaction. A joint venture is a partnership agreement, typically between a landowner and developer, in which each has something to contribute and something to gain. The owner's contribution is the land. Many owners who have held land for a number of years cannot afford to sell outright because the proceeds from such a sale would be heavily taxed. Developing the land, however, provides a depreciation tax shelter and the possibility of receiving a good return on the property's value. On the other hand, the developer's contribution lies in improvements to the land, that is, providing the expertise to put together an office complex or mixed-use development. The owner agrees to accept a certain percentage return based on a negotiated value of the land (called a preferred return). When the center is completed and occupied, the first amount from the cash flow equal to that percentage is paid to the landowner. An equal amount, if available, is then paid to the developer. Remember, the owner's return is not guaranteed but preferred. This means that the owner is paid first from the proceeds of the venture, up to the determined percentage. If the cash flow is less than this percentage, the owner will be paid the maximum amount of money that is available.

Implementing the Joint Venture

To begin the transaction, the owner and the developer enter into an escrow agreement. The owner will not contribute the land to the partnership until the developer has completed certain steps, such as the survey, the financing commitment, letters of intent from major tenants or signed leases. Only then does the owner convey title through escrow to the joint venture. The most difficult stage of the negotiation is between these two points, since the owner will not turn over title to the land until it is absolutely certain the venture will go forward. For the developer, the most important stage involves getting commitments from the major tenants—a necessary step to ensure adequate funding for the project.

50–50 Partnership

The procedure outlined above represents one way of structuring a joint venture. However, if the owner is willing to share in the risks as well as the rewards, a 50–50 partnership may be formed. In this case, the owner will contribute the land, foregoing the preferred return, and sign a construction loan with the developer for half of the projected income from the property. The advantage to this arrangement is that there will be additional income from the rents as the property matures. The owner chooses to share in the anticipated profit increase by relinquishing a low-risk return.

Ground Lease versus Joint Venture

Instead of entering into a joint venture, a landowner may prefer a ground lease transaction, leasing the land for development. With a ground lease, the owner states that the property is worth a certain amount and that a specific percentage return is expected on that stated value. With a joint venture, the amount of return is directly related to the risk the owner takes.

Payment of Commission

A broker receives the joint venture formation fee based on the price of the land contribution. The joint venture entity pays the commission. Fees are usually paid at the time the escrow forms the joint venture (i.e., at the time the land is conveyed in escrow from the owner to the partnership).

You would most likely be involved first with the property owner, who would agree to pay you a commission in the event that you successfully complete a sales transaction, a lease or a joint venture. Ordinarily, the joint venture is not the first approach taken with an owner. If, however, this turns out to be the most viable approach to the property, you will need to work with the owner to understand the option. This may be difficult, particularly if the owner has held the land for a long time and fears the risks involved in a venture.

When the owner has agreed to the transaction, it is important that you make sure the developer understands that the joint venture entity pays your commission. This means that the developer and the property owner are each responsible for half the commission fee.

Other Types of Joint Ventures

There are two other types of joint ventures. The developer may enter into a partnership with (1) a financial institution (lender) or (2) a major tenant. In both cases, the arrangements usually involve large developments. With the first type, a developer will tie up a large piece of property and bring in a financial institution as a partner, most commonly referred to as an equity partner.

DEVELOPMENT FOR A FEE

A less common type of development structuring is one in which a developer (equity or nonequity) agrees to develop an office building as a service to the landowner. In exchange for the service rendered, the developer would receive a negotiated fee from the landowner.

Development for a fee is a less popular method since it requires as much time and effort as traditional methods of development, yet does not carry with it the various benefits that otherwise accrue to the developers.

KNOW DEVELOPERS

In drawing up an inventory of developers for your area, you should know the program and the reputation of each one—their strong and weak points, the type and quality of the projects they have done, their development posture, whether they are equity or nonequity developers or whether they will offer their services on a flat fee schedule. Collect site plans from the different developers and make a study of the space available in their projects.

In the real estate market, many developers rely heavily on brokers. A good-sized developer may have a leasing agent on the staff whose sole responsibility is to get the space rented. This person can be an excellent contact. For example, you may have a tenant whose requirement will be met by existing or proposed space in a developer's center. A leasing agent can help you locate the appropriate space and work out a lease agreement for your tenant.

When initiating contact with developers, be sure to meet with them at their place of business. Use the telephone only for setting an appointment or for follow-up purposes. One effective method of meeting developers is by participating in the National Association of Industrial/Office Parks (N.A.I.O.P).

WORKING WITH DEVELOPERS

You should know something of the protocol expected in dealing with developers. Do not, for example, shop for the best offer for a piece of land by presenting the same property to several different developers at the same time. Take a property to one developer and make it clear that you consider that person the best candidate for this particular piece of property. If developers know you are shopping for the highest price, they are unlikely to make a serious, competitive offer for the property.

A similar problem can develop when you have more than one developer bidding on a site. Each may want to know what the competition is doing. This is a delicate matter to handle. You want to remain on good terms with both developers, yet you must protect the confidence of each one. No broker can serve two masters.

If you are already working with a big developer and another calls to ask you to handle a transaction, make sure there are no conflicts in the categories you have covered. If you are already committed in one area, let the second developer know you cannot work exclusively for his or her firm in the same area. You avoid any misunderstandings and the developer will not become annoyed if you call only once a month rather than twice a week.

Maintaining good relationships with developers is very important. Often in one area only a handful of people are responsible for the majority of the development. If you should happen to antagonize one developer, the word may reach others and it will be difficult for you to restore your credibility.

COMMISSION AGREEMENTS

In every transaction you should draw up a letter of agreement between you and the landowner, stipulating the amount of your commission and a schedule for payment. Usually large amounts of money are involved in these transactions, and brokers' efforts are rewarded only if they receive the commission. Commission agreements, which protect your fee, are discussed in detail in the chapter on Legal Aspects of Office Management.

KNOWING THE MARKET

Besides knowing the program and reputation of each developer in your area, you also should be aware of local laws and zoning ordinances, current tax and rental rates and building requirements and regulations. You can obtain this information from civic organizations, the local chamber of commerce and municipal agencies responsible for zoning and redevelopment. The future state of the market can be gauged by finding out from municipal organizations where new development is being considered.

CONCLUSION

You can earn a substantial income from commissions by successfully working on transactions with developers. Remember, in working with sophisticated professionals, you must maintain a high level of credibility. Keeping on top of the market picture is your responsibility. It requires constant research, analysis and evaluation. Be ready to draw upon everything you have learned from your experience in leasing space. Feel free to ask questions of more experienced salespeople and keep in mind that you will learn much from the developers themselves as you begin to work with them.

Exercise A

1. What are the advantages and disadvantages to landowners of ground leases and joint ventures?

2. What is the difference between an equity and a nonequity developer?

3. How is the commission generally paid in a joint venture transaction?

4. What is meant by *preferred return* and *residual return* in the context of a joint venture?

5. How should the issue of commissions be handled when you decide to work with a developer?

6. What should you know about developers besides the kinds of projects they undertake?

7. Explain what developers might do if they wished to maintain a partial equity position in a development.

Answer A

1. The advantage to landowners of joint ventures is that they provide a depreciation tax shelter and the possibility of receiving a good return on the property's value. The disadvantage is that the rate of return is directly related to the risk the owner takes. The advantage of a ground lease is the certainty of a specific percentage return. The disadvantage is the lower return due to the lower risk.

2. *Equity developers enter a project intending to hold and increase their ownership share. Nonequity developers build projects in order to sell them.*

3. *The developer and the property owner are each responsible for half the commission fee.*

4. *A "preferred return" is where an owner agrees to accept a certain percentage return based on a negotiated value of the land. A "residual return" offers the landowner a percentage of the projected income from the property.*

5. *Prepare a letter of agreement between you and the landowner, stipulating the commission amount and a schedule for payment. Commissions should be paid at the time the escrow forms the venture.*

6. *Know the program and reputation of each developer, including their strong and weak points, the quality of their projects, their development posture, whether they are equity or nonequity developers or whether they offer their services on a flat fee schedule.*

7. *Developers wishing to maintain a partial equity position would show more concern over a center's architectural treatment and the financial qualifications of tenants.*

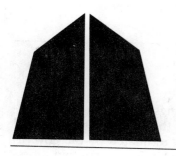

12

Safety and Environmental Issues

INTRODUCTION

In addition to your responsibility for being familiar with the market-place in general, an office salesperson is also responsible for knowledge of specific properties. One area you must take special care to be proficient in is the area of safety issues. These issues are critical to both seller-lessor and buyer-lessee and, of course, to yourself as the intermediary.

Typical safety issues include the presence of asbestos insulation or fireproofing, electrical transformers containing polychlorinated biphenyls (PCBs), underground fuel tanks for back-up generators and soil and groundwater contamination.

UNDERGROUND TANKS

Underground storage tanks present a potential liability for both buyer and seller. Federal law plays a small role in the regulation of underground tanks. However, each state has individual legislation in this area. The most important thing for you as a salesperson to remember is that you have a responsibility to determine from the owner if there is or has been a tank on the property and to disclose that information to the buyer-lessee. The process for discovering and disclosing will be discussed at greater length later in this section.

ASBESTOS

Concern about asbestos in commercial buildings is high. In fact, asbestos was the first material to be regulated by the Federal Occupational Safety and Health Administration. It is now estimated by the government that 20 percent of public and commercial buildings contain asbestos.

Many building owners, concerned about liability for asbestos-related claims, have considered removing all asbestos materials in a building. However, because of the difficulty of removing asbestos, removal can create even greater risk and liability.

Asbestos has been highly regulated in recent years. In 1973, regulations were passed banning the use of spray-applied asbestos materials as building insulation or fireproofing, except in equipment and machinery. Obviously, there are a number of buildings that were built before this ban that have a potential problem. The Environmental Protection Agency's regulations on asbestos apply to "owners and operators" of asbestos emission sources. This includes the building owner. There is liability to the building owner from a disclosure standpoint in selling the property and also as a safety issue for employees, tenants and maintenance workers.

POLYCHLORINATED BIPHENYLS

Polychlorinated biphenyls, more commonly known as PCBs, are present in electrical equipment, including capacitors and transformers. Many office buildings have transformers located in basement or sidewalk vaults or on rooftops. Institutional light fixtures may also contain PCBs.

In 1979, the Environmental Protection Agency placed restrictions on the use of PCB-containing equipment. Responsibility for compliance with these rules lies with both the owner and the operator of the equipment. In addition, the owner of the property on which the equipment is located can be held responsible. This is significant since transformers owned by an electric utility are often located in or adjacent to the building they serve. Thus, a building owner who merely uses utility-owned transformers or owns the property on which they are located may be held liable for any personal injury or property damage resulting from the PCB. For example, building owners have in the past incurred significant costs for cleanup efforts, personal injury and loss of business when transformers have caught on fire. In some cases, the building may have to be closed for years for cleanup.

SOIL AND GROUNDWATER CONTAMINATION

There are extensive and clear guidelines on the management of hazardous wastes. One fact to keep in mind, particularly for office salespeople, is that hazardous waste is not limited to the obviously heavy industrial site. Light industry, mixed-use, warehouse and distribution centers and parking lots can also be major sources of hazardous waste. Under existing regulations, a landowner may be liable for "unauthorized disposals" of hazardous waste on his or her property. This includes any discharge, spilling, dumping, pouring, emitting or leaking of waste. The Environmental Protection Agency may order a cleanup. This order may be given to the current owner of the property, even if the hazardous waste is the result of a former owner or tenant. Both the seller and buyer may be subject to a cleanup order if the property is contaminated, regardless of who was directly responsible for the contamination. For example, if the buyer of a property does not clean up hazardous waste on the site, he or she is contributing to a disposal. No showing of fault is necessary to impose liability. The only issue is whether or not a hazardous substance has been released. Liability is joint and several. That is, each party may be liable for the entire cost of the cleanup. Property owners may be responsible for cleanup costs regardless of whether they owned the property at the time of the release, knew about the contamination or negligently caused the contamination. As you can imagine, this will most likely result in litigation between present and past owners and perhaps tenants. Cases occurred where a bank, because it foreclosed on a mortgage, was considered the owner of a property and held liable for cleanup costs. In addition to cleanup costs, anyone who willfully violates or refuses to comply with an EPA cleanup order is subject to a fine of up to $5,000 for each day such failure to comply continues.

Another aspect of hazardous waste that you must be familiar with is *border-zone legislation*. In some states this legislation limits the owner of property from developing the land for certain uses when his or her property is within a certain distance (typically 2,000 feet) of a disposal of hazardous waste. Any restriction binds not only the landowner but all lessees and successive owners as well.

An important point that an office salesperson must remember is that potential liabilities may be addressed in the sale or lease contract. Therefore, it is particularly important for you to have thoroughly investigated and disclosed the environmental history, condition and use of a property prior to completion of a transaction.

YOUR RESPONSIBILITIES

Because liability for cleanup can be both expensive and retroactive, buyers, sellers, landlords and tenants all must know whether there is any contamination and, if so, the nature and extent. Without such an assessment, sellers risk liability for wastes generated by successive owners or tenants. Buyers may be held responsible for a seller's or tenant's contamination. And tenants may be liable for an owner's or prior tenant's contamination.

There are several steps you, as a responsible office salesperson, must take to investigate any possibility of contamination.

Physical Inspection

The first step in an investigation is a physical inspection. Although it must be stressed that quite often toxic waste is not visible, it is still important to make as thorough a visual evaluation as possible. Among the things to look for on the property and the adjacent site are storage tanks, septic pools, storage drums, a dump site, landfill, any standing water, the drainage system, equipment/automotive service areas and discolored soil.

For office users the strongest likelihood of contamination exists in any site that was built from the 1950s to the 1970s (when asbestos insulation and ceiling tiles were used), any site that was formerly agricultural (due to pesticides), any site with landfill, any site with electrical transformers or any site adjacent to a property with any of these conditions.

Owner/Tenant Inquiry

Your next step is to ask the owner and perhaps the current tenant questions about safety issues. These may include the following questions.

1. Is there any hazardous waste, asbestos or equipment containing PCBs that you know of on your site or any adjacent site?

2. What is the current use of the site?

3. What chemicals and/or equipment is involved in the current use?

4. What use did past owners and tenants make of this property?

5. What use did past owners and tenants make of any adjacent property?

6. What chemicals/equipment were involved in past uses of this property and any adjacent properties?

7. Has an environmental report or violation ever been filed on this site or an adjacent site? (You can check the Environmental Protection Agency National Priority List and Remedial Response Information System for additional information in this area.)

8. What waste disposal methods are used by the current owner-tenant and what methods have been used in the past?

All questions asked and information uncovered must be documented and disclosed.

Testing

Once you have made a verbal and paper investigation, the seller, buyer or tenant may follow it up with testing. Both soil and groundwater can be tested. This should be done by an independent specialist in the field.

If contamination is discovered, the testing company may recommend a variety of cleanup methods, including capping, containment barriers, groundwater collection, pumping and treatment, excavation and removal, on-site treatment, incineration and solidification.

Documentation

There are a number of steps you can take to protect, to the best of your ability, all parties to the transaction.

1. Do your homework. Thoroughly investigate the property, its history and its current use.

2. Document and disclose everything.

3. Use a restrictive covenant if necessary. A restrictive covenant restrains land uses that may cause harm, such as drilling, excavating, building housing, etc.

4. Determine financial responsibility within the sales agreement. You may allocate costs associated with contamination known at the time of sale, costs associated with contamination existing at the time of sale but not discovered until later, costs associated with contamination caused by the buyer or successors and costs associated with contamination of uncertain origin. This will not limit the parties' obligation to the government or third parties. However, it will establish an understanding of the parties' obligations to each other.

Summary

All parties in the transaction are relying on your abilities as a professional to structure a transaction that is mutually beneficial. To fulfill this function, you must be up to date in your knowledge of safety concerns and the specific property involved in the transaction and be able to effectively communicate that information to all parties concerned.

FIGURE 12.1   Buyer's Draft for Purchase of Property

1. Seller's covenants, warranties and representations: The covenants, warranties and representations contained in this paragraph 1 will be effective on the date hereof and at Closing and will survive Closing. Seller covenants, warrants and represents to Buyer, its successors and assigns that:

   (a) No litigation is pending or, to Seller's knowledge, proposed, threatened, or anticipated with respect to the Seller, or with respect to any other matter affecting the Property or the operation thereof.

   (b) Prior to Closing, Seller shall, at its sole cost and expense, and subject to Buyer's reasonable satisfaction, maintain the Property in good repair and in the same condition as of the date of this Agreement, reasonable wear and tear excepted.

   (c) If Seller is notified of any legal proceedings instituted against the Property prior to Closing, Seller shall promptly give notice thereof to Buyer.

   (d) To Seller's knowledge after due inquiry, no electrical transformers, fluorescent light fixtures with ballasts or other equipment containing PCBs are or were located on the Property at any time during or prior to Seller's ownership thereof.

   (e) To Seller's knowledge after due inquiry, no asbestos-containing materials were installed or exposed in the Property through demolition, renovation, or otherwise, at any time or prior to Seller's ownership thereof.

   (f) To Seller's knowledge after due inquiry, no storage tanks for gasoline or any other substance are or were located on the Property at any time during or prior to Seller's ownership thereof.

   (g) The Property and Seller's operations concerning the Property are not in violation of any applicable federal, state or local statute, law or regulation, and no notice from any governmental body has been served upon Seller claiming any violation of any law, ordinance, code or regulation, or requiring or calling attention to the need for, any work, repairs, construction, alterations or installation on or in connection with the Property in order to comply with any laws, ordinances, codes or regulations, with which Seller has not complied. If there are any such notices with which Seller has complied, Seller shall provide Buyer with copies thereof.

2. Release: Buyer expressly releases Seller from any and all liability arising from or connected with the condition of the Property which is discovered after Closing.

3. Indemnity: From and after Closing, Seller shall indemnify, defend and save harmless from all losses or damages resulting from injury to or death of any person and damage to the Property, and any fine, which is occasioned or arises out of any breach of warranty, representation or covenant of Seller under this agreement.

FIGURE 12.2   Seller's Draft

1. Conditions Precedent: Buyer shall have no obligation to purchase the Property from Seller hereunder unless at Closing each and every representation and warranty and covenant contained in paragraph 2 below shall be true and correct on the date of Closing. If any representation, warranty or covenant contained in paragraph 2 below is not true and correct on the date of Closing, Buyer shall elect either to terminate this Agreement or to waive the condition and purchase the Property, and such election shall be Buyer's sole remedy.

2. Seller's Covenants, Warranties and Representations: Seller covenants, warrants and represents to Buyer, its successors and assigns that:

(a) No litigation, and no governmental, administrative or regulatory act or proceeding is pending or, to Seller's knowledge, proposed, threatened or anticipated with respect to the Seller, or with respect to any other matter affecting the Property or the operation thereof.

(b) Prior to Closing, Seller shall, at its sole cost and expense, and subject to Buyer's satisfaction, maintain the Property in good repair and in the same condition as of the date of this Agreement, reasonable wear and tear excepted.

(c) If Seller is notified of any legal or governmental or administrative act or proceeding instituted against the Property prior to Closing, Seller shall promptly give notice thereof to Buyer.

(d) To Seller's knowledge, no asbestos-containing materials were installed in the Property at any time during Seller's ownership thereof. (Include details of any asbestos that was found.)

(e) To Seller's knowledge, all electrical transformers and equipment on the Property are shown in the Building Plans furnished to Buyer.

(f) To Seller's knowledge, no storage tanks for gasoline or any other substance are or were located on the Property at any time during or prior to Seller's ownership thereof.

(g) To Seller's knowledge, the Property and Seller's operations concerning the Property are not in violation of any applicable federal, state or local statute, law or regulation, and no notice from any governmental body has been served upon Seller claiming any violation of any law, ordinance, code or regulation, or requiring or calling attention to the need for any work, repairs, construction, alterations or installation on or in connection with the Property in order to comply with any laws, ordinances, codes or regulations, with which Seller has not complied. If there are any such notices with which Seller has complied, Seller shall provide Buyer with copies thereof.

3. "To Seller's knowledge" Defined: "To Seller's knowledge" means to the actual, but not constructive, knowledge of (name) (title). Buyer has had full opportunity to inspect the Property and examine Seller's records, and Buyer agrees that Seller has no duty to make any investigation as to the matters warranted and represented in paragraph 2 above.

4. Release: From and after Closing, Buyer hereby waives, releases, remises, acquits and forever discharges Seller, its directors, officers, shareholders, employees, and agents and their respective heirs, successors, personal representatives and assigns, of and from any and all suits, causes of action, legal or administrative proceedings, claims, demands, actual damages, punitive damages, losses, costs, liabilities, interest, attorneys' fees and expenses of whatever kind and nature, in law or in equity, known or unknown, which Buyer ever had, now has, hereafter can, shall or may have or acquire or possess or arising out of or in any way connected with directly or indirectly out of, or in any way connected with, based upon, arising out of, (i) Seller's use, maintenance, ownership and operation of the Property prior to Closing, or (ii) the condition, status, quality, nature, contamination or environmental state of the Property.

It is the intention of this agreement that any and all responsibilities and obligations of Seller, and any and all rights or claims of Buyer, its successors and assigns and affiliated entities, arising by virtue of the physical or environmental condition of the Property are by this release provision declared null and void and of no present or future effect as to such parties. Buyer agrees to waive the benefits of Section _____ of the Civil Code of the state of _____ , which provides as follows:

"A general release does not extend to claims which the creditor does not know or suspect to exist in his favor at the time of executing the release, which if known by him must have materially affected his settlement with the debtor."

FIGURE 12.2   (continued)

5. Indemnify: Buyer shall, to the maximum extent permitted by law:

(a) Save, defend, indemnify and hold harmless (herein collectively called "To Indemnify"), Seller, its directors, officers, shareholders, employees and agents, and their respective heirs, successors, personal representatives and assigns (herein collectively called "Indemnified Parties") from and against any and all suits, actions, legal or administrative proceedings, claims, demands, actual damages, fines, punitive damages, losses, costs, liabilities, interest, attorneys' fees (including any such fees and expenses incurred in enforcing this indemnity) (herein collectively called "Damages") resulting from, arising out of or in any way connected with injury to or the death of any person (including, without limitation, any Indemnified Party) or physical damage to property of any kind wherever located and by whomever owned (including, without limitation, that of any Indemnified Party) arising out of or in any way connected with Seller's ownership or use of the Property, including, but not limited to, any such injury, death, damage, or loss arising out of the negligence of the Indemnified Parties.

FIGURE 12.3   Seller's "As Is" Provision

Acceptance of Property "As Is": Buyer acknowledges and agrees that the Property is to be sold and conveyed to, and accepted by Buyer, in an "as is" condition with all faults. Buyer has investigated and has knowledge of operative or proposed governmental laws and regulations (including, but not limited to, zoning, environmental and land use laws and regulations) to which the Property is or may be subject and accepts the Property upon the basis of its review and determination of the applicability and effect of such laws and regulations. Buyer acknowledges that the Property has been used for the production of widgets for many years, and that such production involves the use of solvents and other chemicals. Buyer acknowledges the existence of storage tanks for gasoline on the Property. Buyer acknowledges the use of raw land on the Property for Parking. Buyer acknowledges the existence of asbestos insulation and PCB-laden electrical equipment on the Property. Buyer acknowledges that as a result of such uses and conditions, physical changes, including gasoline and chemical seepage, may have occurred on the Property. Buyer acknowledges that it is entering into this agreement on the basis of Buyer's own investigation of the physical and environmental conditions of the Property, including subsurface conditions, and Buyer assumes the risk that adverse physical and environmental conditions may not have been revealed by its own investigation. Buyer further acknowledges that Seller, its agents and employees and other persons acting on behalf of Seller have made no representation or warranty of any kind in connection with any matter relating to the condition, value, fitness, use or zoning of the Property upon which Buyer has relied directly or indirectly for any purpose. Buyer hereby waives, releases, remises, acquits and forever discharges Seller, Seller's employees, agents or any other person acting on behalf of Seller, of and from any claims, actions, causes of action, demands, rights, damages, costs, expenses or compensation whatsoever, direct or indirect, known or unknown, foreseen or unforeseen, which Buyer now has or which may arise in the future on account of or in any way growing out of or connected with the physical condition of the Property or any law or regulation applicable thereto.

FIGURE 12.4   Seller's Allocation of Testing Responsibility

1. Environmental Conditions:

(a) Seller shall undertake at Seller's expense an investigation to determine the environmental condition of the Property, such review to be completed prior to termination of the Review Period. Such review shall include the sampling of soil and the drilling of observation wells at the locations specified in Exhibit 1 to this Agreement and such additional tests as Seller may reasonably deem necessary to determine the environmental condition of the Property. Buyer may participate in such review and shall have access to all information developed. Buyer agrees that the investigation outlined in Exhibit 1 represents a thorough and reasonable examination of the environmental conditions on the Property.

(b) If the review pursuant to subparagraph 1(a) above identifies the existence of environmental conditions which may be subject to legal requirements for corrective action, Seller may terminate this Agreement.

FIGURE 12.5   Seller's Disclosure of Written Information

Environmental Studies:

Seller has provided Buyer with various environmental studies and reports conducted by independent contractors and various records of Seller concerning, relating to and affecting the Property which identify certain underground tanks, certain contamination of the soil and groundwater of the Property and other environmental information relating to the Property, and correspondence with various governmental entities concerning the Property and Buyer acknowledges having received the reports, records and correspondences that are identified on Exhibit A attached hereto. For reference purposes only, all such reports, records and correspondence identified on Exhibit 1 are referred to collectively as the "Reports." Seller does not warrant the accuracy of any information contained in the Reports.

FIGURE 12.6   Buyer's Proposed Representations Regarding Operating Plant

Seller represents and warrants to Buyer that to Seller's knowledge:

(i) Plant A is used and operated in substantial compliance with applicable local, state and federal laws, ordinances, rules, regulations, and orders, and has all permits and authorizations required for its use and operation.

(ii) No material change has been made in the use or operation of Plant A, and no processes, materials or machinery have been introduced since (date) .

FIGURE 12.7   Allocation of Costs

Post-Closing Corrective Action:

If Buyer within one (1) year following Closing, determines and demonstrates to Seller's reasonable satisfaction that environmental conditions subject to legal requirements for corrective action are present as a result of Seller's operations prior to Closing and that the presence of such conditions was unknown to Buyer before Closing, Buyer's sole remedy shall be to require Seller to correct or make arrangements for the correction of such conditions as are required by law.

FIGURE 12.8   Seller's Indemnification of Buyer for Cleanup

1. Indemnity.

(a) From and after Closing, Seller shall indemnify, defend and save harmless Buyer from and against any and all losses, damages, liabilities, expenses (including reasonable attorneys' fees), fines, penalties and costs arising out of the willful misconduct or negligence of Seller occurring during the exercise of the irrevocable license granted to it pursuant to paragraph _____ hereof.

(b) Seller's liability under the provisions of paragraph 1(a) is expressly conditioned upon Buyer furnishing Seller with prompt written notice of any matter of which Buyer receives actual notice which might give rise to liability on the part of Seller hereunder and Seller having control over the defense of any action, proceeding, claim or demand which might give rise to liability on its part hereunder, and over all negotiations relating to the settlement thereof; provided, however, that Seller shall keep Buyer advised on a reasonably regular basis of the progress thereof and Buyer shall have the right, at its expense, to participate in the defense.

(c) Notwithstanding the indemnity set forth in paragraph 1(a), under no circumstances shall Seller be liable to Buyer or any grantee of Buyer for any special or consequential losses or damages, including loss of use and loss of profits, regardless of cause.

FIGURE 12.9   Cost Splitting: Seller Partially Liable for Two Years

Seller shall indemnify and hold harmless Buyer, from and against eighty percent (80%) of the value of any Damages arising from any environmental contamination present at the Property as a result of Seller's operations prior to Closing to the extent that such Damages in the aggregate exceed Five Hundred Thousand Dollars ($500,000); provided that such indemnity shall not extend to any demand for indemnification made more than two (2) years after Closing.

FIGURE 12.10   Seller's Proposed Restrictive Covenant

Restrictive Covenant. Buyer and Seller hereby agree that the deed delivered pursuant to this purchase and sale agreement will provide as follows:

WHEREAS, Conditions existing on the Property as a result of its use as a manufacturing facility for the processing of widgets make the Property unsuitable for certain uses, and

WHEREAS, The parties hereto desire and intend to restrict the use of the Property in the future so as to reduce the risk of injury or damage to persons and property as a result of the existing conditions,

Now Therefore, in consideration of the mutual promises of the parties hereto, each to the other as covenantor and covenantee, Buyer hereby covenants to Seller, which covenant shall be binding upon all successors in interest to the Property, that the Property or any portion thereof shall not be used for any purpose other than commercial manufacturing or industrial purposes only, at any time during a period of thirty (30) years from and after the date of recordation of this Deed. Said permitted commercial, manufacturing or industrial uses shall not include any agricultural use, any livestock raising or breeding use, any food processing uses, or any playground, sports, recreational, open space, public park, school or hospital uses, or any accessory or incidental use or uses thereto on the Property such as, but not limited to, residential uses of any density or nature whether permanent or temporary. If Buyer, or any successor in interest to the Property, shall cause or permit a breach of said covenant, Seller, or its successors and assigns, may enjoin such unpermitted use and seek other such relief to which it may be entitled.

The covenants contained herein are to run with the land and shall be binding on all parties and persons claiming under them. Buyer agrees that all the restrictions contained in this deed shall be inserted in full in all future deeds of the Property covered by this deed.

13

Sale-Leasebacks

DEFINITION

A sale-leaseback is a transaction in which the owner-tenant of a property sells the property to a buyer and simultaneously leases the property back from the buyer.

The decision to do a sale-leaseback is an economic one. Usually, it is to liquidate real estate equity for use elsewhere. Therefore, your first step as a salesperson when exploring this option with an owner-user is to complete a financial analysis.

ANALYSIS OF A SALE-LEASEBACK

In order to determine if a sale-leaseback makes economic sense, there are four basic questions you need to research.

1. What are the ownership costs for the property?

2. What would the lease costs be for the property?

3. What return could the owner-user receive from an alternative use of the money that is now real estate equity?

4. What are the tax implications of the transaction?

Obviously, the last question is one that demands the attention of the owner-user's tax specialist. However, you must weigh it as a consideration when presenting the sale-leaseback option.

THE PROCESS

There are six steps in the decision-making process for a sale-leaseback.

1. Identify the start date of the analysis and obtain the necessary information.

2. Add up the total ownership inflows and outflows over the ten-year period on an after-tax basis.

3. Add up the total lease costs over the ten-year period after tax.

4. Discount both cash flows (owning/leasing) at varying discount rates.

5. Compare discounted cost differentials to the client's internal yield returns.

6. Review the outcome with the client and the appropriate advisors (tax, etc.). Then let the client make the decision.

Identify a Start Date and Obtain Information

To provide a more accurate assessment of the situation, you will need to do a ten-year analysis using the present year as year one.

Your first step is to estimate how much net equity after tax the owner-user has invested in the property. To do this you must:

1. Estimate the current market value of the building.

2. Subtract out current loan balances.

3. Subtract out tax as if the owner were to sell today.

Example. Market value of property
  – Outstanding loan(s) balance(s)
  – Capital gains tax
  = Net equity after tax

Now you have the owner's beginning investment amount as if he or she had bought the property today. Next, you have to identify the income and expenses related to ownership. These include the operating costs, depreciation schedule, debt service, appreciation, tax effect and the cap rate for resale at the end of the term. This data will allow you to measure both inflows and outflows related to ownership over the ten-year period.

To analyze the sell and leaseback side of the transaction, you assume the owner-user sold the property and executed a triple net lease. (In a triple net lease the lessee assumes payment of all expenses associated with the operation of the property.) Next you identify conventional lease costs for a typical triple net tenant—the rent and expenses at current market rates, the increases per year and the tax consequences. You then have the outflow of the leasing side.

Ownership Inflows and Outflows

Given that you have the needed data on ownership, the total cost of owning the building is computed by adding the initial equity outlay to annual expense outlays and subtracting from that total the income from the resale of the property in year ten.

Example.   Net equity after tax (example 1)
  + Annual cash flows after tax (see calculation)
  <u>− Net resale value</u>
  = Total ownership costs

To calculate the annual cash outflows after tax take:

  Income: (0)
  <u>− Expenses</u>
  = Net operating income (negative)
  <u>− Debt service</u>
  = Cash flow pre-tax

  Net operating income
  − Interest payments
  <u>− Depreciation</u>
  = Taxable income
  <u>× Tax bracket</u>
  = Taxable income/loss

  Cash flow pre-tax
  <u>− Taxable loss</u>
  = Cash flow after tax (annual net outflow, after tax)

Lease Outflows

Given that you have the necessary lease data, the occupancy expense in leasing the property is calculated as follows:

Example.   Triple net lease payments (annual outflows)
  <u>+ Annual lease expenses</u>
  = Annual lease expense, pre-tax

  Annual lease expense, pre-tax
  <u>× (1 − tax bracket)</u>
  = Lease expense per year after tax

Discounting Ownership and Lease Cash Flows

Up to this point, you've assimilated ownership and leasing data and compiled both the total ownership and leasing costs over the analysis time period. Without introducing the time-value of money, we could simply compare these two totals and see which is more costly—owning or renting. Unfortunately a dollar received in ten years is not worth as much as a dollar received today. More specifically, when the owner re-sells the building in year ten, the money he or she receives is worth less per dollar than the money invested in year one. Similarly, the lease costs in year ten do not have the same dollar value as lease costs in year one.

Whenever you have two cash streams involving varying outflows or inflows at different times over a ten-year period, there is no way you can compare the total value of each cash stream on an apple-to-apple basis. Only by selecting a discount rate and calculating the net present value of the cash streams can you compare their relative value dollar-for-dollar. Therefore, the fourth step in the lease versus buy model involves discounting occupancy costs into comparable, net present value terms.

Other Considerations

The sale-leaseback decision rests not only on a comparison of discounted lease and ownership costs, but also on how these costs relate to the business's internal investment yield on operations. For example, business capital may be put to better use in the business operation as opposed to real estate equity. If the company is a widget-maker and the operating profits after tax are 18 percent, the company probably wouldn't want millions tied up in real estate that only yields ten percent. On the other hand, if the inflation rate is extremely low, the company might be better-off owning than renting. In general, it is less costly to own at low discount rates and better to rent for any scenario where the discount rate is high. Thus, for these and other reasons, it is necessary for the sale-leaseback analysis to consider a complete range of discount rates. A critical element to the analysis is to determine the discount rate that the client feels best applies to his or her economic situation.

TYPES OF SALE-LEASEBACKS

The examples given above deal with the most common type of sale-leaseback—that in which the land and building are sold and then leased back. Other varieties of sale-leaseback exist.

Land-Only Sale-Leaseback. Used principally by developers, a land sale-leaseback is where the land component of the property is valued, sold and leased back to the owner, while the ownership of the improvements remains unchanged. The developer typically executes a subordinated ground lease.

The reason for not selling and leasing back the improvements is that, typically, they have depreciation write-off potential. The developer gets the best of both worlds: the nondepreciable land payments are deducted via lease payments, the improvements are depreciated and 100 percent of the land value has been liquidated.

Finally, such arrangements are structured so the buyer-landlord is assured of clear title to land and improvements at the end of the lease term or upon default.

Exchange-Leaseback.   Exchange-Leaseback is a complex transaction having several variations. The two basic types are:

1. The seller-tenant trades his or her facility for a like-kind nonbusiness property and leases back the facility.
2. The seller-tenant trades the facility for the lease itself.

In both cases the transactions are much more technical to structure and require extensive legal, financial and tax advice.

DISCUSSING THE SALE-LEASEBACK OPTION

Obviously, because of the complicated and limited nature of doing a sale-leaseback, saying "Hi, I'm John Jones of ABC Realty and I'm here to talk to you about doing a sale-leaseback," is not an effective opening on a cold-call. However, there are several clues you can listen for in a cold-call. These clues include comments such as the following ones:

1. "Real estate is not our problem. Our problem is capital."
2. "We're getting killed on taxes. We've taken most of our depreciation on this place and two-thirds of our debt service now in principal."
3. "We've got the best profit margin in the business. The problem is we need more facilities to accommodate our growth, and the banks don't like our balance sheet."
4. "We've considered selling, but leasing is always more expensive than owning."
5. "I'm considering refinancing this place so we can get our hands on more capital."

CONCLUSION

As you have seen, the sale-leaseback analysis and decision is an extremely complex one. You as a salesperson are not in a position to serve as sole advisor to a client in this matter. It is very important that he or she also involve financial, legal and tax advisors in the process. However, you can be of great value to a client in providing education on the sale-leaseback option, the process for analysis and giving a general picture of what may be preferable in his or her situation.

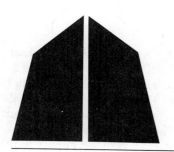

14

Case History

At home one evening in early February, Tom Turner, an office-marketing specialist for Grubb & Ellis, was catching up on a somewhat neglected task—scanning trade journals and the business press for clues to possible deals. An item in *The Wall Street Journal* caught Tom's eye. Morgan, Murphy and Cash, a small but long-established Canadian stockbrokerage firm, had a particularly impressive six-months' earnings report after a steady four-year string of increased quarterly earnings.

Tom was aware that the company had a San Francisco office, but he had no intimate knowledge of the company, nor did he know anyone who worked there. However, the news item made him wonder if such a successful operation might be contemplating an expansion to larger quarters. He decided to investigate.

The next morning Tom called his own stockbroker to ask for a Standard & Poor's fact sheet on Morgan, Murphy and Cash. He also called the Morgan, Murphy and Cash switchboard operator to ask who made the company's real estate decisions. After some calling around, the operator discovered that Donald Cook, the branch manager, handled such decisions.

The Standard & Poor's fact sheet gave Tom a great deal of information. In addition to discussing Morgan, Murphy and Cash's financial standing, it listed the three U.S. and six Canadian cities where the company had offices. Also included were a brief history of the company, outline of types of clients served and size of each of the offices. Corporate headquarters were listed as being in Toronto.

Later that week Tom made a cold call on Morgan, Murphy and Cash. He asked for Mr. Cook, explaining briefly to the receptionist that he was seeking information that would enable him to be of service if the company had any real estate needs. Tom was shown into the branch manager's office.

251

Cook seemed genuinely interested in talking with the Grubb & Ellis salesperson. He said that his company would definitely have to move to larger quarters when its current lease expired. He added that he hadn't thought much about the details of the move. The current lease had 18 months to run and Cook had been postponing the moving decision while he tried to form a clearer idea of his future space needs.

Tom explained that one of his functions was to provide clients with the information needed to make such decisions. To begin the process, he enlisted Cook's aid in filling out a lease survey form, as pictured in exhibit B. The current rent, Cook told him, was $15.00 per square foot. The company had been at its present location for 15 years. The branch manager realized that he would probably have to pay a higher rent per square foot in addition to acquiring more space. But, he hoped that any price increases would be alleviated by the fact that the company, now renting street-level space, was willing to move to an upper-floor location. Although walk-in business had once been a considerable part of a stockbroker's trade, it was no longer a significant factor, said Cook.

Though essentially cooperative, Cook said that he was currently pressured by other matters. He did not wish to pursue the subject of moving until he could devote more time to it. He asked Tom to get back in touch with him in six months.

Back in his office Tom dashed off a thank-you note to Cook for his cooperation (see exhibit A). He also made a note to call him in six months.

Tom called Don Cook again in August. This time the branch manager seemed less friendly. In fact, he hardly seemed to remember the earlier conversation. Cook said he was too busy to consider the matter. Try as he might, Tom was unable to get an appointment. He made a note to himself to try again in two months.

In October, Tom decided to call on Cook in person instead of phoning, since this strategy had at least gotten him in the door the first time. He was admitted to Cook's office, but Cook was still much more distant than he had been during the initial visit. Puzzled, but feeling sure he had done nothing to offend, Tom decided to use the direct approach. He pointed out courteously that Cook seemed less receptive than in their initial visit.

Caught off guard, the branch manager volunteered the reason. A few months after Tom's first visit, Cook had become very friendly with a new member of his local Rotary Club, a residential real estate salesperson, and had signed a tenant representation agreement with him.

Tom did some quick thinking and decided that since Cook had consented to see him, he couldn't be too pleased with his friend's efforts. His distant attitude probably reflected a blend of confusion, embarrassment and self-recrimination for putting himself in that spot.

Tom learned that the agreement was due to expire in two months. He told Cook that while he was certain the residential salesperson was making every effort to serve him, perhaps a specialist in office leasing could increase his chances of finding satisfactory space. Cook promised to let Tom represent him upon expiration of the tenant representation agreement if space had not been found.

Tom was fairly confident that the residential salesperson would not find an acceptable location before the agreement expired. He was tempted to begin compiling a list of buildings Cook might want to consider, but decided against it.

In December, Tom called Cook again. Suitable space had still not been found. This time Tom got an appointment and an opportunity to qualify the client (see exhibits C and D).

During the meeting, Tom established several things about Cook that he had suspected all along. Although undoubtedly knowledgeable about his own field, Cook knew little about his office space needs. He also had no final authority over any change. That decision would be made by the managing partner at corporate headquarters in Toronto. Tom's tactful efforts to arrange a meeting between the Toronto partner, Cook and himself were rebuffed. Cook wanted to make the tentative decision and pass on his recommendation to Toronto.

The San Francisco branch office currently occupied 3,500 square feet. Cook was unsure how much more space it needed. Some quick questions about the number of employees, the office design and the projected rates of business expansion led Tom to conclude that the company needed about 5,000 square feet, preferably with a provision for adding more space later.

Cook told Tom about his company's growing use of electronic equipment—computers, communications cables, market-quotation retrieval systems. The stockbrokerage business was introducing sophisticated new communications techniques so rapidly that new equipment was being added continually.

Morgan, Murphy and Cash was located in the heart of San Francisco's financial district. Cook did not think that that specific location was an advantage for the same reason that a ground-floor location was no longer needed. Most of his big customers were pension-fund managers and other institutional investors who conducted their business by telephone. The branch manager did think the company should maintain a location somewhere in the downtown area, both for prestige and for the convenience of those customers who did like to drop in. New buildings did not appeal to Cook, although he consented to look at them. He felt that an old building with a certain amount of prestige, besides being less expensive than a new one, would complement the "old and reliable" corporate image his company had promoted so successfully. He preferred a ten-year lease, though he was willing to consider anything five years or longer.

As the two men talked, Tom thought of a building on which Grubb & Ellis had an exclusive listing. There were 5,000 square feet available there at $20. The building was 20 years old and well maintained. It had the electrical floor that Morgan, Murphy and Cash's high-technology operation required.

Back at his office, Tom looked through the inventory system and came up with three other properties that seemed to fit Morgan, Murphy and Cash's needs. He worked for part of the next several days preparing his site presentation on four locations. He then made an appointment to show Cook the spaces. Since all four buildings were in downtown San Francisco and Tom was familiar with all of them, he waived his usual preliminary practice tour.

At the beginning of the space tour, Tom presented his client with a packet that included an area map on which buildings were numbered in the order they would be shown. Also included were descriptive brochures from the owners, information on nearby public parking as well as building parking, descriptions of nearby restaurants plus pertinent notes on the area from Tom's own file.

During the space tour, Don Cook was more decisive than Tom had expected. He registered indifference to one site immediately. He very much liked the 20-year-old building that Tom had thought of first, but decided that at $20 per square foot it was too expensive. He narrowed the selection to two of the buildings Tom located in the listing file.

The rental rates on those, too, seemed to bother Cook. They were similar in size and rented in the $19 range. Cook admitted that he had not paid much attention to office-space rental rates for the last several years and that he probably had unrealistic expectations. Tom doubted that the office-space decision maker back in Toronto was that unsophisticated about current market rates. He suspected that Cook was trying to impress the decision maker with his business acumen.

Tom filled out a building economics comparison form, shown in exhibit E for the two buildings in which his client expressed an interest. Then he proceeded to get preliminary concession information from the owners.

At their next meeting, Cook narrowed down his choice to the larger of the two office spaces, a new building that was still in the process of being filled with tenants. The owner offered what even Cook admitted was a generous tenant improvement allowance. But negotiations soon ran into a snag. Because the building was only half rented, the owner insisted on a clause granting him the right to move the tenant to similar space elsewhere in the building within the initial two years of the lease period. Cook would not hear of it. Both sides were adamant. Negotiations ground to a halt and Cook decided to take another look at his second choice. He also decided that this experience justified his initial reservations about the new building.

Negotiations on the second building could not get under way immediately because the owner had gone out of town. The owner returned a few weeks later. Negotiations were about to begin when Tom received a phone call from his tenant. Gary Robinson, the Morgan, Murphy and Cash office-space decision maker had an appointment in Los Angeles and would be stopping off in San Francisco on Tuesday to see Cook. He also would look at the space currently under consideration. Tom had tried several times to arrange a meeting with Robinson, but Cook had always refused, saying that Robinson was unwilling to make the trip until the branch manager had made a preliminary decision. Tom had given up trying to meet Robinson, so the news that he was coming was a pleasant surprise.

Robinson turned out to be a genial person, but his taste in office space by no means matched Don Cook's. He didn't like the second choice of space at all. And when given a description of the 20-year-old building that Cook had turned down, Robinson wanted to see it.

"I don't see why we can't consider it, Don," he said. "We pay nearly that much rent already."

"I thought your current rent was $15.00," said an amazed Tom Turner.

"That was some time ago," said Robinson. "Maybe Don hasn't looked at the lease recently. It has an escalator clause. Our effective rent is now around $16.50."

Suddenly the attractive building with $20 space looked even more attractive to all concerned. But when Tom called to arrange a showing for Robinson, he found that the space had been taken in the six weeks since Cook had refused it.

Tom was back to square one again—almost. Discouraged as he was, he was ahead on one count. Robinson's visit to San Francisco gave Tom an unexpected opportunity to qualify the real decision maker. He now felt confident that he knew what the top man wanted.

Again Tom checked the inventory system. He found a few more listings, but he felt halfhearted about them and couldn't decide whether putting them into a site presentation packet would be worth the effort. They just didn't quite fit the client's needs. Tom was getting discouraged about the entire deal. He decided to put it on the back burner for a few days and concentrate on other transactions.

The next week, while driving home one evening by a new route, Tom saw a "space for rent" sign on a new ten-story building he hadn't noticed before. It was located on the edge of the downtown area. He decided to investigate it in the morning.

Tom learned from the developer, George Stearns, that the building did not have an exclusive agent. He tried to get an exclusive, but Stearns said that he was not willing to sign an exclusive. Tom did manage to sign Stearns for an open listing, as shown in exhibit F.

Stearns took Tom on a tour of several floors. One space in particular looked well suited to Morgan, Murphy and Cash's needs. It was, however, a bit small. The price, $20.50, would probably also disturb the frugal Don Cook. Nevertheless, it had definite advantages. The five-foot modules would make it easy to construct numerous brokers' cubicles. There were also a few larger offices for executives, all of them in efficient sizes. Since the building was not yet filled, the owner might be willing to grant a first right of refusal on additional space. By now both Robinson and Cook were intent on an additional space clause and despite Cook's aversion to new buildings, a new and partially occupied building seemed to offer the best chance of allowing for the future addition of space.

When Tom went home that evening, he couldn't get the new building out of his mind. The more he thought about it, the more it seemed close to perfect for Morgan, Murphy and Cash. The building was laid out around a central core area. Tom had measured the distance from core to window wall and found it ideal. He felt sure that its 4,200 square feet could be designed by a good space planner to fit his client's needs. He also saw the possibility of getting an exclusive listing if he could negotiate this lease to the developer's satisfaction as well as his tenant's needs.

Tom decided that if he could get Stearns to provide space-planning services complete with working drawings, he could sell the idea to Cook. But he was afraid that Stearns would be cold to the proposal. When he called Stearns the next day, the developer did indeed refuse to pay for working drawings. Tom let the matter drop and made an appointment to discuss the space with his client.

Tom reported his findings to Don Cook, adding that there was a good chance he could get a first-right-of-refusal concession. He pointed out that, although the space was more expensive per square foot than the alternatives viewed so far, it was smaller than the others under consideration. Yet it was so well laid out that it would probably be quite adequate with good space planning. Cook was not convinced that the space was large enough, and he refused to hire a highly paid space planner just to confirm his own misgivings. Besides, he said, he didn't want a new building. He went with Tom to look over the building anyway and seemed interested, but repeated his previous objections.

The next day Tom decided it was time to leave Cook alone for a while to do some thinking. But first he wrote a quick letter, reproduced in exhibit G.

At their next meeting, Tom told Stearns that the only concession his client seemed determined to secure, other than a reasonable tenant improvement allowance, was an option on additional space. Stearns turned down the option proposal cold, as Tom expected he would. Tom dropped the subject.

Meanwhile, Tom had contacted Cook again and found that his letter had done some good. Cook now saw that his best alternative lay in going with a new building. He instructed Tom to begin negotiating with Stearns (which Tom had been doing). However, Cook was still unwilling to hire a space planner.

A few days later, Tom returned to the developer's office and told him that his tenant would settle for a first right of refusal on the additional space. Tom revealed that they were a well-known stock brokerage firm that would attract other prestigious tenants to the building. He pointed out that the first right of refusal would cost Stearns absolutely nothing, since it could be exercised only if Stearns had another tenant for the space. So, it could hardly be considered a major concession. Under the circumstances, Tom said, he felt it would be to the developer's advantage to dip into his tenant inducement fund for compensation for a space planner who would stay with the job through the working drawing stage. This time Stearns said yes.

Tom went back to Don Cook to point out that he was now covered on both the equivalent of an expansion option and the services of a space planner—which, even if Tom's hunch about space size proved wrong, would cost Morgan, Murphy and Cash nothing.

J/W Design Associates was hired to make working drawings. Two weeks later they presented Morgan, Murphy and Cash with a detailed plan for space use that left no doubt in Cook's mind that the 4,200 square feet was entirely adequate. Cook approved the space.

Gary Robinson rushed in from Toronto and immediately seconded Cook's vote. Tom presented Stearns with the Morgan, Murphy and Cash proposal. Stearns accepted the proposal without a hitch and agreed to sign an offer to lease as well (shown in exhibit H).

When the two principals met, some minor concessions had to be ironed out. A few new clauses were written into the lease, but essentially the negotiations went smoothly. Morgan, Murphy and Cash moved into their new space in August.

For Tom Turner, the deal ended very well, especially considering its shaky beginning. Just two days after he had sent off thank-you letters to lessor and lessee, he found a new tenant for the space Morgan, Murphy and Cash had vacated. Two months later, he acquired an exclusive listing on Stearns's property.

Exercise A

Check your answers with those given at the end of this exercise.

1. Comment on Tom's technique on his second cold call to Cook of asking point-blank why Cook's attitude had become distant.

2. While waiting for the other broker's tenant representation agree-

ment to expire, was Tom wise not to begin compiling a list of buildings for Cook to visit?

3. What was Tom's biggest mistake in handling the Morgan, Murphy and Cash transaction?

4. Why did Tom ask for an option on additional space although his client didn't feel strongly about it?

5. Why did Tom secure an offer to lease?

6. The client, Don Cook, did a great deal of vacillating on the subject of new buildings. Comment on Tom's handling of this.

7. Generally speaking, how would you rate Tom's handling of the negotiations with George Stearns?

Answer A _____

1. *It was effective. Cook was so taken by surprise that he blurted out his reason. And Tom had very little to lose by being direct, since until then he had been getting nowhere anyway.*

2. *It was the right decision for two reasons. The obvious one is that the broker might have found suitable space within the two months left before his agreement expired. Also, Tom had not yet had an opportunity to qualify his prospect. On either count, he might be wasting time that could be better spent on current prospects.*

3. *His major blunder was in not asking to see the lease on the initial cold call. Had he done so, he would have seen that Morgan, Murphy already paid $16.50. He could probably have sold Cook, and certainly Robinson, on the 20-year-old, $20 building they both liked. Thus he would have collected half of his commission four months earlier, after considerably less work.*

4. *Tom was fairly certain the owner wouldn't agree to the option. But by asking for it, he was able to ask for the first right of refusal as a second choice, making it seem that his tenant was giving up a great deal while the developer was giving up practically nothing.*

5. *He wanted to protect himself and his tenant from a breakdown in negotiations. (For a more detailed answer, see chapter 3.)*

6. *Tom did not handle this well. There was little he could do to qualify Cook on this matter, since the client kept changing his mind. But Tom should have educated him sooner than he did. When he pointed out that new buildings are preferable for tenants who want the right to future additional space and also need many and varied power outlets, Cook was convinced. But Tom would have saved himself a lot of time and effort if he had explained this reality to the client much earlier.*

7. *Tom handled the developer well. First, he pointed out that the prestige his tenant would bring could help Stearns rent his other space to important tenants. Second, after he got the first right of refusal by making it appear to be hardly a concession at all, he placed Stearns in the position of being the one who had not yet given up anything. Then he pressed for the one thing he really wanted—a space planner.*

FIGURE 14.1   Exhibit A

Grubb&Ellis

February 6, 1987

Mr. Donald Cook
Branch Manager
Morgan, Murphy and Cash
700 Vernon Avenue
San Francisco, CA 94217

Dear Don:

I'd like to take this opportunity to thank you for your time and courtesy during our interview earlier today. It was a pleasure meeting you. I sincerely hope that Grubb & Ellis Company can be of service when you decide to move to larger quarters. Our company is a leader in the office marketing field. I am sure that securing the services of our organization would be of great benefit to you.

I look forward to speaking with you in six months.

Sincerely,

Tom Turner
Office Marketing Division

Grubb & Ellis Company   One Montgomery Street, Telesis Tower, San Francisco, CA 94104   (415) 956-1990

FIGURE 14.2   Exhibit B

LEASE SURVEY

San Francisco

OFFICE

COMPANY _____ *Morgan, Murphy and Cash* _____

ADDRESS _____ *700 Vernon Ave.* _____

CITY _____ *San Francisco* _____ PHONE _____ *330-3000* _____

CONTACT _____ *Donald Cook* _____ TITLE _____ *Branch Mgr.* _____

TYPE OF
BUSINESS _____ *Stockbroker* _____

HEADQUARTERS
OR BRANCH _____ *Branch* _____

EXISTING SPACE INFORMATION/FEATURES

TYPE _____

SQUARE FOOTAGE _____ *3,500* _____ PARKING _____ *No* _____

D/H _____ G/L _____ SPRINKLERED YES ☐ NO ☐ SPUR YES ☐ NO ☐ CLEARANCE _____

LEASE EXPIRATION: MONTH _____ *July* _____ YEAR _____ *1988* _____ OWNS YES ☐ NO ☐

RENT: $ _____ *52,500/yr* _____ MONTH _____ *$4,375/mo.* _____ NET _____ GROSS _____

OPTION TERMS _____ *None* _____ EXERCISE DATE _____

COMMENTS: _____ *Now renting ground-floor space in older building. Desires nonground-floor space in next building.*

Many power outlets needed for electronic equipment. Lessee unwilling to discuss details of new space needs now.

Contact in 6 mo.

DATE _____ *2/6/88* _____ REPORT BY _____ *Tom Turner* _____

FIGURE 14.3   Exhibit C

QUALIFYING QUESTIONS

A form to be used during the first call

NEED

1. When does your lease expire? _____

2. When will you be ready to move? _____

3. If we find a building tomorrow that suits your needs, how long will it take for you to sign a lease? _____

_____

4. What experience have you had working with other brokers?

_____

What are you looking for in a new space/location? _____

_____

MONEY

1. How long have you been in business? _____

2. What are your annual sales? _____

3. What is the net worth of the company or person that will sign the lease? _____

4. Normally buildings of the type you have described to me rent in the range of $17 to $19 per square foot. Is this the kind of figure you had budgeted? _____

5. How much money do you have to spend on this purchase?

_____

6. Are you a privately or publicly held company? _____

PERFORM

1. Who will sign the lease? _____

2. What is the process your company uses to approve matters of this type? _____

3. Can we make an appointment to see property for this afternoon or would tomorrow be better? _____

4. When would be the best time to come by and visit your facility, this afternoon or tomorrow? _____

Company Name: _____

Address: _____ Phone: _____

Contact/Title: _____

Person Signing Lease: _____ Phone: _____

Comments: _____

FIGURE 14.4   Exhibit D

12/13/87

MEMO FOR MORGAN, MURPHY AND CASH FILE

Specifications for new space:

Approx. 5,000 square feet
Rent: under $19
Prefers upper-floor location (tenant not willing to pay space premium on either ground floor or "view" location)
Prefers older building
Must have electrical floor
Wants downtown location—not necessarily financial district
Good nearby restaurant (for occasional prestige entertaining) desirable

FIGURE 14.5   Exhibit E

BUILDING ECONOMICS COMPARISON FORM

	BLDG. A		BLDG. B		BLDG. C		BLDG. D	
	sq. ft.		sq. ft.		sq. ft.		sq. ft.	
	ANNUAL	TOTAL	ANNUAL	TOTAL	ANNUAL	TOTAL	ANNUAL	TOTAL
1. Rent								
2. Est. costs—improvements over standard (amortized)								
3. Lease deposit								
4. Moving costs								
5. Telephones								
6. Admin. costs—stationery, etc.								
7. Furniture								
8. Parking costs								
9. Rent escalation								
GRAND TOTAL								

FIGURE 14.6   Exhibit F

NON-EXCLUSIVE AUTHORIZATION OF LEASE

OWNER hereby lists with GRUBB AND ELLIS COMMERCIAL BROKERAGE COMPANY ("Broker") on an open listing basis the right to negotiate a lease or leases on the subject property (the "Property") for a period commencing on ___April 17___ , 19_88_ , and ending at midnight on ___October 17___ , 19 _88_. The Property is located in the City of _San Francisco_ , County of _San Francisco_ , State of _California_ , located at ___1414 Graham Drive___ , and further described as _____

_____

The price and terms of the lease(s) shall be as follows: _4,200 sq.ft. on the Fifth Floor at 1414 Vernon Ave. to be let at $20.50 per sq. ft. per year; lease to include escalator clause to be negotiated with tenant; maximum lease period: 10 years; any lease of longer than 5 years to have rental increase of 35% to become effective at beginning of sixth year._

In consideration of this Authorization and Broker's agreement diligently to pursue the procurement of a tenant or tenants for the Property, Owner agrees to pay Broker a commission or commissions as set forth in the attached SCHEDULE OF COMMISSIONS.

Owner shall pay said commission(s) to Broker if: (a) the Property is leased to tenant(s) by or through Broker prior to the expiration of this Authorization or any extension hereof; or (b) a tenant is procured by or through Broker who is ready, willing and able to lease the Property on the terms above stated or other terms reasonably acceptable to Owner prior to the expiration of this Authorization or any extension hereof; or (c) within one hundred eighty (180) days after the expiration of this Authorization or any extension hereof, the Property is leased to any person or entity with whom Broker has negotiated or to whom Broker has submitted the Property prior to such expiration in an effort to effect a transaction and whose name appears on any list of such persons or entities which Broker shall have mailed to Owner at the address below stated within thirty (30) days following such expiration, provided that if Broker has submitted a written offer to lease or purchase, it shall not be necessary to include the offeror's name on such list.

If a sale or other transfer or conveyance is made by Broker prior to the expiration of this Authorization or any extension hereof, or during the one hundred eighty (180)-day period thereafter, Owner shall pay Broker a commission as set forth in the attached SCHEDULE OF COMMISSIONS.

If during the term of this Authorization or any extension hereof an escrow is opened or negotiations involving the sale, transfer, conveyance or leasing of the Property have commenced and are continuing, in either event with a client of Broker, then the term of this Authorization shall be extended for a period through the closing of such escrow, the termination of such negotiations or the consummation of such transaction, provided this Authorization would otherwise have expired during such period.

Owner agrees to cooperate with Broker in effecting a lease or leases of the Property. Broker is authorized to accept a deposit from any prospective tenant. Broker is further authorized to advertise the Property and shall have the exclusive right to place a sign or signs on the Property if, in Broker's opinion, such would facilitate the leasing thereof.

It is understood that it is illegal for either Owner or Broker to refuse to present, lease or sell to any person because of race, color, religion, national origin, sex, marital status or physical disability.

Owner warrants that he is the owner of record of the Property or has the legal authority to execute this Authorization. Owner agrees to hold Broker harmless from any liability or damages arising from any incorrect information supplied by Owner or any information which Owner fails to supply. Owner acknowledges receipt of a copy of this Authorization and the attached SCHEDULE OF COMMISSIONS, which Owner has read and understands.

If either Owner or Broker commences any litigation to enforce the terms of this Authorization, the prevailing party shall be entitled to receive a reasonable attorney's fee from the other party hereto.

No amendments or alterations in the terms hereof or withdrawal of this Authorization shall be valid or binding unless made in writing and signed by both Owner and Broker.

The heirs, transferees, successors and assigns of the parties hereto are duly bound by the provisions hereof.

DATED: ___April 17___ , 19 _88_   OWNER: _Foremost Enterprises_

ACCEPTED: GRUBB AND ELLIS COMMERCIAL   By _____
                    BROKERAGE COMPANY

                                          By _____

                                          Address: _1414 Graham Drive_

                                          San Francisco, Ca.

By _____   Telephone: _341-9922_

Form 141 Rev. 4/79

FIGURE 14.7   Exhibit G

Grubb&Ellis

April 19, 1988

Mr. Donald Cook
Branch Manager
Morgan, Murphy and Cash
700 Vernon Avenue
San Francisco, CA 94217

Dear Don:

I'm sorry that you don't share my enthusiasm for the space at 1414
Graham Drive.

While I fully appreciate your reasons for wanting an older building that
would better suit Morgan, Murphy and Cash's corporate image, that type
of building is, unfortunately, incompatible with two of your basic needs.
Your business's increasing dependence on sophisticated electronic
equipment could prove prohibitively expensive at some future date should
you find yourself in a building without easy and inexpensive access to
power outlets. Easy access is generally lacking in older buildings.

Also, in a new building the owner is much more likely to agree to some
kind of arrangement on additional future space. This could prove
advantageous to you.

I know that you'll give serious thought to these matters. I'll call you in
about a week to follow up and discuss this further.

Sincerely,

Tom Turner
Office Marketing Division

Grubb & Ellis Company   One Montgomery Street, Telesis Tower, San Francisco, CA 94104 (415) 956-1990

FIGURE 14.8   Exhibit H

OFFER TO LEASE

The undersigned (hereinafter "Tenant") hereby offers to lease the Premises described below on the following terms and conditions:

1. Premises. Located in the City of _San Francisco_ , County of _San Francisco_ , State of _California_ , described as follows: _1414 Graham Drive_

2. Monthly Rent. _$7,175_

3. Term of Lease and Commencement Date. _lease to run for 10 years commencing August 1, 1988 and terminating July 31, 1998_

4. Use of Premises. _stockbrokerage services_

5. Security Deposit; Prepaid Rent. _August rent of $7,175, plus rent for month of July, 1989 of $7,175 to be paid in advance. July, 1989 rent to be paid in lieu of security deposit._

6. Taxes. _to be paid by lessor._

7. Insurance. _Fire and liability insurance to be paid by lessor._

8. Utilities. _Electricity and telephone service to be paid by lessee._

9. Improvements to Premises. _General maintenance plus improvements to the premises to be paid by lessor._

10. Other Terms and Conditions. _____

If this Offer to Lease is not accepted by the Landlord on or before _August 1_ , 19_88_ the Offer shall terminate, and all sums deposited herewith shall be promptly returned to Tenant upon receipt of a written request therefor. Upon acceptance of this Offer to Lease, Landlord is to proceed with the preparation of a Lease, it being expressly understood that this proposal is not binding on either of the parties and that the Lease, when executed by the parties, shall contain their full agreement. In the event the Landlord accepts this Offer to Lease and the parties are for any reason unable to consummate a Lease, all sums deposited herewith shall be promptly returned to Tenant upon receipt of a written request therefor. In consideration of Grubb & Ellis Company presenting this porposal to Landlord, Tenant agrees to conduct all negotiations through Grubb & Ellis Company in the event Tenant commences negotiation to lease or purchase the Premises during the one-year period following the date hereof.

Tenant acknowledges receipt of a copy hereof.

Date _June 19, 1988_   Tenant _Morgan, Murphy and Cash_

San Francisco , _California_   By _____
City   State

Receipt is hereby acknowledged of cash ☐ check ☒ in the sum of _Fourteen Thousand Three Hundred and Fifty Dollars_

_($14,350)_ _____ dollars, to be delivered in accordance with the terms hereof.

Date: _June 19, 1988_   Grubb & Ellis Company
                                              COMMERCIAL BROKERAGE SERVICES

San Francisco , _California_   By _____
City   State

Landlord hereby accepts the foregoing Offer to Lease and appoints Grubb & Ellis Company its agent in connection with the lease of the Premises. Landlord agrees to pay a commission to Grubb & Ellis Company in accordance with the attached Schedule of Commissions. Landlord acknowledges receipt of a copy hereof.

Date: _June 19, 1988_   Landlord _Foremost Enterprises_

San Francisco , _California_   By _____
City   State

NOTICE TO LANDLORD AND TENANT: GRUBB & ELLIS COMPANY IS NOT AUTHORIZED TO GIVE LEGAL OR TAX ADVICE; NO REPRE-SENTATION OR RECOMMENDATION IS MADE BY GRUBB & ELLIS COMPANY OR ITS AGENTS OR EMPLOYEES AS TO THE LEGAL SUFFI-CIENCY, LEGAL EFFECT OR TAX CONSEQUENCES OF THIS DOCUMENT OR ANY TRANSACTION RELATING THERETO, SINCE THESE ARE MATTERS WHICH SHOULD BE DISCUSSED WITH YOUR ATTORNEY.

Form 129 Rev. 1/87

FIGURE 14.9 Exhibit I

OFFICE BUILDING LEASE

THIS LEASE is made and entered into this fifteenth day of ___June___, 19 88 by and between___
___Foremost Enterprises_____ (hereinafter "Landlord") and ___
___Morgan, Murphy and Cash_____ (hereinafter "Tenant").

For and in consideration of the rental and of the covenants and agreements hereinafter set forth to be kept and performed by the Tenant, Landlord hereby leases to Tenant and Tenant hereby leases from Landlord the Premises herein described for the term, at the rental and subject to and upon all of the terms, covenants and agreements hereinafter set forth.

1. PREMISES

1.1 Description. Landlord hereby leases to Tenant and Tenant hereby rents from Landlord those certain Premises (hereinafter "Premises") crosshatched on Exhibit A containing approximately ___4,200 rentable___ square feet on the ___fifth___ floor of that certain office building (hereinafter "Building") located in the City of ___San Francisco___, County of ___San Francisco___, California, commonly known as ___1414 Graham Drive_____ and more particularly described as _____

_____

_____

1.2 Work of Improvement. The obligations of Landlord and Tenant to perform the work and supply the necessary materials and labor to prepare the Premises for occupancy are set forth in detail in Exhibit B. Landlord and Tenant shall expend all funds and do all acts required of them in Exhibit B and shall have the work performed promptly and diligently in a first class workmanlike manner.

2. TERM

2.1 Term. The term of this Lease shall be for ___ten years___ commencing August 1, 1988 ___ and ending on ___July 31, 1998___ unless sooner terminated pursuant to this Lease.

2.2 Delay in Commencement. Tenant agrees that in the event of the inability of Landlord for any reason to deliver possession of the Premises to Tenant on the commencement date set forth in Section 2.1, Landlord shall not be liable for any damage thereby nor shall such inability affect the validity of this Lease or the obligations of Tenant hereunder, but in such case Tenant shall not be obligated to pay rent or other monetary sums until possession of the Premises is tendered to Tenant; provided that if the delay in delivery of possession exceeds sixty (60) days, then the expiration date of the term of the Lease shall be extended by the period of time computed from the scheduled commencement date to the date possession is tendered. In the event Landlord shall not have delivered possession of the Premises within six (6) months from the scheduled commencement date, then Tenant at its option, to be exercised within thirty (30) days after the end of said six (6) month period, may terminate this Lease and upon Landlord's return of any monies previously deposited by Tenant, the parties shall have no further rights or liabilities toward each other.

2.3 Acknowledgement of Commencement Date. In the event the commencement date of the term of the Lease is other than as provided in Section 2.1, then Landlord and Tenant shall execute a written acknowledgment of the date of commencement and shall attach it to the Lease as Exhibit D.

3. RENT.

Tenant shall pay to Landlord as rent for the Premises in advance on the first day of each calendar month of the term of this Lease without deduction, offset, prior notice or demand, in lawful money of the United States, the sum of Seven Thousand One Hundred and Seventy-Five Dollars ($7,175) from 8/1/88-7/31/98, Nine Thousand Six Hundred and Eight Dollars ($9,608) from 8/1/93-7/31/98. If the commencement date is not the first day of a month, or if the Lease termination date is not the last day of a month, a prorated monthly installment shall be paid at the then current rate for the fractional month during which the Lease commences and/or terminates.

Concurrently with Tenant's execution of this Lease, Tenant shall pay to Landlord the sum of Seven Thousand One Hundred and Seventy-Five Dollars ($7,175) _____) as rent for the month(s) of August, 1988 ___

___MONTH'S RENT IN ADVANCE___

4. ~~SECURITY DEPOSIT~~.

Concurrently with Tenant's execution of this Lease, Tenant shall deposit with Landlord the sum of _____

_____ ($_____).

Said sum shall be held by Landlord as a Security Deposit for the faithful performance by Tenant of all of the terms, covenants, and conditions of this Lease to be kept and performed by Tenant during the term hereof. If Tenant defaults with respect to any provision of this Lease, including but not limited to the provisions relating to the payment of rent and any of the monetary sums due herewth, Landlord may (but shall not be required to) use, apply or retain all or any part of this Security Deposit for the payment of any other amount which Landlord may spend by reason of Tenant's default or to compensate Landlord for any other loss or damage which Landlord may suffer by reason of Tenant's default. If any portion of said Deposit is so used or applied, Tenant shall, within ten (10) days after written demand therefor, deposit cash with Landlord in an amount sufficient to restore the Security Deposit to its original amount; Tenant's failure to do so shall be a material breach of this Lease. Landlord shall not be required to keep this Security Deposit separate from its general funds, and Tenant shall not be entitled to interest on such deposit. If Tenant shall

FIGURE 14.9   Exhibit I (continued)

fully and faithfully perform every provision of this Lease to be performed by it, the Security Deposit or any balance thereof shall be returned to Tenant (or, at Landlord's option, to the last assignee of Tenant's interests hereunder) at the expiration of the Lease term and after Tenant has vacated the Premises. In the event of termination of Landlord's interest in this Lease, Landlord shall transfer said Deposit to Landlord's successor in interest whereupon Tenant agrees to release Landlord from liability for the return of such Deposit or the accounting therefor.

5.   TAX AND BUILDING OPERATING COST INCREASES

5.1   **Definitions.** For purposes of this Section, the following terms are herein defined:

(a)   Base Year: the later occurring of (1) the first calendar year in which the Building is assessed as a completed building for tax purposes; or (2) the calendar year in which this Lease commences.   1989

(b)   Building Operating Costs: All costs and expenses of ownership, operation and maintenance of the Building (excluding depreciation on the Building, all amounts paid on loans of Landlord and expenses capitalized for federal income tax purposes) including by way of illustration but not limited to: real and personal property taxes and assessments and any tax in addition to or in lieu thereof, other than taxes covered by Section 5.4, whether assessed against Landlord or Tenant or collected by Landlord or both; utilities; supplies; insurance; license, permit and inspection fees; cost of services of independent contractors (including property management fees); cost of compensation (including employment taxes and fringe benefits) of all persons who perform regular and recurring duties connected with day-to-day operation, maintenance and repair of the Building, its equipment and the adjacent walks, malls and landscaped areas, including janitorial, scavenger, gardening, security, parking, operating engineer, elevator, painting, plumbing, electrical, carpentry, heating, ventilation, air conditioning, window washing, signing and advertising (but excluding persons performing services not uniformly available to or performed for substantially all Building tenants), and rental expense or a reasonable allowance for depreciation of personal property used in the maintenance, operation and repair of the Building.

(c)   Net Rentable Area: the rentable area computed by measuring to the inside finish of permanent outer building walls, to the Premises side of public corridors and/or other permanent partitions and to the center of partitions which separate the adjoining rentable areas with no deductions for columns and projections necessary to the Building structure. On multi-tenant floors, common corridors and toilets, air conditioning rooms, fan rooms, janitorial closets, electrical and telephone closets and any other areas within and exclusively serving that floor are considered common area and for purposes of this Section shall be allocated prorata to the tenants on the floor.

5.2   **Tenant's Share.** In the event the Building Operating Costs incurred by Landlord during any calendar year following the Base Year shall exceed Building Operating Costs incurred by Landlord during the Base Year, Tenant shall pay to Landlord an amount equal to Twelve point Seventy-Five _____ percent (12.75%) of such increase, which share is computed on the basis of the ratio between Net Rentable Area in the Premises and Net Rentable Area in the Building.

5.3   **Payment.** Within ninety (90) days after the end of each calendar year following the Base Year, Landlord shall furnish Tenant a written statement showing in reasonable detail Landlord's Building Operating Costs for the preceding calendar year and the Base Year, and showing the amount, if any, of any increase or decrease in the sums due from Tenant taking into account prior increases paid by Tenant (if any).

Coincidentally with the monthly rent payment next due following Tenant's receipt of such statement, Tenant shall pay to Landlord (in the case of an increase), or Landlord shall credit against the next rent due from Tenant (in the case of a decrease), an amount equal to the sum of (1) the difference between Building Operating Costs for the preceding calendar year and the Base Year less increases paid by Tenant (if any); and (2) one-twelfth (1/12th) said increases for the current calendar year multiplied by the number of rent payments (including the current one) then elapsed in such calendar year. Thereafter the one twelfth (1/12th) shall be paid monthly with the rent until the adjustment the following year pursuant hereto. In no event shall the adjustment entitle Tenant to receive the benefit of a reduction in Building Operating Costs below the level of the initial Base Year during the term hereof.

5.4   **New Taxes.** In addition to rent and other charges to be paid by Tenant hereunder, Tenant shall reimburse to Landlord, within thirty (30) days of receipt of a demand therefore, any and all taxes payable by Landlord (other than net income taxes) whether or not now customary or within the contemplation of the parties hereto: (a) upon, allocable to, or measured by the area of the Premises or on the rent payable hereunder, including without limitation any gross income tax or excise tax levied by the State, any political subdivision thereof, City or Federal Government with respect to the receipt of such rent; or (b) upon or with respect to the possession, leasing, operation, management, maintenance, alteration, repair, use or occupancy by Tenant of the Premises or any portion thereof; or (c) upon or measured by the value of Tenant's personal property, equipment or fixtures located in the Premises; or (d) upon this transaction or any document to which Tenant is a party creating or transferring an interest or an estate in the Premises. Tenant agrees to pay, before delinquency, any and all taxes levied or assessed and which become payable during the term hereof upon Tenant's equipment, furniture, fixtures and other personal property located in the Premises. For the purpose of determining said amount, figures supplied by the County Assessor as to the amount so assessed shall be conclusive. Tenant shall comply with the provisions of any law, ordinance or rule of the taxing authorities which require Tenant to file a report of Tenant's property located in the Premises.

6.   USE

6.1   **Use.** The Premises shall be used and occupied by Tenant for general office purposes and for no other purpose without the prior written consent of Landlord.

6.2   **Suitability.** Tenant acknowledges that neither Landlord nor any agent of Landlord has made any representation or warranty with respect to the Premises or the Building or with respect to the suitability of either for the conduct of Tenant's business, nor has Landlord agreed to undertake any modification, alteration or improvement to the Premises except as provided in this Lease. The taking of possession of the Premises by Tenant shall conclusively establish that the Premises and the Building were at such time in satisfactory condition unless within fifteen (15) days after such date Tenant shall give Landlord written notice specifying in reasonable detail the respects in which the Premises or the Building were not in satisfactory condition.

6.3   **Uses Prohibited.**

(a)   Tenant shall not do or permit anything to be done in or about the Premises nor bring or keep anything therein which will in any way increase the existing rate or affect any fire or other insurance upon the Building or any of its contents (unless Tenant shall pay any increased premium as a result of such use or acts), or cause a cancellation of any insurance policy covering said Building or any part thereof or any of its contents, nor shall Tenant sell or permit to be kept, used or sold in or about said Premises any articles which may be prohibited by a standard form policy of fire insurance.

(b)   Tenant shall not do or permit anything to be done in or about the Premises which will in any way obstruct or interfere with the rights of other tenants or occupants of the Building or injure or annoy them or use or allow the Premises to be used for any unlawful or objectionable purpose, nor shall Tenant cause, maintain or permit any nuisance in or about the Premises. Tenant shall not commit or suffer to be committed any waste in or upon the Premises.

FIGURE 14.9   Exhibit I (continued)

(c) Tenant shall not use the Premises or permit anything to be done in or about the Premises which will in any way conflict with any law, statute, ordinance or governmental rule or regulation or requirement of duly constituted public authorities now in force or which may hereafter be enacted or promulgated. Tenant shall at its sole cost and expense promptly comply with all laws, statutes, ordinances and governmental rules, regulations or requirements now in force or which may hereafter be in force and with the requirements of any board of fire underwriters or other similar body now or hereafter constituted relating to or affecting the condition, use or occupancy of the Premises, excluding structural changes not relating to or affecting the condition, use or occupancy of the Premises, or not related or afforded by Tenant's improvements or acts. The judgment of any court of competent jurisdiction or the admission of Tenant in any action against Tenant, whether Landlord be a party thereto or not, that Tenant has violated any law, statute, ordinance or governmental rule, regulation or requirement, shall be conclusive of the fact as between Landlord and Tenant.

7.   SERVICE AND UTILITIES

7.1   Landlord's Obligations. Landlord agrees to furnish to the Premises during reasonable hours of generally recognized business days, to be determined by Landlord, and subject to the Rules and Regulations of the Building, water, gas and electricity suitable for the intended use of the Premises, heat and air conditioning required in Landlord's judgment for the comfortable use and occupancy of the Premises, scavenger, janitorial and window washing service and elevator service, and security customary in similar buildings in the competing geographical areas. Landlord shall also maintain and keep lighted the common stairs, entries and toilet rooms in the Building.

7.2   Tenant's Obligation. Tenant shall pay for, prior to delinquency, all telephone and all other materials and services, not expressly required to be paid by Landlord, which may be furnished to or used in, on or about the Premises during the term of this Lease.

7.3   Tenants Additional Requirements.

(a) Tenant will not, without the written consent of Landlord, use any apparatus or device in the Premises, including but without limitation thereto, electronic data processing machines, punch card machines and machines using current in excess of 110 volts, which will in any way increase the amount of electricity or water usually furnished or supplied for use of the Premises as general office space; nor connect with electric current, except through existing electrical outlets in the Premises, or water pipes, any apparatus or device, for the purposes of using electric current or water.

(b) If Tenant shall require water or electric current in excess of that usually furnished or supplied for use of the Premises as general office space, Tenant shall first procure the consent of Landlord for the use thereof, which consent Landlord may refuse and Landord may cause a water meter or electric current meter to be installed in the Premises, so as to measure the amount of water and electric current consumed for any such other use. The cost of such meters and of installation, maintenance and repair thereof shall be paid for by Tenant and Tenant agrees to pay Landlord promptly upon demand by Landlord for all such water and electric current consumed as shown by said meters, at the rates charged for such services by the City in which the Building is located or the local public utility, as the case may be, furnishing the same, plus any addtional expense incurred in keeping account of the water and electric current so consumed.

(c) Wherever heat generating machines or equipment are used in the Premises which affect the temperature otherwise maintained by the air conditioning system, Landlord reserves the right to install supplementary air conditioning units in the Premises and the cost thereof, including the cost of installation, operation and maintenance thereof, shall be paid by Tenant to Landlord upon demand by Landlord.

7.4   Non-Liability. Landlord shall not be liable for, and Tenant shall not be entitled to, any abatement or reduction of rent by reason of Landlord's failure to furnish any of the foregoing when such failure is caused by accidents, breakage, repairs, strikes, lockouts or other labor disturbances or labor disputes of any character, or by any other cause similar or dissimilar, beyond the reasonable control of Landlord. Landlord shall not be liable under any circumstances for loss of or injury to property, however occurring, through or in connection with or incidental to failure to furnish any of the foregoing.

8.   MAINTENANCE AND REPAIRS; ALTERATIONS AND ADDITIONS

8.1   Maintenance and Repairs.

(a) Landlord's Obligations. Landlord shall maintain in good order, condition and repair the Building and all other portions of the Premises not the obligation of Tenant or any other tenant in the Building.

(b) Tenant's Obligations.

(i) Tenant at Tenant's sole cost and expense, except for services furnished by Landlord pursuant to Section 7 hereof, shall maintain the Premises in good order, condition and repair including the interior surfaces of the ceilings, walls and floors, all doors, interior windows, exterior windows at or below street level, all plumbing pipes, electrical wiring, switches, fixtures and special items in excess of building standard furnishings, and equipment installed by or at the expense of Tenant. Tenant expressly waives the benefits of any statute now or hereafter in effect which would otherwise afford Tenant the right to make repairs at Landlord's expense or to terminate this Lease because of Landlord's failure to keep the Premises in good order, condition and repair.

(ii) Upon the expiration or earlier termination of this Lease, Tenant shall surrender the Premises in the same condition as received, ordinary wear and tear and damage by fire, earthquake, act of God or the elements alone excepted, and shall promptly remove or cause to be removed at Tenant's expense from the Premises and the Building any signs, notices and displays placed by Tenant. provided Landlord is not at fault in causing the damage.

(iii) Tenant agrees to repair any damage to the Premises or the Building caused by or in connection with the removal of any articles of personal property, business or trade fixtures, machinery, equipment, cabinetwork, furniture, movable partition or permanent improvements or additions, including without limitation thereto, repairing the floor and patching and painting the walls where required by Landlord to Landlord's reasonable satisfaction, all at Tenant's sole cost and expense. Tenant shall indemnify the Landlord against any loss or liability resulting from delay by Tenant in so surrendering the Premises, including without limitation any claims made by any succeeding tenant founded on such delay.

(iv) In the event Tenant fails to maintain the Premises in good order, condition and repair, Landlord shall give Tenant notice to do such acts as are reasonably required to so maintain the Premises. In the event Tenant fails to promptly commence such work and diligently prosecute it to completion, then Landlord shall have the right to do such acts and expend such funds at the expense of Tenant as are reasonably required to perform such work. Any amount so expended by Landlord shall be paid by Tenant promptly after demand with interest at ten percent (10%) per annum from the date of such work. Landlord shall have no liability to Tenant for any damage, inconvenience or interference with the use of the Premises by Tenant as a result of performing any such work.

(c) Compliance with Law. Landlord and Tenant shall each do all acts required to comply with all applicable laws, ordinances, regulations and rules of any public authority relating to their respective maintenance obligations as set forth herein.

8.2   Alterations and Additions.

(a) Tenant shall make no alterations, additions or improvements to the Premises or any part thereof without obtaining the prior written consent of Landlord.

FIGURE 14.9   Exhibit I (continued)

(b) Landlord may impose as a condition to the aforesaid consent such requirements as Landlord may deem necessary in its sole discretion, including without limitation thereto, the manner in which the work is done, a right of approval of the contractor by whom the work is to be performed, the times during which it is to be accomplished, and the requirement that upon written request of Landlord prior to the expiration or earlier termination of the Lease, Tenant will remove any and all permanent improvements or additions to the Premises installed at Tenant's expense and all movable partitions, counters, personal property, equipment, fixtures and furniture.

(c) All such alterations, additions or improvements shall at the expiration or earlier termination of the Lease become the property of Landlord and remain upon and surrendered with the Premises, unless specified pursuant to Section 8.2(b) above.

(d) All articles of personal property and all business and trade fixtures, machinery and equipment, cabinetwork, furniture and movable partitions owned by Tenant or installed by Tenant at its expense in the Premises shall be and remain the property of Tenant and may be removed by Tenant at any time during the Lease term when Tenant is not in default hereunder.

9. ENTRY BY LANDLORD.
Landlord reserves and shall at any and all times have the right to enter the Premises to inspect the same, to supply janitor service and any other service to be provided by Landlord to Tenant hereunder, to submit said Premises to prospective purchasers or tenants, to post notices of non-responsibility and "for lease" signs, and to alter, improve or repair the Premises and any portion of the Building without abatement of rent, and may for that purpose erect scaffolding and other necessary structures where reasonably required by the character of the work to be performed, always providing the entrance to the Premises shall not be blocked thereby, and further providing that the business of Tenant shall not be interfered with unreasonably. Tenant hereby waives any claim for damages for any injury or inconvenience to or interference with Tenant's business, any loss of occupancy or quiet enjoyment of the Premises, and any other loss occasioned thereby. For each of the aforesaid purposes, Landlord shall at all times have and retain a key with which to unlock all of the doors in, upon and about the Premises, excluding Tenant's vaults and safes, and Landlord shall have the right to use any and all means which Landlord may deem proper to open said doors in an emergency, in order to obtain entry to the Premises, and any entry to the Premises obtained by Landlord by any of said means, or otherwise, shall not under any circumstances be construed or deemed to be a forcible or unlawful entry into, or a detainer of, the Premises, or an eviction of Tenant from the Premises or any portion thereof.

10. LIENS.
Tenant shall keep the Premises and any building of which the Premises are a part free from any liens arising out of work performed, materials furnished, or obligations incurred by Tenant and shall indemnify, hold harmless and defend Landlord from any liens and encumbrances arising out of any work performed or materials furnished by or at the direction of Tenant. In the event that Tenant shall not, within twenty (20) days following the imposition of any such lien, cause such lien to be released of record by payment or posting of a proper bond, Landlord shall have, in addition to all other remedies provided herein and by law, the right, but no obligation, to cause the same to be released by such means as it shall deem proper, including payment of the claim giving rise to such lien. All such sums paid by Landlord and all expenses incurred by it in connection therewith including attorney's fees and costs shall be payable to Landlord by Tenant on demand with interest at the rate of ten percent (10%) per annum. Landlord shall have the right at all times to post and keep posted on the Premises any notices permitted or required by law, or which Landlord shall deem proper, for the protection of Landlord and the Premises, and any other party having an interest therein, from mechanics' and materialmen's liens, and Tenant shall give to Landlord at least ten (10) business days prior written notice of the expected date of commencement of any work relating to alterations or additions to the Premises.

11. INDEMNITY

11.1 Indemnity. Tenant shall indemnify and hold Landlord harmless from and defend Landlord against any and all claims of liability for any injury or damage to any person or property whatsoever; (1) occurring in, on or about the Premises or any part thereof; and (2) occurring in, on or about any facilities (including, without prejudice to the generality of the term "facilities", elevators, stairways, passageways, hallways, and parking areas), the use of which Tenant may have in conjunction with other tenants of the Building, when such injury or damage is caused in part or in whole by the act, neglect, fault or omission of any duty with respect to the same by Tenant, its agents, contractors, employees or invitees. Tenant shall further indemnify and hold Landlord harmless from and against any and all claims arising from any breach or default in the performance of any obligation on Tenant's part to be performed under the terms of this Lease, or arising from any act or negligence of Tenant, or any of its agents, contractors, employees and from and against all costs, attorney's fees, expenses and liabilities incurred in the defense of any such claim or any action or proceeding brought thereon. In case any action or proceeding be brought against Landlord by reason of any such claim, Tenant, upon notice from Landlord, shall defend the same at Tenant's expense by counsel reasonably satisfactory to Landlord, provided, however, that Tenant shall not be liable for damage or injury occasioned by the negligence or intentional acts of Landlord and its designated agents or employees unless covered by insurance Tenant is required to provide.

Tenant, as a material part of the consideration to Landlord, hereby assumes all risk of damage to property or injury to persons in, upon or about the Premises from any cause and Tenant hereby waives all claims in respect thereof against Landlord.

11.2 Exemption of Landlord from Liability. Landlord shall not be liable for injury or damage which may be sustained by the person, goods, wares, merchandise or property of Tenant, its employees, invitees or customers, or any other person in or about the Premises caused by or resulting from fire, steam, electricity, gas, water or rain, which may leak or flow from or into any part of the Premises, or from the breakage, leakage, obstruction or other defects of the pipes, sprinklers, wires, appliances, plumbing, air conditioning or lighting fixtures of the same, whether the damage or injury results from conditions arising upon the Premises or upon other portions of the Building of which the Premises are a part, or from other sources. Landlord shall not be liable for any damages arising from any act or neglect of any other tenant of the Building.

12. INSURANCE

12.1 Coverage. Tenant shall, at all times during the term of this Lease, and at its own cost and expense procure and continue in force the following insurance coverage:

(a) Bodily injury and Property Damage Liability insurance with a combined single limit for bodily injury and property damage of not less than $500,000.

(b) Fire and Extended Coverage Insurance, including vandalism and malicious mischief coverage, in an amount equal to the full replacement value of all fixtures, furniture and improvements installed by or at the expense of Tenant.

12.2 Insurance Policies. The aforementioned minimum limits of policies shall in no event limit the liability of Tenant hereunder. The aforesaid insurance shall name Landlord as an additional insured. Said insurance shall be with companies having a rating of not less than AAA in "Best's Insurance Guide". Tenant shall furnish from the insurance companies or cause the insurance companies to furnish certificates of coverage. No such

FIGURE 14.9   Exhibit I (continued)

policy shall be cancellable or subject to reduction of coverage or other modification or cancellation except after thirty (30) days prior written notice to Landlord by the insurer. All such policies shall be written as primary policies, not contributing with and not in excess of the coverage which Landlord may carry. Tenant shall, at least twenty (20) days prior to the expiration of such policies, furnish Landlord with renewals or binders. Tenant agrees that if Tenant does not take out and maintain such insurance, Landlord may (but shall not be required to) procure said insurance on Tenant's behalf and charge Tenant the premiums together with a twenty-five percent (25%) handling charge, payable upon demand. Tenant shall have the right to provide such insurance coverage pursuant to blanket policies obtained by Tenant provided such blanket policies expressly afford coverage to the Premises and to Tenant as required by this Lease.

   12.3   Waiver of Subrogation. Landlord and Tenant each hereby waive any and all rights of recovery against the other or against the officers, employees, agents and representatives of the other, on account of loss or damage occasioned to such waiving party or its property or the property of others under its control to the extent that such loss or damage is insured against under any fire and extended coverage insurance policy which either may have in force at the time of such loss or damage. Tenant shall, upon obtaining the policies of insurance required under this Lease, give notice to the insurance carrier or carriers that the foregoing mutual waiver of subrogation is contained in this Lease.

13. DAMAGE OR DESTRUCTION

   13.1   Partial Damage — Insured. In the event the Premises or the Building are damaged by any casualty which is covered under fire and extended coverage insurance carried by Landlord, then Landlord shall restore such damage provided insurance proceeds are available to pay eighty percent (80%) or more of the cost of restoration and provided such restoration can be completed within sixty (60) days after the commencement of the work in the opinion of a registered architect or engineer appointed by Landlord. In such event this Lease shall continue in full force and effect, except that Tenant shall be entitled to proportionate reduction of rent while such restoration takes place, such proportionate reduction to be based upon the extent to which the restoration efforts interfere with Tenant's business in the Premises.

   13.2   Partial Damage — Uninsured. In the event the Premises or the Building are damaged by a risk not covered by Landlord's insurance or the proceeds of available insurance are less than eighty percent (80%) of the cost of restoration, or if the restoration cannot be completed within sixty (60) days after the commencement of work in the opinion of the registered architect or engineer appointed by Landlord, then Landlord shall have the option either to (1) repair or restore such damage, this Lease continuing in full force and effect, but the rent to be proportionately abated as hereinabove provided, or (2) give notice to Tenant at any time within thirty (30) days after such damage terminating this Lease as of a date to be specified in such notice, which date shall be not less than thirty (30) nor more than sixty (60) days after giving such notice. In the event of the giving of such notice, this Lease shall expire and all interest of Tenant in the Premises shall terminate on such date so specified in such notice and the rent, reduced by any proportionate reduction based upon the extent, if any, to which said damage interfered with the use and occupancy of Tenant, shall be paid to the date of such termination; Landlord agrees to refund to the Tenant any rent theretofore paid in advance for any period of time subsequent to such date.

   13.3   Total Destruction. In the event the Premises are totally destroyed or the Premises cannot be restored as required herein under applicable laws and regulations, notwithstanding the availability of insurance proceeds, this Lease shall be terminated effective the date of the damage.

   13.4   Damage Near End of the Term. Notwithstanding anything to the contrary contained in this Section 13, Landlord shall not have any obligation whatsoever to repair, reconstruct or restore the Premises when the damage resulting from any casualty covered under this Section 13 occurs during the last twelve (12) months of the term of this Lease or any extension thereof.

   13.5   Landlord's Obligations. The Landlord shall not be required to repair any injury or damage by fire or other cause, or to make any restoration or replacement of any panelings, decorations, partitions, railings, floor covering, office fixtures or any other improvements or property installed in the Premises by Tenant or at the direct or indirect expense of Tenant. Tenant shall be required to restore or replace same in the event of damage. Except for abatement of rent, if any, Tenant shall have no claim against Landlord for any damage suffered by reason of any such damage, destruction, repair or restoration; nor shall Tenant have the right to terminate this Lease as the result of any statutory provision now or hereafter in effect pertaining to the damage and destruction of the Premises or the Building, except as expressly provided herein.

14. CONDEMNATION.
If all or any part of the Premises shall be taken or appropriated for public or quasi-public use by right of eminent domain with or without litigation or transferred by agreement in connection with such public or quasi-public use, either party hereto shall have the right at its option exercisable within thirty (30) days of receipt of notice of such taking to terminate this Lease as of the date possession is taken by the condemning authority, provided, however, that before Tenant may terminate this Lease by reason of taking or appropriation as provided hereinabove, such taking or appropriation shall be of such an extent and nature as to substantially handicap, impede or impair Tenant's use of the Premises. If any part of the Building other than the Premises shall be so taken or appropriated, Landlord shall have the right at its option to terminate this Lease. No award for any partial or entire taking shall be apportioned, and Tenant hereby assigns to Landlord any award which may be made in such taking or condemnation, together with any and all rights of Tenant now or hereafter arising in or to the same or any part thereof; provided, however, that nothing contained herein shall be deemed to give Landlord any interest in or to require Tenant to assign to Landlord any award made to Tenant for the taking of personal property and fixtures belonging to Tenant and/or for the interruption of or damage to Tenant's business and/or for Tenant's unamortized cost of leasehold improvements. In the event of a partial taking which does not result in a termination of this Lease, rent shall be abated in the proportion which the part of the Premises so made unusable bears to the rented area of the Premises immediately prior to the taking. No temporary taking of the Premises and/or of Tenant's rights therein or under this Lease shall terminate this Lease or give Tenant any right to any abatement of rent thereunder; any award made to Tenant by reason of any such temporary taking shall belong entirely to Tenant and Landlord shall not be entitled to share therein.

15. ASSIGNMENT AND SUBLETTING

   15.1   Landlord's Consent Required. Tenant shall not assign, transfer, mortgage, pledge, hypothecate or encumber this Lease or any interest therein, and shall not sublet the Premises or any part thereof, without the prior written consent of Landlord and any attempt to do so without such consent being first had and obtained shall be wholly void and shall constitute a breach of this Lease.

   15.2   Reasonable Consent. If Tenant complies with the following conditions, Landlord shall not unreasonably withhold its consent to the subletting of the Premises or any portion thereof or the assignment of this Lease. Tenant shall submit in writing to Landlord (a) the name and legal composition of the proposed subtenant or assignee; (b) the nature of the business proposed to be carried on in the Premises; (c) the terms and provisions of the proposed sublease; (d) such reasonable financial information as Landlord may request concerning the proposed subtenant or assignee.

   15.3   No Release of Tenant. No consent by Landlord to any assignment or subletting by Tenant shall relieve Tenant of any obligation to be performed by Tenant under this Lease, whether occurring before or after such consent, assignment or subletting. The consent by Landlord to any assignment or subletting shall not relieve Tenant from the obligation to obtain Landlord's express written consent to any other assignment or subletting. The acceptance of rent by Landlord from any other person shall not be deemed to be a waiver by Landlord of any provision of this Lease

FIGURE 14.9   Exhibit I (continued)

or to be a consent to any assignment, subletting or other transfer. Consent to one assignment, subletting or other transfer shall not be deemed to constitute consent to any subsequent assignment, subletting or other transfer.

15.4   Attorney's Fees. In the event Landlord shall consent to a sublease or assignment under this Section 15, Tenant shall pay Landlord's reasonable attorney's fees not to exceed $500 incurred in connection with giving such consent.

16. SUBORDINATION

16.1   Subordination. This Lease at Landlord's option shall be subject and subordinate to all ground or underlying leases which now exist or may hereafter be executed affecting the Premises or the land upon which the Premises are situated or both, and to the lien of any mortgages or deeds of trust in any amount or amounts whatsoever now or hereafter placed on or against the land or improvements or either thereof, of which the Premises are a part, or on or against Landlord's interest or estate therein, or on or against any ground or underlying lease without the necessity of the execution and delivery of any further instruments on the part of Tenant to effectuate such subordination. If any mortgagee, trustee or ground lessor shall elect to have this Lease prior to the lien of its mortgage, deed of trust or ground lease, and shall give written notice thereof to Tenant, this Lease shall be deemed prior to such mortgage, deed of trust or ground lease, whether this Lease is dated prior or subsequent to the date of said mortgage, deed of trust, or ground lease or the date of the recording thereof.

16.2   Subordination Agreements. Tenant covenants and agrees to execute and deliver upon demand without charge therefore, such further instruments evidencing such subordination of this Lease to such ground or underlying leases and to the lien of any such mortgages or deeds of trust as may be required by Landlord. Tenant hereby appoints Landlord as Tenant's attorney-in-fact, irrevocably, to execute and deliver any such agreements, instruments, releases or other documents.

16.3   Quiet Enjoyment. Landlord covenants and agrees with Tenant that upon Tenant paying rent and other monetary sums due under the Lease, performing its covenants and conditions under the Lease and upon recognizing purchaser as Landlord pursuant hereto, Tenant shall and may peaceably and quietly have, hold and enjoy the Premises for the term, subject, however, to the terms of the Lease and of any of the aforesaid ground leases, mortgages or deeds of trust described above.

16.4   Attornment. In the event any proceedings are brought for default under ground or any underlying lease or in the event of foreclosure or the exercise of the power of sale under any mortgage or deed of trust made by the Landlord covering the Premises, the Tenant shall attorn to the purchaser upon any such foreclosure or sale and recognize such purchaser as the Landlord under this Lease, provided said purchaser expressly agrees in writing to be bound by the terms of the Lease.

17. DEFAULT; REMEDIES

17.1   Default. The occurrence of any of the following shall constitute a material default and breach of this Lease by Tenant:

(a)   Any failure by Tenant to pay the rent or any other monetary sums required to be paid hereunder (where such failure continues for five (5) days after written notice by Landlord to Tenant);

(b)   The abandonment or vacation of the Premises by Tenant;

(c)   A failure by Tenant to observe and perform any other provision of this Lease to be observed or performed by Tenant, where such failure continues for twenty (20) days after written notice thereof by Landlord to Tenant; provided, however, that if the nature of the default is such that the same cannot reasonably be cured within said twenty (20) day period, Tenant shall not be deemed to be in default if Tenant shall within such period commence such cure and thereafter diligently prosecute the same to completion;

(d)   The making by Tenant of any general assignment or general arrangement for the benefit of creditors; the filing by or against Tenant of a petition to have Tenant adjudged a bankrupt or of a petition for reorganization or arrangement under any law relating to bankruptcy (unless, in the case of a petition filed against Tenant, the same is dismissed within sixty (60) days); the appointment of a trustee or receiver to take possession of substantially all of Tenant's assets located at the Premises or of Tenant's interest in this Lease, where possession is not restored to Tenant within thirty (30) days; or the attachment, execution or other judicial seizure of substantially all of Tenant's assets located at the Premises or of Tenant's interest in this Lease, where such seizure is not discharged within thirty (30) days.

17.2   Remedies. In the event of any such material default or breach by Tenant, Landlord may, at any time thereafter without limiting Landlord in the exercise of any right or remedy at law or in equity which Landlord may have by reason of such default or breach:

(a)   Maintain this Lease in full force and effect and recover the rent and other monetary charges as they become due, without terminating Tenant's right to possession irrespective of whether Tenant shall have abandoned the Premises. In the event Landlord elects not to terminate the Lease, Landlord shall have the right to attempt to re-let the Premises at such rent and upon such conditions and for such a term, and to do all acts necessary to maintain or preserve the Premises as Landlord deems reasonable and necessary without being deemed to have elected to terminate the Lease, including removal of all persons and property from the Premises; such property may be removed and stored in a public warehouse or elsewhere at the cost of and for the account of Tenant. In the event any such re-letting occurs, this Lease shall terminate automatically upon the new Tenant taking possession of the Premises. Notwithstanding that Landlord fails to elect to terminate the Lease initially, Landlord at any time during the term of this Lease may elect to terminate this Lease by virtue of such previous default of Tenant.

(b)   Terminate Tenant's right to possession by any lawful means, in which case this Lease shall terminate and Tenant shall immediately surrender possession of the Premises to Landlord. In such event Landlord shall be entitled to recover from Tenant all damages incurred by Landlord by reason of Tenant's default, including without limitation thereto, the following: (i) the worth at the time of award of any unpaid rent which had been earned at the time of such termination; plus (ii) the worth at the time of award of the amount by which the unpaid rent which would have been earned after termination until the time of award exceeds the amount of such rental loss that is proved could have been reasonably avoided; plus (iii) the worth at the time of award of the amount by which the unpaid rent for the balance of the term after the time of award exceeds the amount of such rental loss that is proved could be reasonably avoided; plus (iv) any other amount necessary to compensate Landlord for all the detriment proximately caused by Tenant's failure to perform his obligations under this Lease or which in the ordinary course of events would be likely to result therefrom; plus (v) at Landlord's election, such other amounts in addition to or in lieu of the foregoing as may be permitted from time to time by applicable State law. Upon any such re-entry Landlord shall have the right to make any reasonable repairs, alterations or modifications to the Premises, which Landlord in its sole discretion deems reasonable and necessary. As used in (i) above, the "worth at the time of award" is computed by allowing interest at the rate of ten percent (10%) per annum from the date of default. As used in (ii) and (iii) the "worth at the time of award" is computed by discounting such amount at the discount date of the U.S. Federal Reserve Bank at the time of award plus one percent (1%). The term "rent", as used in this Section 17, shall be deemed to be and to mean the rent to be paid pursuant to Section 3 and all other monetary sums required to be paid by Tenant pursuant to the terms of this Lease.

FIGURE 14.9   Exhibit I (continued)

17.3   Late Charges. Tenant hereby acknowledges that late payment by Tenant to Landlord of rent and other sums due hereunder will cause Landlord to incur costs not contemplated by this Lease, the exact amount of which will be extremely difficult to ascertain. Such costs include, but are not limited to, processing and accounting charges, and late charges which may be imposed on Landlord by the terms of any mortgage or trust deed covering the Premises. Accordingly, if any installment of rent or any other sum due from Tenant shall not be received by Landlord or Landlord's designee within ten (10) days after such amount shall be due, Tenant shall pay to Landlord a late charge equal to ten percent (10%) of such overdue amount. The parties hereby agree that such late charge represents a fair and reasonable estimate of the costs Landlord will incur by reason of late payment by Tenant. Acceptance of such late charge by Landlord shall in no event constitute a waiver of Tenant's default with respect to such overdue amount nor prevent Landlord from exercising any of the other rights and remedies granted hereunder.

17.4   Default by Landlord. Landlord shall not be in default unless Landlord fails to perform obligations required of Landlord within a reasonable time, but in no event later than thirty (30) days after written notice by Tenant to Landlord and to the holder of any first mortgage or deed of trust covering the Premises whose name and address shall have theretofore been furnished to Tenant in writing, specifying wherein Landlord has failed to perform such obligations; provided, however, that if the nature of Landlord's obligation is such that more than thirty (30) days are required for performance, then Landlord shall not be in default if Landlord commences performance within such thirty-day period and thereafter diligently prosecutes the same to completion.

18. RELOCATION OF PREMISES

18.1   Conditions. For the purpose of maintaining an economical and proper distribution of Tenants throughout the Building acceptable to Landlord, Landlord shall have the right from time to time during the term of this Lease to relocate the Premises in the Building on the following terms and conditions:

(a)   The rented and usable areas of the new location in the Building are of equal size to the existing location (subject to a variation of up to ten percent (10%) provided the amount of rent payable under this Lease is not increased;

(b)   If the then prevailing rental rate for the new location is less than the amount being paid for the existing location, the rent shall be reduced to equal the then prevailing rent for the new location;

(c)   Landlord shall pay the cost of providing tenant improvements in the new location comparable to the tenant improvements in the existing location;

(d)   Landlord shall pay the expenses reasonably incurred by Tenant in connection with such substitution of Premises, including but not limited to costs of moving, door lettering, telephone relocation and reasonable quantities of new stationery;

18.2   Notice. Landlord shall deliver to Tenant written notice of Landlord's election to relocate the Premises, specifying the new location and the amount of rent payable therefore at least thirty (30) days prior to the date the relocation is to be effective. If the relocation of the Premises is not acceptable to Tenant, Tenant for a period of ten (10) days after receipt of Landlord's notice to relocate shall have the right (by delivering written notice to Landlord) to terminate this Lease effective thirty (30) days after delivery of written notice to Landlord.

19. BROKER'S FEE

Upon execution of this Lease by both parties, Landlord shall pay to Grubb and Ellis Commercial Brokerage Company, a licensed real estate broker, a fee of _____ ($_____) for brokerage services heretofore rendered. Landlord further agrees that if Tenant exercises any option granted herein or any option substantially similar thereto, either to extend the term of this Lease, to renew this Lease, to purchase said Premises or any part thereof and/or any adjacent property which Landlord may own or in which Landlord has an interest, or any other option granted herein, or if said Broker is the procuring cause of any other lease or sale entered into between the parties pertaining to the Premises and/or any adjacent property in which Landlord has an interest, then as to any of said transactions, Landlord shall pay Broker a fee in accordance with the commission schedule of Broker in effect at the time of execution of this Lease. Landlord agrees to pay said fee not only on behalf of Landlord but also on behalf of any person, corporation, association, or other entity having an ownership interest in said real property or any part thereof, when such fee is due hereunder. Any transferee of Landlord's interests in this Lease, by accepting an assignment of such interest, shall be deemed to have assumed Landlord's obligation under this Section 19. Said Broker shall be a third party beneficiary of the provisions of this Section.

20. MISCELLANEOUS

20.1   Estoppel Certificate.

(a)   Tenant shall at any time upon not less than ten (10) days' prior written notice from Landlord execute, acknowledge and deliver to Landlord a statement in writing (i) certifying that this Lease is unmodified and in full force and effect (or, if modified, stating the nature of such modification and certifying that this Lease, as so modified, is in full force and effect) and the date to which the rent and other charges are paid in advance, if any, and (ii) acknowledging that there are not, to Tenant's knowledge, any uncured defaults on the part of Landlord hereunder, or specifying such defaults if any are claimed. Any such statement may be conclusively relied upon by any prospective purchaser or encumbrancer of the Premises.

(b)   Tenant's failure to deliver such statement within such time shall be conclusive upon Tenant (i) that this Lease is in full force and effect, without modification except as may be represented by Landlord, (ii) that there are no uncured defaults in Landlord's performance, and (iii) that not more than one month's rent has been paid in advance.

(c)   If Landlord desires to finance or refinance the Building, or any part thereof, Tenant hereby agrees to deliver to any lender designated by Landlord such financial statements of Tenant as may be reasonably required by such lender. Such statements shall include the past three years' financial statements of Tenant. All such financial statements shall be received by Landlord in confidence and shall be used only for the purposes herein set forth.

20.2   Transfer of Landlord's Interest. In the event of a sale or conveyance by Landlord of Landlord's interest in the Premises or the Building other than a transfer for security purposes only, Landlord shall be relieved from and after the date specified in any such notice of transfer of all obligations and liabilities accruing thereafter on the part of Landlord, provided that any funds in the hands of Landlord at the time of transfer in which Tenant has an interest, shall be delivered to the successor of Landlord. This Lease shall not be affected by any such sale and Tenant agrees to attorn to the purchaser or assignee provided all Landlord's obligations hereunder are assumed in writing by the transferee.

20.3   Captions; Attachments; Defined Terms.

(a)   The captions of the paragraphs of this Lease are for convenience only and shall not be deemed to be relevant in resolving any question of interpretation or construction of any section of this Lease.

Form Number 128 (CA) 1/74

FIGURE 14.9 Exhibit I (continued)

(b) Exhibits attached hereto, and addendums and schedules initialed by the parties, are deemed by attachment to constitute part of this Lease and are incorporated herein.

(c) The words "Landlord" and "Tenant", as used herein, shall include the plural as well as the singular. Words used in neuter gender include the masculine and feminine and words in the masculine or feminine gender include the neuter. If there be more than one Landlord or Tenant, the obligations hereunder imposed upon Landlord or Tenant shall be joint and several; as to a Tenant which consists of husband and wife, the obligations shall extend individually to their sole and separate property as well as community property. The term "Landlord" shall mean only the owner or owners at the time in question of the fee title or a tenant's interest in a ground lease of the land underlying the Building. The obligations contained in this Lease to be performed by Landlord shall be binding on Landlord's successor's and assigns only during their respective periods of ownership.

20.4 Entire Agreement. This instrument along with any exhibits and attachments hereto constitutes the entire agreement between Landlord and Tenant relative to the Premises and this Agreement and the exhibits and attachments may be altered, amended or revoked only by an instrument in writing signed by both Landlord and Tenant. Landlord and Tenant agree hereby that all prior or contemporaneous oral agreements between and among themselves and their agents or representatives relative to the leasing of the Premises are merged in or revoked by this Agreement.

20.5 Severability. If any term or provision of this Lease shall, to any extent, be determined by a court of competent jurisdiction to be invalid or unenforceable, the remainder of this Lease shall not be affected thereby, and each term and provision of this Lease shall be valid and be enforceable to the fullest extent permitted by law.

20.6 Costs of Suit.

(a) If Tenant or Landlord shall bring any action for any relief against the other, declaratory or otherwise, arising out of this Lease, including any suit by Landlord for the recovery of rent or possession of the Premises, the losing party shall pay the successful party a reasonable sum for attorneys' fees which shall be deemed to have accrued on the commencement of such action and shall be paid whether or not such action is prosecuted to judgment.

(b) Should Landlord, without fault on Landlord's part, be made a party to any litigation instituted by Tenant or by any third party against Tenant, or by or against any person holding under or using the Premises by license of Tenant, or for the foreclosure of any lien for labor or material furnished to or for Tenant or any such other person or otherwise arising out of or resulting from any act or transaction of Tenant or of any such other person, Tenant covenants to save and hold Landlord harmless from any judgment rendered against Landlord or the Premises or any part thereof, and all costs and expenses, including reasonable attorneys' fees, incurred by Landlord in or in connection with such litigation. provided tenant is judicially found to be liab

(c) If Tenant or Landlord or their successors or assigns shall bring an action against Broker or make Broker a party to litigation arising out of this Lease, Broker shall be entitled to recover reasonable attorney's fees and court costs from either Landlord or Tenant if Broker is adjudged by a court of competent jurisdiction to be without fault in such matter.

20.7 Time; Joint and Several Liability. Time is of the essence of this Lease and each and every provision hereof, except as to the conditions relating to the delivery of possession of the Premises to Tenant. All the terms, covenants and conditions contained in this Lease to be performed by either party, if such party shall consist of more than one person or organization, shall be deemed to be joint and several, and all rights and remedies of the parties shall be cumulative and nonexclusive of any other remedy at law or in equity.

20.8 Binding Effect; Choice of Law. The parties hereto agree that all provisions hereof are to be construed as both covenants and conditions as though the words importing such covenants and conditions were used in each separate paragraph hereof. Subject to any provisions hereof restricting assignment or subletting by Tenant and subject to Section 20.2, all of the provisions hereof shall bind and insure to the benefit of the parties hereto and their respective heirs, legal representatives, successors and assigns. This Lease shall be governed by the laws of the State of California.

20.9 Waiver. No covenant, term or condition or the breach thereof shall be deemed waived, except by written consent of the party against whom the waiver is claimed, and any waiver or the breach of any covenant, term or condition shall not be deemed to be a waiver of any preceeding or succeeding breach of the same or any other covenant, term or condition. Acceptance by Landlord of any performance by Tenant after the time the same shall have become due shall not constitute a waiver by Landlord of the breach or default of any covenant, term or condition unless otherwise expressly agreed to by Landlord in writing.

20.10 Surrender of Premises. The voluntary or other surrender of this Lease by Tenant, or a mutual cancellation thereof, shall not work a merger, and shall, at the option of the Landlord, terminate all or any existing subleases or subtenancies, or may, at the option of Landlord, operate as an assignment to it of any or all such subleases or subtenancies.

20.11 Holding Over. If Tenant remains in possession of all or any part of the Premises after the expiration of the term hereof, with or without the express or implied consent of Landlord, such tenancy shall be from month to month only, and not a renewal hereof or an extension for any further term, and in such case, rent and other monetary sums due hereunder shall be payable in the amount and at the time specified in this Lease and such month to month tenancy shall be subject to every other term, covenant and agreement contained herein.

20.12 Signs

(a) Tenant shall not place or permit to be placed in or upon the Premises, where visible from outside the Premises, or outside the Premises or any part of the Building any signs, notices, drapes, shutters, blinds or displays of any type without the prior written consent of Landlord.

(b) Landlord reserves the right in Landlord's sole discretion to place and locate on the roof, exterior of the Building, and in any area of the Building not leased to Tenant such signs, notices, displays and similar items as Landlord deems appropriate in the proper operation of the Building.

20.13 Reasonable Consent. Except as limited elsewhere in this Lease, wherever in this Lease Landlord or Tenant is required to give its consent or approval to any action on the part of the other, such consent or approval shall not be unreasonably withheld. In the event of failure to give any such consent, the other party shall be entitled to specific performance at law and shall have such other remedies as are reserved to it under this Lease, but in no event shall Landlord or Tenant be responsible in monetary damages for failure to give consent unless said consent is withheld maliciously or in bad faith.

20.14 Interest on Past Due Obligations. Except as expressly provided, any amount due to Landlord not paid when due shall bear interest at ten percent (10%) per annum from the due date. Payment of such interest shall not excuse or cure any default by Tenant under this Lease.

20.15 Rules and Regulations; Parking.

(a) Tenant and Tenant's agents, servants, employees, visitors and licensees shall observe and comply fully and faithfully with all reasonable and non-discriminatory rules and regulations adopted by Landlord for the care, protection, cleanliness and operation of the Building and its Tenants including those annexed to this Lease as Exhibit C and any modification or addition thereto adopted by Landlord, provided Landlord shall give written notice thereof to Tenant. Landlord shall not be responsible to Tenant for the non-performance by any other tenant or occupant of the Building of any of said rules and regulations.

FIGURE 14.9   Exhibit I (concluded)

20.16   **Notices.** All Notices or demands of any kind required or desired to be given by Landlord or Tenant hereunder shall be in writing and shall be deemed delivered forty-eight (48) hours after depositing the notice or demand in the United States mail, certified or registered, postage prepaid, addressed to the Landlord or Tenant respectively at the addresses set forth after their signatures at the end of this Lease.

20.17   **Corporate Authority.** If Tenant is a corporation, each individual executing this Lease on behalf of said corporation represents and warrants that he is duly authorized to execute and deliver this Lease on behalf of said corporation in accordance with a duly adopted resolution of the Board of Directors of said corporation or in accordance with the By-laws of said corporation, and that this Lease is binding upon said corporation in accordance with its terms. If Tenant is a corporaton Tenant shall, within thirty (30) days after execution of this Lease, deliver to Landlord a certified copy of a resolution of the Board of Directors of said corporation authorizing or ratifying the execution of this Lease.

21.   IMPROVEMENTS.   Lessor agrees to furnish and install at Lessor's sole cost and expense all improvements shown on Exhibit B attached hereto and made a part hereof.   In addition, Lessor will sandblast all exterior walls thereby exposing the brick, provide carpeting ($12. per yard grade installed) throughout, put 1" mini blinds on all windows, provide a dropped acoustical ceiling with flush lighting and utilize 9' high vinyl clad walls.   Tenant however will furnish and pay for tenants own furniture, kitchen sink, and any cabinet work and/or shelving.

In Witness Whereof, Landlord and Tenant have executed this Lease the date and year first above written.

Landlord: Tenant:

Foremost Enterprises   Morgan, Murphy and Cash

George Stearns, Owner   Gary Robinson, Managing Partner
Address: Address:

1414 Graham Drive, Second Floor   700 Vernon Avenue

San Francisco, California   San Francisco, California 94217

(If Landlord or Tenant is a corporation, the corporate seal must be affixed and the authorized officers must sign on behalf of the corporation. The Lease must be executed by the President or a Vice President and the Secretary or Assistant Secretary unless the By-laws or a Resolution of the Board of Directors shall otherwise provide, in which event the By-laws or a certified copy of the Resolution, as the case may be, must be furnished.)

THIS LEASE HAS BEEN PREPARED FOR SUBMISSION TO YOUR ATTORNEY WHO WILL REVIEW THE DOCUMENT AND ASSIST YOU TO DETERMINE WHETHER YOUR LEGAL RIGHTS ARE ADEQUATELY PROTECTED. GRUBB AND ELLIS COMMERCIAL BROKERAGE COMPANY IS NOT AUTHORIZED TO GIVE LEGAL OR TAX ADVICE; NO REPRESENTATION OR RECOMMENDATION IS MADE BY GRUBB AND ELLIS COMMERCIAL BROKERAGE COMPANY OR ITS AGENTS OR EMPLOYEES AS TO THE LEGAL SUFFICIENCY, LEGAL EFFECT OR TAX CONSEQUENCES OF THIS DOCUMENT OR ANY TRANSACTION RELATING THERETO. THESE ARE QUESTIONS FOR YOUR ATTORNEY WITH WHOM YOU SHOULD CONSULT BEFORE SIGNING THIS DOCUMENT.

Form Number 128 (CA) 1/74   -9-

FIGURE 14.10   Exhibit J

RULES AND REGULATIONS

1.   No sign, placard, picture, advertisement, name or notice shall be inscribed, displayed or printed or affixed on or to any part of the outside or inside of the Building or the Premises without the written consent of Landlord first had and obtained and Landlord shall have the right to remove any such sign, placard, picture, advertisement, name or notice without notice to and at the expense of Tenant.

All approved signs or lettering on doors shall be printed, painted, affixed or inscribed at the expense of Tenant by a person approved by Landlord.

Landlord shall not place anything or allow anything to be placed near the glass of any window, door, partition or wall which may appear unsightly from outside the Premises; provided, however, that Landlord is to furnish and install a building standard window drapery at all exterior windows.

2.   No Tenant shall obtain for use upon the Premises, ice, drinking or bottled water, towel or other similar service or accept barbering or bootblacking services on the Premises, except from persons authorized by the Landlord and at the hours and under regulations fixed by the Landlord.

3.   The bulletin board or directory of the Building will be provided exclusively for the display of the name and location of Tenant only and Landlord reserves the right to exclude any other names therefrom.

4.   The sidewalks, halls, passages, exits, entrances, elevators and stairways shall not be obstructed by any of the tenants or used by them for any purpose other than for ingress to and egress from their respective Premises. The halls, passages, exits, entrances, elevators, stairways, balconies and roof are not for the use of the general public and the Landlord shall in all cases retain the right to control and prevent access thereto by all persons whose presence in the judgment of the Landlord shall be prejudicial to the safety, character, reputation and interests of the Building and its tenants, provided that nothing herein contained shall be construed to prevent such access to persons with whom the Tenants normally deals in the ordinary course of Tenant's business unless such persons are engaged in illegal activities. No tenant and no employees or invitees of any tenant shall go upon the roof of the Building.

5.   Tenant shall not alter any lock or install any new or additional locks or any bolts on any door of the Premises without the written consent of Landlord.

6.   The toilet rooms, urinals, wash bowls and other apparatus shall not be used for any purpose other than that for which they were constructed and no foreign substance of any kind whatsoever shall be thrown therein and the expense of any breakage, stoppage or damage resulting from the violation of this rule shall be borne by the Tenant who, or whose employees or invitees shall have caused it.

7.   Tenant shall not overload the floor of the Premises or mark, drive nails, screw or drill into the partitions, woodwork or plaster or in any way deface the Premises or any part thereof. No boring, cutting or stringing of wires or laying of linoleum or other similar floor coverings shall be permitted except with the prior written consent of the Landlord and as the Landlord may direct.

8.   No furniture, freight or equipment of any kind shall be brought into the Building without the consent of Landlord and all moving of the same into or out of the Building shall be done at such time and in such manner as Landlord shall designate. Landlord shall have the right to prescribe the weight, size and position of all safes and other heavy equipment brought into the Building and also the times and manner of moving the same in and out of the Building. Safes or other heavy objects shall, if considered necessary by Landlord, stand on wood strips of such thickness as is necessary to properly distribute the weight. Landlord will not be responsible for loss of or damage to any such safe or property from any cause and all damage done to the Building by moving or maintaining any such safe or other property shall be repaired at the expense of Tenant. There shall not be used in any space, or in the public halls of the Building, either by any tenant or others, any hand trucks except those equipped with rubber tires and side guards.

9.   Tenant shall not employ any person or persons other than the janitor of Landlord for the purpose of cleaning the Premises unless otherwise agreed to by Landlord. Except with the written consent of Landlord, no person or persons other than those approved by Landlord shall be permitted to enter the Building for the purpose of cleaning the same. Tenant shall not cause any unnecessary labor by reason of Tenant's carelessness or indifference in the preservation of good order and cleanliness. Landlord shall in no way be responsible to any Tenant for any loss of property on the Premises, however occurring, or for any damage done to the effects of any Tenant by the janitor or any other employee or any other person. Janitor service shall include ordinary dusting and cleaning by the janitor assigned to such work and shall not include cleaning of carpets or rugs, except normal vacuuming, or moving of furniture and other special services. Janitor service will not be furnished on nights when rooms are occupied after 9:30 P.M. Window cleaning shall be done only by Landlord, and only between 6:00 A.M. and 5:00 P.M.

10.   Tenant shall not use, keep or permit to be used or kept any food or noxious gas or substance in the Premises, or permit or suffer the Premises to be occupied or used in a manner offensive or objectionable to the Landlord or other occupants of the Building by reason of noise, odors and/or vibrations, or interfere in any way with other tenants or those having business therein, nor shall any animals or birds be brought in or kept in or about the Premises or the Building. No Tenant shall make or permit to be made any unseemly or disturbing noises or disturb or interfere with occupants of this or neighboring Buildings or Premises or those having business with them whether by the use of any musical instrument, radio, phonograph, unusual noise, or in any other way. No Tenant shall throw anything out of doors or down the passageways.

11.   The Premises shall not be used for manufacturing or for the storage of merchandise except as such storage may be incidental to the use of the Premises for general office purposes. No Tenant shall occupy or permit any portion of his Premises to be occupied as an office for a public stenographer or typist, or for the manufacture or sale of liquor, narcotics, or tobacco in any form, or as a medical office, or as a barber shop or manicure shop. No Tenant shall advertise for laborers giving an address at the Premises. The Premises shall not be used for lodging or sleeping or for any illegal purposes.

FIGURE 14.10 Exhibit J (Concluded)

12. Tenant shall not use or keep in the Premises or the Building any kerosene, gasoline or inflammable or combustible fluid or material, or use any method of heating or air conditioning other than that supplied by Landlord.

13. Landlord will direct electricians as to where and how telephone and telegraph wires are to be introduced. No boring or cutting for wires will be allowed without the consent of Landlord. The location of telephones, call boxes and other office equipment affixed to the Premises shall be subject to the approval of Landlord.

14. All keys to offices, rooms and toilet rooms shall be obtained from Landlord's Building Management Office and Tenant shall not from any other source duplicate, obtain keys or have keys made. The Tenant, upon termination of the tenancy, shall deliver to the Landlord the keys of the offices, rooms and toilet rooms which shall have been furnished or shall pay the Landlord the cost of replacing same or of changing the lock or locks opened by such lost key if Landlord deems it necessary to make such change.

15. No Tenant shall lay linoleum, tile, carpet or other similar floor covering so that the same shall be affixed to the floor of the Premises in any manner except as approved by the Landlord. The expense of repairing any damage resulting from a violation of this rule or removal of any floor covering shall be borne by the Tenant by whom, or by whose contractors employees or invitees, the damage shall have been caused.

16. No furniture, packages, supplies, equipment or merchandise will be received in the Building or carried up or down in the elevators, except between such hours and in such elevators as shall be designated by Landlord.

17. On Sundays, legal holidays and on Saturday commencing at 12:00 noon, and on other days between the hours of 7:00 P.M. and 7:00 A.M. the following day, access to the Building, or to the halls, corridors, elevators or stairways in the Building, or to the Premises may be refused unless the person seeking access is known to the person or employee of the Building in charge and has a pass or is properly identified. The Landlord shall in no case be liable for damages for any error with regard to the admission to or exclusion from the Building of any person. In case of invasion, mob, riot public excitement, or other commotion, the Landlord reserves the right to prevent access to the Building during the continuance of the same by closing the doors or otherwise, for the safety of the Tenants and protection of property in the Building and the Building. Landlord reserves the right to close and keep locked all entrance and exit doors of the Building on Sundays, legal holidays, and on Saturdays commencing at 12:00 noon, and on other days between the hours of 7:00 P.M. and 7:00 A.M., and during such further hours as Landlord may deem advisable for the adequate protection of said Building and the property of its tenants.

18. Tenant shall see that the doors of the Premises are closed and securely locked before leaving the Building and must observe strict care and caution that all water faucets or water apparatus are entirely shut off before Tenant or Tenant's employees leave the Building, and that all electricity shall likewise be carefully shut off, so as to prevent waste or damage, and for any default or carelessness Tenant shall make good all injuries sustained by other tenants or occupants of the Building or Tenant.

19. Landlord reserves the right to exclude or expel from the Building any person who, in the judgment of Landlord, is intoxicated or under the influence of liquor or drugs, or who shall in any manner do any act in violation of any of the rules and regulations of the Building.

20. The requirements of Tenant will be attended to only upon application at the Office of the Building. Employees of Landlord shall not perform any work or do anything outside of their regular duties unless under special instructions from the Landlord, and no employee will admit any person (Tenant or otherwise) to any office without specific instructions from the Landlord.

21. No vending machine or machines of any description shall be installed, maintained or operated upon the Premises without the written consent of the Landlord.

22. Landlord shall have the right, exercisable without notice and without liability to Tenant, to change the name and the street address of the Building of which the Premises are a part.

23. Tenant agrees that it shall comply with all fire and security regulations that may be issued from time to time by Landlord and Tenant also shall provide Landlord with the name of a designated responsible employee to represent Tenant in all matters pertaining to such fire or security regulations.

24. Landlord reserves the right by written notice to Tenant, to rescind, alter or waive any rule or regulation at any time prescribed for the Building when, in Landlord's judgment, it is necessary, desirable or proper for the best interest of the Building and its tenants.

25. Tenants shall not disturb, solicit, or canvass any occupant of the Building and shall cooperate to prevent same.

26. Without the written consent of Landlord, Tenant shall not use the name of the Building in connection with or in promoting or advertising the business of Tenant except as Tenant's address.

27. Landlord shall furnish heating and air conditioning during the hours of 7:00 A.M. to 9:00 P.M. Monday through Friday, and 7:00 A.M. to 12:00 P.M. on Saturday, except for holidays. In the event Tenant requires heating and air conditioning during off hours, Sundays or holidays, Landlord shall on notice provide such services at the rate of $17.50 per hour.

FIGURE 14.11 Exhibit K

Grubb&Ellis

May 29, 1988

Mr. George Stearns
Foremost Enterprises
1414 Graham Drive
San Francisco, CA 94108

RE: Grubb & Ellis Leasing Commission

Tenant: Morgan, Murphy and Cash

Space: 4,200 Sq. Ft. on Fifth Floor

Building: 1414 Graham Drive

Rental: $7,175 per month

Term: 10 years—August 1, 1988 to July 31, 1998

YEARS	INCOME	RATE	COMMISSION
1	$86,100	5%	$4,305.00
2	86,100	5%	4,305.00
3	86,100	5%	4,305.00
4	86,100	4%	3,444.00
5	86,100	4%	3,444.00
6	116,160	2.5%	2,904.00
7	116,160	2.5%	2,904.00
8	116,160	2.5%	2,904.00
9	116,160	2.5%	2,904.00
10	116,160	2.5%	2,904.00

TOTAL COMMISSION DUE $34,323.00

$1/2$ due now $17,161.50
$1/2$ due upon occupance $17,161.50

Note: We have a check for $14,350 from Morgan, Murphy and Cash
representing their first month rental and July 1988 rental, which we can
either credit to your account with us (in which case you should send
$2,811.50) or exchange for a $17,161.50 check. I look forward to hearing
from you.

Sincerely,

Thomas R. Turner
Office Marketing Division

Grubb & Ellis Company   One Montgomery Street, Telesis Tower, San Francisco, CA 94104 (415) 956-1990

FIGURE 14.12   Exhibit L

Grubb&Ellis
SALES & LEASE RECORD

S&L No. 37859   *S&L Code _____

Sale ☐   or Lease ☒   or Sublease ☐

Office No. _____ 3B _____

*Division _____ *Property Type _____

Booking Date _____ 07 / 02 / 88
                    Month Day Year

Total Lease/~~Sale~~ Price ($) $1,011,300

Gross G&E Commission ($/¢) $17,161.50

Net G&E Commission ($/¢) $7,379.45

Close Date _____ 07 / 02 / 83
                  Month Day Year

Source 1 _____ Source 2 _____

Master Record No. _____

Street Address 1414 Graham Drive

City San Francisco   State Ca   Zip 94108

~~Purchaser~~/Tenant Morgan, Murphy and Cash

G&E Client ☒   National Acct. No. __ – _____

User ☐ Developer ☐ Investor ☐ *Investor Code _____

~~Seller~~/Landlord Foremost Enterprises

G&E Client ☐   National Acct. No. __ – _____

User ☐ Developer ☐ Investor ☐ *Investor Code _____

Size 4,200 _____ Sq. Ft. ☒ Acres ☐ Units ☐

Orig. Cross Ref.
S&L No. _____ Office No. _____

Tot. Bal. Owing _____ Due Date ___ / / ___
                                      Month Day Year

Referral No. _____ Office No. _____

COMPUTATION OF GROSS G & E COMMISSION

Receipt of Check From __ Foremost Enterprises _____ $17,161.50

Less: Co-Op Broker (Name/Address) _____   _____

_____ Fed. I.D. No. _____

Less: Co-Op Broker (Name/Address) _____   _____

_____ Fed. I.D. No. _____

Less: Other Payment (Name/Address) _____   _____

_____ Fed. I.D. No. _____

Gross G & E Commission ~~$17,161.50~~

COMPUTATION OF G&E COMMISSIONS

EMPLOYEE			Commission Calculation			COMMISSION										IF APPLICABLE	
NUMBER	INITIAL & LAST NAME		Function *Code	%	X Bracket %	Net %	$	$	$	$	$	$	$	¢	¢	121 (X)	CHECK NO.
3 2 3 0 4	T. Turner		S			55			9	4	3	8	8	2			1578
3 5 4 5 5	W. Manager					1.15				1	9	7	3	6			
3 9 4 4 4	M. Assistant					.85				1	4	5	8	7			
9 9 9 9 9	Net to Grubb & Ellis					43			7	3	7	9	4	5	X	X	1. ☐
X X X X X	Gross G & E Commission					100%		1	7	1	6	1	5	0	X	X	2. ☐

* SEE REVERSE FOR APPROPRIATE CODE

Manager's Approval _W. Manager_____

FORM 500 Revised 1/86   ACCOUNTING NO. 1

S/L No. 37859

FIGURE 14.13   Exhibit M

SALE AND LEASE RECORD
WORKSHEET

Date   August 15, 1988

Address of Property   1414 Graham Drive

Square Feet: 4,200

Lease/Sale Price: $7,175   /mo. $60,900   /yr.

Seller   Foremost Enterprises

Expected Closing Date

Purchaser   Morgan, Murphy and Cash

Lease Starts   8/1/88

Sale/Lease Following is a Breakdown of Commissions:

Co-op Broker None

NAME	%	EXPECTED
Tom Turner	55%	$18,877.65

Net, Grubb & Ellis Co.

Total Commission $18,877.65

Remarks:

Source of Client:

Salesperson: Tom Turner

FIGURE 14.14   Exhibit N

LEASE SUMMARY FORM

LESSEE: _____ *Morgan, Murphy and Cash* _____   ADDRESS: _____ *1414 Graham Dr.* _____

LESSOR: _____ *Foremost Enterprises* _____   LEASE DATE: _____ *May 1, 1988* _____

LEASE TERM: _____ *10* _____ YRS.: _____ *0* _____ MOS., FROM _____ *8/1/88* _____ TO _____ *7/31/98* _____

AREA: _____ × _____ = _____ *4,200* _____ SQ. FT.

RENT: $ _____ *86,100* _____ /YR., $ _____ *7,175* _____ /MO.

RENTAL RATE: $ _____ *1.21* _____ /SQ. FT./yr.

OPTIONS: _____ *None* _____

TAXES: LESSOR ☐   LESSEE ☐   TAX INCREASE ☐

INSURANCE: FIRE: LESSOR ☐   LESSEE ☐

               LIABILITY: LESSOR ☐   LESSEE ☐

MAINTENANCE: INTERIOR: LESSOR ☐   LESSEE ☐

               EXTERIOR: LESSOR ☐   LESSEE ☐

MISCELLANEOUS PROVISIONS: _____

_____

_____

_____

_____

FIGURE 14.15   Exhibit O

Grubb&Ellis

July 30, 1988

Mr. George Stearns
Foremost Enterprises
1414 Graham Drive
San Francisco, CA 94108

Dear George:

Just a reminder that the second half of the leasing commission for the
Morgan, Murphy and Cash lease is due upon their occupancy this week.
The amount payable is $17,161.50.

Please let me know if I can be of further service in facilitating this move or
with any additional real estate needs.

Sincerely,

Tom Turner
Office Marketing Division

Grubb & Ellis Company   One Montgomery Street, Telesis Tower, San Francisco, CA 94104 (415) 956-1990

FIGURE 14.16   Exhibit P

Grubb&Ellis

August 3, 1988

Mr. George Stearns
Foremost Enterprises
1414 Graham Drive
San Francisco, CA 94108

Dear George:

Thank you for the commission check. It has been a pleasure working with you on the Morgan, Murphy and Cash lease. I hope that you found our service completely satisfactory and look forward to working with you again.

Sincerely,

Tom Turner
Office Marketing Division

FIGURE 14.17   Exhibit Q

Grubb&Ellis

August 3, 1988

Mr. Donald Cook
Morgan, Murphy and Cash
1414 Graham Drive
San Francisco, CA 94108

Dear Don:

I'd like to thank you and Gary Robinson for the opportunity to work with you on your recent move. I wish you much success in your expansion at your new location.

I hope that our service was satisfactory. I look forward to working with you again when the need arises.

Sincerely,

Tom Turner
Office Marketing Division

Grubb & Ellis Company   One Montgomery Street, Telesis Tower, San Francisco, CA 94104 (415) 956-1990

FIGURE 14.18   Exhibit R

2/6/87
Talked to Donald Cook, San Francisco branch mgr. of Morgan, Murphy & Cash. Lease expires in 18 mos. Got some info on current space (see file). Says he'll move but doesn't seem to have given it much thought. Contact him 8/1.

8/1
Called Cook for appt. Brushed me off. Call him in 2 mos.

10/2
Saw Cook. He signed Tenant Rep. Agreement with another broker. See him in 2 mos. when it expires.

12/13
Qualified M M & C. Needs 5,000 sq. ft. Wants option or 1st RR on additional space. Uses much electronic equipment. Will use more. Wants to keep downtown location (not necessarily financial district, where it is now). Doesn't want to pay premium on space.

1/8/88
Prepare space presentation on 1200 Winona Dr. and 834 Curry St. for 1/15.

2/24
Saw Gray (A-C Developers). Wants right to move client parking. Cook says no, no, and no.

2/25
Called Perry R.—out of town for 1 mo. Call him 3/26.

3/28
Saw Perry. Will offer only $50,000 tenant improvement, but seemed soft on parking concession.

3/30
Met Robinson. Big shock! M M & C pays $16.50!

4/17
Saw 1414 Graham bldg. George Stearns is developer. Looks good for M M & C. Got open listing.

4/18
Cook doesn't want new bldg. Educate him. Stearns won't bring in space planner.

4/29
Stearns hard-nosed on space option. Who cares? Probably don't need it.

5/10
Stearns says yes on 1st RR.

5/27
Prepare M M & C offer for 6/9.

6/7
Set up lease signing for 6/15.

8/2
Follow-up letters to Cook and Stearns.

Glossary

Accrued items of expense. Incurred expenses that are not yet payable. In a closing statement, accrued expenses of the seller are credited to the purchaser (taxes, wages, interest, etc.).

Acknowledgment. A declaration before a notary public or other officer by a party executing a legal document that the execution is his free and voluntary act and deed.

Acre. A measure of land. One acre is equal to 43,560 square feet or 160 square rods or 4,840 square yards.

Ad valorem. According to value (Latin). This term is generally used to refer to real estate taxes.

Affidavit. A voluntary statement in writing, sworn to before a notary public or other officer.

Agent. One who acts or who has power to act for another. A licensed real estate broker authorized to act under a listing or management agreement executed by a property owner (the principal); this creates a fiduciary relationship under the law of agency. A building manager is the agent of the property owner.

Air-handling light fixture. A light fixture into which air is introduced by means of an air diffuser for quiet, draft-free air distribution.

Air rights. The rights to the use of the space above the physical surface of the land. The surface can be used for some other purpose.

Amortization. The process of paying off a debt together with interest, usually with equal payments at regular intervals over a period of time.

Amortized mortgage. A mortgage loan in which the principal, as well as the interest, is payable in monthly or periodic installments during the term of the loan.

Annual loan constant.   The principal and interest of a loan expressed as the constant annual payment required to retire a debt at a certain rate of interest over a certain period of time.

Appraisal.   An estimate of quantity, quality or value. The process through which conclusions of property value are obtained; also refers to the report setting forth the estimate and conclusion of value.

Approaches to value.   Employed by an appraiser to estimate the value of real estate: cost approach, income approach and market data approach.

Architect.   A person who normally functions as a creator, coordinator, author of the drawings and specifications and the general administrator of construction.

Architectural drawing.   Includes all architectural contracts and drawings such as plot plans, floor plans, elevations, sections, details, schedules, etc., and any architectural drawing that forms a part of the contract documents. Exceptions include mechanical, electrical and structural drawings, as well as specialized data that are normally handled by consultants to the architect or owner.

Assessed value.   The value placed on land and buildings by a township or a county assessor for use in levying annual real estate taxes.

Assignment.   The transfer in writing of an interest in a lease, mortgage or other instrument. The assignor, or lessee, transfers the entire remainder of the term created by the lease, and the assignee becomes liable to the original lessor for rent. Assignor may or may not retain secondary liability for performance under the lease, depending upon the terms of the lease pertaining to assignment.

Bag filter.   A unit within a mechanical system that bellows in a bag form when air flows through, cleaning the air by collecting particles of foreign matter. This system of filtering is rated the most efficient—in a range of 92 to 95 percent.

Banked elevators.   A group of elevators adjacent to each other with a specific demised enclosure.

Bank partition.   The type of space divider usually made of steel and glass and extending only approximately five to six feet up from the floor rather than to the ceiling.

Base lease.   A contract stating the minimum established requirements that are applicable to all tenants.

Base year.   The year of a lease term that is used as the standard when implementing an escalator clause. Operating costs are judged higher or lower during the next year when compared to the base year.

Bay.   An unfinished area or space between a row of columns and the bearing wall. Usually the smallest area into which a building floor can be partitioned.

Bids.   A competitive system in which each bidder submits a sealed proposal to execute construction work for a specified sum. The list of bidders (bid list) is controlled by the client and architect.

Binder.   A preliminary agreement evidencing a meeting of the minds and effective until the principal agreement can be executed.

Block layout.   The preliminary sketch showing different tenants' spaces on various floors. This helps the building management to understand the feasibility of the building.

Board of underwriters.   An organization that fixes rates for fire insurance and other types of coverage. The organization also maintains a laboratory that tests safety factors of materials, substances, electrical equipment, machinery and other apparatus.

Boot.   (See *Fixture boot.*)

Borrowed light. A partition containing glass or plastic panels between an interior dark space and a space illuminated by daylight or high-intensity artificial light.

Buck. (See *Door frame.*)

Building codes. Ordinances that specify minimum construction standards. These ordinances are enforced for the protection of public safety and health.

Building core. The central or arterial part of a multistory building that integrates functions and service needs for established occupants. Such areas are normally composed of toilet facilities, elevator banks, janitors' closets, utilities, mechanical facilities, smoke shafts and stairwells.

Building module. A unit of length and width by which the plan of a building can be standardized and which facilitates the design and layout of office space. The module places constraints on the size and shape of many of the elements of the physical systems. In contrast, buildings of a nonmodular design present many problems for initial design and subsequent alterations.

Building permit. The approval that must be obtained under state or local regulations. Drawings and specifications must be filed with the legal authorities in control of building operations. In Chicago, the legal authority is the City Building Department.

Building shell. The skeleton of a building to which the finished exterior and interior are applied. It includes the building foundation.

Building skin. All the materials that cover a building's shell (see *Building shell*).

Building standard. The specific construction standards that have been established by the owner and architect to achieve a uniform element of design throughout the building and to establish a cost basis for fitting up charges and/or allowances. Such items may be changed only with the approval of the building owner or the managing representative.

Building standards. Building standards that are binding on the tenants are usually set forth in a part of the lease entitled "Rules and Regulations," covering such things as use of common areas, door lettering, signs, noise, odors, moving or installation of equipment, special locks, etc.

Build-to-suit. An agreement between a landlord and a new tenant whereby the landlord assumes the obligation of fitting up the demised space to the tenant's specification within the constraints of building standards. The tenant takes possession when the space is completed.

Cancellation clause. A provision in a lease that confers upon one or both of the parties to the lease the right to terminate the lease upon the occurrence of the condition or contingency set forth in the said clause.

Capitalization. The process of ascertaining the value of a property by the use of a proper investment rate of return and the net income expected to be produced by the property. The formula of net annual income divided by proper capitalization rate is expressed: Income/Rate = Value.

Cash flow. The net operating income of a property minus its debt service.

Cash-on-cash return. A percentage figure arrived at by dividing the cash flow from a property by the total investment in the property and multiplying by 100. Also called Cash yield.

Cash yield. (See *Cash-on-cash return.*)

Caveat emptor. Let the buyer beware (Latin).

Ceiling plenum. A totally enclosed area above the ceiling used for the handling of air.

Certificate of insurance. A certificate issued by an insurance company or its agent. It verifies that a certain insurance policy is in effect for stated amounts and coverages and names those insured.

Certificate of payment. A certificate issued by the architect to the contractor for such amount as the architect decides is properly due. The amount of the certificate is therefore left, subject to the contract's provisions, entirely to the architect's discretion. However, in reaching a decision, the architect is acting not as the owner's agent but in a judicial capacity.

Chain of title. The succession of conveyances from some accepted starting point, usually beginning with the original recorded source, whereby the present holder of real property derives the title.

Change order. An order issued any time there is a change in the specifications, price or time set forth in the building contract as authorized by the owner, architect or engineer.

Channeling. Cutting, chipping or routing a prescribed sectional area in a linear pattern on any surface, usually in concrete or plaster.

Chattels. Personal property items.

Circulation allowance. The space needed to have sufficient access to, from and around workspaces.

Clear span. The amount of floor area clear of interference from columns.

Commitment. A pledge, promise or affirmation of agreement.

Common areas. Areas used by two or more tenants and/or third parties and not under the control of any one tenant.

Comparison year. During the term of a lease with an escalator clause, any year that is compared with a base year for the purpose of establishing a rise or fall in operating costs (see *Base year*).

Condemnation. The taking of private property for public use, with adequate compensation to the owner, under the right of eminent domain.

Condition or conditions. A provision in a deed or a will. It guarantees that, upon the occurrence or nonoccurrence of a certain event, the title of the purchaser or devisee will be limited, enlarged or terminated. A condition in a deed is a restriction that is coupled with a reverter clause.

Consideration. Anything of value given by one party to induce another to enter into a contract. It may be money, personal services or even "love and affection."

Construction allowance. A landlord's contribution to the cost of construction and/or alteration necessary to prepare a space for a tenant's occupancy. This may be an established amount, or it may vary from one kind of transaction to another.

Construction cost. Total expense, plus normal overhead and profit, that must be paid for the job in question.

Construction cost estimate. A figure submitted in advance of construction, not binding unless submitted as a bid. It is used to help arrive at a decision concerning the feasibility of a proposed project.

Constructive eviction. Any disturbance by the landlord of the tenant's possession of leased premises, whereby they are rendered unsuitable for occupancy (the purpose for which they were leased). In such a case, the tenant is not liable for further payment of rent.

Constructive notice. Notice given to the world by the recording of documents with a public official. All persons are charged with knowledge of such documents and their contents, whether or not they have actually examined them.

Contingency fund. A fund established by a developer to cover unforeseen construction costs.

Contract documents. Documents consisting of the agreement and the conditions of the contract (general, supplementary and other conditions). They include the drawings, the specifications, all addenda issued prior to execution of the contract and all modifications thereto. A modification is (1) a written amendment to the contract signed by both parties; (2) a written interpretation issued by the architect in the form of a drawing or otherwise; (3) a change order; or (4) a written order issued by the architect for a minor change in the work.

Contractor.   An individual and/or firm used in performing work on construction projects. There are different classes of contractors, which are normally listed under the heading of *subcontractors*. The function of the subcontractor is to perform a particular task only under the direction and coordination of the *general contractor,* who takes on the responsibility of managing the project in accordance with the construction documents. The general contractor is normally selected through bidding procedures and is totally responsible for completion of the project in a skillful manner that is acceptable to both architect and owner. However, the general contractor may be preselected to handle all work within a particular project. This is usually the case for multistory office buildings where the general contractor is the same for all tenant space construction. The contractor also could be contracted on a time-and-material basis, which may or may not have an upset maximum.

Contractor's affidavit.   A written statement, made under oath before a notary public by a contractor, stating facts regarding the contract, subcontracts, material suppliers and labor and setting forth the amounts paid and unpaid and the balance of payments due.

Convection system.   A system in which heat is transferred through the circulatory motion of air that occurs when the temperature varies due to the difference in air density and the action of gravity. A hot-water or steam radiator is one such system.

Convector.   A heating unit in which air, heated by contact with a heating device in a casing, circulates by convection. This term is often used by the layperson in identifying what is really an induction unit or system, which it resembles. It is usually taken for granted that all systems are the same, and thus it is often used as a generic term when identifying either system.

Conventional mortgage.   A mortgage loan that is not insured or guaranteed by any government agency (FHA or VA).

Conveyance.   A written instrument by which title or an interest in real estate is transferred; a deed.

Core.   (See *Building core.*)

Coring.   A mechanical system of removing a cylindrical section of concrete from the existing floor to gain access to the duct system.

Cost approach.   The process of estimating the value of a property by adding to the estimated land value the appraiser's estimate of the replacement cost of the building, less depreciation.

Cove base.   (See *Wall base.*)

Covenant.   An agreement, written into deeds and other instruments, promising performance or nonperformance of certain acts or stipulating certain uses or nonuses of the property.

Damages.   The estimated reparation in money for an injury sustained.

Damper.   A valve or plate that is operated mechanically or manually to regulate air flow to or from any prescribed point.

Debt service.   The total annual debt payment calculated by multiplying the loan constant by the outstanding loan balance.

Dedication.   The voluntary giving of private property by the owner of a development for some public use (streets, schools, etc.).

Deed.   A written instrument that, when executed and delivered, conveys title to or an interest in real estate.

Deed of trust. Also known as a trust deed, an instrument used to create a mortgage lien by which the mortgagor conveys a title to a trustee who holds it for the benefit of the noteholder (the lender).

Deed restrictions. Clauses in a deed limiting the future uses of the property. Deed restrictions may take many forms. They may limit the density of buildings, dictate the types of structures that can be erected and/or prevent buildings from being used for specific purposes or used at all. Deed restrictions may impose a myriad of limitations and conditions.

Default. Failure to meet an obligation when due or to perform any provision of a lease, mortgage or other agreement.

Demised premises. Premises, or parts of real estate, in which an interest or estate has been transferred temporarily, such as an interest in real property conveyed in a lease.

Demising clause. The clause in a lease whereby the landlord (*Lessor*) leases and the tenant (*Lessee*) takes the property. Demise is synonymous with "lease" or "let."

Demolition clause. A clause within a lease denoting the fact that if or when the ground lease has expired, the building will be demolished per such clause. The lessor must notify the tenants within an established time of such condition.

Depreciation. Loss of value due to all causes. Depreciation usually includes: (1) physical deterioration (ordinary wear and tear); (2) functional depreciation (see *Obsolescence*); and (3) economic obsolescence (causes outside the property).

Design cost or budget cost. Cost based on an agreed-upon concept where specific units have been established.

Design development. The process by which, upon approval of the schematic design, the architect proceeds with development of the plans and elevations of the building. Drawings establishing all major elements and outline specifications are prepared. A revised statement of probable construction cost is usually made at this time.

Developmental planning. Establishing a plan for the current space needs of an office that also takes into account anticipated future needs.

Diffuser. A device for reducing the velocity of air flow from a mechanical duct system supplying air. Its shape is usually circular or square and it is set in the ceiling at predetermined locations to diffuse air within that space.

Door frame. Made of either wood or hollow metal. A frame includes the following components: (a) *head*—the horizontal top portion of the door frame; (b) *jamb*—either the left or right vertical portion of the frame; (c) *sill*—the bottom of the door at floor level; (d) *stop*—a continuous projection around the frame to resist the door from traveling beyond a closing point; (e) *buck*—the subframe of wood or pressed metal to which the door case is fixed.

Doors. The most common types are solid-core wood (S.C.), hollow-core wood (H.C.) or hollow metal (H.M.). All of the doors can be furnished for paint finish; wood doors, when it is requested, may be furnished with any particular wood veneer available, at an additional cost. (One particular type of door that may come up periodically on proposed construction jobs is the class B door. This door of wood or metal, but usually metal, has a two-hour fire rating and is primarily located at stairwells or other enclosures requiring fire protection for at least two hours.)

Dry and wet bulb thermometer. A special thermometer that measures relative humidity.

Duct. A pipe, tube, channel or any other unit necessary for conveying gases, liquids or solid units from one point to another. The term is mostly identified with air-conditioning systems where the transfer of air is necessary. This is accomplished through sheet-metal ducts. The term is also applicable to under-floor duct systems for conveyance of telephone lines and other electrical conductors.

Easement.   A right to use the land of another for a specific purpose, such as a right-of-way or for utilities (see *Incorporeal interest*). An easement appurtenant passes with the land when it is sold.

Economic obsolescence.   Impairment of desirability or useful life or loss in the use and value of property arising from economic forces outside the building or property, such as changes in optimum land use, legislative enactments that restrict or impair property rights and changes in supply-demand relationships.

Effective gross income.   The scheduled gross income of a property minus the vacancy rate.

Egress.   The right to leave a tract of land. Often used in connection with *access*.

Electrified floor.   A floor in a commercial or office building containing ducts that house telephone and power lines, which emerge from the floor at frequent intervals for easy installation of telephones and power equipment.

Eminent domain.   The right of a government or municipal quasi-public body to acquire private property for public use. It is acquired through a court action called condemnation in which the court determines the use is a public use and decides the price or compensation to be paid to the owner.

Encroachment.   A building or some portion of it, or a wall or fence, that extends beyond the land of the owner and illegally intrudes upon land of an adjoining owner, a street or an alley.

Encumbrance.   Any lien, such as a mortgage, tax or judgment lien. It can also be an easement, a restriction on the use of the land or an outstanding dower right that may diminish the value of the property.

Entrepreneurial building.   A building where the landlord is not a major tenant and that is built primarily for its investment-return potential.

Equalization.   The raising or lowering of assessed values for tax purposes in a particular county or taxing district to make them equal to assessments in other counties or districts.

Equity.   The interest or value an owner has in real estate over and above the mortgage against it.

Escalation clause.   A clause in a contract providing for increases or decreases in rent payments in accordance with fluctuations of certain costs or expenses of the landlord.

Escalation payments.   Payments under an escalation clause.

Escrow.   A written agreement between two or more parties providing that certain instruments or property be placed with a third party to be delivered to a designated person upon the fulfillment or performance of some act or condition.

Eviction.   The forced removal, by legal means, of a tenant from the leased premise (see *Constructive eviction*).

Exclusive agency listing.   A listing contract under which the owner appoints a real estate broker as the one exclusive agent for a designated period of time to sell the property on the owner's stated terms, and under which the owner agrees to pay the broker a commission. However, the owner reserves the right to sell without a commission to a prospect not introduced or claimed by the broker (see *Exclusive right to sell*).

Exclusive listing.   A contract to sell property as an agent, whereby the agent is given the exclusive right to sell the property or is made the exclusive agent for its sale.

Exclusive right to sell.   A listing contract in which the owner appoints a real estate broker as the exclusive agent for a designated term. The broker must sell the property on the owner's stated terms, and the owner agrees to pay the broker a commission when the sale is consummated.

Expense ratio. The percentage of gross income that is consumed by the operating expenses of a property.

Expense stop. A ceiling or limit on the dollar amount one party, typically the landlord, will pay in an expense category. This ceiling is determined by adding a percentage or dollar amount to the base year costs.

Exploratory costs. The cost figures collected on the basis of a discussion of possible needs and reviewed with an interested individual (see *Preliminary cost estimates*).

Fee simple. The largest possible estate or absolute right of ownership of real property. It can be held without time limitation and is freely transferable and inheritable.

Fiduciary. A person to whom power or property is entrusted for the benefit of another.

Field observation. (On-site observation.) Observation deemed necessary by the architect to ensure successful completion of the project.

Fin-tube radiation system. A heating convection system that transmits heat through a series of sheet-metal plates spaced at close intervals on a center pipe. The energy of heat transmission is usually through hot water or steam.

First right of refusal. A lease concession that gives a tenant the first right, within a limited period of time, to a designated additional space that another prospective tenant has expressed a desire to lease.

Fit up. (Fitting up.) The construction necessary within the enclosing walls, i.e., the space the tenant is leasing, to divide and improve that tenant's space into a functional layout, including partitions, doors, telephone and electrical outlets, finished surfaces, paint, tile, carpet, etc., and up to the point of furnishing with personal property.

Fixture. Personal property or improvements so attached to the land as to become part of the real property. The right of the tenant to remove fixtures may be given by stipulation in the lease or by separate written agreement between the parties.

Fixture boot. A sheet-metal housing, over air-handling light fixtures, that will receive ducts for conveying conditioned air through such light fixtures to particular areas at certain required quantities.

Flat base. (See *Wall base*.)

Footcandle. A measurement of light level. It is equivalent to the light intensity made by one candle at a distance of one foot.

Footcandles maintained. The level of light that will be maintained after the initial drop-off of footcandles following installation. Usually it will be after the first 100 hours of burning.

Footprint. The shape and configuration of a building.

Foreclosure. A court action initiated by the mortgagee or a lienor for the purpose of having the court order the debtor's real estate sold to pay the mortgage or other lien (mechanic's lien or judgment).

Functional obsolescence. Defects in a building or structure that detract from its value or marketability (see *Obsolescence*).

Garden-type building. A modern, low-rise building typically found in suburban areas, that is built to blend in with its surroundings. Often of stucco exterior.

General lien. A lien on all property, both real and personal, of a debtor.

Glazier. A mechanic responsible for handling and installing glass.

Graduated lease.   A lease that provides for specific increases or decreases in rent at definite times during the term of the lease.

Grantee.   A person to whom an interest in land is conveyed by deed, grant or other written instrument.

Grantor.   A person who transfers his or her interest in land to another by a written instrument.

Gross lease.   A lease of property whereby the lessor is to pay all property charges regularly incurred through ownership (see *Net lease*).

Gross rent multiplier.   A figure that produces an estimate of the property's value when used as a multiplier of the gross income of a property.

Ground lease.   A lease (usually of long duration) of land to a tenant who covenants to erect a building on the premises. The building is security for rentals. If the tenant defaults, the landlord may foreclose on the lease (see *Subordinated ground lease*).

Hard construction costs.   The costs of constructing a building shell plus most of the covering materials.

Hardware.   General term that includes the following: (a) hinges, butt or pivot; (b) lever handles, knobs or pulls; (c) latchset, lockset, magnetic and friction catches; and (d) door closers, door holds, door bumpers.

Highest and best use.   That possible use of land that will produce the greatest net income and thereby develop the highest land value.

High rise.   An inexact term, usually denoting a building of steel frame construction regardless of the building height.

Hold harmless.   (See *Save harmless*.)

Holding area.   A space or room, usually in the freight-docking area where deliveries to a tenant (or the building management) may be held until delivered; sometimes also called a receiving area.

Holding over.   The act of a tenant retaining possession of the premises longer than the term expressed in the lease.

HVAC.   An abbreviation for heating, ventilating and air conditioning.

Improvements on land.   Usually privately owned structures such as buildings, fences, driveways and retaining walls erected so that a site can be used.

Improvements to land.   Usually publicly owned structures such as curbs, sidewalks, streetlights and sewers constructed to enable the development of privately owned land.

Income approach.   The process of estimating the value of an income-producing property by capitalization of the annual net income expected to be produced by the property during its remaining useful life.

Incorporeal interest.   Nonpossessory rights in real estate. For example, it could be an easement or right-of-way.

Inducements.   Negotiable points in a lease resolved in the tenant's favor in an effort to induce them to sign the lease. Also called concessions, typically inducements include free rent and an increased tenant improvement allowance.

Induction system.   A mechanical system normally located on the periphery of a building at the base of the window walls. Forced air is thermostatically controlled to temper its flow by heating or cooling the interior air. This process is controlled by the current climatic conditions at the exterior and the demands of the spaces within the building (see *Convection system* and *Convector*).

Industrial district or park.   A controlled parklike development designed to accommodate specific types of industry. It provides public utilities, streets, railroad sidings, water, sewage facilities, etc.

Installment contract.   A contract for the sale of real estate wherein the purchase price is paid in installments over an extended period of time by the purchaser, who is in possession. Title is retained by the seller until the final payment.

Insured.   The indemnified person(s) or company(ies) who receive the proceeds of insurance in the event of insurable loss or damage.

Interest rate.   The percentage of the principal sum charged by a lender for its use, usually for a yearly period.

Interior partitions.   All types of interior nonload-bearing partitions that enclose or subdivide tenant space. May be of steel, wood, glass, masonry or combinations of these materials. Such partitions may be either movable or nonmovable, prefabricated or built on the job.

Jamb.   (see *Door frame.*)

Joint tenants.   Two or more landowners who have been specifically named in one conveyance as joint tenants. Upon the death of a joint tenant, the surviving joint tenant or tenants receive the deceased tenant's interest by the right of survivorship, which is the important element of joint tenancy.

Judgment clause.   A provision in notes, leases and contracts by which the debtor, lessee, etc., authorizes any attorney to go into court and confess judgment against him for a default in payment.

Judgment lien.   A charge, or lien, upon the lands of a debtor. The court decree, which must be properly entered, declares that the debtor is indebted and fixes the amount of the indebtedness.

Land contract.   A contract for the purchase of real estate on an installment basis. Upon payment of the last installment, the deed is delivered to the purchaser (see *Installment contract*).

Latent defect.   (*Hidden defect*). A physical deficiency or construction defect not readily ascertainable from a reasonable inspection of the property, such as a defective septic tank or underground sewage system, improper plumbing or electrical liner.

Lease.   A contract whereby, for a consideration (usually termed rent), one who is entitled to the possession of real property transfers such rights to another for life, for a term of years, month to month or at will.

Leasehold.   The interest or estate that a lessee of real estate holds under the provisions of a lease.

Lessee.   The tenant in a lease.

Lessor.   The landlord in a lease.

Letter of Intent.   (see *Offer to lease.*)

Levy.   To impose or assess a tax on a person or property. The amount of taxes to be imposed in a given district.

License.   Permission given by the landlord for a person to enter the premises of a tenant for a particular purpose. A license is of temporary character, purely a personal right, and cannot be sold. It is revocable.

Lien.   A right given by law to a creditor to have a debt or charge satisfied out of the property of the debtor. It applies to a particular piece or pieces of real or personal property.

Limited partnership.   A partnership arrangement that limits the partner's liability to the amount invested and also limits the profit he or she can make. A limited partner is not permitted to have a voice in the management.

Listing contract.   An agreement between a landowner (as principal) and a licensed real estate broker (as agent) by which the broker is employed as agent to sell the real estate on the landowner's terms within a given time, for which service the landowner agrees to pay a commission (see *Open listing, Exclusive agency listing* and *Exclusive right to sell*).

Live load.   A load that may be removed or replaced on a structure but is not necessarily a dynamic load. It includes the impact effect, such as people walking on a surface.

Low rise.   A building not of steel-frame construction and, hence, necessarily only one to a few stories high.

Market data approach.   The process of estimating the value of property through the examination and comparison of actual sales of comparable properties.

Market value.   The highest price that a buyer ready, willing and able but not compelled to buy, would pay, and the lowest a seller ready, willing and able but not compelled to sell, would accept.

Mechanic's lien.   A lien established by law in favor of those who provide labor or material for the improvement of real estate.

Metal pan.   An architectural term for a preformed sheet-metal unit that is set in place to receive a plastic material (concrete, terrazzo, etc.). It is frequently used for ceiling or stair construction.

Millwork.   Finished carpentry work, wood processing done in the mill or factory, as distinguished from handwork on the job.

Miscellaneous area.   Area, other than workspaces, that requires equipment accommodating special construction, furnishing or interior-design treatments.

Modular system.   (See *Building module.*)

Module.   (See *Building module.*)

Month-to-month tenancy.   A tenancy from month to month is generally created when no definite lease term is specified by the parties and the rent is payable monthly. Such a lease may be written or oral, and can be terminated by either party at the end of any month. Otherwise, it is renewed automatically from month to month on the same terms.

Mortgage.   A conditional transfer or pledge of real property as security for the payment of a debt.

Mortgagee.   A lender.

Mortgage lien.   A claim on real estate given to the mortgagee when the mortgagor executes a mortgage or trust deed to secure his or her note.

Mortgagor.   A borrower who conveys real property as security for a loan.

Mullions.   Metal strips placed at regular intervals along a window line. They are designed to receive a wall partition in a manner ensuring a smooth, soundproof connection.

Multipersonnel areas.   Areas within a tenant's space (open or enclosed) providing workspaces for more than one occupant. They require interior and access circulation allowances.

Net lease.   Lease under which the tenant pays the agreed-upon rent plus utilities and taxes.

Net-net lease.   Lease under which the tenant pays the agreed-upon rent plus utilities, taxes, insurance and maintenance.

Net-net-net lease.   Lease under which the tenant pays the agreed-upon rent plus all costs of maintenance and repair. Also called *triple net lease.*

Net operating income (NOI).   The effective gross income from a property minus operating expenses.

Noninstitutional building.   (See *Entrepreneurial building.*)

Notary public.   An officer appointed by the governor with authority to take the acknowledgment of persons executing documents and to sign the certificate and affix a seal.

Notice.   Information about or warning of something. Notice may be by personal observation or by written or oral message from another person.

Obsolescence. Lessening of value due to being out of date (obsolete) as a result of changes in design and use; an element of depreciation.

Offer to lease. An agreement that binds the lessor to continuing negotiations in good faith once a qualified tenant has been found, until all negotiating points have been covered. In effect, it takes the space off the market during the negotiating period. Also called a *letter of intent.*

Open listing. A listing contract under which the broker's commission is contingent upon the broker producing a buyer before the property is sold by the owner or another broker.

Option. A contractual agreement giving one party a privilege of demanding, within a specified time, the carrying out of a transaction upon stipulated terms.

Pass-through. Expenses or a portion of expenses associated with tenancy that are "passed through" from the landlord to the tenant who then pays them.

Percentage lease. Lease under which the tenant pays a fixed minimum monthly rent plus a percentage of his or her gross monthly income in excess of that minimum. Used primarily in retail leases.

Perimeter drapery pocket. A linear area along the interior of the exterior window wall that is recessed at some dimension above the ceiling to accommodate drapery tracks.

Perimeter space. A prescribed area at the outer periphery of a building.

Personal property. Items (chattels) that do not fit the definition of realty; movable objects.

Plenum. (See *Ceiling plenum.*)

Plumbing walls. Walls provided along areas, as in kitchens and washrooms, where there are no provisions for pipe shafts.

Possession. Right of an owner to occupy property; when the property is occupied by a tenant, the owner has constructive possession by right of title.

Power cells. (See *Under-floor ducts.*)

Preliminary cost estimates. First estimates, which are recognized as ballpark figures and arrived at before detailed data have been made available to the estimator.

Preliminary costs. Expenditures that are made before the main project is begun, such as feasibility studies, subsoil exploration, financing commitments, etc.

Prepaid items of expense. In the preparation of a closing statement, prorations of prepaid items of expense that are credited to the seller.

Prime tenant. A tenant who occupies a great portion of the space available within a given building that may, in addition, be owned by that tenant.

Principal. (1) A sum lent or employed as a fund or investment, as distinguished from its income or profits; (2) the original amount (as of a loan) of the total due and payable at a certain date; (3) a party to a transaction, as distinguished from an agent.

Principal and agent. The relation created by express or implied contract or by law whereby one party delegates the transaction of some lawful business, with more or less discretionary power, to another who undertakes to manage the affair and render an account thereof.

Procuring cause. "A broker will be regarded as the 'procuring cause' of a sale, so as to be entitled to commission, if his efforts are the foundation on which the negotiations resulting in a sale are begun" *Coles* versus *Pattison,* 189 Okl. 160, 114 P. 2d 457, 458.

Pro forma. A set of figures projecting costs and income on a proposed new property. Used as a basis for capitalization.

Programming.   A system in which specific requirements of the client are determined in written form and, when approved by the client, become the basis for all future planning. The effects of successful programming will be felt by the client as long as he or she lives with the facility executed. The client will have a flexible enclosure able to house immediate and long-range needs without disrupting his or her operation during growth periods.

Public corridor.   The space that leads to different tenants' spaces from a service core.

Punch list.   A list prepared by the architect, designer and owner and formally submitted to the contractor to note any deficiencies when they check all completed construction, which assures verification that such work has been accomplished in a good, workmanlike manner in respect to the contract documents.

Purchase-money mortgage.   A note secured by a mortgage or trust deed given by a buyer (as mortgagor) to a seller (as mortgagee) as part of the purchase price of the real estate.

Quiet enjoyment.   A covenant, usually inserted into leases and conveyances on the part of the grantor, promising that the tenant or grantee shall enjoy possession of the premises in peace and without disturbance.

Quiet-title suit.   A suit to remove a defect, cloud or questionable claim against the title to property.

Real estate broker.   Any person, copartnership, association or corporation who, for a compensation or valuable consideration, sells or offers for sale, buys or offers to buy, or negotiates the purchase, sale, or exchange of real estate, or who leases or offers to lease or rents or offers for rent any real estate or the improvements thereon for others. Such a broker must secure a state license. For a license to be issued to a firm, it is usually required that all active partners and officers must be licensed real estate brokers.

Real estate salesperson.   Any person who, for a compensation or valuable consideration, is employed either directly or indirectly by a real estate broker to sell or offer to sell, or buy or offer to buy or negotiate the purchase, sale or exchange of real estate or to lease, rent or offer for rent any real estate or to negotiate leases thereof or the improvements thereon.

REALTOR®.   A registered trademark term reserved for the sole use of active members of local boards of REALTORS® affiliated with the National Association of REALTORS®.

Recapture.   A clause in a lease agreement providing for lessor's retaking or recovering possession of the premises, usually by cancellation of the lease under certain conditions.

Receiving area.   (See *Holding area.*)

Recording.   The act of entering a record of documents affecting or conveying interest in real estate in a county recorder's office. Until recorded, a deed or mortgage generally is not effective against subsequent purchasers or mortgages or other third parties (see *Constructive notice*).

Redemption period.   A period established by state laws during which the property owner has the right to redeem his or her real estate from a foreclosure or tax sale by paying the sale price, interest and costs. (Many states do not have mortgage-redemption laws.)

Rentable area.   The importance of this subject dictates the following detailed definition. In the United States and Canada there are three methods of measuring rentable area in office buildings. All three measure the total square footage.

1.   International Association of Building Owners and Managers. From the inside of the outside wall (or in new buildings from the glass line) to the

outside of the inside wall (or hall wall) and center to center on the division walls. Columns are included.

2. General Services Administration. Same as above except all columns, division walls, service closets, etc., are included. Net usable space only. In making leases to the federal government, this method must be used.

3. So-called New York Method. Space is measured right across the floor from glass line to glass line, subtracting only elevator shafts and stairwells. In the case of multiple occupancy on one floor, the common space—usable and nonusable—is apportioned among the tenants according to the size of their respective areas.

Replacement cost.   The new cost of replacing the subject property with property having exactly the same utility and amenities.

Restriction.   A limitation placed upon the use of property. It is contained in the deed or other written instrument in the chain of title.

Reversionary interest.   A right to the future enjoyment of property that is presently in the possession of or is occupied by another.

Revisions.   Changes in the work that require the architect to provide substitute drawings or revise the original working drawings. Each revision on the drawings should be identified graphically to illustrate the point of changes, and the date should be circled to indicate when the revision was made.

Right-of-way.   The right or privilege to pass across the lands of another; an easement.

Sales contract.   A contract containing the complete terms of the agreement between seller and buyer for the sale of a particular parcel or parcels of real estate.

Save harmless.   To indemnify another; to secure another against loss or damage or claims of a third party. Often referred to as *hold harmless*.

Scheduled gross income.   The rental rate of a property multiplied by the total rentable space.

Schematic design.   (1) A design concerning the building program resulting from inspection of the site and conferences with the client. The client's needs and requirements are carefully analyzed. Zoning regulations and codes affecting the work are studied. Sketches and statements of probable construction costs are prepared for the owner's approval. (2) A suggested plan, design or program of action.

Settlement.   The process at the closing of a sale of real estate, negotiated by a real estate broker, whereby the broker usually accounts to the principal for the *earnest money* deposit and deducts commission and advances by use of a form of settlement statement.

Shell.   (See *Building shell.*)

Shop drawings.   Drawings made by the various trades reflecting construction of items on the contract documents—a necessary step between the architect's drawings and actual construction. Shop drawings speak not merely the language of the trade but the language of the shop in which work is to be done.

Signal-zone closet.   A closet that holds communication equipment; e.g., telephone or intercom systems.

Sill.   (See *Door frame.*)

Skin.   (See *Building skin.*)

Slab.   The reinforced concrete floor between beams, supporting columns or walls. Also, any large, thin area of concrete such as a wall, roof or balcony is a slab.

Soft construction costs. Costs of constructing and leasing a building other than the costs of building the actual physical structure.

Space analysis. An analysis of an existing office situation to locate problem areas and to provide a basis for judgment in evaluating major changes. Also, it can be in the form of planning tools that will be used by the client in developing a planning decision. This includes space standards, adjacency requirements and space requirements.

Space planning. Architecturally designing any space with all the amenities and mechanical gadgets to make it more functional for the occupants. Besides amenities, gadgets and good communication systems, it includes better sound and light control within the space.

Space standards. The standard-size spaces for particular functions—a necessary tool in planning for any growing organization. The absence of standards leads to a situation where space is allocated to offices in a haphazard, nonfunctional manner.

Special assessment. A charge against real estate made by a unit of government to cover the proportionate cost of an improvement such as a street or sewer.

Special facilities. Workspace for one or more occupants designed to accommodate the special equipment required for their work.

Special-warranty deed. A form of deed whereby the grantor covenants against lawful claims of all persons claiming by, through or under the grantor only.

Specifications. A detailed and exacting statement of what is to be done. Their careful preparation is the best insurance for trouble-free execution of the work and satisfactory completion of the project.

Specific lien. A lien that affects or is attached to only a certain specific parcel of land or piece of property.

Speculative building. An *entrepreneurial building* where construction is undertaken without a prior lease commitment from a prime tenant or tenants.

Staging area. A place to store and work with materials and equipment prior to their movement into the space where they will finally be used.

Statute of frauds. A state law that requires certain classes of contracts, engagements and/or transfers of interest in real estate to be made in writing in order to be enforceable in a court of law. Details of this law vary from one state to another. (The original Statute of Frauds was passed in England in 1677.)

Straight wall base. (See *Wall base.*)

Sublease. A lease executed by the lessee of an estate to a third person that conveys the same estate for a shorter term, or a portion of the estate for the same or a shorter term, is a sublease. When the entire estate is sublet for the entire remainder of the term, it is called an assignment.

Subordinated ground lease. A ground lease in which the lessor (owner) places his right in relation to the structure behind that of others, such as the holder of the construction loan or permanent mortgage (see *Ground lease*).

Subordination. An agreement by which a lienholder, a lessee or one having an interest or claim in or against personal or real property places the interest behind that of another.

Subrogation. The act of replacing one person with another in regard to a legal right, interest or obligation; substitution such as an insured transferring claim rights to the insurance carrier in return for direct payment of the loss.

Substitution clause. That portion of the work letter that specifies what materials may be substituted for the standard constructive materials ordinarily supplied by the landlord.

Survey.   The process of measuring land to determine its size, location and physical description; also, the map or plat showing the results of a survey.

Syndication.   A combining of persons or firms to accomplish a joint venture that is of mutual interest.

Task lighting.   Overhead lighting systems that provide each workspace with individual overhead lighting controls. Designed to conserve energy by lighting only work areas that are occupied at any given time.

Tax rate (real estate).   Generally quoted as so many dollars per $100 of *assessed value,* the general real estate tax is made up of the taxes levied on real estate by various governmental agencies and municipalities, such as the city, the county, school districts, park districts, etc.

Tenancy at sufferance.   A tenancy that exists when, after expiration of a lease, the tenant remains in possession without the consent of the landlord or the person entitled to possession. No notice is required to terminate this tenancy.

Tenancy at will.   One wherein the landlord agrees that the tenant may stay in possession after expiration of the lease and pay rent for the time the space is occupied, until either landlord or tenant desires to terminate the tenancy.

Tenant representation agreement.   A contract under which a client agrees to work through no salesperson except the one designated in the agreement.

Thermopane.   A brand name (now used generally) for a window-glass construction that has insulating qualities. Two layers of glass are separated by an air space. Also called double-glazing insulating glass.

Thermostat.   A device actuated by temperatures that regulates and controls dampers, valves, switches or other mechanisms.

Title.   Evidence of the right a person has to the ownership and possession of land.

Title defect.   Any legal right held by others to claim property or to make demands upon the owner.

Title insurance policy.   A policy insuring an owner or mortgagee against loss by reason of defects in the title to a parcel of real estate, other than those encumbrances, defects and matters that are specifically excluded by the policy.

Topography.   Surface features of land, such as elevation, ridges, slope and contour.

Trade(s).   A classification of worker skills; carpenters, electricians, sheet-metal workers, etc.

Trade fixtures.   Articles installed by a tenant under terms of a lease and removable by the tenant before the lease expires. These remain personal property; they are not true fixtures.

Traffic-flow study.   A careful study made by the space planner of the interactions among different departments, operations and/or person-to-person contacts in the given space to avoid confusion and create better function and communication. (A typical example: stenos and their offices.)

Transfer lobby.   A floor area in a building where passengers must transfer from an elevator that has brought them from a lower level to a different elevator that serves higher levels of the building. An inconvenience.

Transfer tax.   A levy on a deed transfer signified by affixing stamps to a deed.

Triple net lease.   (See *Net-net-net lease.*)

Trust deed.   An instrument used to create a mortgage lien by which the mortgagor conveys title to a trustee who holds it for the benefit of the noteholder (the lender).

Trustee's deed.   A deed executed by a trustee that conveys land held in a trust.

Twindows. Windows built of double panes of glass with space between the panes. Designed to conserve energy by improving building insulation.

Under-floor ducts (electrical and telephone raceways). The underfloor distribution system provided in the structural slab to meet electrical and telephone needs on the floor. The system should be designed not only to take care of a specific arrangement of furniture or equipment but to provide for logical rearrangement or reasonable increase in service equipment.

Unit office space. Fully enclosed or semi-enclosed space, providing workspace for a single occupant and involving a circulation provision required to access the space.

Usable area. Any area in a given floor that could be used by the tenant. This area includes a point from the perimeter glass line to demising walls; it also includes column areas within such a space.

Usury. The charging of interest at a rate in excess of the maximum legal rate.

Value. The power of a thing to command other goods in exchange; the present worth of future rights to income and benefits arising from ownership.

Voidable. A valid act that may be avoided or declared void.

Volume per square foot. The method of estimating probable total construction cost by multiplying the adjusted gross building volume in square feet by a predetermined cost per unit of volume.

Waiver of lien. The intentional or voluntary relinquishment of the right to a mechanic's lien. It is routinely signed by contractors when they are paid for their work.

Wall base. A defined material applied to the base of walls for general protection and finish. Although it can be provided in various materials, the primary material is vinyl or rubber. The base is available in various heights and colors. It is also available as a *straight* or *flat base,* for carpeted areas, or a *cove base,* which is normally used for tile floors as a maintenance and finish advantage.

Warranty deed. A deed that contains a covenant or assurance by the grantor of real property for him- or herself and heirs to the effect that he or she is the owner and will defend and protect the grantee against claims.

Waste. An unreasonable or improper use, abuse, mismanagement or omission of duty regarding the care or title to real estate by one rightfully in possession.

Water closet (W.C.). A toilet.

Wet columns. Columns where provisions are made to have a plumbing fixture for drinking fountains, sink, etc.; the pipes are taken through the small enclosure (chase) against the column.

Working drawings. Detailed floor-space plans that diagram all improvements to be made. They are designed as instructions to the various contractors involved.

Work letter. That part of the lease stated in detail pertaining to all work that is to be done for a tenant by a landlord.

Wrap-around mortgage. A technique in which the lender assumes payment of the existing mortgage and gives a new, increased mortgage to the borrower at a higher interest rate. The new mortgage "wraps around" the existing one. With the trend in today's mortgage market toward rising interest rates and appreciated property values, wraparound mortgaging has gained increased acceptance.

Zoning ordinance. Exercise of policy power by a municipality in regulating and controlling the character and use of property.

Index